How to Change the World

the World

Tales of Marx and Marxism

Eric Hobsbawm

To the memory of George Lichtheim

ABACUS

This collection first published in Great Britain in 2011 by Little, Brown
Reprinted 2011 (four times)
This paperback edition published in 2012 by Abacus

A CIP catalogue record for this book
is available from the British Library.

ISBN 978-0-3491-2352-3

Typeset in Baskerville by M Rules
Printed and bound in Great Britain by
Clays Ltd, St Ives plc

Papers used by Abacus are from well-managed forests
and other responsible sources.

MIX
Paper from
responsible sources
FSC® C104740

Abacus
An imprint of
Little, Brown Book Group
100 Victoria Embankment
London EC4Y 0DY

An Hachette UK Company
www.hachette.co.uk

www.littlebrown.co.uk

Eric Hobsbawm was born in Alexandria in 1917 and educated in Austria, Germany and England. He is a Fellow of the British Academy and of the American Academy of Arts and Sciences, a Foreign Member of the Japan Academy, with honorary ees from universities in several countries. He taught until ement at Birkbeck College, University of London, and then the New School for Social Research in New York. In addition *The Age of Revolution*, *The Age of Capital*, *The Age of Empire* and *The Age of Extremes*, his books include *Bandits*, *Revolutionaries*, *common People* and his memoir, *Interesting Times*.

Contents

Foreword

This book, a collection of many of my writings in this field from 1956 to 2009, is essentially a study of the development and posthumous impact of the thought of Karl Marx (and the inseparable Frederick Engels). It is not a history of Marxism in the traditional sense, although its core comprises six chapters I wrote for a very ambitious multi-volume *Storia del Marxismo* published by the house of Einaudi in Italian (1978–82) of which I was co-planner and co-editor. These, revised, sometimes extensively rewritten and supplemented by a chapter on the period of Marxist recession since 1983, constitute over half the contents of the book. In addition it contains some further studies in what scholarly jargon calls 'the reception' of Marx and Marxism; an essay on Marxism and labour movements since the 1890s, an initial version of which was originally given as a lecture in German to the Linz International Conference of Labour Historians; and three introductions to particular works: Engels' *Condition of the Working Class*, the *Communist Manifesto*, and Marx's views on pre-capitalist social formations in the important set of 1850s manuscripts known in their published form as *Grundrisse*. The only post-Marx/Engels Marxist specifically discussed in this book is Antonio Gramsci.

About two thirds of these texts have not been published in

English or at all. Chapter 1 is a largely expanded and rewritten contribution to a public conversation on Marx held under the auspices of the Jewish Book Week in 2007. Likewise chapter 12. Chapter 15 has not been published before.

Who are the readers I had in mind when I wrote these studies, now collected together? In some cases (chapters 1, 4, 5, 16, perhaps 12) simply the men and women interested in finding out more about the subject. However, most of the chapters are aimed at readers with a more specific interest in Marx, Marxism, and the interaction between the historical context and the development and influence of ideas. What I have tried to provide for both is a sense that the discussion of Marx and Marxism cannot be confined either to the debate for or against, the political and ideological territory occupied by the various and changing brands of Marxists and their antagonists. For the past 130 years it has been a major theme in the intellectual music of the modern world, and through its capacity to mobilise social forces a crucial, at some periods a decisive presence in the history of the twentieth century. I hope that my book will help readers to reflect on the question of what its and humanity's future will be in the twenty-first century.

Eric Hobsbawm
London, January 2011

I

MARX AND ENGELS

1

Marx Today

I

In 2007 a Jewish Book Week took place less than two weeks before the anniversary of Karl Marx's death (14 March) and within a short walking distance of the place with which he is most closely associated in London, the Round Reading Room of the British Museum. Two very different socialists, Jacques Attali and I, were there to pay our posthumous respects to him. And yet, when you consider the occasion and the date, this was doubly unexpected. One cannot say Marx died a failure in 1883, because his writings had begun to make an impact in Germany and especially among intellectuals in Russia, and a movement led by his disciples was already on the way to capturing the German labour movement. But in 1883 there was little enough to show for his life's work. He had written some brilliant pamphlets and the torso of an uncompleted major piece, *Das Kapital*, work on which hardly advanced in the last decade of his life. 'What works?' he asked bitterly when a visitor questioned him about his works. His major political effort since the failure of the 1848 revolution, the so-called First

International of 1864–73, had foundered. He had established no place of significance in the politics or the intellectual life of Britain, where he lived for over half his life as an exile.

And yet, what an extraordinary posthumous success! Within twenty-five years of his death the European working-class political parties founded in his name, or which acknowledged his inspiration, had between 15% and 47% of the vote in countries with democratic elections – Britain was the only exception. After 1918 most of them became parties of government, not only of opposition, and remained so after the end of fascism, but most of them then became anxious to disclaim their original inspiration. All of them are still in existence. Meanwhile disciples of Marx established revolutionary groups in non-democratic and third-world countries. Seventy years after Marx's death, one third of the human race lived under regimes ruled by communist parties which claimed to represent his ideas and realise his aspirations. Well over 20% still do, though their ruling parties have, with minor exceptions, dramatically changed their policies. In short, if one thinker left a major indelible mark on the twentieth century, it was he. Walk into Highgate cemetery, where a nineteenth-century Marx and Spencer – Karl Marx and Herbert Spencer – are buried, curiously enough within sight of each other's grave. When both were alive, Herbert was the acknowledged Aristotle of the age, Karl a guy who lived on the lower slopes of Hampstead on his friend's money. Today nobody even knows Spencer is there, while elderly pilgrims from Japan and India visit Karl Marx's grave and exiled Iranian and Iraqi communists insist on being buried in his shade.

The era of communist regimes and mass communist parties came to an end with the fall of the USSR, for even where they survive, as in China and in India, in practice they have abandoned the old project of Leninist Marxism. And when it did, Karl Marx found himself once again in no-man's land. Communism had claimed to be his only true heir, and his ideas had been largely identified with it. For even the dissident Marxist or Marxist-Leninist tendencies that established a few footholds here and there after Khrushchev denounced Stalin in 1956 were almost certainly ex-communist breakaways. So, for most of the first twenty years after the centenary of his death, he became strictly yesterday's man and no longer worth bothering about. Some journalist has even suggested that this discussion tonight is trying to rescue him from 'the dustbins of history'. Yet today Marx is, once again, very much a thinker for the twenty-first century.

I don't think too much should be made of a BBC poll that showed British radio listeners voting him the greatest of all philosophers, but if you type his name into Google he remains the largest of the great intellectual presences, exceeded only by Darwin and Einstein, but well ahead of Adam Smith and Freud.

There are, in my view, two reasons for this. The first is that the end of the official Marxism of the USSR liberated Marx from public identification with Leninism in theory and with the Leninist regimes in practice. It became quite clear that there were still plenty of good reasons to take account of what Marx had to say about the world. And notably – this is the second reason – because the globalised capitalist world that emerged in the 1990s was in crucial ways uncannily like the world anticipated by Marx in the *Communist Manifesto*. This became clear in the public reaction to the 150th anniversary of this astonishing little pamphlet in 1998 – which was, incidentally, a year of dramatic upheaval in the global economy. Paradoxically, this time it was the capitalists and not the socialists who rediscovered him: the socialists were too discouraged to make much of this anniversary. I recall my amazement when I was approached by the editor of the inflight magazine of United Airlines, 80% of whose readers must be American business travellers. I'd written a piece on the *Manifesto*; he thought his readers would be interested in a debate on the *Manifesto*, and could he use something from my piece? I was even more amazed when, at lunch some time around the turn of the century, George Soros asked me what I thought of Marx. Knowing how widely our views differed, I wanted to avoid an argument so I gave an ambiguous answer. 'That man,' said Soros, 'discovered something about capitalism 150 years ago that we must take notice of.' And so he had. Soon after that writers who had never, so far as I am aware, been communists began to look at him again seriously, as in Jacques Attali's new life and study of Marx. Attali also thinks Karl Marx has much left to say to those who want the world to be a different and better society from the one we have today. It is good to be reminded that even from this point of view we need to take account of Marx today.

By October 2008, when the London *Financial Times* published its headline 'Capitalism in Convulsion', there could no longer be any doubt that he was back on the public scene. While global capitalism is undergoing its greatest disruption and crisis since the early 1930s, he is unlikely to make his exit from it. On the other hand, the Marx of the twenty-first century will almost certainly be very different from the Marx of the twentieth.

What people thought about Marx in the last century was dominated by three facts. The first was the division between countries in which revolution was on the agenda and those in which it wasn't, i.e. – speaking very broadly – the countries of developed capitalism in the North Atlantic and Pacific regions and the rest. The second fact follows from the first: Marx's heritage naturally bifurcated into a social-democratic and reformist heritage and a revolutionary heritage, overwhelmingly dominated by the Russian Revolution. This became clear after 1917 because of the third fact: the collapse of nineteenth-century capitalism and nineteenth-century bourgeois society into what I have called the 'Age of Catastrophe', between, say, 1914 and the late 1940s. That crisis was so severe as to make many doubt whether capitalism could recover. Was it not destined to be replaced by a socialist economy, as the far from Marxist Joseph

Schumpeter predicted in the 1940s? In fact capitalism did recover, but not in its old form. At the same time in the USSR a socialist alternative appeared to be immune to breakdown. Between 1929 and 1960 it did not seem unreasonable, even to many non-socialists who disapproved of the political side of these regimes, to believe that capitalism was running out of steam and the USSR was proving that it might outproduce it. In the year of Sputnik this did not sound absurd. That it was, became abundantly evident after 1960.

These events and their implications for policy and theory belong to the period after Marx's and Engels' death. They lie beyond the range of Marx's own experience and assessments. Our judgement of twentieth-century Marxism is not based on the thinking of Marx himself, but on posthumous interpretations or revisions of his writing. At most we can claim that in the later 1890s, during what was the first intellectual crisis of Marxism, the first generation of Marxists, those who had been in personal contact with Marx, or more likely with Frederick Engels, were already beginning to discuss some of the issues that became relevant in the twentieth century, notably revisionism, imperialism and nationalism. Much of later Marxist discussion is specific to the twentieth century and not to be found in Karl Marx, notably the debate on what a socialist economy could or should actually be like, which emerged largely out of the experience of the war economies of 1914–18 and the post-war quasi-revolutionary or revolutionary crises.

Thus the claim that socialism was superior to capitalism as a way to ensure the most rapid development of the forces of production could hardly have been made by Marx. It belongs to the era when inter-war capitalist crisis confronted the USSR of the Five-Year plans. Actually, what Karl Marx claimed was not that capitalism had reached the limits of its capacity to boost the forces of production, but that the jagged rhythm of capitalist growth produced periodic crises of overproduction which would, sooner or later, prove incompatible with a capitalist way of running the economy and generate social conflicts which it would not survive. Capitalism was by its nature incapable of framing the subsequent economy of social production. This, he supposed, would necessarily be socialist.

Hence it is not surprising that 'socialism' was at the core of twentieth-century debates and assessments of Karl Marx. This was not because the project of a socialist economy is specifically Marxist – it isn't – but because all Marxist-inspired parties shared such a project and the communist ones actually claimed to have instituted it. In its twentieth-century form this project is dead. 'Socialism' as applied in the USSR and the other 'centrally planned economies', that is to say theoretically market-less state-owned and -controlled command economies, has gone and will not be revived. Social-democratic aspirations to build socialist economies had always been ideals for the future, but even as formal aspirations they had been abandoned by the end of the century.

How much of the model of socialism in the minds of social democrats, and the socialism established by communist regimes, was Marxian? Here it is crucial that Marx himself deliberately abstained from specific statements about the economics and economic institutions of socialism and said nothing about the concrete shape of communist society, except that it could not be constructed or programmed, but would evolve out of a socialist society. Such general remarks as he made on the subject, as in the *Critique of the Gotha Programme* of the German social democrats, hardly gave his successors specific guidance, and indeed these gave no serious thought to what they considered would be an academic problem or a utopian exercise until after the revolution. It was enough to know that it would be based – to quote the famous 'clause 4' of the Labour Party's constitution – 'on the common ownership of the means of production' which was generally understood as achievable by nationalising the country's industries.

Curiously enough, the first theory of a centralised socialist economy was not worked out by socialists but by a non-socialist

Italian economist, Enrico Barone, in 1908. Nobody else thought about it before the question of nationalising private industries came on the agenda of practical politics at the end of the First World War. At that point socialists faced their problems quite unprepared and without guidance from the past or anyone else.

'Planning' is implicit in any kind of socially managed economy, but Marx said nothing concrete about it, and when it was tried in Soviet Russia after the revolution it had largely to be improvised. Theoretically this was done by devising concepts (such as Leontief's input-output analysis) and providing the relevant statistics. These devices were later to be widely taken up in non-socialist economies. In practice it was done by following the equally improvised war economies of World War One, especially the German one, perhaps with special attention to the electrical industry about which Lenin was informed by political sympathisers among executives in German and American electrical firms. A war economy remained the basic model of the Soviet planned economy, that is to say an economy where certain targets are fixed in advance – ultra-speedy industrialisation, winning a war, making an atom-bomb or getting men on the moon – and then plans to achieve them by allocating resources whatever the short-term cost. There is nothing exclusively socialist about this. Working towards a priori targets may be done with more or less sophistication, but the Soviet economy never really got beyond this. And, though it tried from 1960 on, it could never get out of the catch-22 implicit in trying to fit markets into a bureaucratic command structure.

Social democracy modified Marxism in a different way either by postponing the construction of a socialist economy or, more positively, by devising different forms of a mixed economy. Insofar as social-democratic parties remained committed to the creation of a fully socialist economy, this implied some thought about the subject. The most interesting thinking came from non-Marxist thinkers like the Fabians Sidney and Beatrice Webb, who envisaged a gradual transformation of capitalism to socialism by a series of irreversible and cumulative reforms and who therefore gave some political thought to the institutional shape of socialism, though none to its economic operations. The chief Marxian 'revisionist', Eduard Bernstein, finessed the problem by insisting that the reformist movement was everything and the final aim had no practical reality. In fact, most social-democratic parties which became parties of government after World War One settled for the revisionist policy, in effect leaving the capitalist economy to operate subject to meeting some of the demands of labour. The *locus classicus* of this attitude was Anthony Crosland's *The Future of Socialism* (1956), which argued that as post-1945 capitalism had solved the problem of producing a society of plenty, public enterprise (in the classical form of nationalisation or otherwise) was not necessary and the only task of socialists was to ensure an equitable distribution of the national wealth. All this was a long way from Marx, and indeed from the traditional socialist vision of socialism as essentially a non-market society, which probably Karl Marx also shared.

Let me just add that the more recent debate between economic neo-liberals and their critics about the role of the state and publicly owned enterprises is not a specifically Marxist or even socialist debate in principle. It rests on the attempt since the 1970s to translate a pathological degeneration of the principle of laissez-faire into economic reality by the systematic retreat of states from any regulation or control of the activities of profit-making enterprise. This attempt to hand over human society to the (allegedly) self-controlling and wealth- or even welfare-maximising market, populated (allegedly) by actors in rational pursuit of their interests, had no precedent in any earlier phase of capitalist development in any developed economy, not even the USA. It was a *reductio ad absurdum* of what its ideologists read into Adam Smith, as the correspondingly extremist 100% state-planned command economy of the USSR was of what the Bolsheviks read into Marx. Not surprisingly, this 'market fundamentalism', closer to theology than economic reality, also failed.

The disappearance of the centrally planned state economies and the virtual disappearance of a fundamentally transformed society from the aspirations of the demoralised social-democratic parties have eliminated much of the twentieth-century debates on socialism. They were some way from Karl Marx's own thinking, though very largely inspired by him and conducted in his name. On the other hand, in three respects Marx remained an enormous force: as an economic thinker, as a historical thinker and analyst, and as the recognised founding father (with Durkheim and Max Weber) of modern thinking about society. I am unqualified to express an opinion on his continued, but clearly serious, significance as a philosopher. Certainly what never lost contemporary relevance is Marx's vision of capitalism as a historically temporary mode of the human economy and his analysis of its ever-expanding and concentrating, crisis-generating and self-transforming modus operandi.

II

What is the relevance of Marx in the twenty-first century? The Soviet-type model of socialism – the only attempt to build a socialist economy so far – no longer exists. On the other hand there has been an enormous and accelerating progress of globalisation and the sheer wealth-generating capacity of humans. This has reduced the power and scope of economic and social action by nation-states and therefore the classical policies of social-democratic movements, which depended primarily on pressing reforms on national governments. Given the prominence of market fundamentalism it has also generated extreme economic inequality within countries and between regions and brought back the element of catastrophe to the basic cyclical rhythm of the capitalist economy, including what became its most serious global crisis since the 1930s.

Our productive capacity has made it possible, at least potentially, for most human beings to move from the realm of necessity into the realm of affluence, education and unimagined life choices, although most of the world's population have yet to enter it. Yet for most of the twentieth century socialist movements and regimes still operated essentially within this realm of necessity, even in the rich countries of the West where a society of popular affluence emerged in the twenty post-1945 years. However, in the realm of affluence the aim of adequate food, clothing, housing, jobs to provide income and a welfare system to protect people against the hazards of life, though necessary, is no longer a sufficient programme for socialists.

A third development is negative. As the spectacular expansion of the global economy has undermined the environment, the need to control unlimited economic growth has become increasingly urgent. There is a patent conflict between the need to reverse or at least to control the impact of our economy on the biosphere and the imperatives of a capitalist market: maximum continuing growth in the search for profit. This is the Achilles heel of capitalism. We cannot at present know whose arrow will be fatal to it.

So how are we to see Karl Marx today? As a thinker for all humanity and not only for a part of it? Certainly. As a philosopher? As an economic analyst? As a founding father of modern social science and guide to the understanding of human history? Yes, but the point about him which Attali has rightly emphasised is the universal comprehensiveness of his thought. It is not 'interdisciplinary' in the conventional sense but integrates all disciplines. As Attali writes, 'Philosophers before him have thought of man in his totality, but he was the first to apprehend the world as a whole which is at once political, economic, scientific and philosophical.'

It is perfectly obvious that much of what he wrote is out of date, and some of it is not or no longer acceptable. It is also evident that his writings do not form a finished corpus but are, like all thought that deserves the name, an endless work in progress. Nobody is any longer going to turn it into a dogma, let alone an institutionally buttressed orthodoxy. This would certainly have shocked Marx himself. But we should also reject the idea that there is a sharp difference between a 'correct' and an 'incorrect' Marxism. His mode of enquiry could produce different results and political perspectives. Indeed it did so with Marx himself, who envisaged a possible peaceful transition to power in Britain and the Netherlands, and the possible evolution of the Russian village community into socialism. Kautsky and even Bernstein were heirs of Marx as much (or, if you like, as little) as Plekhanov and Lenin. For this reason I am sceptical of Attali's distinction between a true Marx and a series of subsequent simplifiers or falsifiers of his thought – Engels, Kautsky, Lenin. It was as legitimate for the Russians, the first attentive readers of *Capital*, to see his theory as a way for moving countries like theirs from backwardness to modernity through economic development of the Western type as it was for Marx himself to speculate whether a direct transition to socialism could not take place on the basis of the Russian village commune. Probably, if anything, it was more in line with the general run of Karl Marx's own thought. The case against the Soviet experiment was not that socialism could only be constructed after the whole world had first gone capitalist, which is not what Marx said, or can be firmly claimed to have believed. It was empirical. It was that Russia was too backward to produce anything other than a caricature of a socialist society – 'a Chinese empire in red' as Plekhanov is said to have warned. In 1917 this would have been the overwhelming consensus of all Marxists, including even most Russian Marxists. On the other hand the case against the so-called 'Legal Marxists' of the 1890s, who took the Attali view that the main job of Marxists was to develop a flourishing industrial capitalism in Russia, was also empirical. A liberal capitalist Russia wouldn't come about either under tsarism.

And yet a number of central features of Marx's analysis remain valid and relevant. The first, obviously, is the analysis of the irresistible global dynamic of capitalist economic development and its capacity to destroy all that came before it, including even those parts of the heritage of the human past from which capitalism had itself benefited, such as family structures. The second is the analysis of the mechanism of capitalist growth by generating internal 'contradictions' – endless bouts of tensions and temporary resolutions, growth leading to crisis and change, all producing economic concentration in an increasingly globalised economy. Mao dreamed of a society constantly renewed by unceasing revolution; capitalism has realised this project by historical change through what Schumpeter (following Marx) called unending 'creative destruction'. Marx believed that this process would eventually lead – it would have to lead – to an enormously concentrated economy – which is exactly what Attali meant when he said in a recent interview that the number of people who decide what happens in it is of the order of 1,000, or at most 10,000. This Marx believed would lead to the supersession of capitalism, a prediction that still sounds plausible to me but in a different way from what Marx anticipated.

On the other hand, his prediction that it would take place by the 'expropriation of the expropriators' through a vast proletariat leading to socialism was not based on his analysis of the mechanism of capitalism, but on separate a priori assumptions. At most it was based on the prediction that industrialisation would produce populations largely employed as manual wageworkers, as was happening in England at the time. This was correct enough as a middle-range prediction, but not, as we know, in the long term. Nor, after the 1840s, did Marx and Engels expect it to produce the politically radicalising pauperisation that they hoped for. As was obvious to both, large sections of the proletariat were not getting poorer in any absolute sense. Indeed, an American observer of the solidly proletarian congresses of the German Social Democratic Party in the 1900s observed that the comrades there looked 'a loaf or two above poverty'. On the other hand, the evident growth of economic inequality between different parts of the world and between classes does not necessarily produce Marx's 'expropriation of the expropriators'. In short, hopes for the future were read into his analysis but did not derive from it.

The third is best put in the words of the late Sir John Hicks, an economics Nobel laureate. 'Most of those who wish to fit into place a general course of history,' he wrote, 'would use the Marxist categories or some modified version of them, since there is little in the way of alternative versions that is available.'

We cannot foresee the solutions of the problems facing the world in the twenty-first century, but if they are to have a chance of success they must ask Marx's questions, even if they do not wish to accept his various disciples' answers.

2

Marx, Engels and
pre-Marxian Socialism

I

Marx and Engels were relative latecomers to communism. Engels declared himself a communist late in 1842, Marx probably not until the latter part of 1843, after a more prolonged and complex settling of accounts with liberalism and Hegel's philosophy. Even in Germany, a political backwater, they were not the first. German journeymen (*Handwerksgesellen*) working abroad had already made contact with organised communist movements, and produced the first native German communist theorist, the tailor Wilhelm Weitling, whose first work had been published in 1838 (*Die Menschheit, wie sie ist und wie sie sein sollte*). Among the intellectuals Moses Hess preceded, and indeed claimed to have converted, the young Frederick Engels. However, the question of priority in German communism is unimportant. By the early 1840s a flourishing socialist and communist movement, both theoretical and practical, had existed for some time in France, Britain and the USA. How much did the young Marx and Engels know about these movements? What did they owe to them? In what relation does their own socialism stand to their predecessors' and contemporaries'? These questions will be discussed in the present chapter.

Before doing so we may briefly dismiss the pre-historic figures of communist theory, though historians of socialism usually pay their respects to them, since even revolutionaries like to have ancestors. Modern socialism does not derive from Plato or Thomas More, or even from Campanella, though the young Marx was sufficiently impressed with his *City of the Sun* to plan its inclusion in an abortive 'Library of the best foreign socialist writers' he projected with Engels and Hess in 1845.[1] Such works had some interest for nineteenth-century readers, since one of the main difficulties of communist theory for urban intellectuals was that the actual operations of communist society appeared to have no precedent and were difficult to make plausible. The name of More's book, indeed, became the term used to describe any attempt to sketch the ideal society of the future, which in the nineteenth century meant primarily a communist one: utopia. Inasmuch as at least one utopian communist, E. Cabet (1788–1856), was an admirer of More, the name was not ill-chosen. Nevertheless, the normal procedure of the pioneer socialists and communists of the early nineteenth century, if sufficiently given to study, was not to derive their ideas from some remote author, but to discover, or have their attention drawn to, the relevance of some earlier theoretical architect of ideal commonwealths when about to construct their own critique of society or utopia; and then to use and praise him. The fashion for utopian – not necessarily communist – literature in the eighteenth century made such works familiar enough.

Nor, in spite of varying degrees of familiarity with them, were the numerous historical examples of Christian communist establishments among the inspirers of modern socialist and communist ideas. How far the older ones (like the descendants of the sixteenth-century Anabaptists) were widely known at all is unclear. Certainly the young Engels, who cited various such communities as proof that communism was practicable, confined himself to relatively recent examples: Shakers, (whom he regarded as 'the first people to set up a society on the basis of community of goods . . . in the whole world'),[2] Rappites and Separatists. Insofar as they were known, they also primarily confirmed an already existing desire for communism more than they inspired it.

It is not possible to dismiss quite so summarily the ancient religious and philosophical traditions which, with the rise of modern capitalism, acquired or revealed a new potential for social criticism, or confirmed an established one, because the revolutionary model of a liberal-economic society of unrestrained individualism conflicted with the social values of virtually every hitherto known community of men and women. For the educated minority, to whom practically all socialist, as indeed any other social theorists belonged, they were embodied in a chain or network of philosophical thinkers, and most notably in a tradition of Natural Law stretching back to classical antiquity. Though some eighteenth-century philosophers were engaged in modifying such traditions to fit in with the new aspirations of a liberal-individualist society, philosophy carried with it from the past a strong heritage of communalism, or even, in several cases, the belief that a society without private property was in some sense more 'natural' or at any rate historically prior to one with private property. This was even more marked in Christian ideology. Nothing is easier than to see the Christ of the Sermon on the Mount as 'the first socialist' or communist, and though the majority of early socialist theorists were not Christians, many later members of socialist movements have found this reflection useful. Insofar as these ideas were embodied in a succession of texts, commenting upon, adding to and criticising their predecessors, which were part of the formal or informal education of social theorists, the idea of a 'good society', and specifically a society not based on private property, was at least a marginal part of their intellectual heritage. It is easy to laugh at Cabet, who lists a huge array of thinkers from Confucius to Sismondi and passing through Lycurgus, Pythagoras, Socrates, Plato, Plutarch, Bossuet, Locke, Helvetius, Raynal and Benjamin Franklin, as recognising in his communism the realisation of their fundamental ideas – and indeed Marx and Engels made fun of such intellectual genealogy in the *German Ideology*.[3] Nevertheless, it represents a genuine element of continuity between the traditional critique of what was wrong in society and the new critique of what was wrong in bourgeois society; at least for the literate.

Insofar as such older texts and traditions embodied communal concepts, they actually reflected something of the powerful elements in European – mainly rural – pre-industrial societies, and the even more obvious communal elements in the exotic societies with which Europeans came into contact from the sixteenth century. The study of such exotic and 'primitive' societies played a notable role in the formation of western social criticism, particularly in the eighteenth century, as witness the tendency to idealise them as against 'civilised' society, whether in the form of the 'noble savage', the free Swiss or Corsican peasant, or otherwise. At the very least, as in Rousseau and other eighteenth-century thinkers, it suggested that civilisation also implied the corruption of some prior and in some ways more just, equal and benevolent human state. It might even suggest that such societies before private property ('primitive communism') provided models of what future societies should once again aspire to, and proof that it was not impracticable. This line of thought is certainly present in nineteenth-century socialism, and not least in Marxism, but, paradoxically, it emerges much more strongly towards the end of the century than in its early decades – probably in connection with Marx's and Engels' increasing acquaintance and preoccupation with primitive communal institutions.[4] With the exception of Fourier, the early socialists and communists show no tendency to look back, even out of the corner of their eye, towards a 'primitive happiness' which could in some sense serve as a model for the future felicity of mankind; and this in spite of the fact that the most familiar model for the speculative construction of perfect societies, throughout the sixteenth to eighteenth centuries, was the utopian novel, purporting to recount what the traveller had encountered in the course of some journey to remote areas of the earth. In the struggle between tradition and progress, the primitive and the civilised, they were firmly committed on one side. Even Fourier, who identified the primitive state of man with Eden, believed in the ineluctability of progress.

The word 'progress' brings us to what was clearly the main intellectual matrix of early modern socialist and communist critiques of society, namely the eighteenth-century (and in particular the French) Enlightenment. At least this was Frederick Engels' firm opinion.[5] What he stressed above all was its systematic rationalism. Reason provided the basis of all human action and the formation of society, and the standard against which 'all previous forms of society and government, all the old ideas handed down by tradition' were to be rejected. 'Henceforth superstition, injustice, privilege and oppression were to be superseded by eternal truth, eternal justice, equality grounded in Nature and the inalienable rights of man.'[6] The rationalism of the Enlightenment implied a fundamentally critical approach to society, logically including bourgeois society. Yet the various schools and currents of the Enlightenment provided more than merely a charter for social criticism and revolutionary change. They provided the belief in the capacity of man to improve his conditions, even – as with Turgot and Condorcet – in his perfectibility, the belief in human history as human progress towards what must eventually be the best possible society, and social criteria by which to judge societies more concrete than reason in general. The natural rights of man were not merely life and liberty, but also 'the pursuit of happiness', which revolutionaries, rightly recognising its historical novelty (Saint-Just), transformed into the conviction that 'happiness is the only object of society'.[7]

Even in its most bourgeois and individualist form, such revolutionary approaches contributed to encourage a socialist critique of society when the time was propitious. We are unlikely to regard Jeremy Bentham as any kind of socialist. Yet the young Marx and Engels (perhaps more the latter than the former) saw Bentham as a link between the materialism of Helvetius and Robert Owen who 'proceeded from Bentham's system to found English communism', while 'only the proletariat and the Socialists . . . have succeeded in developing his teachings a step forwards'.[8] Indeed, both went so far as to propose Bentham's inclusion – if only as a consequence of that of William Godwin's *Political Justice* – in their projected 'Library of the best foreign socialist writers'.[9]

The specific debt of Marx to schools of thought produced within the Enlightenment – e.g. in the field of political economy and philosophy – need not be discussed in this connection. The fact remains that they rightly saw their predecessors, the 'utopian' socialists and communists, as belonging to illuminism. Insofar as they traced the socialist tradition back beyond the French Revolution, it was to the philosophical materialists Holbach and Helvetius, and to the illuminist communists Morelly and Mably – the only names from this early period (with the exception of Campanella) to figure in their projected Library.

Nevertheless, though he appears to have had no great direct influence on Marx and Engels, the role of one particular thinker in the formation of later socialist theory must be briefly considered: J.-J. Rousseau. Rousseau can hardly be called a socialist, for though he developed what was to be the most popular version of the argument that private property is the source of all social inequality, he did not argue that the good society must socialise property, only that it must ensure its equal distribution. Though he agreed with it, he did not even develop in any detail the theoretical concept that 'property is theft', which was later popularised by Proudhon – but, as witness its elaboration by the Girondin Brissot, did not in itself imply socialism either.[10] Yet two observations must be made about him. First, the view that social equality must rest on common ownership of wealth and central regulation of all productive labour is a natural extension of Rousseau's argument. Second, and more important, the political influence of Rousseau's egalitarianism on the Jacobin left, out of which the first modern communist movements emerged, is undeniable. In his defence, Babeuf appealed to Rousseau.[11] The communism whose acquaintance Marx and Engels first made had *equality* as its central slogan;[12] and Rousseau was its most influential theorist. Inasmuch as socialism and communism in the early 1840s were French – as they largely were – Rousseauist egalitarianism was one of the original components. The Rousseauist influence on classical German philosophy should not be forgotten either.

II

As already suggested, the unbroken history of communism as a modern social movement begins on the left wing of the French Revolution. A direct line of descent links Babeuf's *Conspiracy of the Equals* through Buonarroti with Blanqui's revolutionary societies of the 1830s; and these in turn, through the 'League of the Just' – later, the 'Communist League' – of the German exiles which they inspired, with Marx and Engels, who drafted the *Communist Manifesto* on its behalf. It is natural that Marx's and Engels' projected 'Library' of 1845 was to have begun with two branches of 'socialist' literature: with Babeuf and Buonarroti (following upon Morelly and Mably) who represent the openly communist wing, and with the left-wing critics of the formal equality of the French Revolution and the Enragés (the 'Cercle Social', Hébert, Jacques Roux, Leclerc). Yet the theoretical interest of what Engels was to call 'an ascetic communism, deriving from Sparta' (*Werke* 20, p.18) was not great. Even the communist writers of the 1830s and 1840s do not seem to have impressed Marx and Engels as theorists. Indeed Marx argued that it was the crudeness and one-sidedness of this early communism which 'allowed other socialist doctrines such as those of Fourier, Proudhon etc. to appear in distinction from it, not by accident but by necessity'.[13] Though Marx read their writings – even such relatively minor figures as Lahautière (1813–82) and Pillot (1809–77) – he clearly owed little to their social analysis, which was chiefly significant in formulating the class struggle as one between 'proletarians' and their exploiters.

However, babouvist and neo-babouvist communism was significant in two ways. In the first place, unlike most of the utopian socialist theory, it was profoundly embedded in politics, and therefore embodied not only a theory of revolution but a doctrine of political praxis, of organisation, strategy and tactics, however limited. Its chief representatives in the 1830s – Laponneraye (1808–49), Lahautière, Dézamy, Pillot and above all Blanqui – were active revolutionaries. This, as well as their organic connection with the history of the French Revolution, which Marx studied intensively, made them highly relevant to the development of his thought. In the second place, though the communist writers were mainly marginal intellectuals, the communist movement of the 1830s visibly attracted the workers. This fact, noted by Lorenz von Stein, clearly impressed Marx and Engels, who later recalled the proletarian character of the communist movement of the 1840s, as distinct from the middle-class character of most utopian socialism.[14] Moreover, it was from this French movement, which adopted the name 'communist' around 1840,[15] that German communists, including Marx and Engels, took the name of their views.

The communism which emerged in the 1830s from the neo-babouvist and essentially political and revolutionary tradition of France fused with the new experience of the proletariat in the capitalist society of the early industrial revolution. That is what made it into a 'proletarian' movement, however small. Insofar as communist ideas rested directly upon such experience, they were clearly likely to be influenced by the country in which an industrial working class already existed as a mass phenomenon – Great Britain. It is thus no accident that the most prominent of the French communist theorists of the time, Etienne Cabet (1788–1856), was inspired not by neo-babouvism but by his experiences in England during the 1830s, and especially by Robert Owen, and therefore belongs rather to the utopian socialist current. Yet insofar as the new industrial and bourgeois society could be analysed by any thinker within the regions directly transformed by one or the other aspect of the 'dual revolution' of the bourgeoisie – the French Revolution and the (British) Industrial Revolution – such analysis was not so directly linked with the actual experience of industrialisation. It was, in fact, simultaneously and independently undertaken in both Britain and France. This analysis forms a major basis for the subsequent development of Marx's and Engels' thought. It may be observed, incidentally, that, thanks to Engels' British connection, Marxian communism was from the outset under British as well as French intellectual influence, whereas the remainder of the German socialist and communist left was acquainted with little more than French developments.[16]

Unlike the word 'communist', which always signified a programme, the word 'socialist' was primarily analytical and critical. It was used to describe those who held a particular view of human nature (e.g. the fundamental importance of 'sociability' or the 'social instincts' in it), which implied a particular view of human society, or those who believed in the possibility or necessity of a particular mode of social action, notably in public affairs (e.g. intervention in the operations of the free market). It was soon realised that such views were likely to be developed by or to attract those who favoured equality, such as the disciples of Rousseau, and to lead to interference with property rights – the point was already made by eighteenth-century Italian opponents of the Enlightenment and of 'socialists'[17] –

but it was not entirely identified with a society based on the fully collective ownership and management of the means of production. Indeed, it did not become completely so identified in general usage until the emergence of socialist political parties in the late nineteenth century, and some may argue that it is not completely identified even today. Hence evident non-socialists (in the modern sense) could, even in the late nineteenth century, describe themselves or be described as 'socialists', like the *Kathedersozialisten* of Germany or the British Liberal politician who declared 'we are all socialists now'. This programmatic ambiguity extended even to movements regarded as socialist by socialists. It should not be forgotten that one of the major schools of what Marx and Engels called 'utopian socialism', the Saint-Simonians, was 'more concerned with collective regulation of industry than with co-operative ownership of wealth'.[18] The Owenites who first used the word in England (1826) – but only described themselves as 'socialists' several years later – described the society they aspired to as one of 'co-operation'.

Yet in a society in which the antonym of 'socialism', 'individualism',[19] itself implied a specific liberal-capitalist model of the competitive unrestricted market economy, it was natural that 'socialism' should also carry a programmatic connotation as the general name for all aspirations to organise society on an associationist or co-operative model, i.e. based on co-operative rather than private property. The word continued to be imprecise though, from the 1830s on, it was associated primarily with the more or less fundamental reshaping of society in this sense. Its adherents ranged from social reformers to freaks.

Two aspects of early socialism must therefore be distinguished: the critical and the programmatic. The critical consisted of two elements, a theory of human nature and society, mainly derived from various currents of eighteenth-century thought, and an analysis of the society produced by the 'dual revolution', sometimes in the framework of a view of historical development or 'progress'. The first of these was of no great interest to Marx and Engels, except insofar as it led (in British rather than French thought) to political economy. We shall consider this below. The second evidently influenced them very much. The programmatic aspect also consisted of two elements: a variety of proposals to create a new economy on the basis of co-operation, in extreme cases by the foundation of communist communities; and an attempt to reflect on the nature and the characteristics of the ideal society which was thus to be brought about. Here again, Marx and Engels were uninterested in the first. Utopian community-building they rightly regarded as politically negligible, as indeed it was. It never became a movement of any practical significance outside the USA, where it was rather popular in both a secular and a religious form. At best it served as an illustration of the practicability of communism. The politically more influential forms of associationism and co-operation, which exercised a substantial appeal to both British and French artisans and skilled workers, they either knew little about at the time (e.g. the Owenite 'labour exchanges' of the 1830s) or distrusted. Retrospectively, Engels compared Owen's 'labour bazaars' with Proudhon's proposals.[20] In Louis Blanc's remarkably successful *Organisation du Travail* (ten editions 1839–48) they clearly are not considered significant, and insofar as Marx and Engels were, they opposed them.

On the other hand the utopian reflections on the nature of communist society influenced Marx and Engels very substantially, though their hostility to the drafting of such prospectuses for the communist future has led many subsequent commentators to underestimate this influence. Very nearly everything that Marx and Engels said about the concrete shape of communist society is based on earlier utopian writings, e.g. the abolition of the distinction between town and country (derived, according to Engels, from Fourier and Owen)[21] and the abolition of the state (from Saint-Simon),[22] or it is based on a critical discussion of utopian themes.

Pre-Marxian socialism is therefore embedded in the later work of Marx and Engels, but in a doubly distorted form. They made a highly selective use of their predecessors, and also their mature and late writings do not necessarily mirror the impact which the early socialists made upon them in their formative period. Thus the youthful Engels was clearly much less impressed with the Saint-Simonians than the later Engels, while Cabet, who does not figure in *Anti-Dühring* at all, is not infrequently referred to in the writings before 1846.[23]

However, almost from the start Marx and Engels singled out three 'utopian' thinkers as especially significant: Saint-Simon, Fourier and Robert Owen. In this respect the late Engels maintains the judgement of the early forties.[24] Owen stands slightly apart from the other two, and not only because he was clearly introduced to Marx (who can hardly have known him, since his works were as yet untranslated) by Engels, who was in close contact with the Owenite movement in England. Unlike Saint-Simon and Fourier, Owen is usually described by the Marx and Engels of the early 1840s as a 'communist'. Engels then, as later, was especially impressed by the practical common sense and businesslike manner with which he designed his utopian communities ('from an expert's standpoint, there is little to be said against the actual detailed arrangements' – *Werke* 20, p.245). Owen's single-minded hostility to the three great obstacles to social reform, 'private property, religion and marriage in its present form' (ibid.), also clearly appealed to him. Moreover, the fact that Owen, himself a capitalist entrepreneur and factory-owner, criticised the actual bourgeois society of the Industrial Revolution, gave his critique a specificity which the French socialists lacked. (That he had also, in the 1820s and 1830s, attracted substantial working-class support does not seem to have been appreciated by Engels, who only knew the Owenite socialists of the 1840s).[25] Nevertheless, Marx had no doubt that theoretically Owen was notably inferior to the French.[26] The major theoretical interest of his writings, as with those of the other British socialists whom Marx later studied, lay in their economic analysis of capitalism, i.e. in the manner in which they derived socialist conclusions from the premises and arguments of bourgeois political economy.

'In Saint-Simon we find the breadth of view of genius, thanks to which almost all ideas of later socialists, which are not strictly economic, are contained in his work in embryo.'[27] There is no doubt that Engels' later judgement reflects the very considerable debt which Marxism owes to Saint-Simonism, though, curiously enough, there is not much reference to the Saint-Simonian school (Bazard, Enfantin et al.) which actually turned the ambiguous if brilliant intuitions of their master into something like a socialist system. The extraordinary influence of Saint-Simon (1759–1825) on a variety of significant and often brilliant talents, not only in France but abroad (Carlyle, J.S. Mill, Heine, Liszt), is a fact of European cultural history in the era of Romanticism which is not always easy to appreciate today by those who read his actual writings. If these contain a consistent doctrine, it is the central importance of productive industry which must make the genuinely productive elements in society into its social and political controllers and shape the future of society: a theory of industrial revolution. The 'industrialists' (a Saint-Simonian coinage) form the majority of the population and include the productive entrepreneurs – including, notably, the bankers – the scientists, technological innovators and other intellectuals, and the labouring people. Insofar as they contain the latter, who incidentally function as the reservoir from which the former are recruited, Saint-Simon's doctrines attack poverty and social inequality, while he totally rejects the French Revolution's principles of liberty and equality as individualist and leading to competition and economic anarchy. The object of social institutions is to 'faire concourir les principales institutions à l'accroissement du bien-être des prolétaires', defined simply as 'la classe la plus nombreuse' (*Organisation Sociale*, 1825). On the other hand, insofar as the 'industrialists' are entrepreneurs and technocratic planners, they oppose not only the idle and parasitic ruling classes, but also the anarchy of bourgeois-liberal capitalism, of which he provides an early critique. Implicit in him is the recognition that industrialisation is fundamentally incompatible with an unplanned society.

The emergence of the 'industrial class' is the result of history. How much of Saint-Simon's views were his own, how much influenced by his secretary (1814–17), the historian Augustin Thierry, need not concern us. At all events social systems are determined by the mode of organisation of property, historic evolution rests on the development of the productive system, and the power of the bourgeoisie on its possession of the means of production. He appears to hold a rather simple view of French history as class struggle, dating back to the conquest of the Gauls by the Franks, which was elaborated by his followers into a more specific history of the exploited classes which anticipates Marx: slaves are succeeded by serfs, and these by nominally free but propertyless proletarians. However, for the history of his own times, Saint-Simon was more specific. As Engels later noted with admiration, he saw the French Revolution as a class struggle between nobility, bourgeois and propertyless masses. (His followers extended this by arguing that the Revolution had liberated the bourgeois, but the time had now come to liberate the proletarian.)

Apart from history, Engels was to stress two other major insights: the subordination, indeed eventually the absorption, of politics into economics and consequently the abolition of the state in the society of the future: the 'administration of things' replacing the 'government of men'. Whether or not this Saint-Simonian phrase is to be found in the writings of the founder, the concept is clearly there. Yet a number of other concepts which have become part of Marxism, as of all subsequent socialism, can also be traced back to the Saint-Simonian school, though not perhaps explicitly to Saint-Simon himself. 'The exploitation of man by man' is a Saint-Simonian phrase; so is the formula slightly altered by Marx to describe the distributive principle of the first phase of communism: 'From each according to his abilities, to each ability according to its work'; so is the phrase, singled out by Marx in the *German Ideology*, that 'all men must be assured the free development of their natural capacities'. In short, Marxism was evidently much indebted to Saint-Simon, though the exact nature of the debt is not easy to define, since the Saint-Simonian contribution cannot always be distinguished from other contemporary ones. Thus the discovery of the class struggle in history was likely to be made by anyone who studied, or even who had lived through, the French Revolution. It was indeed ascribed by Marx to the bourgeois historians of the French Restoration. At the same time the most important of these (from Marx's point of view), Augustin Thierry, had, as we have seen, been closely linked with Saint-Simon at one period of his life. Still, however we define the influence, it is not in doubt. The uniformly favourable treatment of Saint-Simon by Engels, who noted that 'he positively suffered from a plethora of ideas' and whom he actually compared to Hegel as 'the most encyclopedic mind of his age', speaks for itself.[28]

The mature Engels praised Charles Fourier (1772–1837) mainly on three grounds: as a brilliant, witty and savage critic of bourgeois society, or rather of bourgeois behaviour;[29] for his advocacy of women's liberation; and for his essentially dialectical conception of history. (The last point seems to belong more to Engels than to Fourier.) Yet the first impact which Fourier's thought made on him, and that which has perhaps left the most profound traces in Marxian socialism, was his analysis of labour. Fourier's contribution to the socialist tradition was idiosyncratic. Unlike other socialists he was suspicious of progress, and shared a Rousseauist belief that humanity had somehow taken the wrong turning in adopting civilisation. He was suspicious of industry and technical advance, though prepared to accept and use it, and convinced that the wheel of history could not be turned back. He was also – in this respect like several other utopians – suspicious of Jacobin popular sovereignty and democracy. Philosophically he was an ultra-individualist whose supreme aim for humanity was the satisfaction of all individuals' psychological urges, and the attainment of maximum enjoyment by the individual. Since – to quote Engels' first recorded impressions of him[30] – 'each individual has an inclination or preference for a particular kind of work, the sum of all individual inclinations must, by and large, constitute a sufficient force to satisfy the needs of all. From this principle there follows: if all individuals are allowed to do and not to do whatever corresponds to their personal inclinations, the needs of all will be satisfied,' and he demonstrated 'that . . . *absolute inactivity* is nonsense, and has never existed nor can it ever exist . . . He further demonstrates that labour and enjoyment are identical, and it is the irrationality of the present social order which separates the two.' Fourier's insistence on the emancipation of women, with the explicit corollary of radical sexual liberation, is a logical extension – indeed perhaps the core – of his utopia of the liberation of all personal instincts and impulses. Fourier was certainly not the only feminist among the early socialists, but his passionate commitment made him perhaps the most powerful, and his influence may be detected in the radical turn of the Saint-Simonians in this direction.

Marx himself was perhaps more aware than Engels of the possible conflict between Fourier's view of labour as the essential satisfaction of a human instinct, identical with play, and the full development of all human capacities which both he and Engels believed communism would ensure, though the abolition of the division of labour (i.e. of permanent functional specialisation) might well produce results which could be interpreted on Fourierist lines ('to hunt in the morning, to fish in the afternoon, to rear cattle in the evening, and criticise after dinner').[31] Indeed, later he specifically rejected Fourier's conception of labour as 'mere fun, mere amusement'[32] and in doing so implicitly rejected the Fourierist equation between self-realisation and instinctual liberation. Fourier's communist humans were men and women as nature had made them, liberated from all repression; Marx's communist men and women were more than this. Nevertheless, the fact that the mature Marx specifically reconsiders Fourier in his most serious discussion of labour as human activity suggests the significance of this writer for him. As for Engels, his continuing laudatory references to Fourier (e.g. in the *Origin of the Family*) attest to a permanent influence, and to his permanent sympathy for the only utopian socialist writer who can still be read today with the same sense of pleasure, illumination – and exasperation – as in the early 1840s.

The utopian socialists thus provided a critique of bourgeois society, the outlines of a historical theory, the confidence that socialism was not only realisable but called for at this historical moment, and a great deal of thinking about what the human arrangements in such a society would be like (including individual human behaviour). Yet they had striking theoretical and practical deficiencies. They had both a minor and a major practical weakness. They were mixed up, to put it mildly, with various kinds of romantic eccentricity ranging from the penetratingly visionary to the psychically unhinged, from mental confusion, not always to be excused by the overflow of ideas, to curious cults and exalted quasi-religious sects. In short, their followers tended to make themselves ridiculous and, as the young Engels observed of the Saint-Simonians, 'once something has been made ridiculous, it is hopelessly lost in France'.[33] Marx and Engels, while regarding the fantastic elements in the great utopians as the necessary price for their genius or originality, could hardly envisage much of a practical role in the socialist transformation of the world for increasingly odd and often increasingly isolated groups of cranks.

Second, and more to the point, they were essentially apolitical, and thus, even in theory, provided no effective means by which such a transformation could be achieved. The exodus into communist communities was no more likely to produce the desired results than the earlier appeals of a Saint-Simon to Napoleon, Tsar Alexander or the great Paris bankers. The utopians (with the exception of the Saint-Simonians, whose chosen instrument, the dynamic capitalist entrepreneurs, drew them away from socialism) did not recognise any special class or group as the vehicle of their ideas, and even when (as Engels later recognised in the case of Owen) they appealed to the workers, the proletarian movement played no distinctive part in their plans, which were addressed to all who ought to – but generally failed to – recognise the obvious truth they alone had discovered. Yet doctrinal propaganda and education, especially in the abstract form which the young Engels criticised in the British Owenites, would never succeed by themselves. In short, as he saw clearly from his British experience, 'socialism, which goes far beyond French communism in its basis, in its development lags behind it. It will have for a moment to revert to the French point-of-view, in order subsequently to go beyond it.'[34] The French point of view was that of the revolutionary – and political – class struggle of the proletariat. As we shall see, Marx and Engels were even more critical of the non-utopian developments of early socialism into various kinds of co-operation and mutualism.

Among the numerous theoretical weaknesses of utopian socialism, one stood out dramatically: its lack of an economic analysis of private property which 'the French socialists and communists . . . had not only criticised in various ways but also "transcended" [*aufgehoben*] in a utopian manner',[35] but which they had not systematically analysed as the basis of the capitalist system and of exploitation. Marx himself, stimulated by Engels' early *Outline of a Critique of Political Economy* (1843–4),[36] had come to the conclusion that such an analysis must be the core of communist theory. As he later put it, when describing his own process of intellectual development, political economy was 'the anatomy of civil society' (Preface to *Critique of Political Economy*). It was not to be found in the French 'utopian' socialists. Hence his admiration and (in *The Holy Family*, 1845) extended defence of P.-J. Proudhon (1809–65), whose *What is Property?* (1840) he read towards the end of 1842, and whom he immediately went out of his way to praise as 'the most consistent and acute socialist writer'.[37] To say that Proudhon 'influenced' Marx or contributed to the formation of his thought is an exaggeration. Even in 1844 he compared him in some respects unfavourably as a theorist with the German tailor-communist Wilhelm Weitling,[38] whose only real significance was that (like Proudhon himself) he was an actual worker. Yet, though he regarded Proudhon as an inferior mind to Saint-Simon and Fourier, he nevertheless appreciated the advance he made upon them, which he later compared to that of Feuerbach over Hegel; and, in spite of his subsequent and increasingly bitter hostility to Proudhon and his followers, he never modified his view.[39] This was not so much because of the economic merits of the work, for 'in a strictly scientific history of political economy the work would be hardly worth a mention'. Indeed, Proudhon was not and never became a serious economist. He praised Proudhon not because he had anything to learn from him, but because he saw him as pioneering that very 'critique of political economy' which he himself recognised as the central theoretical task, and he did so all the more generously because Proudhon was both an actual worker and unquestionably an original mind. Marx did not have to advance far in his economic studies before the deficiencies of Proudhon's theory struck him more forcibly than its merits: they are flayed in the *Poverty of Philosophy* (1847).

None of the other French socialists exercised any significant influence on the formation of Marxian thought.

III

The triple origin of Marxian socialism in French socialism, German philosophy and British political economy is well known: as early as 1844 Marx observed something like this international division of intellectual labour in 'the European proletariat'.[40] This chapter is concerned with the origins of Marxian thought only insofar as it is to be found in pre-Marxian socialist or labour thought, and consequently it deals with Marxian economic ideas only insofar as these were originally derived from, or mediated through, such thought, or insofar as Marx discovered anticipations of his analysis in it. Now British socialism was in fact intellectually derived from classical British political economy in two ways: through Owen from Benthamite utilitarianism, but above all through the so-called 'Ricardian socialists' (some of them originally utilitarians), notably William Thompson (1775–1833), John Gray (1799–1883), John Francis Bray (1809–97) and Thomas Hodgskin (1787–1869). These writers are significant, not only for using Ricardo's labour theory of value to devise a theory of economic exploitation of the workers, but also for their active connection with socialist (Owenite) and working-class movements. There is in fact no evidence that even Engels knew many of these writings in the early 1840s, and Marx certainly did not read Hodgskin, 'the most cogent socialist among pre-Marxian writers',[41] until 1851, after which he expressed his appreciation with his usual scholarly conscientiousness.[42] That these writers were eventually to make a contribution to Marx's economic studies is perhaps better known than the British contribution – radical rather than socialist – to the Marxian theory of economic crisis. As early as 1843–4 Engels acquired – it would seem from John Wade's *History of the Middle and Working Classes* (1835)[43] – the view that crises with a regular periodicity were an integral aspect of the operations of the capitalist economy, using the fact to criticise Say's Law.

Compared with these links with British left-wing economists, Marx's debt to continental ones is slighter. Insofar as French socialism had an economic theory, it developed in connection with the Saint-Simonians, possibly under the influence of the heterodox Swiss economist Sismondi (1773–1842), especially through Constantin Pecqueur (1801–87), who has been described as 'a link between Saint-Simonism and Marxism' (Lichtheim). Both were among the first economists to be seriously studied by Marx (1844). Sismondi is frequently quoted, Pecqueur discussed in *Capital* III. Neither, however, is included in the *Theories on Surplus Value*, though Marx at one point wondered whether to include Sismondi. On the other hand the British Ricardian socialists are: Marx was, after all, the last and overwhelmingly the greatest of Ricardian socialists himself.

Yet if we can pass briefly over what he approved or developed in the left-wing economics of his day, we must also briefly consider what he rejected. He rejected what he saw as 'bourgeois' (*Communist Manifesto*) and later 'petty-bourgeois' or otherwise misguided attempts to deal with the problems of capitalism by such means as credit reform, currency manipulation, rent reform, measures to inhibit capitalist concentration by the abolition of inheritance or other means, even if they were intended to benefit not small individual proprietors but associations of workers operating within, and eventually designed to replace, capitalism. Such proposals were widespread on the left, including parts of the socialist movement. Marx's hostility to Sismondi, whom he respected as an economist, to Proudhon, whom he did not, as well as his criticism of John Gray derive from this view. At the time when he and Engels formed their own communist views, these weaknesses in contemporary left-wing theory did not detain them much. However, from the mid-1840s on they increasingly found themselves obliged to pay greater critical attentions to them in their political practice, and consequently in theory.

IV

What of the German contribution to the formation of their thought? Economically and politically backward, the Germany of Marx's youth possessed no socialists from whom he could learn anything of importance. Indeed, until almost the moment of Marx's and Engels' conversion to communism, and indeed in some ways until after 1848, it is misleading to speak of a socialist or communist left distinct from the democratic and Jacobin tendencies which formed the radical opposition to reaction and princely absolutism in the country. As the *Communist Manifesto* pointed out, in Germany (unlike France and Britain) the communists had no option other than to march in common with the bourgeoisie against absolute monarchy, feudal landed property and petty-bourgeois conditions (*die Kleinbürgerei*),[44] while encouraging the workers to become clearly conscious of their opposition to the bourgeois. Politically, and ideologically, the German radical left looked westwards. Ever since the German Jacobins of the 1790s, France had provided the model, the place of refuge for political and intellectual refugees, the source of information about progressive tendencies: in the early 1840s even Lorenz von Stein's survey of socialism and communism there served chiefly as such, in spite of the author's intention, which was to criticise these doctrines. In the meantime a group, mainly consisting of travelling German journeymen craftsmen working in Paris, had separated from the post-1830 liberal refugees in France to adapt French working-class communism for their own purposes. The first clear German version of communism was therefore revolutionary and proletarian in a primitive way.[45] Whether the radical young intellectuals of the Hegelian left wished to stop at democracy or advance politically and socially beyond it, France provided the intellectual models and catalyst for their ideas.

Among these journeymen craftsmen Moses Hess (1812–75) was significant, not so much for his intellectual merits – for he was far from a clear thinker – but because he became a socialist before the rest and succeeded in converting a whole generation of young intellectual rebels. His influence on Marx and Engels was crucial in 1842–5, though very soon both ceased to take him seriously. His own brand of 'True Socialism' (mainly a sort of Saint-Simonism translated into Feuerbachian jargon) was not destined to be of much significance. It is chiefly remembered because it has been embalmed in Marx's and Engels' polemics against it (in the *Communist Manifesto*), which were mainly directed against the otherwise forgotten and forgettable Karl Grün (1817–87). Hess, whose intellectual development converged for a while with Marx's, to the point where in 1848 he may well have regarded himself as Marx's follower, suffered from his inadequacies both as a thinker and as a politician, and must be content with the role of the eternal precursor: of Marxism, of the German labour movement, and finally of Zionism.

However, if German pre-Marxian socialism is not very important in the genesis of Marxian ideas – except, as it were, biographically – a word must be said of the German non-socialist critique of liberalism, which struck notes potentially classifiable as 'socialist' in the ambiguous nineteenth-century sense of the word. The German intellectual tradition contained a powerful component hostile to any form of eighteenth-century 'Enlightenment' (and therefore to liberalism, individualism, rationalism and abstraction – e.g. to any form of the Benthamite or Ricardian arguments), one devoted to an organicist conception of history and society, which found expression in German Romanticism, initially a militantly reactionary movement, though in some ways Hegelian philosophy provided a sort of synthesis of the Enlightenment and the romantic view. German political practice, and consequently German applied social theory, was dominated by the activities of an all-embracing state administration. The German bourgeoisie – a late developer as an entrepreneurial class – did not, on the whole, demand either political supremacy or unrestricted economic liberalism, and a large part of its vocal members consisted in any case of servants of the state in one form or another. Neither as civil servants (including professors) nor as entrepreneurs did German liberals tend to have an unqualified belief in the unrestricted free market. Unlike France and Britain, the country bred writers who hoped that the complete development of a capitalist economy, such as was already visible in Britain, could be avoided, and with it the problems of mass poverty, by a combination of state planning and social reform. The theories of such men might actually come quite close to a kind of socialism, as in J.K. Rodbertus-Jagetzow (1805–75), a conservative monarchist (he was briefly Prussian minister in 1848) who in the 1840s elaborated an underconsumptionist critique of capitalism and a doctrine of 'state socialism' based on a labour theory of value. For propagandist purposes this was to be used in the Bismarckian era as a proof that Imperial Germany was as 'socialist' as any social democrat, not to mention as a proof that Marx himself had plagiarised an upstanding conservative thinker. The accusation was absurd, for Marx only read Rodbertus around 1860 when his views were fully formed, and Rodbertus could 'at best have taught Marx how not to go about his task and how to avoid the grossest errors'.[46] The controversy has long been forgotten. On the other hand it may well be argued that the type of attitude and argument exemplified by Rodbertus was influential in the formation of Lassalle's kind of state socialism (the two men were associated for a while).

It need hardly be said that these non-socialist versions of anti-capitalism not only played no role in the formation of Marxian socialism[47] but were actively combated by the young German left on account of their obvious conservative associations. What may be called 'romantic' theory belongs to the pre-history of Marxism only in its least political form, i.e. that of 'natural philosophy' for which Engels always kept a slight fondness (cf. his preface to *Anti-Dühring*, 1885), and insofar as it had been absorbed into classical German philosophy in its Hegelian form. The conservative and liberal tradition of state intervention in the economy, including state ownership and management of industries, merely confirmed them in the view that the nationalisation of industry by itself was not socialist.

Thus neither the German economic, social or political experience nor the writings designed specifically to deal with its problems contributed anything of great significance to Marxian thought. And indeed it could hardly have been otherwise. As has been often observed, not least by Marx and Engels, the issues which in France and England appeared concretely in political and economic form, in the Germany of their youth appeared only in the costume of abstract philosophical enquiry. Conversely, and no doubt for this reason, the development of German philosophy at this period was considerably more impressive than that of philosophy in other countries. If this deprived it of contact with the concrete realities of society – there is no actual reference in Marx to the 'propertyless class' whose problems 'cry out to heaven in Manchester, Paris and Lyons' before the autumn of 1842^{48} – it provided a powerful capacity to generalise, to penetrate beyond the immediate facts. To realise its full potential, however, philosophical reflection had to be transformed into a means of acting upon the world, and speculative philosophical generalisation had to be married to the concrete study and analysis of the actual world of bourgeois society. Without this marriage the German socialism sprung from a political radicalisation of philosophic development, mainly Hegelian, was likely to produce at best that German or 'true' socialism which Marx and Engels lampooned in the *Communist Manifesto*.

The initial steps of this philosophical radicalisation took the form of a critique of religion and later (since the topic was more politically sensitive) the state, these being the two chief 'political' issues with which philosophy was directly concerned as such. The two great pre-Marxian landmarks of this radicalisation were Strauss's *Life of Jesus* (1835) and particularly Feuerbach's by now clearly materialist *Wesen des Christenthums* (1841). The crucial significance of Feuerbach as a stage between

Hegel and Marx is familiar, though the continued central role of the critique of religion in the mature thought of Marx and Engels is not always so clearly appreciated. However, at this vital stage of their radicalisation, the young German politico-philosophical rebels could draw directly upon the radical and even socialist tradition, since the most familiar and consistent school of philosophical materialism, that of eighteenth-century France, was linked not only with the French Revolution, but even with early French communism – Holbach and Helvetius, Morelly and Mably. To this extent French philosophic development contributed to, or at least encouraged, the development of Marxist thought, as the British philosophical tradition did through its seventeenth- and eighteenth-century thinkers, directly or via political economy. However, fundamentally the process by which the young Marx 'turned Hegel the right way up' took place within classical German philosophy, and owed little to the pre-Marxian revolutionary and socialist traditions except a sense of the direction it was to move in.

V

Politics, economics and philosophy, the French, British and German experience, 'utopian' socialism and communism, were fused, transformed and transcended in the Marxian synthesis during the 1840s. It is surely no accident that this transformation should have taken place at this historical moment.

Some time around 1840 European history acquired a new dimension: the 'social problem', or (seen from another point of view) potential social revolution, both expressed typically in the phenomenon of the 'proletariat'. Bourgeois writers became systematically conscious of the proletariat as an empirical and political problem, a class, a movement – in the last analysis a power for overturning society. At one end this consciousness found expression in systematic enquiries, often comparative, on the conditions of this class (Villermé for France in 1840, Buret for France and Britain in 1840, Ducpétiaux for various countries in 1843), at the other in historical generalisations already reminiscent of the Marxian argument:

> But this is the content of history: no major historical antagonism disappears or dies out unless there emerges a new antagonism. Thus the general antagonism between the rich and the poor has been recently polarised into the tension between capitalists and the hirers of labour on the one hand and the industrial workers of all kinds on the other; out of this tension there emerges an opposition whose dimensions become more and more menacing with the proportional growth of the industrial population. (art. 'Revolution' in Rotteck and Welcker, *Lexicon der Staatswissenschaften* XIII, 1842).[49]

We have already seen that a revolutionary and consciously proletarian communist movement emerged at this time in France, and indeed that the very words 'communist' and 'communism' came into currency around 1840 to describe it. Simultaneously a massive proletarian class movement, closely observed by Engels, reached its peak in Britain: Chartism. Before it, earlier forms of 'utopian' socialism in western Europe retreated to the margins of public life, with the exception of Fourierism, which flourished modestly, but persistently, in the proletarian soil.[50]

A new and more formidable fusion of the Jacobin-revolutionary-communist and the socialist-associationist experience and theories became possible on the basis of a visibly growing and mobilising working class. Marx, the Hegelian, seeking for the force which would transform society by its negation of existing society, found it in the proletariat, and though he had no concrete acquaintance with it (except through Engels) and had not given the operations of capitalist and political economy much thought, immediately began to study both. It is an error to suppose that he did not seriously concentrate his mind on economics before the early 1850s. He began his serious studies not later than 1844.

What precipitated this fusion of social theory and social movement was the combination of triumph and crisis in the developed, and apparently paradigmatic, bourgeois societies of France and Britain during this period. Politically the revolutions of 1830 and the corresponding British reforms of 1832–5 established regimes which evidently served the interests of the predominant part of the liberal bourgeoisie, but fell spectacularly short of political democracy. Economically, industrialisation, already dominant in Britain, was visibly advancing on parts of the continent – but in an atmosphere of crisis and uncertainty which appeared to many to put in question the entire future of capitalism as a system. As Lorenz von Stein, the first systematic surveyor of socialism and communism (1842), put it:

> There is no longer any doubt that for the most important part of Europe political reform and revolution are at an end; social revolution has taken their place and towers over all movements of the peoples with its terrible power and serious doubts. Only a few years ago, what now confronts us seemed but an empty shadow. Now it faces all Law as an enemy, and all efforts to compress it into its former nothingness are vain.[51]

Or as Marx and Engels were to put it a few years later, 'A spectre is haunting Europe – the spectre of Communism.'

The Marxian transformation of socialism would therefore hardly have been historically possible before the 1840s. Nor, perhaps, would it have been possible within the main bourgeois countries themselves, where both the radical political and working-class movements, and radical social and political theory, were deeply embedded in a long history, tradition and practice from which they found it hard to emancipate themselves. As subsequent history was to show, the French left was long resistant to Marxism, in spite of – indeed because of – the strength of the autochthonous revolutionary and associationist tradition; and the British labour movement remained unreceptive to Marxism for even longer, in spite of – indeed because of – its home-grown success in developing a conscious class movement and a critique of exploitation. Without the French and British contribution, the Marxian synthesis would have been quite impossible; and, as has been suggested, the biographical fact that Marx established a lifelong partnership with Engels, with his unique experience of Britain (not least as a practising Manchester capitalist), was undoubtedly important. Nevertheless, it was perhaps more likely that the new phase of socialism should be developed not at the centre of bourgeois society, but on its German margin, and by means of a reconstruction of the all-embracing speculative architecture of German philosophy.

The actual development of Marxian socialism lies beyond the scope of this chapter. Here we need merely recall that it differed from its predecessors in three respects. First, it replaced a partial critique of capitalist society with a comprehensive critique, based on an analysis of the fundamental (in this instance economic) relation determining that society. The fact that analytically it penetrated deeper than the superficial phenomena accessible to empirical criticism implied an analysis of the 'false consciousness' which stood in the way, and of the (historical) reasons for it. Second, it set socialism in the framework of an evolutionary historical analysis, which explained both why it emerged as a theory and a movement when it did, and why the historic development of capitalism must in the end generate a socialist society. (Incidentally, unlike the earlier socialists, for whom the new society was a finished thing which had only to be instituted in a final form, according to whatever the preferred model was, at the suitable moment, Marx's future society itself continues to evolve historically, so that only its very general principles and outlines can be predicted, let alone designed.) Third, it clarified the mode of the transition from the old to the new society: the proletariat would be its carrier, through a class movement engaged in a class struggle which would achieve its object only through revolution – 'the expropriation of the expropriators'. Socialism had ceased to be 'utopian' and become 'scientific'.

In fact, the Marxian transformation had not only replaced but also absorbed its predecessors. In Hegelian terms, it had 'sublated' them (*aufgehoben*). For most purposes other than the writing of academic theses, they have either been forgotten, form part of the pre-history of Marxism, or (as in the case of some Saint-Simonian strains) developed in ideological directions which have nothing to do with socialism. At most, like Owen and Fourier, they survive among educational theorists. The only socialist writer of the pre-Marxist period who still maintains some significance as a theorist within the general area of socialist movements is Proudhon, who continues to be cited by the anarchists (not to mention, from time to time, the French ultra-right and various other anti-Marxists). This is in some ways unfair to men who, even when below the illuminations of the best utopians, were original thinkers with ideas which, if proposed today, would often be taken quite seriously. Yet the fact remains that, as socialists, they are today of interest chiefly to the historian.

This should not mislead us into supposing that pre-Marxian socialism died immediately Marx developed his characteristic views. Even nominally, Marxism did not become influential in labour movements until the 1880s, or at the earliest the 1870s. The history of Marx's own thought and his political and ideological controversies cannot be understood unless we recall that, for the remainder of his life, the tendencies he criticised, combated or had to come to terms with within the labour movement were primarily those of the pre-Marxian radical left, or those deriving from it. They belonged to the progeny of the French

Revolution, whether in the form of radical democracy, Jacobin republicanism or the neo-babouvist revolutionary proletarian communism surviving under the leadership of Blanqui. (This last was a tendency with which, on political grounds, Marx found himself allied from time to time.) Occasionally they sprang from, or at least had been precipitated by, that same left Hegelianism or Feuerbachianism through which Marx himself had passed, as in the case of several Russian revolutionaries, notably Bakunin. But in the main they were the offspring, indeed the continuation of, pre-Marxian socialism.

It is true that the original utopians did not survive the 1840s; but then, as doctrines and movements they had already been moribund in the early forties, with the exception of Fourierism which, in a modest way, flourished until the revolution of 1848 in which its leader, Victor Considérant, therefore found himself playing an unexpected and unsuccessful role. On the other hand various kinds of associationism and co-operative theories, partly derived from utopian sources (Owen, Buchez), partly developed on a less messianic basis in the 1840s (Louis Blanc, Proudhon), continued to flourish. They even maintained, in an increasingly shadowy way, the aspiration to transform the whole of society on co-operative lines, from which they had originally been derived. If this was so even in Britain, where the dream of a co-operative utopia that would emancipate labour from capitalist exploitation was diluted into co-operative shopkeeping, it was even more alive in other countries, where the co-operation of producers remained dominant. For most workers in Marx's lifetime this *was* socialism; or rather the socialism which gained working-class support, even in the 1860s, was one which envisaged independent groups of producers without capitalists but supplied by society with enough capital to make them viable, protected and encouraged by public authority but in turn with collective duties to the public. Hence the political significance of Proudhonism and Lassalleanism. This was natural in a working class whose politically conscious members consisted largely of artisans or those close to the artisan experience. Moreover, the dream of the independent productive unit controlling its own affairs did not merely belong to men (and much more rarely women) who were not yet fully proletarian. In some ways this primitive 'syndicalist' vision also reflected the experience of proletarians in the workshops of the mid-nineteenth century.

It would thus be a mistake to say that pre-Marxian socialism died out in Marx's time. It survived among Proudhonians, Bakuninite anarchists, among later revolutionary syndicalists and others, even when these later learned, for want of any adequate theory of their own, to adopt much of the Marxian analysis for their own purposes. Yet from the middle 1840s on it can no longer be said that Marx derived anything from the pre-Marxist tradition of socialism. After his extended dissection of Proudhon (*The Poverty of Philosophy*, 1847), it can no longer even be said that the critique of pre-Marxian socialism played a major part in the formation of his own thought. By and large, it formed part of his political polemics rather than of his theoretical development. Perhaps the only major exception is the *Critique of the Gotha Programme* (1875), in which his shocked protests against the German Social Democratic Party's unjustified concessions to the Lassalleans provoked him into a theoretical statement which, if probably not new, had at any rate not been publicly formulated by him before. It is also possible that the development of his ideas on credit and finance owed something to the need to criticise the belief in various currency and credit nostrums which remained popular in labour movements of the Proudhonist type. However, by the mid-1840s Marx and Engels had, on the whole, learned all they could from pre-Marxian socialism. The foundations of 'scientific socialism' had been laid.

3

Marx, Engels and Politics

The present chapter deals with the political ideas and views of Marx and Engels, that is to say their views both about the state and its institutions, and about the political aspect of the transition from capitalism to socialism – the class struggle, revolution, the mode of organisation, strategy and tactics of the socialist movement, and similar matters. Analytically these were, in a sense, secondary problems. 'Legal relations as well as forms of State could not be understood from themselves . . . but are rooted in the material conditions of life', in that 'civil society' whose anatomy was political economy (Preface, *Critique of Political Economy*). What determined the transition from capitalism to socialism were the internal contradictions of capitalist development, and more particularly the fact that capitalism inevitably generated its grave-digger, the proletariat, 'a class always increasing in numbers, and disciplined, united, organised by the very process of capitalist production itself' (*Capital* I, chapter XXXII). Moreover, while state power was crucial to class rule the authority of capitalists over workers as such 'is vested in its bearers only as a personification of the requirements of labour standing above the labourer. It is not vested in them in their capacity as political or theocratic rulers, in the way that it used to be in former modes of production' (*Werke* 1, iii, p.888). Hence politics and the state do not need to be integrated into the basic analysis, but can be brought in at a later stage.[1]

In practice, of course, the problems of politics were not secondary for active revolutionaries, but primary. Hence an enormous amount of Marx's writings deals with these. Yet these writings differ in character from his main theoretical work. Though he never completed his comprehensive economic analysis of capitalism, its torso exists in various large manuscripts destined for publication or actually published. Marx also devoted systematic attention to the critique of social philosophy and what may be called the philosophical analysis of the nature of bourgeois society and communism in the 1840s. There is no analogous systematic theoretical effort about politics. His writings in this field take the form, almost entirely, of journalism, inquests on the immediate political past, contributions to discussion within the movement, and private letters. Engels, however, though even his writings on the subject are mainly in the nature of commentaries on current politics, attempted a more systematic treatment of these subjects in *Anti-Dühring*, but mainly in various writings after Marx's death.

The precise nature of Marx's and to a lesser extent Engels' views is therefore often unclear, especially about matters which did not particularly preoccupy them; which indeed they may have wished to discourage, because 'what blinds people most is above all the illusion of an autonomous history of state constitutions, legal systems, and the ideological representations in all special fields' (Engels to Mehring, *Werke* 39, p.96ff). Engels himself admitted, late in life, that though he and Marx were right to emphasise first and foremost 'the derivation of political, juridical and other ideological conceptions from the basic economic facts', they had somewhat neglected the formal side of this process for the content. This applies not only to the analysis of political, legal and other institutions as ideology, but also – as he pointed out in the well-known letters glossing the materialist conception of history – to the relative autonomy of these super-structural elements. There are considerable gaps in the known ideas of Marx and Engels on these topics, and consequently there are uncertainties about what they were, or might have been.

It is evident that these gaps did not worry Marx or Engels, since they would certainly have filled them, if such an analysis had proved necessary in the course of their concrete political praxis. Thus there is hardly any specific reference to law in Marx's writings; but Engels had no difficulty in improvising a discussion on jurisprudence (in collaboration with Kautsky) when this seemed opportune (1887).[2] Nor is there much diffi-culty in understanding why Marx and Engels did not bother to fill some theoretical gaps which seem obvious to us. The histor-ical epoch in which and about which they wrote was not merely quite different from ours, but also (except for some overlap in the last years of Engels' life) quite different from the one in which Marxist parties developed into mass organisations or oth-erwise into significant political forces. Indeed, Marx's and Engels' actual situation as active communists was only occa-sionally comparable to that of their Marxist followers who led or were politically active in these later movements. For though Marx, perhaps more than Engels, played an important role in practical politics, especially during the 1848 revolution as editor of the *Neue Rheinische Zeitung* and in the First International, nei-ther ever led or belonged to political parties of the kind which became characteristic of the movement in the period of the Second International. At most they advised those who led them; and their leaders (e.g. Bebel), in spite of their enormous admi-ration and respect for Marx and Engels, did not always accept their advice. The only political experience of Marx and Engels which might be compared with that of some later Marxist organisations was their leadership of the Communist League

(1847–52) to which, for this reason, Leninists have tended to refer back since 1917. Marx's and Engels' specific political thinking was inevitably marked by the specific historical situations they confronted, though perfectly capable of being extended and developed to confront others.

We should nevertheless distinguish between that part of their thought which was simply ad hoc and that part which was cumulative, inasmuch as a coherent analysis underlay it, which was gradually shaped, modified and elaborated in the light of successive historical experiences. This is notably the case with the two problems of State and Revolution, which Lenin correctly linked in his attempt to present this analysis systematically.

Marx's own thinking about the state began with the attempt to settle accounts with the Hegelian theory on the subject in the *Critique of Hegel's Philosophy of Law* (1843). At this stage Marx was a democrat but not yet a communist, and his approach thus has some similarity with Rousseau's, though students who have attempted to establish direct links between the two thinkers have been defeated by the undoubted fact that 'Marx never gave any indication of being remotely aware of [this alleged debt to Rousseau]',[3] and indeed appears to misinterpret that thinker. This text anticipated some aspects of Marx's later political ideas; notably, in a vague way, the identification of the state with a specific form of production-relations ('private property'), the state as a historical creation, and its eventual dissolution (*Auflösung*), together with that of 'civil society' when democracy ends the separation of state and people. However, it is chiefly notable as a critique of orthodox political theory, and consequently forms the first and last occasion on which Marx's analysis operates systematically in terms of constitutions, problems of representation etc. We note his conclusion that constitutional forms were secondary to social content – both the USA and Prussia were equally based on a social order of private property – and his critique of government by (e.g. parliamentary) representatives, i.e. by introducing democracy as a *formal* part of the state rather than recognising it as its essence.[4] Marx envisaged a system of democracy in which participation and representation would no longer be distinct, 'a working, not a parliamentary body' in the words he later applied to the Paris Commune,[5] though its formal details, in 1843 as in 1871, were left obscure.

The early communist form of Marx's theory of the state sketched out four main points: the essence of the state was political power, which was the official expression of the opposition of classes within bourgeois society; it would consequently cease to exist in communist society; in the present system it represented not a general interest of society but the interest of the ruling class(es); but with the revolutionary victory of the proletariat it would, during the expected transition period, not disappear immediately but take the temporary form of 'the proletariat organised as a ruling class' or the 'dictatorship of the proletariat' (though this phrase was not used by Marx until after 1848).

These ideas, though consistently maintained for the remainder of Marx's and Engels' lives, were considerably elaborated, particularly in two respects. First, the concept of the state as class power was modified, particularly in the light of the Bonapartism of Napoleon III in France and the other post-1848 regimes which could not be simply described as the rule of a revolutionary bourgeoisie (see below). Second, mainly after 1870, Marx, but more especially Engels, outlined a more general model of the historical genesis and development of the state as a consequence of the development of class society, most fully formulated in the *Origin of the Family* (1884), which incidentally forms the starting-point of Lenin's later discussion. With the growth of irreconcilable and unmanageable class antagonisms in society 'a power apparently standing above society became necessary for the purpose of moderating this conflict and keeping it within the bounds of "order"', i.e. to prevent the class conflict from consuming both the classes and society 'in sterile struggle'.[6] Though plainly 'as a rule' the state represents the interests of the most powerful and economically dominant class which by its control acqired new means of holding down the oppressed, it should be noted that Engels accepts both the general social function of the state, at least negatively, as a mechanism to prevent social disintegration, and also that he accepts the element of concealment of power, or rule by mystification or ostensible consent implicit in the state's appearance of standing above society. The mature Marxian theory of the state was thus considerably more sophisticated than the simple equation: state = coercive power = class rule.

Since Marx and Engels believed both in the eventual dissolution of the state and in the necessity of a transitional (proletarian) state, as well as in the necessity of social planning and management up to, at least, the first stage of communism ('socialism'), the future of political authority raised complex problems, which their successors have not solved either in theory or practice. Since the 'state' as such was defined as the apparatus for ruling men, the apparatus of management which would survive it could be accepted as confined to 'the administration of things', and therefore no longer a state.[7] The distinction between the government of men and the administration of things was probably taken over from earlier socialist thought. It had been made familiar especially by Saint-Simon. The distinction becomes more than a semantic device only on certain utopian or at any rate very optimistic assumptions, e.g. the belief that the 'administration of things' would be technically rather simpler and less specialised than it has so far turned out to be, and thus within the scope of non-specialist citizens – Lenin's ideal of every cook being able to govern the state. There seems no doubt that Marx shared this optimistic outlook.[8] Nevertheless, during the transitional period the rule of men, or in Engels' more precise phrase the 'intervention of state power in social relations' (*Anti-Dühring*), would disappear only gradually. When it would begin to disappear in practice, and how it would disappear, remained in obscurity. Engels' famous passage in *Anti-Dühring* merely states that this would happen 'of itself' by 'withering away'. For practical purposes we can read little into the purely tautological formal statement that this process would begin with 'the first act in which the state will appear as the real representative of the whole of society', the conversion of the means of production into social property, because it merely says that in representing the whole of society it is no longer classifiable as a state.

Marx's and Engels' preoccupation with the disappearance of the state is interesting not for what prognoses can actually be read into it, but chiefly as powerful evidence of their hopes for and conception of the future communist society: all the more powerful because their forecasts on this matter contrast with their habitual reluctance to speculate about an unpredictable future. The legacy they left to their successors on this problem remained puzzling and uncertain.

One further complication of their theory of the state must be briefly mentioned. Insofar as it was not merely an apparatus of rule, but one based on *territory* (*Origin of Family*, *Werke* 21, p.165), the state also had a function in bourgeois economic development as the 'nation', the unit of this development; at least in the form of a number of large territorial units of this kind (see below). The future of these units is not discussed by Marx or Engels, but their insistence on the maintenance of national unity in some centralised form after the revolution, though raising problems noted by Bernstein and confronted by Lenin,[9] is not in doubt. Marx always disclaimed federalism.

Marx's ideas on revolution, equally naturally, began with the analysis of the major revolutionary experience of his era, that of France from 1789 on.[10] France was to remain for the rest of his life the 'classical' exemplification of class struggle in its revolutionary form and the major laboratory of historical experiences in which revolutionary strategy and tactics were formed, However, from the moment he made contact with Engels, the

French experience was supplemented with the experience of the mass proletarian movement, for which Britain was then and remained for several decades the only significant example.

The crucial episode of the French Revolution from both points of view was the Jacobin period. It stood in an ambiguous relation to the bourgeois state[11] since the nature of that state was to provide a free field for the anarchic operations of bourgeois/civil society, while in their different ways both the Terror and Napoleon sought to force them into a state-directed framework of community/nation, the one by subordinating them to 'permanent revolution' – first used in this connection by Marx (*Holy Family*, p.130) – the other to permanent conquest and war. The real bourgeois society first emerged after Thermidor, and eventually the bourgeoisie discovered its effective form, 'the *official* expression of its *exclusive* power, and the *political* recognition of its *specific* interests', in 'the constitutional parliamentary state' (*Repräsentativstaat*) in the revolution of 1830 (ibid. p.132).

Yet as 1848 approached, another aspect of Jacobinism was emphasised. It alone achieved the total destruction of the relics of feudalism, which might otherwise have proceeded over decades. Paradoxically this was due to the intervention in the revolution of a 'proletariat' as yet too immature to be able to achieve its own objectives.[12] The argument remains relevant, even though we would not today regard the Sansculotte movement as 'proletarian', for it raises the crucial problem of the role of the popular classes in a bourgeois revolution, and of the relations between bourgeois and proletarian revolution. These were to be the major themes of the *Communist Manifesto*, the writings of 1848 and the post-1848 discussions. They were to remain a major theme of Marx's and Engels' political thinking and of twentieth-century Marxism. Moreover, insofar as the coming of bourgeois revolution provided a possibility, following the Jacobin precedent, of leading to regimes which went *beyond* bourgeois rule, Jacobinism also suggested some political characteristics of such regimes, e.g. centralism and the role of the legislative power.

The experience of Jacobinism therefore threw light on the problem of the transitional revolutionary state, including the 'dictatorship of the proletariat', a much-debated concept in subsequent Marxist discussion. The term first entered Marxian analysis – whether it was derived from Blanqui is unimportant – in the aftermath of the defeat of 1848–9, i.e. in the setting of a possible new edition of something like the 1848 revolutions. Subsequent reference to it occurs chiefly in the aftermath of the Paris Commune and in connection with the perspectives of the German Social Democratic Party in the 1890s. Though it never ceased to be a crucial element in Marx's analysis[13] the political context in which it was discussed thus changed profoundly. Hence some of the ambiguities of subsequent debate.

Marx himself never seems to have used the term 'dictatorship' to describe a specific institutional form of government, but always only to describe the *content* rather than the form of group or class rule. Thus for him the 'dictatorship' of the bourgeoisie could exist with or without universal suffrage.[14] However, it is probable that in a revolutionary situation, when the main object of the new proletarian regime must be to gain time by immediately taking 'the necessary measures to intimidate the mass of the bourgeoisie sufficiently',[15] such rule would tend to be more overtly dictatorial. The only regime actually described by Marx as a dictatorship of the proletariat was the Paris Commune, and the political characteristics of it which he emphasised were the opposite of dictatorial (in the literal sense). Engels cited both the 'democratic republic' as its specific political form, 'as the French Revolution already demonstrated',[16] and the Paris Commune. However, since neither Marx nor Engels set out to construct a universally applicable model of the *form* of the dictatorship of the proletariat, or to predict all types of situations in which it might be in force, we can conclude no more from their observations than that it ought to combine the democratic transformation of the political life of the masses with measures to prevent counter-revolution by the

defeated ruling class. We have no textual authority for speculations about what their attitude would have been to the
post-revolutionary regimes of the twentieth century, except that
they would almost certainly have given the greatest initial priority to the maintenance of revolutionary proletarian power
against the dangers of overthrow. An army of the proletariat
was the precondition of its dictatorship.[17]

As is well known, the experience of the Paris Commune suggested important amplifications to Marx's and Engels' thought
on the state and the proletarian dictatorship. The old state
machinery could not be simply taken over, but had to be eliminated; Marx here seems to have thought primarily of Napoleon
III's centralised bureaucracy, as well as army and police. The
working class 'had to secure itself against its own representatives
and officials' in order to avoid 'the transformation of the state
and state organs from servants of society into its masters' as had
happened in all previous states.[18] Though this change has been
interpreted in subsequent Marxist discussion chiefly as the need
to safeguard the revolution against the dangers of the surviving
old state machinery, the danger envisaged applies to *any* state
machinery which is allowed to establish autonomous authority,
including that of the revolution itself. The resulting system, discussed by Marx in connection with the Paris Commune, has
been the subject of intensive debate ever since. Little about it is
unambiguously clear except that it is to consist of 'responsible
(elected) servants of society' and not of a 'corporation standing
above society'.[19]

Whatever its precise form, the rule of the proletariat over the
defeated bourgeoisie has to be maintained during a period of
transition of uncertain and doubtless variable length, while capitalist society is gradually transformed into communist society. It
seems clear that Marx expected government, or rather its social
costs, to 'wither away' during this period.[20] Though he distinguished between 'the first phase of communist society, as it
has emerged after long labour-pains from capitalist society' and 'a

higher phase', when the principle 'from each according to ability, to each according to need' can be applied, because the old motivations and limitations on human capacity and productivity will have been left behind,[21] no sharp chronological separation between the two phases seems envisaged. Since Marx and Engels rigidly refused to paint pictures of the future communist society, any attempt to piece their fragmentary or general observations on this subject together to form one must be avoided as misleading. Marx's own comments on those points suggested to him by one unsatisfactory document (the *Gotha Programme*) are obviously not comprehensive. They are mainly confined to restating general principles.

Throughout the post-revolutionary prospect is presented as a lengthy, complex, by no means necessarily linear and essentially at present unpredictable process of development. 'The general demands of the French bourgeoisie before 1789 were more or less established, as – *mutatis mutandis* – are the immediate demands of the proletariat today. They were more or less standard for all the countries of capitalist production. However, no pre-revolutionary Frenchman of the eighteenth century had the slightest idea, a priori, of the way in which these demands of the French bourgeoisie were actually to be carried out.'[22] Even after the revolution, as he observed in connection with the Commune, 'the replacement of the economic conditions of the slavery of labour by those of free and associated labour can only be the progressive work of time', that 'the present "spontaneous operation of the natural laws of capital and landed property" can only be replaced by "the spontaneous operation of the laws of social economy of free and associated labour" in the course of a lengthy process of development of new conditions',[23] as had happened in the past with the slave and feudal economies. The revolution could only initiate this process.

This caution about predicting the future was largely due to the fact that the chief maker and leader of the revolution, the proletariat, was itself a class in process of development. The

broad outlines of Marx's and Engels' views on this development, evidently based in the main on Engels' British experience
of the 1840s, are presented in the *Communist Manifesto*: a progress
from individual rebellion through localised and sectional economic struggles, first informal, then increasingly organised
through labour unions, to 'one national struggle between
classes', which must also be a political struggle for power. 'The
organisation of the workers as a class' must be 'consequently
into a political party'. This analysis was substantially maintained for the remainder of Marx's life, though slightly modified
in the light of capitalist stability and expansion after 1848, as
well as of the actual experience of organised labour movements.
As the prospect of economic crises precipitating immediate
workers' revolt receded, Marx and Engels became somewhat
more optimistic about the possibility of successes for the workers' struggle within the framework of capitalism, by means of
trade union action or the achievement of favourable legisla-
tion,[24] though the argument that the workers' wage depended to
some extent on a customary or acquired living-standard as well
as on market forces is already sketched by Engels in 1845.[25] It
follows that the pre-revolutionary development of the working
class would be more prolonged than Marx and Engels had
hoped or expected before 1848.

In discussing these problems it is difficult but essential to
avoid reading a century of subsequent Marxist controversies
back into the text of the classic writings. In Marx's lifetime the
essential task, as he and Engels saw it, was to generalise the
labour movement into a class movement, to bring into the open
the aim implied in its existence, which was to replace capitalism
by communism, and most immediately to turn it into a political
movement, a working-class party separate from all parties of the
possessing classes and aiming at the conquest of political power.
Hence it was vital for the workers neither to abstain from political action, nor to allow any separation of their 'economic
movement from their political activity'.[26] On the other hand the

nature of that party was secondary, so long as it was a class party.[27] It must not be confused with later concepts of 'party', and no coherent doctrine about these is to be found in their writings. The word itself was initially used in the very general sense current in the mid-nineteenth century, which included both the supporters of a particular set of political views or cause and the organised members of a formal group. Though Marx and Engels in the 1850s frequently used the word to describe the Communist League, the former *Neue Rheinische Zeitung* group or the relics of both, Marx carefully explained that the League, like earlier revolutionary organisations, 'was merely an episode in the history of the party, which forms spontaneously and everywhere in the soil of society', i.e. 'the party in the wider historical sense'.[28] In this sense Engels could speak of the workers' party as a political party 'being already in existence in most countries' (1871).[29] Evidently from the 1870s Marx and Engels favoured, where possible, the constitution in some form of an *organised* political party, so long as this was not a sect; and in the parties formed by their followers or under their influence, problems of internal organisation, party structure and discipline etc. naturally called forth suitable expressions of opinion from London. Where no such parties existed, Engels continued to use the term 'party' for the sum total of the political (i.e. electoral) bodies expressing the independence of the working class, irrespective of their organisation; 'never mind how, so long as it is a separate workers' party'.[30] They showed little except incidental interest in the problems of party structure, organisation or sociology which were to preoccupy later theorists.

Conversely, 'sectarian "etiquettes" must be avoided . . . The general aims and tendencies of the working class arise from the general conditions in which it finds itself. Therefore these aims and tendencies are found in the whole class, although the movement is reflected in their heads in the most varied forms, more or less imaginary, more or less related to these conditions. Those who best understand the hidden meaning of the class struggle which is unfolding before our eyes – the Communists – are the last to commit the error of approving or furthering sectarianism' (1870).[31] The party must aim to be the organised class, and Marx and Engels never deviated from the declaration of the *Manifesto*, that the communists did not form a separate party opposed to other working-class parties, or set up any sectarian principles of their own by which to shape and mould the proletarian movement.

All Marx's political controversies in his later years were in defence of the triple concept of (a) a *political* class movement of the proletariat; (b) a revolution seen not simply as a once-for-all transfer of power to be followed by some sectarian utopia, but as a crucial moment initiating a complex and not readily predictable period of transition; and (c) the consequently necessary maintenance of a system of political authority, a 'revolutionary and transitory form of the state'.[32] Hence the particular bitterness of his opposition to the anarchists, who rejected all of them.

It is thus vain to seek in Marx for the anticipation of such later controversies as those between 'reformists' and 'revolutionaries', or to read his writings in the light of subsequent debates between right and left in the Marxist movements. That they have been so read is part of the history of Marxism, but belongs to a later stage of its history. The issue for Marx was not whether labour parties were reformist or revolutionary, or even what these terms implied. He recognised no conflict in principle between the everyday struggle of the workers for the improvement of their conditions under capitalism and the formation of a political consciousness which envisaged the replacement of capitalist by socialist society, or the political actions which led to this end. The issue for him was how to overcome the various kinds of immaturity which held up the development of proletarian class parties, e.g. by keeping them under the influence of various kinds of democratic radicalism (and therefore of bourgeoisie or petty-bourgeoisie), or by trying to identify it with various kinds of utopias or patent formulas for achieving socialism, but above all by diverting it from the necessary unity of economic and political struggle. It is an anachronism to identify Marx with either a 'right' or 'left', 'moderate' or 'radical' wing in the international or any other labour movement. Hence the irrelevance as well as the absurdity of arguments about whether Marx at any point ceased to be a revolutionary and became a gradualist.

What form the actual transfer of power, and indeed the subsequent transformation of society, would take would depend on the degree of development of the proletariat and its movement, which reflected both the stage reached in capitalist development and its own process of learning and maturing by praxis. It would naturally depend on the socio-economic and political situation at the time. Since Marx patently did not propose to wait until the proletariat had become a large numerical majority and class polarisation had reached an advanced stage, he certainly conceived of the class struggle as continuing after the revolution, though 'in the most rational and humane manner'.[33] Before and for an undefined period after the revolution the proletariat must thus be expected to act politically as the core and leader of a class coalition, its advantage being that, thanks to its historic position, it could be 'acknowledged as the only class capable of social initiative', even though still a minority. It is not too much to say that Marx saw the only 'dictatorship of the proletariat' he actually analysed, the Paris Commune, as destined ideally to proceed by something like a popular front of 'all classes of society which do not live by others' labour' under the leadership and hegemony of the workers.[34] However, these were matters of concrete assessment. They merely confirm that Marx and Engels did not rely on the spontaneous operation of historical forces, but on political action within the limits of what history made possible. At all stages of their lives they consistently analysed situations with action in their minds.

The assessment of these changing situations must therefore be considered.

We may distinguish three phases of the development of their analysis: from the mid-1840s to the mid-1850s; the following twenty-five years, when a lasting victory of the working class did not seem on the immediate agenda; and Engels' last years, when the rise of proletarian mass parties appeared to open new perspectives of transition in the advanced capitalist countries. Elsewhere a modification of the earlier analyses remained valid. We shall consider the international aspects of their strategy separately below.

The '1848' perspective rested on the assumption, which proved correct, that a crisis of the old regimes would lead to widespread social revolution, and on the assumption, which proved incorrect, that the development of the capitalist economy had proceeded far enough to make possible the eventual triumph of the proletariat as the outcome of such a revolution. The actual working class, however defined, was at this time clearly a small minority of the population, except in Britain where – against Engels' prediction – no revolution took place. Moreover, it was both immature and barely organised. The prospects of proletarian revolution therefore rested on two possibilities. Either (as Marx, in some ways anticipating Lenin, foresaw) the German bourgeoisie would prove unable or unwilling to make its own revolution, and an embryonic proletariat, led by communist intellectuals, would take over its leadership,[35] or (as in France) the radicalisation of bourgeois revolution initiated by the Jacobins could be continued.

The first possibility clearly proved quite unrealistic. The second still seemed possible even after the defeat of 1848–9. The proletariat had taken part in the revolution as a subaltern but important member of a class alliance ranging leftwards from sections of the liberal bourgeoisie. In such a revolution possibilities of radicalisation arose at various moments, as moderates decided that the revolution had gone far enough, while radicals wished to press further with demands 'which were, or seemed, at least in part, to be in the interest of the great mass of the people'.[36] In the French Revolution this radicalisation had only served to reinforce the victory of the moderate bourgeoisie. However, the potential polarisation of class antagonisms during the capitalist era, as in the France of 1848–9, between a now united and reactionary bourgeois ruling class and a front of all other classes, grouped round the proletariat, might for the first time make it possible that a defeat of the bourgeoisie could make 'the proletariat, made wise by defeat, into the decisive factor'. This historical reference back to the French Revolution lost much of its point with the triumph of Louis Napoleon.[37] Of course much – in the event too much – depended on the specific dynamic of the revolution's political development, since the continental working classes, including the Parisian, had behind them a very inadequate development of the capitalist economy.

The major task of the proletariat was therefore the radicalisation of the next revolution from which, once the liberal bourgeoisie had gone over to the 'party of order', the more radical 'democratic party' was likely to emerge as victor. This was the 'maintenance of the revolution in permanence' which forms the chief slogan of the Communist League in 1850[38] and which was to be the basis of a shortlived alliance between Marxians and Blanquists. Among the democrats the 'republican petty-bourgeoisie' was the most radical, and as such the most dependent on proletarian support. It was the stratum which must primarily both put pressure on the proletariat, and be combated by it. Yet the proletariat remained a small minority and therefore required allies, even as it sought to replace the petty-bourgeois democrats as the leader of the revolutionary alliance. We may note in passing that during 1848–9 Marx and Engels, like most of the left, underestimated the revolutionary or even the radical potential of the countryside, in which they took little interest. Only after the defeat, perhaps under the impetus of Engels (whose *Peasant War*, 1850, already showed an acute interest in the subject), did Marx come to envisage, at least for Germany, 'some second edition of the peasant war' to back proletarian revolution (1856). The revolutionary development thus envisaged was complex and perhaps lengthy. Nor was it possible to predict at which stage of it the 'dictatorship of the proletariat' might arise. However, the basic model was evidently a more or less rapid transition from an initial liberal phase through a radical-democratic one to one led by the proletariat.

Until the world capitalist crisis of 1857 failed to lead to revolution in any country, Marx and Engels continued to hope for, and indeed expect, a new and revised edition of 1848. Thereafter, for some two decades, they had no hope of any imminent and successful proletarian revolution, though Engels maintained his perennial youthful optimism better than Marx. Certainly they did not expect much of the Paris Commune and were careful to avoid optimistic statements about it during its brief lifetime. On the other hand the rapid worldwide development of the capitalist economy, and especially of industrialisation in western Europe and the USA, now generated massive proletariats in various countries. It was on the growing strength, class consciousness and organisation of these labour movements that they now pinned their hopes. It must not be assumed that this made a fundamental difference to their political perspectives. As we have seen, the actual revolution, in the sense of the (presumably violent) transfer of power, could take place at various stages of the lengthy process of working-class development, and would in turn initiate a lengthy process of post-revolutionary transition. The postponement of the actual transfer of power to some later stage of working-class and capitalist development would no doubt affect the nature of the subsequent transition period, but though it might disappoint revolutionaries eager for action, it could hardly change the essential character of the predicted process. Nevertheless, the point about this period of Marx's and Engels' political strategy is that, though willing to plan for any eventuality, they did not consider a successful transfer of power to the proletariat imminent or probable.

The advance of mass socialist parties, particularly after 1890, for the first time created the possibility, in some economically developed countries, of a direct transition to socialism under proletarian governments which had come to power directly. This development occurred after Marx's death, and we therefore do not know how he would have confronted it, though there are some signs that he might have done so in a more flexible and less 'orthodox' manner than Engels did.[39] However, since Marx died before the temptation to identify himself with a flourishing mass Marxist party of the German proletariat was so great, this is a matter for speculation. There is some evidence that it was Bebel who persuaded Engels that a direct transition to power now became possible, bypassing 'the intermediate radical-bourgeois stage'[40] which had previously been regarded as necessary in countries which had failed to make a bourgeois revolution. At all events, it seemed that henceforth the working class would no longer be a minority, with luck at the head of a broad revolutionary alliance, but a vast stratum growing towards a majority, organised as a mass *party* and rallying allies from other strata *round that party*. Herein lay the difference between the new situation and that (still unique) of Britain, in which the proletariat formed the majority in a decisively capitalist economy and had achieved 'a certain degree of maturity and universality', but – for reasons into which Marx hardly bothered to enquire – had failed to develop a corresponding political class movement.[41] To this perspective of a 'revolution of the majority' achievable through mass socialist parties, Engels devoted his last writings, though these must be read to some extent as reactions to a specific (German) situation in this period.

Three peculiarities characterised the new historical situation with which Engels now attempted to come to terms. There was

virtually no precedent for mass socialist working-class parties of
the new sort and none for what increasingly became common,
single, national 'social-democratic' parties virtually without
competition on the left, as in Germany. The conditions which
allowed them to develop, and which became increasingly
common after 1890, were legality, constitutional politics and
the extension of the right to vote. Conversely, the prospects of
revolution, as traditionally conceived, were now substantially
changed (the international changes will be considered below).
The debates and controversies of socialists in the era of the
Second International reflect the problems arising out of these
changes. Engels was only partly involved in their early stages,
and they certainly became acute only after his death. Indeed it
may be argued that he never fully worked out the possible implications of the new situation. Nevertheless, his opinions were
obviously relevant to them, helped to shape them, and were to
be the subject of much textual debate, because of the very
impossibility of identifying them with any one of the diverging
trends.

What was to give rise to particular controversy was his insistence on the new possibilities implicit in universal suffrage, and
his abandonment of the old insurrectionary perspectives – both
clearly formulated in one of his last writings, the *aggiornamento* of
Marx's *Class Struggles in France* (1895). It was the combination of
both which was controversial: the statement that the German
bourgeoisie and government 'are much more afraid of the legal
than of the illegal action of the workers' party, of electoral success than of rebellion'.[42] Yet in fact, in spite of some ambiguity
in Engels' last writings, he certainly cannot be read as approving
or implying the legalistic and electoralistic illusions of later
German and other social democrats.

He abandoned the old insurrectionary hopes, not only for
technical reasons, but also because the clearer emergence of
class antagonisms which made possible the mass parties also
made more difficult the old insurrections with which all strata of

the population sympathised. Reaction would thus now be able to gather support from much larger sectors of the middle strata: '"The people" will therefore always appear divided and thus a powerful lever disappears, which was so effective in 1848.'[43] Yet he refused – even for Germany – to abandon thoughts on armed confrontation and with his usual and excessive optimism predicted a German revolution for 1898–1904.[44] Indeed, his immediate argument in 1895 tried to show little more than that, in the then situation, parties like the SPD had most to gain by utilising their legal possibilities. Violent and armed confrontation was thus likely to be initiated not by insurrectionaries but from the right against the socialists. This continued a line of argument already sketched out by Marx in the 1870s[45] in connection with countries in which there was no constitutional obstacle to the election of a socialist national government. The suggestion here was that the revolutionary struggle would then (as in the French Revolution and the American Civil War) take the form of a fight between a 'legitimate' government and counter-revolutionary 'rebels'. There is no reason to suppose that Engels ever disagreed with Marx's then view that 'no great movement has been born without the shedding of blood'.[46] Engels clearly saw himself not as abandoning revolution, but simply as adapting the revolutionary strategy and tactics to a changed situation, as he and Marx had done all their lives. It was the discovery that the growth of mass social-democratic parties did not lead to some form of confrontation but to some form of integration of the movement into the existing system which threw doubt on his analysis. If he is to be criticised, it is for underestimating this possibility.

On the other hand he was keenly aware of the dangers of opportunism – 'the sacrifice of the future of the movement for the sake of its present'[47] – and did his best to safeguard the parties against these temptations by recalling, and indeed largely systematising the main doctrines and experiences of what was now coming to be called 'Marxism', by stressing the need for 'socialist science',[48] by insisting on the essentially proletarian base of socialist advance,[49] and especially by establishing the limits beyond which political alliances, compromises and programmatic concessions for the sake of winning electoral support became impermissible.[50] Yet in fact – and against Engels' intention – this contributed, especially in the German party, to the widening of the gap between theory and doctrine on the one hand, actual political practice on the other. It was the tragedy of Engels' last years, as we can now see, that his lucid, realistic and often immensely perspicacious comments on the concrete situation of the movements served not to influence their practice but to reinforce a general doctrine increasingly separate from them. His prediction proved only too accurate: 'What can the consequence of all this be, except that the party will suddenly, at the moment of decision, not know what to do, that there is unclarity and uncertainty about the most decisive points, because these points have never been discussed?'[51]

Whatever the prospects of the working-class movement, the political conditions for the conquest of power were complicated by the unexpected transformation of bourgeois politics after the defeat of 1848. In the countries which had undergone revolution the 'ideal' political regime of the bourgeoisie, the constitutional parliamentary state, was either not achieved or (as in France) abandoned for a new Bonapartism. In short, the bourgeois revolution had failed in 1848 or led to unpredicted regimes whose nature probably preoccupied Marx more than any other problem concerning the bourgeois state: to states plainly serving the bourgeoisie's interest, but not directly representing it as a class.[52] This raised the wider question, which is far from having exhausted its interest, of the relations between a ruling class and the centralised state apparatus, originally developed by the absolutist monarchies, strengthened by bourgeois revolution in order to achieve 'the bourgeois unity of the nation' which was the condition of capitalist development, but constantly tending to establish its autonomy vis-à-vis all classes, including the bourgeoisie.[53] (This is the starting-point for the argument that the victorious proletariat cannot merely take over the state machinery, but must break it.) This vision of the convergence of class and state, economy and 'power elite', clearly anticipates much of twentieth-century development. So does Marx's attempt to provide French Bonapartism with a specific social basis, in this instance the post-revolutionary petty-bourgeois peasantry, i.e. a class 'incapable of asserting their class interests in their own name . . . They cannot represent themselves, but must be represented. Their representative must at the same time appear as their master, as an authority above them, as an unrestricted government power protecting them from other classes and sending rain and sunshine from above'.[54] Here various forms of later demagogic populism, fascism etc., are anticipated.

Why such forms of rule should prevail was not clearly analysed by Marx and Engels. Marx's argument that bourgeois-democratic government had exhausted its possibilities and that a Bonapartist system, the ultimate bulwark against the proletariat, would therefore also be the last form of rule before proletarian revolution,[55] evidently proved mistaken. In a more general form a 'class-balance' theory of such Bonapartist or absolutist regimes was eventually formulated by Engels (mainly in *Origin of the Family*), based on various formulations of Marx derived from the French experience. These ranged from the sophisticated analysis in the *18th Brumaire* of how the fears and internal divisions of the 'party of order' in 1849–51 had 'destroyed all conditions of its own regime, the parliamentary regime, in the course of its struggle against the other classes of society' to simplified statements that it rested 'on the fatigue and impotence of the two antagonistic classes of society'.[56] On the other hand Engels, as so often theoretically more modest but also more empirical, pursued the suggestion that Bonapartism was acceptable to the bourgeoisie because it did not want to be bothered with, or 'has not the stuff for', governing directly.[57] Apropos of Bismarck, joking about Bonapartism as 'the religion of the bourgeoisie', he argued that this class could (as in Britain) let an aristocratic oligarchy conduct the actual government in its interest, or in the absence of such an oligarchy adopt 'Bonapartist semi-dictatorship' as the 'normal' form of government. This fruitful hint was not elaborated till later, in connection with the peculiarities of bourgeois-aristocratic coexistence in Britain,[58] but rather as an incidental observation. At the same time Marx and Engels after 1870 maintained, or reverted to, the emphasis on the constitutional-parliamentary character of the typical bourgeois regime.

But what was to happen to the old perspective of a bourgeois revolution, to be radicalised and transcended by 'permanent revolution', in the states where 1848 had simply been defeated and the old regimes re-established? In one sense the very fact that the revolution had taken place proved that the problems it raised *must* be solved: 'the real [i.e. historical] as distinct from the illusory tasks of a revolution are always solved as a result of it'.[59] In this instance they were solved 'by its testamentary executors, Bonaparte, Cavour and Bismarck.' But though Marx and Engels recognised this fact, and even welcomed it – with mixed feelings – in the case of Bismarck's 'historically progressive' achievement of German unity, they did not fully work out its implications. Thus the support of a 'historically progressive' step taken by a reactionary force might conflict with the support of political allies on the left who happened to be opposed to it. In fact this happened over the Franco-German war, which Liebknecht and Bebel opposed on anti-Bismarckian grounds (supported by most of the ex-1848 left) while Marx and Engels inclined privately to support it up to a point.[60] There is a danger in supporting 'historically progressive achievements' irrespective of who carries them out, except of course *ex post facto*. (Marx's dislike and contempt for Napoleon III saved him from similar dilemmas over Italian unification.)

However, more seriously, there was the question of how to assess the undoubted concessions made from above to the bourgeoisie (e.g. by Bismarck), sometimes even described as 'revolutions from above'.[61] Though regarding them as historically inevitable, Engels – Marx wrote little on this topic – was slow to abandon the view that they were impermanent. Either Bismarck would be forced towards a more bourgeois solution, or the German bourgeoisie 'would once more be compelled to do its political duty, to oppose the present system, so that at long last there will be some progress again'.[62] Historically he was right, for in the course of the next seventy-five years the Bismarckian compromise and Junker power were swept away, though in ways unpredicted by him. However, in the short run – and in their general theory of the state – Marx and Engels did not quite come to terms with the fact that the compromise solutions of 1849–71 were, for most of the European bourgeois classes, substantially the equivalent of another 1848 and not a poor substitute for it. They showed little signs of wanting or needing more power or a more completely and unequivocally bourgeois state – as Engels himself hinted.

Under these circumstances the fight for 'bourgeois democracy' continued, but without its former content of bourgeois revolution. Though this fight, increasingly conducted under working-class leadership, won rights which enormously facilitated the mobilisation and organisation of mass working-class parties, there was no real evidence for the late Engels' view that the democratic republic, 'the logical [*konsequente*] form of bourgeois rule', would also be the form in which the conflict between bourgeoisie and proletariat would be polarised and finally fought out.[63] The character of the class struggle and of bourgeois-proletarian relations within the democratic republic, or its equivalent, remained cloudy. In short, it must be admitted that the question of the political structure and function of the bourgeois state in a developed and stable capitalism did not receive systematic consideration in the writings of Marx and Engels, in the light of the historical experience of the developed countries after 1849. This does not diminish the brilliance, and in many cases the profundity, of their insights and observations.

However, to consider Marx's and Engels' political analysis without its international dimension is to play *Othello* as though it did not take place in Venice. The revolution was for them essentially an international phenomenon, not simply an aggregate of national transformations. Their strategy was essentially international. Not for nothing does Marx's Inaugural Address to the First International conclude with a call to the working classes to penetrate the secrets of international politics and to take an active part in them.

An international policy and strategy was essential not only because an international state system existed, which affected the chances of survival of any revolution, but more generally, because the development of world capitalism necessarily proceeded through the formation of separate socio-political units, as is implied in Marx's almost interchangeable use of the terms 'society' and 'nation'.[64] The world created by capitalism, though increasingly unified, was 'a universal interdependence of nations' (*Communist Manifesto*). The fortunes of revolution, moreover, depended on the system of international relations, because history, geography, uneven strength and uneven development placed its development in each country at the mercy of what happened elsewhere, or gave it international resonance.

Marx's and Engels' belief in capitalist development through a number of separate ('national') units is not to be confused with a belief in what was then called 'the principle of nationality' and today 'nationalism'. Though initially they found themselves attached to a deeply nationalist republican-democratic left, since this was the only effective left, nationally or internationally, before and during 1848, they rejected nationalism and the self-determination of nations as an end in itself, as they rejected the democratic republic as an end in itself.[65] Many of their followers were to be less careful to draw the line between proletarian socialists and petty-bourgeois (nationalist) democrats. That Engels never lost some of the German nationalism of his youth and the associated national prejudices, especially against the Slavs, is common knowledge.[66] (Marx was rather less affected by such feelings.) Yet his belief in the progressive character of German unity, or support for German victory in wars, was not based on German nationalism, though it certainly gave him pleasure as a German. For much of their lives both Marx and Engels regarded France rather than their own country as decisive for the revolution. Their attitude to Russia, long the chief target for their attack and contempt, changed as soon as a Russian revolution became possible.

Thus they may be criticised for underestimating the political force of nationalism in their century, and for failing to provide an adequate analysis of this phenomenon, but not for political or theoretical inconsistency. They were not in favour of nations as such, and still less in favour of self-determination for any or all nationalities as such. As Engels observed with his habitual realism: 'There is no country in Europe in which different nationalities are not placed under the same government ... And in all probability it will always be so.'[67] As analysts they recognised that capitalist society developed through the subordination of local and regional interests to large units – probably, they hoped from the *Manifesto* on, eventually into a genuine world society. They recognised, and in the perspective of history approved, the formation of a number of 'nations' through which this historic process and progress operated, and for this reason rejected federalist proposals 'to replace that unity of great peoples which, if originally brought about by force, has nevertheless today become a powerful factor of social production'.[68] Initially they recognised and approved the conquest of backward areas in Asia and Latin America by advanced bourgeois nations for similar reasons. They correspondingly accepted that many smaller nations had no such justification for independent existence, and some might actually cease to exist as nationalities; though here they were clearly blind to some contrary processes visible at the time, as among the Czechs. Personal feelings, as Engels explained to Bernstein,[69] were secondary, though when they coincided with political judgement (as with Engels on the Czechs) they left undue room for the expression of national prejudice and – as was to appear later – for what Lenin was to call 'great nation chauvinism'.

On the other hand, as revolutionary politicians Marx and Engels favoured those nations and nationalities, great or small, whose movements objectively assisted the revolution and opposed those which found themselves, objectively, on the side of reaction. In principle they took the same attitude to the policies of states. The chief legacy they thus left to their successors was the firm principle that nations and movements of national liberation were not to be regarded as ends in themselves, but only in relation to the process, interests and strategies of world revolution. In most other respects they left a heritage of problems, not to mention a number of deprecatory judgements which had to be explained away by socialists trying to build movements among peoples dismissed by the founding fathers as unhistorical, backward or doomed. Except for the basic principle, later Marxists were left to construct a theory of 'the national question' with little aid from the classics. It must be pointed out that this was due not only to the greatly changed historical circumstances of the imperialist era, but also to Marx's and Engels' failure to develop more than a very partial analysis of the national phenomenon.

History determined the three major phases of their international revolutionary strategy: up to and including 1848, 1848–71, and from 1871 to Engels' death.

The decisive stage of the future proletarian revolution was the region of bourgeois revolution and advanced capitalist development, i.e. somewhere in the area of France, Britain, the German lands and conceivably the USA. Marx and Engels showed little except incidental interest in the lesser and politically not decisive 'advanced' countries until the development of socialist movements there called for comments on their affairs. In the 1840s revolution in this zone could reasonably be expected, and did indeed take place, though, as Marx recognised,[70] it was doomed by the failure of Britain to take part in it. On the other hand, except for Britain, no real proletariat or proletarian class movement as yet existed.

In the generation after 1848 rapid industrialisation produced both growing working classes and proletarian movements, but the prospect of social revolution in the 'advanced' zone grew increasingly improbable. Capitalism was stable. During this period Marx and Engels could only hope that some combination of internal political tension and international conflict might possibly produce a situation out of which revolution might emerge, as indeed it did in France in 1870–1. However, in the final period, which was once again one of capitalist crisis on a global scale, the situation changed. In the first place, mass working-class parties, largely under Marxist influence, transformed the prospects of internal development in 'advanced' countries. In the second, a new element of social revolution emerged on the margins of developed capitalist society, in Ireland and Russia. Marx himself first became aware of both at about the same time in the late 1860s. (The first specific reference to the possibilities of a Russian revolution occurs in 1870.)[71] Though Ireland ceased to play much part in Marx's calculations after the collapse of Fenianism,[72] Russia became increasingly important: its revolution could 'give the signal for a workers' revolution in the west, so that both complement each other' (1882).[73] The major significance of a Russian revolution would, of course, lie in its transformation of the situation in the developed countries.

These changes in the perspectives of revolution determined a major change in Marx's and Engels' attitude to war. They were no more pacifist in principle than they were republican democrats or nationalists in principle. Nor, since they knew war to be Clausewitz's 'continuation of politics by other means' did they believe in an exclusive economic causation of war, at least in their lifetime. There is no suggestion of this in their writings.[74] Briefly, in the first two phases, they expected war to advance their cause directly, and the hope of war played a major, sometimes a decisive part in their calculations. From the late 1870s on – the turning point came in 1879–80[75] – they saw a general war as an obstacle in the short run to the advance of the movement. Moreover, in his last years Engels became increasingly convinced of the terrible character of the new and probably global war which he predicted. It would, he said prophetically, have 'only one certain result: mass butchery on a hitherto unheard-of scale, exhaustion of Europe to a hitherto unheard-of degree, and finally the collapse of the entire old system' (1886).[76] He expected such a war to end in the victory of the proletarian party, but since a war was 'no longer necessary' to achieve revolution he naturally hoped that 'we shall avoid all this butchery' (1885).[77]

There were two main reasons why a war was initially an integral and necessary part of the revolutionary strategy, including Marx's and Engels'. First, it was necessary to overcome Russia, the main bulwark of European reaction, the guarantor and restorer of the conservative status quo. Russia itself was at this stage immune to internal subversion, except on its western flank in Poland, whose revolutionary movement therefore long played a major role in the Marx–Engels international strategy. Revolution would be lost unless it turned into a European war of liberation against Russia, and conversely such a war would extend the range of the revolution by disintegrating the East European empires. 1848 had extended it to Warsaw, Debreczen and Bucharest, wrote Engels in 1851; the next revolution must extend to St Petersburg and Constantinople.[78] Such a war must inevitably involve England, the consistent adversary of Russia in the East, which must oppose a Russian predominance in Europe, and this would have the additional and crucial advantage of undermining the other great pillar of the status quo, a stable capitalist Britain dominating the world market – perhaps even bringing the Chartists to power.[79] The defeat of Russia was the essential international condition of progress. It may be that Marx's somewhat obsessional campaign against the British foreign minister Palmerston was coloured by his disappointment at the refusal of Britain to run the risk of a major disruption of the European balance of power by a general war. For, in the absence of a European revolution – and perhaps even in the presence of one – a major European war against Russia without England was impossible. Conversely, when a Russian revolution became probable, such a war was no longer an indispensable condition of revolution in the advanced countries, though the failure of the Russian revolution to take place in his lifetime tempted the late Engels once again to see Russia as the ultimate bulwark of reaction.

Second, such a war was the only way to unify and radicalise the European revolutions – a process for which the French revolutionary wars of the 1790s provided a precedent. A revolutionary France, returning to the internal and external traditions of Jacobinism, was the obvious leader of such a war-alliance against tsarism, both because France initiated European revolution and because it would possess the most formidable revolutionary army. This hope was also disappointed in 1848, and though France continued to play a crucial role in Marx's and Engels' calculations – and indeed both fairly consistently underestimated the stability and achievements of the Second Empire and expected its imminent overthrow – from the 1860s on France could no longer play the central role in European revolution formerly assigned to it.

But if, in the 1848 period, a war was seen as the logical outcome and extension of European revolution, as well as the condition of its success, in the next twenty years it had to be seen as the most important hope of destabilising the status quo, and thus releasing the internal tensions within the countries. The hope that this would be achieved by economic crisis died in

1857.[80] Never thereafter did Marx or Engels seriously place similar short-term hopes on any economic crisis, not even in 1891.[81] Their calculation was correct: the wars of this period had the predicted effect, though not in the manner hoped for by Marx and Engels, for they brought about no revolution in any major European country except France, whose international role, as we have seen, had changed. Hence, as already suggested, Marx and Engels were now increasingly forced into the novel position of deciding between the international policies of existing powers, all of them bourgeois or reactionary.

This was, of course, largely academic so long as Marx and Engels remained quite unable to influence the policies of Napoleon III, Bismarck or any other statesman, and there were no socialist and labour movements whose attitude governments had to take into account. Moreover, though sometimes the 'historically progressive' policy was fairly clear – Russia was to be opposed, the North to be supported against the South in the American Civil War – the complexities of Europe left endless room for inconclusive speculation and debate. It is by no means evident that Marx and Engels were more right than Lassalle in the attitude they took towards the Italian War of 1859,[82] though in practice the attitude of neither side mattered much at the time. When there were mass socialist parties which might feel obliged to give support to one bourgeois state in conflict with another, the political implications of such debates would become more serious. Certainly one reason why the late Engels (and even the late Marx) began to turn away from calculations that international war might be an instrument of revolution was the discovery that it would lead to 'the recrudescence of chauvinism in all countries'[83] which would serve the ruling classes and weaken the now growing movements.

If the prospects of revolution in the period after 1848 were not good, it was largely because Britain was the main bulwark of capitalist stability, as Russia was that of reaction. 'Russia and England are the two great cornerstones of the actual European

system.'[84] In the long run the British would only get into movement once the country's world monopoly was at an end, and this
began to happen in the 1880s and was on various occasions
analysed and welcomed by Engels. As the prospect of Russian
revolution undermined one cornerstone of the system, the end
of Britain's world monopoly undermined the other, though even
in the 1890s Engels' expectations of the British movement
remained rather modest.[85] In the short run Marx hoped to
'accelerate social revolution in England', which he regarded as
the most important task of the First International – and not an
entirely unrealistic one, since 'it is the only country in which the
material conditions for (working-class) revolution have developed
to a certain degree of maturity'[86] – through Ireland. Ireland
split the British workers on racial lines, gave them an apparent
joint interest in exploiting another people, and provided the economic base for the British landed oligarchy, whose overthrow
must be the first step in Britain's advance.[87] The discovery that a
national liberation movement in an agrarian colony could
become a crucial element in revolutionising an advanced empire
anticipated Marxist developments in the era of Lenin. Nor is it
an accident that in Marx's mind it was associated with that other
new discovery, the potential of revolution in agrarian Russia.[88]

In the final phase of Marx's, or more precisely Engels' strategy
the international situation was fundamentally transformed by
the prolonged global capitalist depression, the decline in Britain's
world monopoly, the continued industrial advance of Germany
and the USA, and the probability of revolution in Russia.
Moreover, for the first time since 1815 a world war was visibly
approaching, observed and analysed with remarkable prophetic
acumen and military expertise by Engels. Nevertheless, as we
have seen, the international policy of the powers now played a
much smaller, or rather a more negative role in their calculations.
It was considered chiefly in the light of its repercussions on the
fortunes of the growing socialist parties and as an obstacle rather
than as a possible aid to their advance.

In a sense, Engels' interest in international politics was increasingly concentrated within the labour movement which, in his final years, was once again organised as an International. For the actions of each movement could reinforce, advance or inhibit the others. This is clear from his writings, though we need not read too much into his occasional comparison of the situation in the 1890s with that before 1848.[89] Moreover, it was natural to assume that the fortunes of socialism would be determined in Europe (in the absence of a strong movement in the USA) and on the movements in the main continental powers, now also including Russia (in the absence of a strong movement in Britain). However welcome they were, Engels did not give much thought to the movements in Scandinavia or the Low Countries, practically none to those in the Balkans, and tended to regard any movements in colonial countries as irrelevant side-shows or consequences of metropolitan developments. Beyond reasserting the firm principle that 'the victorious proletariat cannot force any kind of "happiness" on any foreign people without undermining its own victory' (ibid. p.358), he hardly considered the problem of colonial liberation seriously.[90] Indeed, it is surprising how little attention he paid to these problems which, almost as soon as his ashes had been scattered, forced themselves upon the international left in the form of the great debate on imperialism. 'We have', he told Bernstein in 1882, 'to work for the liberation of the West European proletariat, and to subordinate all other aims to this purpose.'[91]

Within this central area of proletarian advance the international movement was now one of national parties, and had to be so, unlike before 1848.[92] This raised the problem of coordinating their operations and of what to do about conflicts which arose out of particular national claims and presumptions in individual movements. Some of these could be tactfully postponed into an indefinite future by suitable formulas, e.g. about eventual self-determination,[93] though socialists in Russia and Austro-Hungary were more aware than Engels that others could not.

Barely more than a year after Engels' death, Kautsky frankly admitted that 'Marx's old position' on the Poles, the Eastern Question and the Czechs could no longer be maintained.[94] Moreover, the unequal strength and strategic importance of various movements raised minor, but troublesome difficulties. Thus the French had traditionally assumed 'a mission as world liberators and thereby the right to stand at the head' of the international movement.[95] But France was no longer in a position to maintain this role, and the French movement, divided, confused and heavily infiltrated with petty-bourgeois radical republicanism or other distracting elements, was disappointing – and indisposed to listen to Marx and Engels.[96] Engels even suggested at one point that the Austrian movement might replace the French as the 'avant garde'.

Conversely, the spectacular growth of the German movement, not to mention its close association with Marx and Engels, now made it clearly into the main force for international socialist advance.[97] Though Engels did not believe in the subordination of other movements to a leading party, except possibly at the moment of immediate action,[98] it was clear that the interests of world socialism would best be served by the progress of the German movement. This view was not confined only to German socialists. It was still very much present in the early years of the history of the Third International. On the other hand the view, also expressed by Engels in the early 1890s, that in a European war the victory of Germany against a Franco-Russian alliance would be desirable[99] was not shared in other countries, though the prospect of revolution arising out of defeat, which he held out to the French and Russians, was certainly to be accepted by Lenin. It is idle to speculate what Engels would have thought in 1914, had he still been alive then, and quite illegitimate to suppose that he would have held the same views as in the 1890s. It is also probable that most socialist parties would have decided to support their government, even if the German party had been unable to appeal to the authority of

Engels. Nevertheless, the heritage he left to the International on questions of international relations and especially on war and peace was an ambiguous one.

How can we sum up the general heritage of ideas about politics which Marx and Engels left to their successors? In the first place, it stressed the subordination of politics to historical development. The victory of socialism was historically inevitable because of the process summarised by Marx in the famous passage on the historical tendency of capitalist accumulation in *Capital* I, culminating in the prophecy about the 'expropriation of the expropriators'.[100] Socialist political effort did not create 'the revolt of the working class, a class always increasing in numbers, and disciplined, united, organised, by the very mechanism of capitalist production itself'; it rested upon it. Fundamentally the prospects of socialist political effort depended on the stage which capitalist development had reached, both globally and in specific countries, and a Marxist analysis of the situation in this light therefore formed the necessary basis for socialist political strategy. Politics was embedded in history, and the Marxian analysis showed how powerless it was to achieve its ends if not so embedded; and conversely, how invincible the working-class movement, which was.

In the second place, politics was nevertheless crucial, insofar as the inevitably triumphant working class must and would be organised politically (i.e. as a 'party') and would aim at the transfer of political power, which would be followed by a transitional system of state authority under the proletariat. Political action was thus the essence of the proletarian role in history. It operated *through* politics, i.e. within the limits set by history – choice, decision and conscious action. Probably in the lifetime of Marx and Engels as well as during the Second International, the main criterion which distinguished Marxians from most other socialists, communists and anarchists (except those in the Jacobin tradition) and from 'pure' trade union or cooperative movements, was the belief in the essential role of politics before, during and after the revolution. It may have been overemphasised because of Marx's controversy with Proudhonian and Bakuninite anarchists, but there is no doubt of its major significance. For the post-revolutionary period, the implications of this attitude were as yet academic. For the pre-revolutionary period they necessarily involved the proletarian party in all kinds of political activity under capitalism.

In the third place, they saw such politics essentially as a class struggle within states which represented the ruling class or classes, except for certain special historical conjunctures such as those of class-balance. As Marx and Engels championed materialism against idealism in philosophy, so also they consistently criticised the view that the state stood above classes, represented the common interest of all society (except negatively, as a safeguard against its collapse), or was neutral between classes. The state was a historical phenomenon of class society, but while it existed as a state it represented class rule – though not necessarily in the agitationally simplified form of an 'executive committee of the ruling class'. This imposed limits both on the involvement of proletarian parties in the political life of the bourgeois state and on what it could be expected to concede to them. The proletarian movement thus operated both within the confines of bourgeois politics and outside them. Since power was defined as the main content of the state, it would be easy to assume (though Marx and Engels did not do so) that power was the only significant issue in politics and in the discussion of the state at all times.

Fourthly, the transitional proletarian state, whatever functions it maintained, must eliminate the separation between the people and government as a special set of governors. One would say it had to be 'democratic', if this word were not identified in common parlance with a specific institutional type of government by periodically elected assemblies of parliamentary representatives, which Marx rejected. Still, in a sense not identified with specific institutions, and reminiscent of certain aspects of Rousseau, it was 'democracy'. This has been the most difficult part of Marx's legacy for his successors, since – for reasons which go beyond the present discussion – all actual attempts to realise socialism along Marxian lines so far have found themselves strengthening an independent state apparatus (as have non-socialist regimes), while Marxists have been reluctant to abandon the aspiration so firmly regarded by Marx as an essential aspect of the development of the new society.

Finally, and to some extent deliberately, Marx and Engels left to their successors a number of empty or ambiguously filled spaces in their political thought. Since the actual forms of political and constitutional structure before the revolution were relevant to them only insofar as they facilitated or inhibited the development of the movement, they gave little systematic attention to them, though commenting freely on a variety of concrete cases and situations. Since they refused to speculate about the details of the coming socialist society and its arrangements, or even about the details of the transitional period after the revolution, they left their successors little more than a very few general principles with which to confront it. Thus they provided no concrete guidance of practical use on such problems as the nature of the socialisation of the economy or the arrangements for planning it. Moreover, there were some subjects on which they provided no guidance, general, ambiguous or even out of date, at all, because they never felt the need to consider them.

Yet what must be stressed is not so much what later Marxists could or could not derive in detail from the legacy of the founders, or what they would have to think out for themselves, but its extreme originality. What Marx and Engels rejected, persistently, militantly and polemically, was the traditional approach of the revolutionary left of their day, including all earlier socialists,[101] an approach which has still not lost its temptations. They rejected the simple dichotomies of those who set out to replace the bad society by the good, unreason by reason, black by white. They rejected the a priori programmatic models of the various brands of the left, not without noting that while each brand had such a model, up to and sometimes including the most elaborate blueprints of utopia, few of these models were in agreement with each other. They also rejected the tendency to devise fixed operational models – e.g. to prescribe the exact form of the revolutionary change, declaring all others to be illegitimate; to reject or to rely exclusively on political action, etc. They rejected ahistorical voluntarism.

Instead, they placed the action of the movement firmly into the context of historical development. The shape of the future and the tasks of action could be discerned only by discovering the process of social development which would lead to them, and this discovery itself became possible only at a certain stage of development. If this limited the vision of the future to a few rough structural principles, by excluding speculative forecasts, it gave to socialist hopes the certainty of historical inevitability. In terms of concrete political action, to decide what was necessary and possible (both globally and in specific regions and countries) required an analysis of both historical development and concrete situations. Thus political decision was inserted into a framework of historical change, which did not depend on political decision. Inevitably, this made the communists' tasks in politics both ambiguous and complex.

They were ambiguous because the general principles of the Marxian analysis were too wide to provide specific policy guidance, if such were required. This applies particularly to the problems of revolution and the subsequent transition to socialism. Generations of commentators have scrutinised the texts for a clear statement of what the 'dictatorship of the proletariat' would be like and failed, because the founders were primarily concerned to establish the historical necessity of such a period. It was complex, because Marx's and Engels' attitude to the *forms* of political action and organisation, as distinct from their *content*, and to the formal institutions among which they operated, was so largely determined by the concrete situation in which they found themselves that they could not be reduced to any set of *permanent* rules. At any given moment and in any specific country or region, the Marxian political analysis could be formulated as a set of policy recommendations (as, for instance, in the Addresses of the General Council in 1850), but they did not, by definition, apply to situations different from the ones for which they were compiled – as Engels pointed out in his later thoughts on Marx's *Class Struggles in France*. But post-Marxian situations were inevitably different from those in Marx's lifetime, and insofar as they contained similarities, these could only be discovered by a historical analysis both of the situation Marx had faced and the one to which later Marxists sought his guidance. All this made it virtually impossible to derive from the classic writings anything like a manual of strategic and tactical instruction, dangerous even to use them as a set of precedents, though they have nevertheless been so used. What could be learned from Marx was his method of facing the tasks of analysis and action rather than ready-made lessons to be derived from classic texts.

And this is certainly what Marx would have wished his followers to learn. Yet the translation of Marxian ideas into the inspiration of mass movements, parties and organised political groups inevitably was to bring with it what E. Lederer once called 'the well-known fore-shortened, simplifying stylisation which brutalises thought, and to which every great idea is and must be exposed, if it is to set masses into movement'.[102] A guide to action was constantly tempted to allow itself to be turned into dogma. In no part of Marxian theory has this been so damaging to both theory and movement as in the field of Marx's and Engels' political thinking. But it represents what Marxism became, perhaps inevitably, perhaps not. It represents a derivation from Marx and Engels, all the more so since the texts of the founders acquired classic or even canonical status. It does not represent what Marx and Engels thought and wrote, and only sometimes how they acted.

4

On Engels' The Condition of the Working Class in England

Frederick Engels, it is hard to remember, was twenty-four years old when he wrote *The Condition of the Working Class*. He was exceptionally well qualified for the task. He came from a wealthy family of cotton manufacturers in Barmen, in the Rhineland, and one which had, moreover, been astute enough to establish a branch (Ermen & Engels) in the very centre of the economy of industrial capitalism, in Manchester itself. The young Engels, surrounded by the horrors of early industrial capitalism and reacting against the narrow and self-righteous pietism of his home, took the usual road of progressive young German intellectuals in the late 1830s. Like his slightly older contemporary Karl Marx he became a 'left Hegelian' – Hegel's philosophy then dominated higher education in the Prussian capital, Berlin – leaned increasingly towards communism and began to contribute to various periodicals and publications in which the German left attempted to formulate its critique of society. Soon he considered himself a communist. It is not clear whether the decision to settle in England for a while was his or his father's. Probably both favoured it for different reasons: old Engels in order to remove his revolutionary son from the agitation of

Germany and turn him into a solid businessman, young Engels in order to be in the centre of modern capitalism and near the great movements of the British proletariat, which he already recognised as the crucial revolutionary force in the modern world.

Engels left for England in the autumn of 1842, making his first personal contact with Marx on the way, and remained there for the better part of two years, observing, studying, and formulating his ideas.[1] By the early months of 1844 he was certainly at work on the book, though most of the writing was done in the winter of 1844–5. The work appeared in its final form in Leipzig, in the summer of 1845, with a preface and dedication (in English) 'to the working classes of Great Britain'.[2] It was published in English, with slight revisions by the author but substantial prefaces in 1887 (American edition) and 1892 (British edition). It thus took the best part of a half-century for this masterpiece about early industrial England to reach the country which was its subject. Since then, however, it has been familiar to every student of the Industrial Revolution, if only by name.

The idea of writing a book about the condition of the labouring classes was not in itself original. By the 1830s it had become clear to every intelligent observer that the economically advanced parts of Europe faced a social problem which was no longer simply that of 'the poor' but of a historically unprecedented class, the proletariat. The 1830s and 1840s, a decisive period in the evolution of capitalism and the working-class movement, therefore saw books, pamphlets and inquiries into the condition of the working classes multiplying all over western Europe. Engels' book is the most eminent piece of writing of this kind, though L. Villermé's *Tableau de l'Etat Physique et Moral des Ouvriers employés dans les Manufactures de Coton, de Laine et de Soie* (1840) deserves mention as a very distinguished piece of social investigation. It was also clear that the problem of the proletariat was not merely local or national, but international.

Buret compared English and French conditions (*La misère des classes laborieuses en France et en Angleterre*, 1840) and Ducpétiaux compiled data on the conditions of young workers all over Europe in 1843. Engels' book was therefore not an isolated literary phenomenon, a fact which has led anti-Marxists periodically to accuse him of plagiarism when unable to think of anything better.[3]

However, it differed from apparently similar contemporary works in several ways. Firstly it was, as Engels himself justly claimed, the first book in Britain or any other country which dealt with the working class as a whole and not merely with particular sections and industries. Secondly, and more important, it was not merely a survey of working-class conditions, but a general analysis of the evolution of industrial capitalism, of the social impact of industrialisation and its political and social consequences – including the rise of the labour movement. In fact, it was the first large-scale attempt to apply the Marxist method to the concrete study of society, and probably the first work by either Marx or Engels which the founders of Marxism regarded as sufficiently valuable to merit permanent preservation.[4] However, as Engels makes clear in the 1892 preface, his book did not yet represent a mature Marxism but rather 'one of the phases of its embryonic development'. For the mature and fully formulated interpretation we must go to Marx's *Capital*.

Argument and Analysis

The work begins with a brief sketch of that Industrial Revolution which transformed British society and created, as its chief product, the proletariat (chapters I–II). This is the first of Engels' pioneering achievements, for the *Condition* is probably the earliest large work whose analysis is systematically based on the concept of the Industrial Revolution, which was then novel and tentative, having only been invented in British and French socialist discussions during the 1820s. Engels' historical account of this transformation lays no claim to historical originality. Though still useful, it has been superseded by later and fuller works.

Socially Engels sees the transformations brought about by the Industrial Revolution as a gigantic process of concentration and polarisation, whose tendency is to create a growing proletariat, an increasingly small bourgeoisie of increasingly large capitalists, both in an increasingly urbanised society. The rise of capitalist industrialism destroys the petty commodity producers, peasantry, and petty-bourgeoisie, and the decline of these intermediate strata, depriving the worker of the possibility of becoming a small master, confines him to the ranks of the proletariat which thus becomes 'a definite class in the population, whereas it had only been a transitional stage towards entering into the middle classes'. The workers therefore develop class consciousness – the term itself is not used by Engels – and a labour movement. Here is another of Engels' major achievements. In Lenin's words 'he was among the first to say that the proletariat is *not only* a class that suffers; that it is precisely its shameful economic situation which irresistibly drives it forward, and obliges it to struggle for its final emancipation'.[5]

However, this process of concentration, polarisation and urbanisation is not fortuitous. Large-scale mechanised industry requires growing capital investments, its division of labour requires the accumulation of large numbers of proletarians. Such large units of production, even when built in the countryside, attract communities round them, which will produce a surplus labour force, so that wages fall and other industrialists are attracted. Thus industrial villages grow into cities which continue to expand, because of the economic advantages they provide for industrialists. Though industry will tend to migrate from the higher urban to the lower rural wages, this will in turn plant the seeds of urbanism in the countryside.

For Engels the great cities are therefore the most typical

locations of capitalism and he discusses them in chapter III. There unrestrained exploitation and competition appear in their most naked form: 'everywhere barbarous indifference, hard selfishness on one side, unspeakable misery on the other, everywhere social war, every man's house a fortress, everywhere marauders who plunder under the protection of the law'. In this anarchy those who own no means of life and production are defeated and reduced to labouring for a pittance or to star-vation when unemployed. And what is worse, to a life of profound insecurity, in which the worker's future is utterly unknown and unsettled. In fact, it is governed by the laws of capitalist competition which Engels discusses in chapter IV.

The workers' wage fluctuates between a minimum subsis-tence rate – though this is not a rigid concept for Engels – which is set by the workers' competition with one another but limited by their inability to work below subsistence, and a maximum, set by the competition of capitalists with one another in times of labour shortage. The average wage is likely to be somewhat above the minimum: how much depends on the customary or acquired standard of living of the workers. But certain kinds of labour, notably in industry, require better qualified workers, and their average wage level is therefore higher than the rest, though part of this higher level also reflects the higher cost of living in the cities. (This higher urban and industrial wage level also helps to enlarge the working class by attracting rural and foreign – Irish – immigrants.) However, the competition between workers creates a permanent 'surplus population' – what Marx was later to call the industrial reserve army – which keeps down the stan-dard of all.

This is so despite the expansion of the whole economy that arises from the cheapening of goods through technological progress, which increases demand and reabsorbs many of the workers it displaces into new industries, and from Britain's industrial world monopoly. Hence population grows, production increases, and so does the demand for labour. Nevertheless, the 'surplus population' is kept in being because of the operation of the periodic cycle of prosperity and crisis, which Engels was one of the first to recognise as an integral part of capitalism, and for which he was one of the first to suggest a precise periodicity.[6] The recognition of a reserve army as a permanently essential part of capitalism and of the trade cycle, represents two further important pieces of theoretical pioneering. Since capitalism operates through fluctuations, it *must* have a permanent reserve of workers, except at the very peak of the booms. The reserve is composed partly of proletarians, partly of potential proletarians – countrymen, Irish immigrants, people from economically less dynamic occupations.

What kind of working class does capitalism produce? What are its conditions of life, what sort of individual and collective behaviour do these material conditions create? Engels devotes the greater part of his book (chapters III, V–XI) to the description and analysis of these matters and in doing so produces his most mature contribution to social science, an analysis of the social impact of capitalist industrialisation and urbanisation which is still in many respects unsurpassed. It must be read and studied in detail. The argument can be briefly summarised as follows. Capitalism pitchforks the new proletariat, often composed of immigrants from pre-industrial backgrounds, into a social hell in which they are ground down, underpaid or starved, left to rot in slums, neglected, despised, and coerced, not only by the impersonal force of competition but by the bourgeoisie as a class, which regards them as objects and not as men, as 'labour' or 'hands' and not as human beings (chapter XII). The capitalist, supported by bourgeois law, imposes his factory discipline, fines them, causes them to be jailed, imposes his wishes on them at will. The bourgeoisie as a class discriminates against them, evolves the Malthusian population theory against them, and imposes on them the cruelties of the Malthusian 'New Poor Law' of 1834. However, this systematic dehumanisation also keeps the workers out of the reach of bourgeois ideology and illusion – for instance of bourgeois egoism, religion and morality. Progressive industrialisation and urbanisation forces them to learn the lessons of their social situation and in concentrating them, makes them aware of their power. 'The closer the workers are associated with industry the more advanced they are.' (However, Engels also observes the radicalising effect of mass immigration, as among the Irish.)

The workers face their situation in different ways. Some succumb to it, allowing themselves to be demoralised: but the increase in drunkenness, vice, crime and irrational spending is a *social* phenomenon, the creation of capitalism, and not to be explained by the weakness and shiftlessness of individuals. Others submit passively to their fate and exist as best they can as respectable law-abiding citizens, take no interest in public affairs and thus actually help the middle class to tighten the chains which bind the workers. But real humanity and dignity are to be found only in the fight against the bourgeoisie, in the labour movement which the workers' conditions inevitably produce.

This movement passes through various stages. Individual revolt – crime – may be one, machine-wrecking another, though neither are universally found. Trade unionism and strikes are the first general forms taken by the movement. Their importance lies not in their effectiveness but in the lessons of solidarity and class consciousness which they teach. The political movement of Chartism marks a yet higher level of development. Side by side with these movements socialist theories were evolved by middle-class thinkers who had, Engels argues, remained largely outside the labour movement until 1844, though capturing a small minority of the best workers. But the movement must move towards socialism, as the crisis of capitalism advances.

As Engels saw it in 1844 this crisis would inevitably develop in one of two ways. Either American (or possibly German) competition would put an end to the British industrial monopoly and precipitate a revolutionary situation, or the polarisation of society would proceed until the workers, by then the great majority of the nation, would realise their strength and seize power. (It is interesting to observe that Engels' argument lays no stress on the absolute long-term pauperisation of the proletariat.) However, given the intolerable conditions of the workers and the crisis of the economy, a revolution was likely before these tendencies had worked themselves out. Engels expected it to occur between the next two economic depressions, i.e. between 1846–7 and the middle 1850s.

Immature though the work is, Engels' scientific achievements are nevertheless remarkable. His faults were chiefly those of youth and to some extent of historical foreshortening. For some of the mistakes there is a sound historical explanation. At the time Engels wrote British capitalism was at the most acute stage of the first of its great periods of secular crisis, and he came to England at almost the worst period of what was certainly the most catastrophic economic slump of the nineteenth century, that of 1841–2. It was by no means entirely unrealistic to think of the crisis period of the 1840s as the final agony of capitalism and the prelude to revolution. Engels was not the only observer who thought of it in this way.

We now know that this was not the final crisis of capitalism, but the prelude to a major period of expansion, based partly on the massive development of the capital goods industries – railways, iron and steel, as against the textiles of the earlier phase – partly on the conquest of yet wider spheres of capitalist activity in hitherto undeveloped countries, partly on the defeat of the agrarian vested interests, partly on the discovery of new and effective methods of exploiting the working classes which, incidentally, made it possible eventually for their real incomes to rise substantially. We also know that the revolutionary crisis of 1848, which Engels foresaw with considerable accuracy, did not affect Britain. This was largely due to a phenomenon of uneven development, which he could hardly have foreseen. For while on the continent the corresponding stage of economic development reached its most acute crisis in 1846–8, in Britain the equivalent point had been reached in 1841–2. By 1848 the new period of expansion, whose first symptom was the vast 'railway boom' of 1844–7, was already under way. The British equivalent of the 1848 revolution was the Chartist general strike of 1842. The crisis which precipitated continental revolutions, in Britain merely interrupted a period of rapid recovery. Engels happened to be particularly unfortunate in writing at a time when this could not be clear. Even today statisticians still argue about exactly where, between 1842 and 1848, to place the boundary mark which separates the 'bleak years' from the golden Victorian boom of British capitalism. We can hardly blame Engels for not seeing it more clearly.

Nevertheless, the unbiased reader can only regard the short-comings of Engels' book as incidental, and must be far more impressed with its achievements. These were due not only to Engels' obvious personal talent, but also to his communism. It was this which gave him an economic, social and historical per-spicacity so signally superior to that of the contemporary champions of capitalism. The good social scientist, as Engels showed, could only be a person free from the illusions of bour-geois society.

Engels' Description of England in 1844

How far is Engels' description of the British working class in 1844 reliable and comprehensive? How far has subsequent research confirmed his statements? Our judgement of the historical value of the book must depend largely on the answer to these questions. He has often been criticised, from the 1840s, when V.A. Huber and B. Hildebrand agreed with his facts, but thought his interpretation too gloomy, to the Cold War years when editors argued that 'historians may no longer regard Engels' book as an authoritative work which gives a valuable picture of social England in the 1840s'.[7] The first view is tenable, the second is nonsense.

Engels' account is based on first-hand observation and on other available sources. He evidently knew industrial Lancashire intimately, particularly the Manchester area, and paid visits to the main industrial towns of Yorkshire – Leeds, Bradford, Sheffield – as well as spending some weeks in London. Nobody has seriously suggested that he misrepresented what he saw. Of the descriptive chapters it is clear that a large part of III, V, VII, IX and XII are based on first-hand observation, and such knowledge plainly illuminates the other chapters also. It must not be forgotten that Engels was (unlike most other foreign visitors) no mere tourist, but a Manchester businessman who knew the businessmen among whom he lived, a communist who knew and worked with the Chartists and early socialists, and – not least through his relations with the Irish factory girl Mary Burns and her relatives and friends – a man with considerable first-hand knowledge of working-class life. His book is thus an important primary source for our knowledge of industrial England at this time.

For the rest of the book, and for confirmation of his own observations, Engels relied on other informants as well as on printed evidence, taking care to allow for the political bias of such evidence, by quoting where possible from sources sympathetic to capitalism. (See the last paragraph of his preface.) Though not exhaustive, his documentation is good and full. Though there are a number of slips in transcribing it (some later corrected by Engels) and a tendency to summarise the authorities rather than to quote verbatim, the accusation that he selects and misquotes his evidence is untenable. His hostile editors have been unable to find more than a handful of examples of what they consider 'misrepresentation' in a large volume, and most of these accusations are either trivial or wrong.[8] There are indeed available sources which he did not utilise, but some of these present if anything an even more scarifying picture. By all sensible standards the *Condition* is an excellently documented work, handled with a sound grasp of evidence.

Accusations such as that he painted proletarian conditions in unnecessarily dark colours or failed to appreciate the benevolence of the British bourgeoisie can be shown to be wrong. The careful reader will find no basis for the contention that Engels described all workers as destitute or starving, their standard of living as one of bare subsistence, the proletariat as an undifferentiated mass of paupers, or for many of the other extreme statements which have been ascribed to him by critics who have not always read his text. He did not deny that improvements in working-class conditions had been made (see the summary at the end of chapter III). He did not present the bourgeoisie as a single black-hearted mass (see the long footnote at the end of chapter XII). His hatred of what the bourgeoisie represented and what made it behave as it did was not a naive hatred for men of ill will as distinct from men of good will. It was part of the critique of the inhumanity of capitalism which automatically turned the exploiters collectively into a 'deeply demoralised class, incurably corrupted by selfishness, corroded in their very being'.

The critics' objection to Engels is often only their reluctance to admit his facts. No man, communist or otherwise, could have visited England from abroad in those years without a sense of shocked horror, which plenty of respectable bourgeois liberals expressed in words as inflammatory as Engels' own – but without his analysis.

'Civilisation works its miracles,' wrote de Tocqueville of Manchester, 'and civilised man is turned back almost into a savage.'

'Every day that I live,' wrote the American Henry Colman, 'I thank Heaven that I am not a poor man with a family in England.'

We can find plenty of statements about the harsh utilitarian indifference of the industrialists to set beside Engels'.

The truth is that Engels' book remains today, as it was in 1845, by far the best single book on the working class of the period. Subsequent historians have regarded and continue to regard it as such, except for a recent group of critics, motivated by ideological dislike. It is not the last word on the subject, for 125 years of research have added to our knowledge of working-class conditions, especially in the areas with which Engels had no close personal acquaintance. It is a book of its time. But nothing can take its place in the library of every nineteenth-century historian and everyone interested in the working-class movement. It remains an indispensable work and a landmark in the fight for the emancipation of humanity.

5

On the Communist Manifesto*

In the spring of 1847 Karl Marx and Frederick Engels agreed to join the so-called League of the Just (Bund der Gerechten), an off-shoot of the earlier League of the Outlaws (Bund der Geächteten), a revolutionary secret society formed in Paris in the 1830s under French revolutionary influence by German journeymen – mostly tailors and woodworkers – and still mainly composed of such expatriate artisan radicals. The League, convinced by their 'critical communism', offered to publish a manifesto drafted by Marx and Engels as its policy document, and also to modernise its organisation along their lines. Indeed it was so reorganised in the summer of 1847, renamed League of the Communists (Bund der Kommunisten), and committed to the object of 'the overthrow of the bourgeoisie, the rule of the proletariat, the ending of the old society which rests on class contradiction (*Klassengegensätzen*) and the establishment of a new society without classes or private property'.[1] A second congress of the League, held in London in November–December 1847, formally accepted the objects and

*The present chapter was written as an introduction to an edition of the *Communist Manifesto* on its 150th anniversary in 1998.

new statutes and invited Marx and Engels to draft the new manifesto expounding the League's aims and policies.

Though both Marx and Engels prepared drafts, and the document clearly represents the joint views of both, the final text was almost certainly written by Marx – after a stiff reminder by the Executive, for Marx, then as later, found it hard to complete his texts except under the pressure of a firm deadline. The virtual absence of early drafts might suggest that it was written rapidly.[2] The resulting document of twenty-three pages, entitled *Manifesto of the Communist Party* (more generally known since 1872 as the *Communist Manifesto*) was 'published in February 1848' and printed in the office of the Workers' Educational Association (better known as the Communistischer Arbeiterbildungsverein, which survived until 1914) at 46 Liverpool Street in the City of London.

This small pamphlet was almost certainly by far the most influential single piece of political writing since the French Revolutionary *Declaration of the Rights of Man and Citizen*. By good luck it hit the streets only a week or two before the outbreak of the revolutions of 1848, which spread like a forest fire from Paris across the continent of Europe. Although its horizon was firmly international – the first edition hopefully, but wrongly, announced the impending publication of the *Manifesto* in English, French, Italian, Flemish and Danish – its initial impact was exclusively German. Small though the Communist League was, it played a not insignificant part in the German revolution, not least through the newspaper *Neue Rheinische Zeitung* (1848–9), which Karl Marx edited. The first edition of the *Manifesto* was reprinted three times in a few months, serialised in the *Deutsche Londoner Zeitung*, reset and corrected in April or May 1848 in thirty pages, but dropped out of sight with the failure of the 1848 revolutions. By the time Marx settled down to his lifelong exile in England in 1849 it had become sufficiently scarce for Marx to think it worth reprinting section III of the *Manifesto* ('Socialistische und kommunistische Literatur') in the last issue of his London magazine *Neue Rheinische Zeitung, politisch-ökonom-ische Revue* (November 1850), which had hardly any readers.

Nobody would have predicted a remarkable future for it in the 1850s and early 1860s. A small new edition was privately issued in London by a German émigré printer, probably in 1864, and another small edition in Berlin in 1866, the first ever actually published in Germany. Between 1848 and 1868 there seem to have been no translations, apart from a Swedish version, probably published at the end of 1848, and an English one in 1850, significant in the bibliographical history of the *Manifesto* only because the translator seems to have consulted Marx, or (since she lived in Lancashire) more probably Engels. Both versions sank without trace. By the middle 1860s virtually nothing that Marx had written in the past was any longer in print.

Marx's prominence in the International Working Men's Association (the so-called 'First International', 1864–72) and the emergence, in Germany, of two important working-class parties, both founded by former members of the Communist League, who held him in high esteem, led to a revival of interest in the *Manifesto*, as in his other writings. In particular, his eloquent defence of the Paris Commune of 1871 (commonly known as *The Civil War in France*) gave him considerable notoriety in the press as a dangerous leader of international subversion, feared by governments. More specifically, the treason trial of the German Social Democratic Party leaders Wilhelm Liebknecht, August Bebel and Adolf Hepner in March 1872 gave the document unexpected publicity. The prosecution read the text of the *Manifesto* into the court record, and thus gave the social democrats their first chance of publishing it legally, and in a large print-run, as part of the court proceedings. As it was clear that a document published before the 1848 revolution might need some updating and explanatory commentary, Marx and Engels produced the first of the series of prefaces which have since usually accompanied new editions of the *Manifesto*.[2] For legal reasons the preface could not be widely distributed at the time, but in fact the 1872 edition (based on the 1866 edition) became the foundation of all subsequent editions. Meanwhile, between 1871 and 1873, at least nine editions of the *Manifesto* appeared in six languages.

In the next forty years the *Manifesto* conquered the world, carried forward by the rise of the new (socialist) labour parties, in which the Marxist influence rapidly increased in the 1880s. None of these chose to be known as a Communist Party until the Russian Bolsheviks returned to the original title after the October Revolution, but the title *Manifesto of the Communist Party* remained unchanged. Even before the Russian Revolution of 1917 it had been issued in several hundred editions in some thirty languages, including three editions in Japanese and one in Chinese. Nevertheless, its main region of influence was in the central belt of Europe, stretching from France in the west to Russia in the east. Not surprisingly the largest number of editions were in the Russian language (seventy), plus thirty-five more in the languages of the Tsarist Empire: eleven in Polish, seven in Yiddish, six in Finnish, five in Ukrainian, four in Georgian and two in Armenian. There were fifty-five editions in German plus, for the Habsburg empire, another nine in Hungarian and eight in Czech (but only three in Croat and one each in Slovak and Slovene); thirty-four in English (covering the USA also, where the first translation appeared in 1871); twenty-six in French; and eleven in Italian – the first not until 1889.[3] Its impact in southwestern Europe was small: six editions in Spanish (and this including the Latin American editions), one in Portuguese. So was its impact in southeastern Europe: seven editions in Bulgarian, four in Serb, four in Romanian, and a single edition in Ladino, presumably published in Salonica. Northern Europe was moderately well represented with six editions in Danish, five in Swedish and two in Norwegian.[4]

This uneven geographical distribution reflected not only the uneven development of the socialist movement, and of Marx's own influence, as distinct from other revolutionary ideologies such as anarchism, but should also remind us that there was no strong correlation between the size and power of social-democratic and labour parties and the circulation of the *Manifesto*. Thus until 1905 the German Social Democratic Party (SPD) with its hundreds of thousands of members and millions of voters published new editions of the *Manifesto* in print-runs of not more than 2000–3000 copies. The party's *Erfurt Programme* of 1891 was published in 120,000 copies while it appears to have published not many more than 16,000 copies of the *Manifesto* over the eleven years from 1895 to 1905, the year in which the circulation of its theoretical journal *Die Neue Zeit* was 6400.[5] The average member of a mass Marxist social-democratic party was not expected to pass examinations in theory. Conversely, the seventy pre-revolutionary Russian editions represented a combination of organisations, illegal for most of the time, whose total membership cannot have been more than a few thousand. Similarly the thirty-four English editions were published by and for the scattering of Marxist sects in the Anglo-Saxon world, operating on the left flank of such labour and socialist parties as existed. This was the milieu in which 'the clearness of a comrade could be gauged invariably from the number of earmarks on his *Manifesto*'.[6] In short, the readers of the *Manifesto*, though part of the new and rising socialist labour parties and movements, were almost certainly not a representative sample of their membership. They were men and women with a special interest in the theory that underlay such movements. This is probably still the case.

This situation changed after the October Revolution, at all events in the communist parties. Unlike the mass parties of the Second International (1889–1914), those of the Third (1919–43) expected all their members to understand, or at least to show some knowledge of, Marxist theory. The dichotomy between effective political leaders uninterested in writing books and the 'theorists' like Karl Kautsky, known and respected as such but not as practical political decision-makers, faded away. Following

Lenin all leaders were now supposed to be important theorists, since all political decisions were justified on grounds of Marxist analysis, or, more likely, by reference to the textual authority of 'the classics': Marx, Engels, Lenin and, in due course, Stalin. The publication and popular distribution of Marx's and Engels' texts therefore became far more central to the movement than in the days of the Second International. They ranged from series of the smaller writings, probably pioneered by the German *Elementarbücher des Kommunismus* during the Weimar Republic, and suitably selected compendia of readings, such as the invaluable *Selected Correspondence of Marx and Engels*, to *Selected Works of Marx and Engels* in two, later three volumes, and the preparation of their *Collected Works* (*Gesamtausgabe*) – all backed by the (for these purposes) unlimited resources of the Soviet Communist Party, and often printed in the Soviet Union in a variety of foreign languages.

The *Communist Manifesto* benefited from this new situation in three ways. Its circulation undoubtedly grew. The cheap edition published in 1932 by the official publishing houses of the American and British Communist Parties in 'hundreds of thousands' of copies has been described as 'probably the largest mass edition ever issued in English'.[7] Its title was no longer a historical survival, but now linked directly to current politics. Since a major state now claimed to represent Marxist ideology, the *Manifesto*'s standing as a text in political science was reinforced, and it accordingly entered the teaching programme of universities, destined to expand rapidly after the Second World War, and where the Marxism of intellectual readers was to find its most enthusiastic public in the 1960s and 1970s.

The USSR emerged from the Second World War as one of the two superpowers in the world, heading a vast region of communist states and dependencies. Western communist parties (with the notable exception of the German one) emerged from the war stronger than they had ever been or were likely to be. Though the Cold War had begun, in the year of its centenary the *Manifesto* was no longer published simply by communist or other Marxist editors but in large print-runs by non-political publishers with introductions by prominent academics. In short, it was no longer only a classic Marxist document, it had become a political classic *tout court*.

It remains one, even after the end of Soviet communism and the decline of Marxist parties and movements in many parts of the world. In states without censorship, almost certainly anyone within reach of a good bookshop, and certainly anyone within reach of a good library, not to mention the internet, can have access to it. The object of a new edition is therefore not so much to make the text of this astonishing masterpiece available, and still less to revisit a century of doctrinal debates about the 'correct' interpretation of this fundamental document of Marxism. It is to remind ourselves that the *Manifesto* still has plenty to say to the world in the twenty-first century.

II

What does it have to say?

It is, of course, a document written for a particular moment in history. Some of it became obsolete almost immediately – for instance the tactics recommended for communists in Germany, which were not those in fact applied by them during the 1848 revolution and its aftermath. More of it became obsolete as the time separating the readers from the date of writing length-ened. Guizot and Metternich have long retired from leading governments into history books, the Tsar (though not the Pope) no longer exists. As for the discussion of 'Socialist and Communist Literature', Marx and Engels themselves admitted in 1872 that even then it was out of date.

More to the point, with the lapse of time the language of the *Manifesto* was no longer that of its readers. For example, much has been made of the phrase that the advance of bourgeois society had rescued 'a considerable part of the population from the idiocy of rural life'. But while there is no doubt that Marx at this time shared the usual townsman's contempt for, as well as ignorance of, the peasant milieu, the actual and analytically more interesting German phrase ('dem Idiotismus des Landlebens entrissen') referred not to 'stupidity' but to 'the narrow horizons', or 'the isolation from the wider society' in which people in the countryside lived. It echoed the original meaning of the Greek term *idiotes* from which the current meaning of 'idiot' or 'idiocy' is derived, namely 'a person concerned only with his own private affairs and not with those of the wider community'. In the course of the decades since the 1840s, and in movements whose members, unlike Marx, were not classically educated, the original sense had evaporated and was misread.

This is even more evident in its political vocabulary. Terms such as 'Stand' ('estate'), 'Demokratie' ('democracy') and 'Nation/national' either have little application to today's politics or no longer have the meaning they had in the political or philosophical discourse of the 1840s. To take an obvious example, the 'Communist Party' whose manifesto our text claimed to be had nothing to do with the parties of modern democratic politics or the 'vanguard parties' of Leninist communism, let alone the state parties of the Soviet and Chinese type. None of these as yet existed. 'Party' still meant essentially a tendency or current of opinion or policy, although Marx and Engels recognised that once this found expression in class movements, it developed some kind of organisation ('diese Organisation der Proletarier zur Klasse, und damit zur politischen Partei'). Hence the distinction in part IV between the 'already constituted workers' parties . . . the Chartists in England and the agrarian Reformers in North America' and the others, not yet so constituted.[8] As the text made clear, Marx's and Engels' Communist Party at this stage was no kind of organisation, nor did it attempt to establish one, let alone an organisation with a specific programme distinct from other organisations.[9] Incidentally, the actual body on whose behalf the *Manifesto* was written, the Communist League, is nowhere mentioned in it.

Moreover, it is clear that the *Manifesto* was not only written in and for a particular historical situation, but also that it represented one phase – a relatively immature phase – in the development of Marxian thought. This is most evident in its economic aspects. Though Marx had begun to study political economy seriously from 1843, he did not seriously set out to develop the economic analysis expounded in *Capital* until he arrived in his English exile after the 1848 revolution and acquired access to the treasures of the British Museum Library, in the summer of 1850. Thus the distinction between the proletarian's sale of his *labour* to the capitalist, and the sale of his *labour power*, which is essential to the Marxian theory of surplus value and exploitation, had clearly not yet been made in the *Manifesto*. Nor did the mature Marx hold the view that the price of the commodity 'labour' was its cost of production, i.e. the cost of the physiological minimum of keeping the worker alive. In short, Marx wrote the *Manifesto* less as a Marxian economist than as a communist Ricardian.

And yet, though Marx and Engels reminded readers that the *Manifesto* was a historical document, out-of-date in many respects, they promoted and assisted the publication of the 1848 text, with relatively minor amendments and clarifications.[10] They recognised that it remained a major statement of the analysis which distinguished their communism from all other projects for the creation of a better society. In essence this analysis was historical. Its core was the demonstration of the historical development of societies, and specifically of bourgeois society, which replaced its predecessors, revolutionised the world, and in turn necessarily created the conditions for its inevitable supersession. Unlike Marxian economics, the 'materialist conception of history' which underlay this analysis had already found its mature formulation in the middle 1840s. It remained substantially unchanged in later years.[11] In this respect the *Manifesto* already was a defining document of Marxism. It embodied the historical vision, though its general outline remained to be filled in by fuller analysis.

III

How will the *Manifesto* strike the reader who comes to it for the first time? The new reader can hardly fail to be swept away by the passionate conviction, the concentrated brevity, the intellectual and stylistic force of this astonishing pamphlet. It is written, as though in a single creative burst, in lapidary sentences almost naturally transforming themselves into the memorable aphorisms which have become known far beyond the world of political debate: from the opening 'A spectre is haunting Europe – the spectre of communism' to the final 'The proletarians have nothing to lose but their chains. They have a world to win.'[12] Equally uncommon in nineteenth-century German writing, it is written in short apodictic paragraphs, mainly of one to five lines, in only five cases out of more than two hundred, of fifteen or more lines. Whatever else it is, *The Communist Manifesto* as political rhetoric has an almost biblical force. In short, it is impossible to deny its compelling power as literature.[13]

However, what will undoubtedly also strike the contemporary reader is the *Manifesto*'s remarkable diagnosis of the revolutionary character and impact of 'bourgeois society'. The point is not simply that Marx recognised and proclaimed the extraordinary achievements and dynamism of a society he detested, to the surprise of more than one later defender of capitalism against the red menace. It is that the world transformed by capitalism which he described in 1848, in passages of dark, laconic eloquence, is recognisably the world of the early twenty-first century. Curiously, the politically quite unrealistic optimism of two revolutionaries of twenty-eight and thirty years has proved to be the *Manifesto*'s most lasting strength. For though the 'spectre of communism' did indeed haunt politicians, and though Europe was living through a major period of economic and social crisis, and was about to erupt in the greatest continent-wide revolution of its history, there was plainly no adequate ground for the *Manifesto*'s belief that the moment for the overthrow of capitalism was approaching ('the bourgeois revolution in Germany can only be the prelude to an immediately following proletarian revolution'). On the contrary. As we now know, capitalism was poised for its first era of triumphant global advance.

What gives the *Manifesto* its force is two things. The first is its vision, even at the outset of the triumphal march of capitalism, that this mode of production was not permanent, stable, 'the end of history', but a temporary phase in the history of humanity, and, like its predecessors, one due to be superseded by another kind of society (unless – the *Manifesto*'s phrase has not been much noted – it founders 'in the common ruin of the contending classes'). The second is its recognition of the necessary *long-term* historical tendencies of capitalist development. The revolutionary potential of the capitalist economy was already evident; Marx and Engels did not claim to be the only ones to recognise it. Since the French Revolution some of the tendencies they observed were plainly having substantial effect – for instance the decline of 'independent or but loosely connected provinces, with separate interests, laws, governments and systems of taxation' before nation-states 'with one government, one code of laws, one national class interest, one frontier and one customs-tariff'. Nevertheless, by the late 1840s what 'the bourgeoisie' had achieved was a great deal more modest than the miracles ascribed to it in the *Manifesto*. After all, in 1850 the world produced no more than 71,000 tons of steel (almost 70% in Britain) and had built fewer than 24,000 miles of railroads (two-thirds of these in Britain and the USA).

Historians have had no difficulty in showing that even in Britain the Industrial Revolution (a term specifically used by Engels from 1844 on)[14] had hardly created an industrial or even a predominantly urban country before the 1850s. Marx and Engels described not the world as it had already been transformed by capitalism in 1848, but predicted how it was logically destined to be transformed by it.

We now live in a world in which this transformation has largely taken place, even though readers of the *Manifesto* in the third millennium of the western calendar will no doubt observe the continued acceleration of its advance. In some ways we can even see the force of the *Manifesto*'s predictions more clearly than the generations between us and its publication. For until the revolution in transport and communications since the Second World War, there were limits to the globalisation of production, to 'giving a cosmopolitan character to production and consumption in every country'. Until the 1970s industrialisation remained overwhelmingly confined to its regions of origin. Some schools of Marxists could even argue that capitalism, at least in its imperialist form, so far from 'compel[ling] all nations, on pain of extinction, to adopt the bourgeois mode of production', was by its nature perpetuating, or even creating, 'underdevelopment' in the so-called Third World. While one third of the human race lived in economies of the Soviet communist type, it seemed as though capitalism would never succeed in compelling all nations 'to become bourgeois themselves'. It would not 'create a world after its own image'. Again, before the 1960s the *Manifesto*'s announcement that capitalism brought about the destruction of the family seemed not to have been verified, even in the advanced Western countries, where today something like half the children are born to or brought up by single mothers, and half of all households in big cities consist of single persons.

In short, what might in 1848 have struck an uncommitted reader as revolutionary rhetoric or, at best, as plausible prediction can now be read as a concise characterisation of capitalism at the start of the new millennium. Of what other document of the 1840s can this be said?

IV

However, if today we must be struck by the acuteness of the *Manifesto*'s vision of the then remote future of a massively globalised capitalism, the failure of another of its forecasts is equally striking. It is now evident that the bourgeoisie has not produced 'above all, its own gravediggers' in the proletariat. 'Its fall and the victory of the proletariat' have not proved 'equally inevitable'. The contrast between the two halves of the *Manifesto*'s analysis in its section on 'Bourgeois and Proletarians' calls for more explanation after over 150 years than at the time of its centenary.

The problem lies not in Marx's and Engels' vision of a capitalism which necessarily transformed most of the people earning their living in this economy into men and women who depend for their livelihood on hiring themselves out for wages or salaries. It has undoubtedly tended to do so, though today the incomes of some who are technically employees hired for a salary, such as corporation executives, can hardly count as proletarian. Nor does it lie essentially in their belief that most of this working population would consist of a workforce of *industrial* labour. While Great Britain remained quite exceptional as a country in which wage-paid manual workers formed the absolute majority of the population, the development of industrial production required massive and growing inputs of manual labour for well over a century after the *Manifesto*. Unquestionably this is no longer the case in modern capital-intensive high-tech production, a development not considered in the *Manifesto*, though in fact in his more mature economic studies Marx himself envisaged the possible development of an increasingly labourless economy, at least in a post-capitalist era.[15] Even in the old industrial economies of capitalism, the percentage of people employed in manufacturing industry remained stable until the 1970s, except for the USA, where the decline set in a little earlier. Indeed, with very few exceptions such as Britain, Belgium and the USA, in 1970 industrial workers probably formed a larger proportion of the total occupied population in the industrial and industrialising world than ever before.

In any case, the overthrow of capitalism envisaged by the *Manifesto* did not rely on the prior transformation of the *majority* of the occupied population into proletarians, but on the assumption that the situation of the proletariat in the capitalist economy was such that, once organised as a necessarily political class movement, it could take the lead and rally round itself the discontent of other classes, and thus acquire political power as 'the independent movement of the immense majority in the interests of the immense majority'. Thus the proletariat would 'rise to be the leading class of the nation, . . . constitute itself *the* nation'.[16]

Since capitalism has not been overthrown we are apt to dismiss this prediction. Yet, utterly improbable though it looked in 1848, the politics of most European capitalist countries were to be transformed by the rise of organised political movements basing themselves on the class-conscious working class, which had barely made its appearance outside Great Britain. Labour and socialist parties emerged in most parts of the 'developed' world in the 1880s and became mass parties in states with the democratic franchise which they did so much to bring about. During and after World War One, as one branch of 'proletarian parties' followed the revolutionary road of the Bolsheviks, another branch became the sustaining pillars of a democratised capitalism. The Bolshevik branch is no longer of much significance in Europe, or parties of this kind have assimilated to social democracy. Social democracy, as understood in the days of Bebel or even Clement Attlee, was fighting a rearguard action in the 1990s. However, at the end of the century, the descendants of the social-democratic parties of the Second International, sometimes under their original names, were the parties of government in all except two Western European states (Spain and Germany), in both of which they had in the past provided the government and were likely to do so again.

In short, what is wrong is not the *Manifesto*'s prediction of the central role of the political movements based on the working class (and still sometimes specifically bearing the class name, as in the British, Dutch, Norwegian and Australasian Labour Parties). It is the proposition that 'of all the classes that confront the bourgeoisie today, the proletariat alone is a really revolutionary class', whose inevitable destiny, implicit in the nature and development of capitalism, is to overthrow the bourgeoisie: 'Its fall and the victory of the proletariat are equally inevitable.'

Even in the notoriously 'hungry forties', the mechanism which was to assure this, namely the inevitable pauperisation of the labourers,[17] was not totally convincing; unless on the assumption, implausible even then, that capitalism was in its final crisis and about to be *immediately* overthrown. It was a double mechanism. Pauperisation, in addition to its effect on the workers' movement, proved that the bourgeoisie was 'unfit to rule because it is incompetent to assure an existence to its slave within his slavery, because it cannot help letting him sink into such a state, that it has to feed him instead of being fed by him'. So far from providing the profit which fuelled the engine of capitalism, labour now drained it away. But, given the enormous economic potential of capitalism so dramatically expounded in the *Manifesto* itself, why was it inevitable that capitalism could not provide a livelihood, however miserable, for most of its working class, or alternatively, that it could not afford a welfare system? That 'pauperism [in the strict sense] develops even more rapidly than population and wealth'?[18] If capitalism had a long life before it – as became obvious very soon after 1848 – this did not have to happen, and indeed it did not.

The *Manifesto*'s vision of the historic development of 'bourgeois society', including the working class which it generated, did not necessarily lead to the conclusion that the proletariat would overthrow capitalism and, in so doing, open the way to the development of communism, because vision and conclusion did not derive from the same analysis. The aim of communism, adopted before Marx became 'Marxist', was not derived from the analysis of the nature and development of capitalism but from a philosophical, indeed an eschatological argument about human nature and destiny. The idea – fundamental for Marx from then on – that the proletariat was a class which could not liberate itself without thereby liberating society as a whole first appears as 'a philosophical deduction rather than a product of observation'.[19] As George Lichtheim put it: 'the proletariat makes its first appearance in Marx's writings as the social force needed to realise the aims of German philosophy', as Marx saw it in 1843–4.[20]

At this time Marx knew little more about the proletariat than that 'it is coming into being in Germany only as a result of the rising industrial development', and this was precisely its potential as a liberating force, since, unlike the poor masses of traditional society, it was the child of a '*drastic dissolution* of society' and therefore by its existence 'proclaim[ed] the *dissolution of the hitherto existing world order*'. He knew even less about labour movements, though a great deal about the history of the French Revolution. In Engels he acquired a partner who brought to the partnership the concept of the 'Industrial Revolution', an understanding of the dynamics of capitalist economy as it actually existed in Britain, and the rudiments of an economic analysis,[21] both leading him to predict a future social revolution, to be made by an actual working class about which, living and working in Britain in the early 1840s, he knew a great deal. Marx's and Engels' approaches to 'the proletariat' and communism complemented one another. So did their conception of the class struggle as a motor of history, in Marx's case derived largely from the study of the French Revolutionary period, in Engels' from the experience of social movements in post-Napoleonic Britain. It is no surprise that they found themselves (in Engels' words) 'in agreement in all theoretical fields'.[22] Engels brought to Marx the elements of a model which demonstrated the fluctuating and self-destabilising nature of the operations of the capitalist economy – notably the outlines of a theory of economic crises[23] – and empirical material about the rise of the British working-class movement and the revolutionary role it could play in Britain.

In the 1840s the conclusion that society was on the verge of revolution was not implausible. Nor was the prediction that the working class, however immature, would lead it. After all, within weeks of the publication of the *Manifesto* a movement of Paris workers overthrew the French monarchy, and gave the signal for revolution to half Europe. Nevertheless, the tendency for capitalist development to generate an essentially *revolutionary* proletariat could not be deduced from the analysis of the nature of capitalist development. It was one possible consequence of this development, but could not be shown to be the only possible one. Still less could it be shown that a successful overthrow of capitalism by the proletariat must necessarily open the way to communist development. (The *Manifesto* claims no more than that it would then initiate a process of very gradual change.)[24] Marx's vision of a proletariat whose very essence destined it to emancipate all humanity and end class society by its overthrow of capitalism represents a hope read into his analysis of capitalism, but not a conclusion necessarily imposed by that analysis.

What the *Manifesto*'s analysis of capitalism could undoubtedly lead to, especially when extended by Marx's analysis of economic concentration, which is barely hinted at in 1848, is a more general and less specific conclusion about the self-destructive forces built into capitalist development. It must reach a point – and nowadays not only Marxists will accept this – where 'the bourgeois relations of production and exchange, bourgeois property relations, modern bourgeois society, which has conjured up such gigantic means of production and exchange, is like the sorcerer who is no longer able to control the powers of the underworld he has called up . . . Bourgeois relations have become too narrow to encompass the wealth created by them.'

It is not unreasonable to conclude that the 'contradictions' inherent in a market system based on 'no other nexus between human beings than naked self-interest, than callous "cash payment"', a system of exploitation and of endless accumulation, can never be overcome; that at some point in a series of transformations and restructurings the development of this essentially self-destabilising system will lead to a state of affairs that can no longer be described as capitalism. Or, to quote the later Marx, when 'centralisation of the means of production and the socialisation of labour at last reach a point where they become incompatible with their capitalist integument' and that 'integument is burst asunder'.[25] By what name the subsequent state of affairs is described is immaterial. However, as the effects of the world economic explosion on the world environment demonstrate, it will necessarily have to mark a sharp shift away from private appropriation to social management on a global scale.

It is extremely unlikely that such a 'post-capitalist society' would correspond to the traditional models of socialism, and still less to the 'really existing' socialisms of the Soviet era. What forms it might take, and how far it would embody the humanist values of Marx's and Engels' communism, would depend on the political action through which this change came about. For this, as the *Manifesto* holds, is central to the shaping of historical change.

V

In the Marxian view, however we describe that historic moment when 'the integument is burst asunder', politics will be an essential element in it. The *Manifesto* has been read primarily as a document of historical inevitability, and indeed its force derived largely from the confidence it gave its readers that capitalism was inevitably destined to be buried by its gravediggers, and that now and at no earlier era in history the conditions for emancipation had come into being. Yet, contrary to widespread assumptions, inasmuch as it believes that historical change proceeds through men making their own history, it is not a determinist document. The graves have to be dug by or through human action.

A determinist reading of the argument is indeed possible. It has been suggested that Engels tended towards it more naturally than Marx, with important consequences for the development of Marxist theory and the Marxist labour movement after Marx's death. However, though Engels' own earlier drafts have been cited as evidence,[26] in fact it cannot be read into the *Manifesto* itself. When it leaves the field of historical analysis and enters the present, it is a document of choices, of political possibilities rather than probabilities, let alone certainties. Between 'now' and the unpredictable time when 'in the course of development' there would be 'an association in which the free development of each is the condition of the free development of all' lies the realm of political action.

Historical change through social praxis, through collective action, is at its core. The *Manifesto* sees the development of the proletariat as the 'organisation of the proletarians into a class and consequently into a political party'. The 'conquest of political power by the proletariat' ('the winning of democracy') is 'the first step in the workers' revolution', and the future of society hinges on the subsequent political actions of the new regime (how 'the proletariat will use its political supremacy'). The commitment to *politics* is what historically distinguished Marxian socialism from the anarchists, and from the successors of those socialists whose rejection of all political action the *Manifesto* specifically condemns. Even before Lenin, Marxian theory was not just about 'what history shows us will happen', but also about 'what must be done'. Admittedly, the Soviet experience of the twentieth century has taught us that it might be better not to do 'what must be done' under historical conditions which virtually put success beyond reach. But this lesson might also have been learned from considering the implications of the *Communist Manifesto*.

But then, the *Manifesto* – it is not the least of its remarkable qualities – is a document which envisaged failure. It hoped that the outcome of capitalist development would be 'a revolutionary reconstitution of society at large' but, as we have already seen, it did not exclude the alternative: 'common ruin'.

Many years later another Marxian rephrased this as the choice between socialism and barbarity. Which of these will prevail is a question which the twenty-first century must be left to answer.

6

Discovering the Grundrisse[*]

The place of the *Grundrisse* in Marx's *oeuvre* and its fortunes are in many respects peculiar. In the first place, they are the only example of a major set of Marx's mature writings which, for practical purposes, were entirely unknown to Marxists for more than half a century after Karl Marx's death; and indeed almost completely unavailable until almost a century after the composition of the manuscripts which have been brought together under this name. Whatever the debates about their significance, the writings of 1857–8, clearly part of the intellectual effort that was to produce *Das Kapital*, represent Marx in his maturity, not least as an economist. This distinguishes the *Grundrisse* from the other earlier posthumous addition to the Marxian corpus, the 1932 *Fruehschriften*. The exact place of these writings of the early forties in Marx's theoretical development has been much debated, rightly or wrongly, but there can be no such disagreement about the maturity of the writings of 1857–8.

[*]Foreword to Marcello Musto (ed.), *Karl Marx's* Grundrisse: *Foundations of the Critique of Political Economy 150 years Later* (Routledge, London, 2008).

In the second place, and somewhat surprisingly, the entire publication of the *Grundrisse* took place under what may safely be regarded as the least favourable conditions for any original development of Marx studies and Marxist thinking, namely in the USSR and the German Democratic Republic, at the height of the era of Stalin. The publication of texts by Marx and Engels remained a matter subject to the imprimatur of political authority even later, as editors engaged in foreign editions of their works have had reason to discover. It is still not clear how the obstacles to publication were overcome, including the purging of the Marx-Engels Institute and the elimination and eventual murder of its founder and director, or how Paul Weller, who was in charge of work on the manuscript from 1925 to 1939, survived the terror of 1936–8 to do so. It may have helped that the authorities did not quite know what to make of this large and difficult text. However, they plainly had their doubts about its precise status, not least because Stalin's view was that draft manuscripts were of less importance than the three volumes of *Capital* which reflected Marx's mature position and views. The *Grundrisse* were not in fact fully published in a Russian translation until 1968–9, and neither the original (Moscow) German edition of 1939–41 nor its 1953 (Berlin) reprint were published as parts of the (incomplete) Soviet edition of Marx's and Engels' collected works usually known by the acronym MEGA (only 'in the format of MEGA'), or as part of the Marx–Engels *Werke*. However, unlike the *Fruehschriften* of 1844, which disappeared from the official Marx corpus after their original appearance in MEGA (1932), they actually were published in the USSR, even at the peak of the Stalin era.

The third peculiarity is the long-lasting uncertainty about the status of the 1857–8 manuscripts which is reflected in the fluctuating name of the papers in the Marx-Engels-Lenin Institute of the 1930s until they acquired their title *Grundrisse* shortly before going to print. Indeed, the exact nature of their relation to the published texts of *Das Kapital* as written by Marx and reconstructed by Engels, and the fourth volume of *Theories of Surplus Value*, compiled by Kautsky from Marx's notes of 1861–3, remains a matter of debate. Kautsky, who went through them, does not seem to have known what to do about them. He published two extracts from them in his review *Die Neue Zeit*, but no more. These were the brief *Bastiat and Carey* (1904), which made little impact, and the so-called Introduction to the *Critique of Political Economy* (1903), never completed and therefore not published in 1859 with the book of the same name which was to become an early text for those wishing to extend Marxist interpretation beyond prevailing orthodoxies, notably the Austro-Marxists. To date it is probably the most widely discussed part of the *Grundrisse*, although at least one commentator in the latest book on the subject questions whether these two pieces form part of it. The rest of the manuscripts remained unpublished, and indeed unknown to commentators, until Ryazanov and his collaborators in Moscow acquired photocopies of them in 1923, put them in order and planned to publish them in the MEGA. It is interesting to speculate what impact they might have had if they had been published in 1931, as originally planned. The date of their actual publication – at the end of 1939 and a week after Hitler's invasion of the USSR in 1941 – meant that they remained almost totally unknown in the West until the 1953 reprint in East Berlin, although rare copies reached the USA and from 1948 on the work was analysed, but not published before 1967–8, by the great pioneer explicator of the *Grundrisse*, Roman Rosdolsky (1898–1965), recently arrived in the USA via Auschwitz and various other concentration camps. It is difficult to believe that the bulk of the original German edition, 'sent to the front as material for agitation against German soldiers and later to camps as study materials for prisoners of war' achieved their theoretical or practical objectives.

Why the full reprint of 1939/41, which became the *editio principes* for the international reception of the *Grundrisse*, was published in East Germany in 1953, some years before the publication of the Marx–Engels *Werke*, and deliberately unconnected with these, we do not know, though some plausible suggestions have been made. With one exception, the work did not begin to make a serious mark on Marx studies until the 1960s. That exception is the section on 'Forms that precede capitalist production', which was first published separately in Russian in 1938 (as, somewhat earlier, was the chapter on money), translated into Japanese in 1947, in German in 1952, a text immediately translated into Hungarian, Japanese and Italian (1953–4), and certainly discussed among Marxist historians in the English-speaking world. The English translation, with an explicatory introduction (1964), was soon published in Spanish versions in Argentina and Franco's Spain (1966–7). Presumably its special interest for Marxist historians and social anthropologists helps to explain the wide distribution of this text, well before the availability of the full *Grundrisse*, and also its specific relevance to the much-disputed Marxist analysis of Third World societies. It threw light on the 'Asiatic mode of production' debate, controversially revived in the West by works like Wittfogel's *Oriental Despotism* (1957).

The *Rezeptionsgeschichte* of the 1857–8 manuscripts really begins with the major effort, following the crisis of 1956, to free Marxism from the straitjacket of Soviet orthodoxy, both within and outside the no longer monolithic communist parties. Since they did not belong to the canonical corpus of 'the classics' but were unquestionably by Marx, both the 1844 writings and the 1857–8 manuscripts could be regarded inside communist parties as the basis for a legitimate opening of hitherto closed positions. The almost simultaneous international discovery of Gramsci's writings – the first publication of his writings in the USSR was in 1957–9 – had the same function. The belief that the *Grundrisse* had the potential for heterodoxy is shown by the appearance of unofficial freelance translations such as those of the reformists of the French Editions Anthropos (1968) and, under the auspices of the *New Left Review*, Martin Nicolaus (1971). Outside the communist parties the *Grundrisse* had the function of justifying a non-communist but unquestionable Marxism, but this did not become politically significant until the era of student rebellions in the 1960s, although their significance had already been recognised in the 1950s by scholarly Germans close to the Frankfurt tradition, but not in the milieu of political activism, like Lichtheim and the young Habermas. Student radicalisation in rapidly expanding universities also provided a larger body of readers than could have been expected in the past for extremely difficult texts such as these. But for this commercial publishers like Penguin Books would surely not have been prepared to publish the *Grundrisse*, even as part of a 'Pelican Marx Library'. In the meantime the text had been, more or less reluctantly, accepted as an integral part of the corpus of Marx's writings in the USSR, being added to the previous edition of the Marx–Engels works in 1968–9, though in a smaller edition than *Capital*. Publication in Hungary and Czechoslovakia soon followed, and, after the end of Mao, in China.

It is thus not easy to separate the debates on the *Grundrisse* from the political setting in which they took place, and which stimulated them. In the 1970s, when they were at their most intense, they also suffered from a generational or cultural handicap, namely the loss of most of the (mainly Central and East European) pioneer generation of Marxian textual scholars of monumental devotion and learning, men like David Ryazanov and Roman Rosdolsky. Some serious efforts were indeed made by younger Trotskyist intellectuals to build on the earlier analyses of the place of the 1857–8 manuscripts in the development of Marx's thought, and more specifically on their place in the general plan of what became the torso of *Capital*. However, prominent Marxist theoretical polemics might be launched by writers like Louis Althusser in France and Antonio Negri in Italy with a frankly insufficient formation in Marxian literature and received by young men and women who themselves might well as yet lack much knowledge of the texts, or ability to judge the past controversies about them, if only for linguistic reasons.

The present collective volume appears at a time when Marxist parties and movements are only rarely significant actors on the global scene and when debates about their doctrines, strategies, methods and objectives are no longer the inevitable framework of debates about the writings of Marx, Engels and their followers. And yet it also comes out at a time when the world appears to demonstrate the perspicacity of Marx's insight into the economic modus operandi of the capitalist system. Perhaps this is the right moment to return to a study of the *Grundrisse* less constricted by the temporary considerations of left-wing politics between Khrushchev's denunciation of Stalin and the fall of Gorbachev. It is an enormously difficult text in every respect, but also an enormously rewarding one, if only because it provides the only guide to the full range of the treatise of which *Capital* is only a fraction, and a unique introduction to the methodology of the mature Marx. It contains analyses and insights, for instance about technology, that take Marx's treatment of capitalism far beyond the nineteenth century, into the era of a society where production no longer requires mass labour, of automation, the potential of leisure, and the transformations of alienation in such circumstances. It is the only text that goes some way beyond Marx's own hints of the communist future in the *German Ideology*. In short, it has been rightly described as 'Marx's thought at its richest'.

7

Marx on pre-Capitalist Formations

I

In 1857–8 Karl Marx was composing a bulky manuscript in preparation for his *Critique of Political Economy* and *Capital*. It was published under the title *Grundrisse der Kritik der Politischen Ökonomie* in Moscow, 1939–41, though some small extracts had appeared in the *Neue Zeit* in 1903–4. The time and place of publication caused the work to be virtually unknown until 1952 when a section of it was published as a pamphlet in Berlin, and 1953, when the entire *Grundrisse* were republished in the same city. This 1953 German edition long remained the only accessible one. The *Grundrisse* thus belong to that large group of Marx and Engels manuscripts which were never published during their authors' lifetime, and have become available for adequate study only since 1930.* Most of them, such as the *Economic-Philosophical Manuscripts of 1844*, which have figured a

---

*This chapter was written as the introduction to a section of the *Grundrisse*, known in English as *Pre-Capitalist Economic Foundations* (Lawrence & Wishart, London, 1964). References in the chapter are to that edition.

great deal in subsequent discussions, belong to the youth of both Marx and Marxism. The *Grundrisse*, however, belong to his full maturity. They are the outcome of a decade of intensive study in England, and clearly represent the stage of his thought which immediately precedes the drafting of *Capital* during the early 1860s, for which, as already observed, they provide preliminary work. The *Grundrisse* are therefore the last major writings of the mature Marx to have reached the public.

Under the circumstances, their neglect is very surprising. This is especially true of the sections, headed 'Formen die der Kapitalistischen Produktion vorhergehen', in which Marx attempts to grapple with the problem of pre-capitalist historic evolution. For these are not unimportant or casual notes. The *Formen* do not merely represent – as Marx himself proudly wrote to Lassalle (12 November 1858) – 'the result of fifteen years' research, that is to say of the best years of my life', they show Marx at his most brilliant and profound, and are also in many ways the indispensable pendant to the superb Preface to the *Critique of Political Economy*, which was written shortly after and presents historical materialism in its most pregnant form. It can be said without hesitation that any Marxist historical discussion which does not take into account the *Grundrisse* – that is to say virtually all such discussion before 1941, and (unfortunately) much of it since – must be reconsidered in the light of them.

There are, however, obvious reasons for this neglect. The *Grundrisse* were, as Marx wrote to Lassalle, 'monographs, written at widely varying periods, for my own clarification and not for publication'. Not only do they require from the reader an easy familiarity with Marx's idiom of thought – i.e. with his entire intellectual evolution and especially with Hegelianism – but they are also written in a sort of private intellectual shorthand which is sometimes impenetrable, in the form of rough notes interspersed with asides which, however clear they may have been to Marx, are often ambiguous to us. Anyone who has tried to translate the manuscript or even to study and interpret it, will know that it is sometimes quite impossible to put the meaning of some sibylline passage beyond all reasonable doubt.

Even if Marx had taken the trouble to make his meaning clear, it would still be far from easy, because his analysis is conducted at a very high level of generality, that is to say in highly abstract terms. In the first place Marx is concerned – as in the Preface to the *Critique* – to establish the general mechanism of *all* social change: the formation of social relations of production which correspond to a definite stage of development of the material forces of production; the periodic development of conflicts between the forces and relations of production; the 'epochs of social revolution' in which the relations once again adjust themselves to the level of the forces. This general analysis does not imply any statement about specific historical periods, forces and relations of productions whatever. Thus the word 'class' is not even mentioned in the Preface, for classes are merely special cases of social relations of production at particular – though admittedly very long – periods of history. And the only actual statement about historic formations and periods is the brief, unsupported and unexplained list of the 'epochs in the progress of the economic formation of society' – namely, the 'Asiatic, ancient, feudal and modern bourgeois', of which the final one is the last 'antagonistic' form of the social process of production.

The *Formen* are both more general and more specific than the Preface, though they too – it is important to note this at the outset – are not 'history' in the strict sense. In one aspect, the draft attempts to discover in the analysis of social evolution the characteristics of *any* dialectical, or indeed of any satisfying theory on any subject whatever. It seeks to possess, and indeed it does possess, those qualities of intellectual economy, generality and unbroken internal logic, which scientists incline to call 'beauty' or 'elegance', and it pursues them, by the use of Hegel's dialectical method, though on a materialist and not an idealist basis.

This immediately brings us to the second aspect. The *Formen* seek to formulate the *content* of history in its most general form. This content is *progress*. Neither those who deny the existence of historical progress nor those who (often basing themselves on the writings of the immature Marx) see Marx's thought merely as an ethical demand for the liberation of man will find any support here. For Marx progress is something objectively definable, and at the same time pointing to what is desirable. The strength of the Marxist belief in the triumph of the free development of all men depends not on the strength of Marx's hope for it, but on the assumed correctness of the analysis that this is indeed where historical development eventually leads mankind.

The objective basis of Marx's humanism, but of course also, and simultaneously, of his theory of social and economic evolution, is his analysis of man as a social animal. Man – or rather men – perform *labour*, i.e. they create and reproduce their existence in daily practice, breathing, seeking food, shelter, love, etc. They do this by operating *in* nature, taking from nature (and eventually consciously changing nature) for this purpose. This interaction between man and nature is, and produces, social evolution. Taking from nature, or determining the use of some bit of nature (including one's own body), can be, and indeed is in common parlance, seen as appropriation, which is therefore originally merely an aspect of labour. It is expressed in the concept of *property* (which is not by any means the same thing as the historically special case of *private* property). In the beginning, says Marx, 'the relationship of the worker to the objective conditions of his labour is one of ownership; this is the natural unity of labour with its material [*sachliche*] prerequisites' (p.67). Being a social animal man develops both co-operation and a *social division of labour* (i.e. specialisation of functions), which is not only made possible by, but increases the further possibilities of, producing a *surplus* over and above what is needed to maintain the individual and the community of which he is a part. The existence of both the surplus and the social division of labour makes possible *exchange*. But initially both production and exchange have as their object merely *use* – i.e. the maintenance of the producer and his community. These are the main analytical bricks out of which the theory is built, and all are in fact expansions or corollaries of the original concept of man as a social animal of a special kind.[1]

Progress of course is observable in the growing emancipation of man from nature and his growing control over nature. This emancipation – i.e. from the situation as given when primitive men go about their living, and from the original and spontaneous (or as Marx says *naturwüchsig* – 'as grown up in nature') relations which emerge from the process of the evolution of animals into human groups – affects not only the forces but also the relations of production. And it is with the latter aspect that the *Formen* deals. On the one hand, the relations men enter into as a result of the specialisation of labour – and notably *exchange* – are progressively clarified and sophisticated, until the invention of *money* and with it of *commodity production* and exchange, provides a basis for procedures unimaginable before, including capital accumulation. (This process, while mentioned at the outset (p.67), is not its major subject.) On the other hand, the double relation of labour-property is progressively broken up, as man moves further from the *naturwüchsig* or spontaneously evolved primitive relation with nature. It takes the form of a progressive 'separation of free labour from the objective conditions of its realisation – from the means of labour [*Arbeitsmittel*] and the material of labour . . . Hence, above all, the separation of the labourer from the earth as his natural laboratory' (p.67). Its final clarification is achieved under capitalism, when the worker is reduced to nothing but labour-power, and conversely, we may add, property to a control of the means of production entirely divorced from labour, while in the process of production there is a total separation between use (which has no direct relevance) and exchange and accumulation (which is the direct object of production). This is the process which, in its possible variations of type, Marx attempts to analyse. Though particular social-economic formations, expressing particular phases of this evolution, are very relevant, it is the entire process, spanning the centuries and continents, which he has in mind. Hence his framework is chronological only in the broadest sense, and problems of, let us say, the transition from one phase to another are not his primary concern, except in so far as they throw light on the long-term transformation.

But at the same time this process of the emancipation of man from his original natural conditions of production is one of human *individualisation*. 'Man is only individualised [*vereinzelt sich*] through the process of history. He appears originally as a generic being, a tribal being, a herd animal . . . Exchange itself is a major agent of this individualisation. It makes the herd animal superfluous and dissolves it' (p.96). This automatically implies a transformation in the relations of the individual to what was originally the community in which he functioned. The former community has been transmuted, in the extreme case of capitalism, into the dehumanised social mechanism which, while it actually makes individualisation possible, is outside and hostile to the individual. And yet this process is one of immense possibilities for humanity. As Marx observes in a passage full of hope and splendour (pp.84–5):

The ancient conception, in which man always appears (in however narrowly national, religious or political a definition) as the aim of production, seems very much more exalted than the modern world, in which production is the aim of man and wealth the aim of production. In fact, however, when the narrow bourgeois form has been peeled away, what is wealth, if not the universality of needs, capacities, enjoyments, productive powers, etc., of individuals, produced in universal exchange? What, if not the full development of human control over the forces of nature – those of his own nature as well as those of so-called 'nature'? What, if not the absolute elaboration of his creative dispositions, without any preconditions other than antecedent historical evolution which makes the totality of this evolution – i.e. the evolution of all human powers as such, unmeasured by any *previously established* yardstick – an end in itself? What is this, if not a situation where man does not reproduce himself in any determined form, but produces his totality? Where he does not seek to remain something formed by the past, but is in the absolute movement of becoming? In bourgeois political economy – and in the epoch of production to which it corresponds – this complete elaboration of what lies within man appears as the total alienation, and the destruction of all fixed, one-sided purposes as the sacrifice of the end in itself to a wholly external compulsion.

Even in this most dehumanised and apparently contradictory form, the humanist ideal of free individual development is nearer than it ever was in all previous phases of history. It only awaits the passage from what Marx calls, in a lapidary phrase, the pre-historic stage of human society – the age of class societies of which capitalism is the last – to the age when man is in control of his fate, the age of communism.

Marx's vision is thus a marvellously unifying force. His model of social and economic development is one which (unlike Hegel's) can be applied to history to produce fruitful and original results rather than tautology; but at the same time it can be presented as the unfolding of the logical possibilities latent in a few elementary and almost axiomatic statements about the nature of man – a dialectical working out of the contradictions of labour/property, and the division of labour.[2] It is a model of facts, but, seen from a slightly different angle, the *same* model provides us with value-judgements. It is this multi-dimensionality of Marx's theory which causes all but the dim-witted or prejudiced to respect and admire Marx as a thinker, even when they do not agree with him. At the same time, especially when Marx himself makes no concessions to the requirements of an outside reader, it undoubtedly adds to the difficulty of this text.

One example of this complexity must be particularly mentioned: it is Marx's refusal to separate the different academic disciplines. It is possible to do so in his stead. Thus the late J. Schumpeter, one of the more intelligent critics of Marx, attempted to distinguish Marx the sociologist from Marx the economist, and one could easily separate out Marx the historian. But such mechanical divisions are misleading, and entirely contrary to Marx's method. It was the bourgeois academic economists who attempted to draw a sharp line between static and dynamic analysis, hoping to transform the one into the other by injecting some 'dynamising' element into the static system, just as it is the academic economists who still work out a neat model of 'economic growth', preferably expressible in equations, and relegate all that does not fit into the province of the 'sociologists'. The academic sociologists make similar distinctions on a rather lower level of scientific interest, the historians on an even humbler one. But this is not Marx's way. The social relations of production (i.e. social organisation in its broadest sense) and the material forces of production, to whose level they correspond, cannot be divorced. 'The economic structure of society is formed by the totality of these relations of production' (Preface, *Werke* 13, p.8). Economic development cannot be simplified down into 'economic growth', still less into the variation of isolated factors such as productivity or the rate of capital accumulation, in the way of the modern vulgar economist who used to argue that growth is produced when more than, say, 5% of the national income is invested.[3] It cannot be discussed except in terms of particular historic epochs and particular social structures. His discussion of various pre-capitalist modes of production is a brilliant example of this, and incidentally illustrates how entirely wrong it is to think of historical materialism as an *economic* (or for that matter a *sociological*) interpretation of history.[4]

Yet even if we are firmly aware that Marx must not be divided up into segments according to the academic specialisations of our time, it may still be difficult to grasp the unity of his thought, partly because the mere effort at systematic and lucid exposition tends to lead us to discuss its different aspects *seriatim* instead of simultaneously, and partly because the task of scientific research and verification must at some stage lead us to do the same. This is one reason why some of Engels' writings, which have clear exposition as their object, give the impression of somewhat over-simplifying or thinning out the density of Marx's thought. Some later Marxist expositions, such as Stalin's *Dialectical and Historical Materialism*, have gone much further in this direction, too far. Conversely, the wish to emphasise the dialectical unity and interdependence of Marx may produce merely vague generalisations about dialectics or such observations as that the superstructure is not mechanically or in the short run determined by the base, but reacts back upon it and may from time to time dominate it. Such statements may be of pedagogic value, and serve as warnings against over-simplified views of Marxism (and it is as such that e.g. Engels made them in his well-known letter to Bloch), but do not really advance us much farther. There is, as Engels observed to Bloch,[5] one satisfactory way of avoiding these difficulties. It is 'to study this theory further from its original sources and not at second-hand'. It is for this reason that the *Formen*, in which the reader may follow Marx *while he is actually thinking*, deserve such close and admiring study.

Most readers will be interested in one major aspect: Marx's discussion of the epochs of historic development, which forms the background to the brief list given in the Preface to the *Critique of Political Economy*. This is in itself a complex subject, which requires us to know something of the development of Marx's and Engels' thinking on history and historical evolution, and of the fortunes of their main historic periodisations or divisions in subsequent Marxist discussion.

The classical formulation of these epochs of human progress occurs in the Preface to the *Critique of Political Economy*, of which the *Grundrisse* are a preliminary draft. There Marx suggested that 'in broad outlines we can designate the Asiatic, the ancient, the feudal and the modern bourgeois modes of production as so many epochs in the progress of the economic formation of society'. The analysis which led him to this view, and the theoretical model of economic evolution which it implies, are not discussed in the Preface, though various passages in the *Critique*, and in *Capital* (especially vol. III), form part of it or are difficult to understand without it. The *Formen*, on the other hand, deal almost wholly with this problem. They are therefore essential reading for anyone who wishes to understand Marx's ways of thinking in general, or his approach to the problem of historical evolution and classification in particular.

This does not mean that we are obliged to accept Marx's list of historical epochs as given in the Preface, or in the *Formen*. As we shall see, few parts of Marx's thought have been more revised by his most devoted followers than this list – not necessarily with equal justification – and neither Marx nor Engels rested content with it for the remainder of their lives. The list, and a good deal of the discussion in the *Formen* which lies behind it, are the outcome not of theory but of observation. The general theory of historical materialism requires only that there should be a succession of modes of production, though not necessarily any particular modes, and perhaps not in any particular predetermined order.[6] Looking at the actual historical record, Marx thought that he could distinguish a certain number of socio-economic formations and a certain succession. But if he had been mistaken in his observations, or if these had been based on partial and therefore misleading information, the general theory of historical materialism would remain unaffected. Now it is generally agreed that Marx's and Engels' observations on pre-capitalist epochs rest on far less thorough study than Marx's description and analysis of capitalism. Marx concentrated his energies on the study of capitalism, and he dealt with the rest of history in varying degrees of detail, but mainly in so far as it bore on the origins and development of capitalism. Both he and Engels were, so far as history goes, exceptionally well-read laymen, and both their genius and their theory enabled them to make immeasurably better use of their reading than any of their contemporaries. But they relied on such literature as was available to them, and this was far scantier than it is at present. It is therefore useful to survey briefly what Marx and Engels knew of history and what they could not yet know. This does not mean that their knowledge was *insufficient* for the elaboration of their theories of pre-capitalist societies. It may very well have been perfectly adequate. It is an occupational kink of scholars that the mere accumulation of volumes and articles advances understanding. It may merely fill libraries. Nevertheless, a knowledge of the factual basis of Marx's historical analysis is evidently desirable for its understanding.

So far as the history of classical (Greco-Roman) antiquity was concerned, Marx and Engels were almost as well equipped as the modern student who relies on purely literary sources, though the great bulk of archaeological work and the collection of inscriptions, which have since revolutionised the study of classical antiquity, were not available to them when the *Formen* were written, and neither were the papyri. (Schliemann did not begin his excavations at Troy until 1870 and the first volume of Mommsen's *Corpus Inscriptionum Latinarum* did not appear until 1863.) As classically educated men they had no difficulty in reading Latin and Greek, and we know that they were familiar with even quite recondite sources such as Jornandes, Ammianus Marcellinus, Cassiodorus and Orosius.[7] On the other hand neither a classical education nor the material then available made a serious knowledge of Egypt and the ancient Middle East possible. Marx and Engels did not in fact deal with this region in this period. Even casual references to it are relatively scarce;

though this does not mean that Marx and Engels[8] overlooked its historical problems.

In the field of oriental history their situation was rather different. There is no evidence that before 1848 either Marx or Engels thought or read much on this subject. It is probable that they knew no more about oriental history than is contained in Hegel's *Lectures on the Philosophy of History* (which is not illuminating) and such other information as might be familiar to Germans educated in that period. Exile in England, the political developments of the 1850s and above all Marx's economic studies rapidly transformed their knowledge. Marx himself clearly derived some knowledge of India from the classical economists whom he read or re-read in the early 1850s (J.S. Mill's *Principles*, Adam Smith, Richard Jones's *Introductory Lecture* in 1851).[9] He began to publish articles on China (14 June) and India (25 June) for the *New York Daily Tribune* in 1853. It is evident that in this year both he and Engels were deeply preoccupied with the historical problems of the Orient, to the point where Engels attempted to learn Persian.[10] In the early summer of 1853 their correspondence refers to the Rev. C. Foster's *A Historical Geography of Arabia*, Bernier's *Voyages*, Sir William Jones, the orientalist, and parliamentary papers on India, and Stamford Raffles' *History of Java*.[11] It is reasonable to suppose that Marx's views on Asiatic society received their first mature formulation in these months. They were, as will be evident, based on far more than cursory study.

On the other hand Marx's and Engels' study of west European feudalism appears to have proceeded in a different manner. Marx was abreast of current research on medieval agrarian history, which meant in the main the works of Hanssen, Meitzen and Maurer,[12] who are already referred to in *Capital*, vol. I, but in fact there is little sign that at this period he was seriously interested in the problems of the evolution of medieval agriculture or serfdom. (The references are in connection with the actual serfdom of Eastern Europe and especially Romania.) It was not until *after* publication of *Capital*, vol. I (i.e. also after the substantial drafting of *Capital*, vols. II and III) that this problem evidently began to preoccupy the two friends, notably from 1868, when Marx began seriously to study Maurer, whose works he and Engels henceforth regarded as the foundation of their knowledge in this field.[13] However, Marx's own interest appears to have lain in the light Maurer and others threw on the original peasant community, rather than on serfdom, though Engels seems from the start to have been interested in this aspect also, and elaborated it on the basis of Maurer in his account of *The Mark* (written 1882). Some of the very last letters exchanged between the two in 1882 deal with the historical evolution of serfdom.[14] It seems clear that Marx's interest in the subject grew towards the end of his life, when the problems of Russia preoccupied him increasingly. The sections of *Capital*, vol. III, which deal with the transformations of rent show no sign of any detailed study of the literature on Western feudal agriculture.

Marx's interest in the medieval origins of the bourgeoisie and in feudal trade and finance was – as is evident from *Capital*, vol. III – very much more intensive. It is clear that he studied not merely general works on the Western Middle Ages, but, so far as they were then available, the specialised literature about medieval prices (Thorold Rogers), and medieval banking and currency and medieval trade.[15] Of course the study of these subjects was in its infancy in the period of Marx's most intensive work in the 1850s and 1860s, so that some of his sources both on agrarian and commercial history must be regarded as long obsolete.[16]

In general, Engels' interest in the Western, and especially the Germanic Middle Ages was much livelier than Marx's. He read a great deal, including primary sources and local monographs, drafted outlines of early German and Irish history, was keenly aware of the importance not only of linguistic evidence but of archaeology (especially the Scandinavian work which Marx already noted as outstanding in the 1860s) and was as keenly aware as any modern scholar of the crucial importance of such economic documents of the dark ages as the Polyptych of Abbot Irmino of St Germain. However, one cannot escape the impression that, like Marx, his real interest lay in the ancient peasant community more than in manorial development.

So far as primitive communal society is concerned, Marx's and Engels' historic views were almost certainly transformed by the study of two authors: Georg von Maurer, who attempted to demonstrate the existence of communal property as a stage in German history, and above all Lewis Morgan, whose *Ancient Society* (1877) provided the basis of their analysis of primitive communalism. Engels' *The Mark* (1882) is based on the former, and his *Origin of the Family, Private Property and the State* (1884) is heavily, and equally frankly, indebted to the latter. Maurer's work (which, as we have seen, began to make its chief impact on the two friends in 1868) they considered in a sense as a liberation of scholarship from the romantic medievalism which reacted against the French Revolution. (Their own lack of sympathy with such romanticism may explain something of their own relative neglect of Western feudal history.) To look back beyond the Middle Ages to the primitive epochs of human history, as Maurer did, appeared to be consonant with the socialist tendency, even though the German scholars who did so were not socialists.[17] Lewis Morgan, of course, grew up in a utopian-socialist atmosphere, and clearly outlined the relation between the study of primitive society and the future. It was therefore only natural that Marx, who encountered his work soon after its publication and immediately noted the similarity of its results with his own, welcomed and used it; as usual acknowledging his debt with the scrupulous scientific honesty which was so characteristic of him as a scholar. A third source which Marx used abundantly in his later years was the very full literature of Russian scholarship, especially the work of M.M. Kovalevsky.

At the time the *Formen* were written, Marx's and Engels' knowledge of primitive society was therefore only sketchy. It was not based on any serious knowledge of tribal societies, for modern anthropology was in its infancy, and in spite of Prescott's work (which Marx read in 1851 and evidently utilised in the *Formen*) so was our knowledge of pre-Columbian civilisation in the Americas. Until Morgan, most of their views about it were based partly on classical authors, partly on oriental material, but mainly on material from early medieval Europe or the study of communal survivals in Europe. Among these the Slavonic and East European ones played an important part, for the strength of such survivals in those parts had long attracted the attention of scholars. The division into four basic types – oriental (Indian), Greco-Roman, Germanic and Slavonic (see p.95) – fits in with the state of their knowledge in the 1850s.

As for the history of capitalist development, Marx was already a considerable expert by the end of the 1850s, on the basis not so much of the literature of economic history, which then hardly existed, but of the voluminous literature of economic theory, of which he had a profound knowledge. In any case the nature of his knowledge is sufficiently familiar. A glance at the bibliographies attached to most editions of *Capital* will illustrate it. Admittedly by modern standards the information available in the 1850s and 1860s was extremely defective, but we should not for this reason write it off, especially when utilised by a man of Marx's acuteness of mind. Thus it may be argued that our knowledge of the sixteenth-century price-rise and the role of American bullion in it has only been put on a sound documentary basis since about 1929, or indeed even later. It is easy to forget that at least one basic work on this subject was already available before Marx's death,[18] and even easier to forget that long before this enough was known in general about the subject to permit an intelligent discussion of it, such as that of Marx in the *Critique of Political Economy*.[19] I need hardly add that both Marx and Engels kept abreast of subsequent work in this field.

So much for the general state of Marx's and Engels' historical knowledge. We may summarise it as follows. It was (at all events in the period when the *Formen* were drafted) thin on pre-history, on primitive communal societies and on pre-Columbian America, and virtually non-existent on Africa. It was not impressive on the ancient or medieval Middle East, but markedly better on certain parts of Asia, notably India, but not on Japan. It was good on classical antiquity and the European Middle Ages, though Marx's (and to a lesser extent Engels') interest in this period was uneven. It was, for the times, outstandingly good on the period of rising capitalism. Both men were, of course, close students of history. However, it is probable that there were two periods in Marx's career when he occupied himself more particularly with the history of pre-industrial or non-European societies: the 1850s, i.e. the period which precedes the drafting of the *Critique of Political Economy*, and the 1870s, after the publication of *Capital* I and the substantial drafting of *Capital* II and III, when Marx appears to have reverted to historical studies, most notably about Eastern Europe, and primitive society; perhaps in connection with his interest in the possibilities of revolution in Russia.

II

Let us next follow the evolution of Marx's and Engels' views on historical periodisation and evolution. The first stage of this is best studied from the *German Ideology* of 1845–6, which already accepts (what was of course not in itself new) that various stages in the social division of labour correspond to various forms of property. The first of these was communal, and corresponded to 'the undeveloped stage of production where a people sustains itself by hunting, fishing, cattle-raising or at most by farming'.[20]

At this stage social structure is based on the development and modification of the kinship group and its internal division of labour. This kinship group (the 'family') tends to develop within itself not only the distinction between chieftains and the rest, but also slavery, which develops with the increase in population and needs, and the growth of external relations, whether of war or barter. The first main advance of the social division of labour consists of the separation of industrial and commercial from agricultural labour, and therefore leads to the distinction between and opposition of town and country. This in turn leads to the second historic phase of property relations, the 'communal and state property of antiquity'. Marx and Engels see its origins in the formation of cities by the union (by agreement or conquest) of tribal groups, slavery continuing to subsist. Communal city property (including that of the citizens over the city slaves) is the main form of property, but side by side with this private property emerges, though at first subordinate to the communal. With the rise first of mobile, later and especially of immobile private property, this social order decays, and so does the position of the 'free citizens', whose position *vis-à-vis* the slaves was based on their collective status as primitive tribesmen.

By now the social division of labour is already rather elaborate. Not only does the division between town and country exist, and even in time between states representing urban and rural interests, but within the city, the division between industry and overseas trade; and of course, that between free men and slaves. Roman society was the ultimate development of this phase of evolution.[21] Its basis was the city, and it never succeeded in going beyond its limitations.

The third historic form of property, 'feudal or rank ownership',[22] follows chronologically though in fact the *German Ideology* suggests no logical connection between them, but merely notes the succession and the effect of the mixture of broken-down Roman and conquering tribal (Germanic) institutions. Feudalism appears to be an *alternative* evolution out of primitive communalism, under conditions in which no cities develop, because the density of population over a large region is low. The *size* of the area seems to be of decisive importance, for Marx and Engels suggest that 'feudal development starts on a much more extensive territory, and one prepared by the Roman conquests and the spread of agriculture connected with these'.[23] Under these circumstances the countryside and not the city is the point of departure of social organisation. Once again communal property – which in effect turns into the collective property of the feudal lords as a group, backed by the military organisation of the Germanic tribal conquerors – is its basis. But the exploited class in opposition to which the feudal nobility organised its hierarchy, and rallied its armed retainers, was not one of slaves but of serfs. At the same time a parallel division existed in the towns. There the basic form of property was the private labour of individuals, but various factors – the needs of defence, competition and the influence of the surrounding feudal organisation of the countryside – produced an analogous social organisation: the guilds of master craftsmen or merchants, which in time confronted the journeymen and apprentices. *Both* landed property worked by serf labour and small-scale craft work with apprentices and journeymen are at this stage described as the 'main form of property' under feudalism (*Haupteigentum*). The division of labour was relatively undeveloped, but expressed chiefly in the sharp separation of various 'ranks' – princes, nobles, clergy and peasants in the countryside, masters, journeymen, apprentices and eventually a 'plebs' of day-labourers in the cities. This territorially extensive system required relatively large political units in the interests both of the landed nobility and the cities: the feudal monarchies, which therefore became universal.

The transition from feudalism to capitalism, however, is a product of feudal evolution.[24] It begins in the cities, for the separation of town and country is the fundamental and, from the birth of civilisation to the nineteenth century, constant element in and expression of the social division of labour. Within the cities, which once again arose in the Middle Ages, a division of labour between production and trade developed, where it did not already survive from antiquity. This provided the basis of long-distance trade, and a consequent division of labour (specialisation of production) between different cities. The defence of the burghers against the feudalists and the interaction between the cities produced a *class* of burghers out of the burgher-groups of individual towns. 'The bourgeoisie itself gradually develops as the conditions for its existence arise, splits into different factions again after the division of labour has taken place, and eventually absorbs all existing possessing classes (while developing the majority of the property-less and a part of the hitherto property-owning classes into a new class, the proletariat), to the degree that all existing property is transformed into commercial or industrial capital.' Marx adds the note: 'In the first instance it absorbs those branches of labour which belong directly to the state, subsequently all more or less ideological estates.'[25]

So long as trade has not become worldwide, and is not based on large-scale industry, the technological advances due to these developments remain insecure. They may, being locally or regionally based, be lost in consequence of barbarian invasions or wars, and local advances need not be generalised. (We note in passing that the *German Ideology* here touches on the important problem of historical decay and regression.) The crucial development in capitalism is therefore that of the world market.

The first consequence of the division of labour between towns is the rise of manufactures independent of the guilds, based (as in the pioneer centres of Italy and Flanders) on foreign trade, or (as in England and France) on the internal market. These rest also on a growing density of the population – notably in the countryside – and a growing concentration of capital inside and outside the guilds. Among these manufacturing occupations, weaving (because it depended on the use of machinery, however crude) proved the most important. The growth of manufactures in turn provided means of escape for feudal peasants, who had hitherto fled into the cities, but had been increasingly excluded from them by guild exclusiveness. The source of this labour was partly the former feudal retainers and armies, partly the population displaced by agricultural improvements and the substitution of pasture for tillage.

With the rise of manufactures nations begin to compete as such, and mercantilism (with its trade wars, tariffs and prohibitions) arises on a national scale. Within the manufactures the relation of capitalist and labourer develops. The vast expansion of trade as the result of the discovery of the Americas and the conquest of the sea-route to India, and the mass import of overseas products, notably bullion, shook the position both of feudal landed property and of the labouring class. The consequent change in class relations, conquest, colonisation 'and above all the extension of markets into a world market which now became possible and indeed increasingly took place'[26] opened a new phase in historical development.

We need not follow the argument further at this point, beyond noting that the *German Ideology* records two further periods of development before the triumph of industry, up to the middle of the seventeenth century and thenceforward to the end of the eighteenth, and also suggests that the success of Britain in industrial development was due to the concentration of trade and manufacture in that country during the seventeenth century, which gradually created 'a relative world market for the benefit of this country, and thereby a demand for its manufacturing products, which could no longer be satisfied by the hitherto existing forces of industrial production'.[27]

This analysis is clearly the foundation of the historical sections of the *Communist Manifesto*. Its historical basis is slender – classical antiquity (mostly Roman) and Western and Central Europe. It recognises only three forms of class society: the slave society of antiquity, feudalism and bourgeois society. It seems to suggest the first two as *alternative* routes out of primitive communal society, linked only by the fact that the second established itself on the ruins of the first. No mechanism for the breakdown of the former was outlined, though one is probably implicit in the analysis. Bourgeois society in turn is seen to arise, as it were, in the interstices of feudal society. Its growth is sketched entirely – at least to begin with – as that of and within the cities, whose connection with agrarian feudalism is chiefly that of drawing their original population and its reinforcements from former serfs. There is as yet no serious attempt to discover the sources of the surplus population which is to provide the labour force for towns and manufactures, the remarks about this being too sketchy to bear much analytical weight. It must be regarded as a very rough and provisional hypothesis of historical development, though some of the incidental observations it contains are suggestive and some brilliant.

The stage of Marx's thought represented by the *Formen* is considerably more sophisticated and considered, and it is of course based on far greater and more varied historical studies, this time not confined to Europe. The chief innovation in the table of historical periods is the 'Asiatic' or 'oriental' system, which is incorporated into the famous Preface to the *Critique of Political Economy*.

Broadly speaking, there are now three or four alternative routes out of the primitive communal system, each representing a form of the social division of labour already existing or implicit within it: the *oriental*, the *ancient*, the *Germanic* (though Marx of course does not confine it to any one people) and a somewhat shadowy *Slavonic* form which is not further discussed, but has affinities with the *oriental* (pp.88, 97). One important distinction between these is the historically crucial one of systems which resist and those which favour historical evolution. The model of 1845–6 barely touches on this problem, though as we have seen, Marx's view of historical development was never simply unilinear, nor did he ever regard it as a mere record of progress. Nevertheless, by 1857–8 the discussion is considerably more advanced.

Ignorance of the *Formen* has resulted in the discussion of the oriental system in the past being based chiefly on Marx's and Engels' earlier letters and on Marx's articles on India (both 1853),[28] where it is characterised – in line with the views of the earliest foreign observers – by 'the absence of property in land'. This was thought due to special conditions, requiring exceptional centralisation, e.g. the need for public works and irrigation schemes in areas which could not be otherwise effectively cultivated. However, on further consideration, Marx evidently held that the fundamental characteristic of this system was 'the self-sustaining unity of manufacture and agriculture' within the village commune, which thus 'contains all the conditions for reproduction and surplus production within itself' (pp.70, 83, 91), and which therefore resisted disintegration and economic evolution more stubbornly than any other system (p.83). The theoretical absence of property in 'oriental despotism' thus masks the 'tribal or communal property' which is its base (pp.69–71). Such systems may be decentralised or centralised, 'more despotic or more democratic' in form, and variously organised. Where such small community-units exist as part of a larger unity, they may devote part of their surplus product to pay 'the costs of the (larger) community, i.e. for war, religious worship, etc.', and for economically necessary operations such as irrigation and the maintenance of communications, which will thus appear to be done by the higher community, 'the despotic government suspended above the small communities'. However, this alienation of the surplus product contains the germs of 'seignorial *dominium* in its original sense' and feudalism (villeinage) may develop out of it. The 'closed' nature of the communal units means that cities hardly belong in the economy at all, arising 'only where the location is particularly favourable to external trade, or where the ruler and his satraps exchange their revenue (surplus product) for labour, which they expend as a labour fund' (p.71). The Asiatic system is therefore not yet a class society, or if it is a class society, then it is the most primitive form. Marx appears to regard Mexican and Peruvian societies as belonging to the same genus, as also certain Celtic societies, though complicated – and perhaps elaborated – by the conquest of some tribes or communities by others (pp.70, 88). I note that it does not *exclude* further evolution, but admits it only as a luxury, as it were; only in so far as it can develop on the surplus given by or extorted from the basic self-sustaining economic units of the tribe or village.

The second system emerging from primitive society – 'the product of a more dynamic historical life' (p.71) – produces the *city*, and through it, the *ancient* mode, an expansionist, dynamic, changing society (pp.71–7 and *passim*); 'the city with its attached territory [*Landmark*] formed the economic whole' (p.79). In its developed form – but Marx is careful to insist on the long process which precedes it, as well as on its complexity – it is characterised by chattel-slavery. But this in turn has its economic limitations, and had to be replaced by a more flexible and productive form of exploitation, that of dependent peasants by lords, *feudalism*, which in turn gives way to *capitalism*.

A third type has as its basic unit neither the village community nor the city, but 'each separate household, which forms an independent centre of production (manufacture merely the domestic subsidiary labour of women, etc.)' (p.79). These separate households are more or less loosely linked with one another (provided they belong to the same tribe) and occasionally unite 'for war, religion, the settlement of legal disputes, etc.' (p.80), or for the use – by the individually self-sufficient households – of communal pastures, hunting territory, etc. The basic unit is thus weaker and potentially more 'individualist' than the village community. This Marx calls the *Germanic* type, though, I repeat, he clearly does not confine it to any one people.[29] Since the *ancient* and the *Germanic* types are distinguished from the *oriental* type, we may infer that Marx regarded the *Germanic* type in its way as also more potentially dynamic than the oriental, and this is indeed not unlikely.[30] Marx's observations on this type are tantalisingly sketchy, but we know that he and Engels left the way open for a direct transition from primitive society to feudalism, as among the Germanic tribes.

The division between town and country (or agricultural and non-agricultural production) which was fundamental to Marx's analysis in 1845–6 thus remains fundamental in the *Formen*, but it is both more broadly based and more elegantly formulated:

> Ancient history is the history of cities, but of cities founded on agriculture and landed property; Asian history is a kind of undifferentiated unity of town and country (the large city, properly speaking, must be regarded merely as a princely camp superimposed on the real economic structure); the Middle Ages (Germanic period) starts with the countryside as the location of history, whose further development then proceeds by the opposition of town and country; modern history is the urbanisation of the countryside, not, as among the ancients, the ruralisation of the city (pp.77–8).

However, while these different forms of the social division of labour are clearly alternative forms of the break-up of communal society, they are apparently presented – in the Preface to the *Critique of Political Economy*, though not specifically in the *Formen* – as *successive* historical stages. In the literal sense this is plainly untrue, for not only did the Asiatic mode of production co-exist with all the rest, but there is no suggestion in the argument of the *Formen*, or anywhere else, that the ancient mode evolved out of it. We ought therefore to understand Marx not as referring to chronological succession, or even to the evolution of one system out of its predecessor (though this is obviously the case with capitalism and feudalism), but to evolution in a more general sense. As we saw earlier, 'Man only becomes an individual [*vereinzelt sich selbst*] by means of the historical process. He appears originally as a generic being, a tribal being, a herd animal.' The different forms of this gradual individualisation of man, which means the break-up of the original unity, correspond to the different stages of history. Each of these represents, as it were, a step away from 'the original unity of a specific form of (tribal) community and the property in nature connected with it, or the relation to the objective conditions of production as naturally existing [*Naturdaseins*]' (p.94). They represent, in other words, steps in the evolution of private property.

Marx distinguishes four analytical, though not chronological, stages in this evolution. The first is direct communal property, as in the oriental, and in a modified form the Slavonic system, neither of which, it would seem, can as yet be regarded as fully formed class societies. The second is communal property continuing as the substratum of what is already a 'contradictory', i.e. class, system, as in the ancient and the Germanic forms. The third stage arises, if we are to follow Marx's argument, not so much through feudalism as through the rise of *crafts* manufacture, in which the independent craftsman (organised corporatively in guilds) already represents a far more individual form of the control over the means of production, and indeed of consumption, which allows him to live while he produces. It would seem that what Marx has in mind here is a certain autonomy of the craft sector of production, for he deliberately excludes the manufactures of the ancient orient, though without giving reasons. The fourth stage is that in which the proletarian arises; that is to say in which exploitation is no longer conducted in the crude form of the appropriation of *men* – as slaves or serfs – but in the appropriation of 'labour'. 'For Capital the worker does not constitute a condition of production, but only labour. If this can be performed by machinery, or even by water or air, so much the better. And what capital appropriates is not the labourer but his labour – and not directly, but by means of exchange' (p.99).

It would seem – though in view of the difficulty of Marx's thought and the elliptical quality of his notes one cannot be sure – that this analysis fits into a schema of the historical stages in the following way. The oriental (and Slavonic) forms are historically closest to man's origins, since they conserve the functioning primitive (village) community in the midst of the more elaborate social superstructure, and have an insufficiently developed class system. (Of course, we may add, that at the time Marx was writing he observed that both these systems were disintegrating under the impact of the world market and their special character was therefore disappearing.) The ancient and Germanic systems, though also primary – i.e. not *derived* from the oriental – represent a somewhat more articulated form of evolution out of primitive communalism; but the 'Germanic system' as such does not form a special socio-economic formation. It forms the socio-economic formation of feudalism in conjunction with the medieval town (the locus of the emergence of the autonomous craft production). This combination then, which emerges during the Middle Ages, forms the third phase. Bourgeois society, emerging out of feudalism, forms the fourth. The statement that the Asiatic, ancient, feudal and bourgeois formations are 'progressive' does not therefore imply any simple unilinear view of history, nor a simple view that all history is progress. It merely states that each of these systems is in crucial respects further removed from the primitive state of man.

III

The next point to be considered is the internal dynamic of these systems: what makes them rise and decline? This is relatively simple for the oriental system, whose characteristics make it resistant to disintegration and economic evolution, until wrecked by the external force of capitalism. Marx tells us too little about the Slavonic system at this stage to permit much comment. On the other hand his views of the internal contradiction of the ancient and feudal systems are complex, and raise some difficult problems.

Slavery is the chief characteristic of the ancient system, but Marx's view on its basic internal contradiction is more complex than the simple view that slavery imposes limits to further economic evolution and thus produces its own breakdown. It should be noted in passing that the basis of his analysis appears to be the West Roman rather than the Greek half of the Mediterranean. Rome begins as a community of peasants, though its organisation is urban. Ancient history is 'a history of cities founded on landed property and agriculture' (p.77). It is not an entirely equal community, for tribal developments combined with inter-marriages and conquests already tend to produce socially higher and lower kin groups, but the Roman citizen is essentially a landowner, and 'the continuation of the commune is the reproduction of all its members as self-sustaining peasants, whose surplus time belongs precisely to the commune, the (communal) labour of war, etc.' (p.74). For war is the commune's primary business, because the only threat to its existence comes from other communities which seek its land, and the only way to secure each citizen land as population expands is to occupy that land by force (p.71). But the very warlike and expansive tendencies of such peasant communities must lead to the break-up of the peasant qualities which are their basis. Up to a point slavery, the concentration of landed property, exchange, a monetary economy, conquest, etc., are compatible with the foundations of this community. Beyond this point they must lead to its breakdown, and must make the evolution of society or of the individual impossible (pp.83–4). Even *before* the development of a slave economy, therefore, the ancient form of social organisation is crucially limited, as is indicated by the fact that with it the development of productivity is not and cannot be a fundamental preoccupation. 'Among the ancients we never encounter an enquiry into which forms of landed property, etc., are the most productive, create maximum wealth . . . The enquiry is always about which kind of property creates the best citizen. Wealth as an end in itself appears only among a few trading peoples – monopolists of the carrying trade – who live in the pores of the ancient world like the Jews in medieval society' (p.84).

Two major factors therefore tend to undermine it. The first is the social differentiation within the community, against which the peculiar ancient combination of communal and private landed property provides no safeguard. It is possible for the individual citizen to *lose* his property – i.e. the basis of his citizenship. The more rapid the economic development, the more is this likely: hence the ancient suspicion of trade and manufacture, which are best left to freedmen, clients or foreigners, and the citizens' 'belief in the dangers of intercourse with foreigners, desire to exchange surplus products, etc. Second, of course, there is slavery. For the very necessity to restrict citizenship (or what amounts to the same thing, landed property) to members of the conquering community leads naturally to the enslavement or enserfment of the conquered. 'Slavery and serfdom are therefore simply further developments of property based on tribalism' (p.91). Hence 'the preservation of the community implies the destruction of the conditions on which it rests, and turns into its opposite' (p.93). The 'commonwealth', first represented by all citizens, is represented by the aristocratic patricians, who remain the only ones to be full landowners against the lesser men and the slaves and by the citizens against the non-citizens and slaves. The actual economic contradictions of a slave economy are not discussed by Marx in this context at all. At the very general level of his analysis in the *Formen*, they are merely a special aspect of the fundamental contradiction of ancient society. Nor does he discuss why in antiquity it was slavery rather than serfdom which developed. One may conjecture that it was because of the level of productive forces and the complexity of the social relations of production already reached in the ancient Mediterranean.

The breakdown of the ancient mode is therefore implicit

in its socio-economic character. There seems to be no logical reason why it must lead *inevitably* to feudalism, as distinct from other 'new forms, combinations of labour' (p.93) which would make higher productivity possible. On the other hand a direct transition from the ancient mode to capitalism is excluded.

When we come to feudalism, out of which capitalism *did* develop, the problem becomes very much more puzzling, if only because Marx tells us so little about it. No sketch of the internal contradictions of feudalism, comparable to that of the ancient mode, is to be found in the *Formen*. Nor is there ever any real discussion of serfdom (any more than of slavery). Indeed these two relations of production often appear bracketed together, sometimes as 'the relation of domination and subordination', in contrast to the position of the free labourer.[31] The element within feudal society from which capitalism derives appears to be, in 1857–8 as in 1845–6, the *city* – more specifically the city merchants and craftsmen (see pp.97–8, 100). It is the emancipation of ownership in the means of production from its communal basis, such as occurs among the medieval crafts, which provides the basis of the separation of 'labour' from the 'objective conditions of production'. It is the same development – the formation of the 'working owner' by the side of and outside landed property – the craft and urban evolution of labour – which is 'not . . . an aspect [*Akzident*] of landed property and subsumed under it' (p.100), which provides the basis of the evolution of the capitalist.

The role of agricultural feudalism in this process is not discussed, but would seem to be rather negative. It must, at the right moment, make it possible for the peasant to be separated from the soil, the retainer from his lord, in order to turn him into a wage-labourer. Whether this takes the form of the dissolution of villeinage (*Hörigkeit*), of the private property or possession of yeomen or peasant tenants, or of various forms of clientship, is irrelevant. The important thing is that none of these should stand in the way of the transformation of men into at least potentially free labour.

However, though this is not discussed in the *Formen* (but in *Capital* III), serfdom and other analogous relations of dependence differ from slavery in economically significant ways. The serf, though under the control of the lord, is in fact an economically independent producer; the slave is not.[32] Take away lords from serfdom and what is left is small commodity production; separate plantations and slaves and (until the slaves do something else) no kind of economy is left. 'Hence what is required are conditions of personal dependence, personal unfreedom in whatever form, the attachment of men as an adjunct to the land, villeinage in the proper sense of the word' (*Capital* III, p.841). For under conditions of serfdom the serf produces not merely the labour surplus which his lord, in one form or another, appropriates, but he can also accumulate a profit for himself. Since, for various reasons, in economically primitive and undeveloped systems such as feudalism there is a tendency for the surplus to remain unchanged as a conventional magnitude, and since 'the use of [the serf's] labour power is by no means confined to agriculture, but includes rural domestic manufactures, there is here the possibility of a certain economic evolution . . .' (*Capital* III, pp.844–5).

Marx discusses these aspects of serfdom no more than the internal contradictions of slavery, because in the *Formen* it is not his business to outline an 'economic history' of either. Indeed, as elsewhere – though here in a rather more general form – he is not concerned with the internal dynamics of pre-capitalist systems except in so far as they explain the preconditions of capitalism.[33] Here he is interested merely in two negative questions: why could 'labour' and 'capital' not arise out of pre-capitalist socio-economic formations other than feudalism? And why did feudalism in its agrarian form allow them to emerge, and not impose fundamental obstacles to their emergence?

This explains obvious gaps in his treatment. As in 1845–6,

there is no discussion of the specific *modus operandi* of feudal agriculture. There is no discussion of the specific relationship between the feudal city and countryside, or why the one should produce the other. On the other hand there is the implication that European feudalism is *unique*, for no other form of this system produced the medieval city, which is crucial to the Marxian theory of the evolution of capitalism. In so far as feudalism is a general mode of production existing outside Europe (or perhaps Japan, which Marx nowhere discusses in detail), there is nothing in Marx to authorise us to look for some 'general law' of development which might explain its tendency to evolve into capitalism.

What *is* discussed in the *Formen* is the 'Germanic system', i.e. a particular sub-variety of primitive communalism, which therefore tends to evolve a particular type of social structure. Its crux, as we have seen, seems to be scattered settlement in economically self-sustaining family units, as against the peasant city of the ancients: 'Every individual household contains an entire economy, forming as it does an independent centre of production (manufacture merely the domestic subsidiary labour of the women, etc.). In the ancient world the city with its attached territory [*Landmark*] formed the economic whole, in the Germanic world it is the individual homestead' (p.79). Its existence is safeguarded by its bond with other similar homesteads belonging to the same tribe, a bond expressed in the occasional assembly of all homesteaders for the purpose of war, religion, settlement of disputes, and in general for mutual security (p.80). In so far as there is common property, as in pastures, hunting grounds, etc., it is used by each member as an individual, and not as in ancient society, as a representative of the commonwealth. One might compare the ideal of Roman social organisation to an Oxford or Cambridge college, whose fellows are co-possessors of land and buildings only in so far as they form a body of fellows, but who cannot, as individuals, be said to 'own' it or any part of it. The Germanic system might then be comparable to a housing co-operative in which the individual occupation of a man's flat depends on his union and continued co-operation with other members, but in which nevertheless individual possession exists in an identifiable form. This looser form of community, which implies a greater potentiality of economic individualisation, makes the 'Germanic system' (via feudalism) the direct ancestor of bourgeois society.

How this system evolves into feudalism is not discussed, though various possibilities of internal and external social differentiation (e.g. by the effect of war and conquest) present themselves. One may hazard the guess that Marx attached considerable importance to military organisation (since war is, in the Germanic as in the ancient system, 'one of the earliest tasks of all such primitive [*naturwüchsig*] communities, both for the preservation and the acquisition of its property') (p.89). This is certainly the later line of explanation in Engels' *Origin of the Family*, where kingship arises out of the transformation of gentile military leadership among the Teutonic tribes. There is no reason for supposing that Marx would have thought differently.

What were the internal contradictions of feudalism? How did it evolve into capitalism? These problems have increasingly pre-occupied Marxist historians, as in the vigorous international discussion arising out of M.H. Dobb's *Studies in the Development of Capitalism* in the early 1950s and the slightly subsequent debate on the 'fundamental economic law of feudalism' in the USSR. Whatever the merits of either discussion – and those of the first appear to be rather greater than those of the second – both of them are evidently handicapped by the absence of any indication of Marx's own views on the subject. It is not impossible that Marx might have agreed with Dobb that the cause of feudal decline was 'the inefficiency of Feudalism as a system of production, coupled with the growing needs of the ruling class for revenue' (*Studies*, p.42), though Marx appears, if anything, to stress the relative inflexibility of the demands of the feudal ruling class, and its tendency to fix them conventionally.[34] It is equally possible that he would have approved of R.H. Hilton's view that 'the struggle for rent was the "prime mover" in feudal society',[35] though he would almost certainly have rejected as over-simplified Porshnev's view that the simple struggle of the exploited masses was such a prime mover. But the point is that Marx nowhere appears to anticipate any of these lines of argument; certainly not in the *Formen*.

If any of the participants in these discussions can be said to follow his identifiable trails, it is P.M. Sweezy, who argues (following Marx) that feudalism is a system of production for use,[36] and that in such economic formations 'no boundless thirst for surplus labour arises from the nature of production itself' (*Capital* I, p.219, chapter X, section 2). Hence the main agent of disintegration was the growth of trade, operating more particularly through the effects of the conflict and interplay between a feudal countryside and the towns which developed on its margin (*Transition*, pp.2, 7–12). This line of argument is very similar to that of the *Formen*.

For Marx the conjunction of three phenomena is necessary to account for the development of capitalism out of feudalism: first, as we have seen, a rural social structure which allows the peasantry to be 'set free' at a certain point; second, the urban craft development which produces specialised, independent, non-agricultural commodity production in the form of the crafts; and third, accumulations of monetary wealth derived from trade and usury (Marx is categorical on this last point (pp.107–8)). The formation of such monetary accumulations 'belongs to the pre-history of bourgeois economy' (p.113); nor are they as yet capital. Their mere existence, or even their apparent predominance, does not automatically produce capitalist development, otherwise 'ancient Rome, Byzantium, etc., would have ended their history with free labour and capital' (p.109). But they are essential.

Equally essential is the urban craft element. Marx's observations on this are elliptic and allusive, but its importance in his analysis is clear. It is above all the element of craft skill, pride and organisation which he stresses.[37] The main importance of the formation of the medieval craft appears to be that, by developing 'labour itself as skill determined by craft [it becomes] a property itself, and not merely the source of property' (p.104), and thus introduces a potential separation between labour and the other conditions of production, which expresses a higher degree of individualisation than the communal and makes possible the formation of the category of free labour. At the same time it develops special skills and their instruments. But in the craft-guild stage 'the instrument of labour is still so intimately merged with living labour, that it does not truly circulate' (p.108). And yet, though it cannot *by itself* produce the labour market, the development of exchange production and money can only create the labour market 'under the precondition of urban *craft activity*, which rests *not* on capital and wage labour but on the organisation of labour in guilds, etc.' (p.112)

But all these also require the potentially soluble rural structure. For capitalism cannot develop without 'the involvement of the entire countryside in the production not of use – but of exchange-values' (p.116). This is another reason why the ancients, who, while contemptuous and suspicious of the crafts, had produced a version of 'urban craft activity', could not produce large-scale industry (ibid). What precisely makes the rural structure of feudalism thus soluble, apart from the characteristics of the 'Germanic system' which is its substratum, we are not told. And indeed, in the context of Marx's argument at this point, it is not necessary to probe further. A number of effects of the growth of an exchange-economy are mentioned in passing (e.g. pp.112–113). It is also noted that 'in part this process of separation [of labour from the objective conditions of production – food, raw materials, instruments] took place without [monetary wealth]' (p.113). The nearest thing to a general account (pp.114ff) implies that capital first appears sporadically or *locally* (Marx's emphasis) *alongside* (Marx's emphasis) the old modes of production, but subsequently breaks them up everywhere.

Manufacture for the foreign market arises first on the basis of long-distance trade and in the centres of such trade, not in the guild-crafts, but in the least skilled and guild-controlled rural supplementary trades such as spinning and weaving, though also of course in such urban branches directly connected with shipping as shipbuilding. On the other hand in the countryside the peasant tenant appears, as does the transformation of the rural population into free day-labourers. All these manufactures require the pre-existence of a mass market. The dissolution of serfdom and the rise of manufactures gradually transform all branches of production into capitalist ones, while in the cities a class of day-labourers, etc., outside the guilds provides an element in the creation of a proper proletariat (pp.114–17).[38]

The destruction of the rural supplementary trades creates an *internal* market for capital based on the substitution of manufacture or industrial production for the former rural supply of consumer goods. 'This process arises automatically [*von selbst*] from the separation of the labourers from the soil and from their property (though even only serf property) in the conditions of production' (p.118). The transformation of urban crafts into industry proceeds later, for it requires a considerable advance of productive methods in order to be capable of factory production. At this point Marx's manuscript which deals specifically with pre-capitalist formations ends. The phases of capitalist development are not discussed.

IV

We must next consider how far Marx's and Engels' subsequent thinking and study led them to modify, amplify and follow up the general views expressed in the *Formen*.

This was notably the case in the field of the study of primitive communalism. It is certain that Marx's own historical interests after the publication of *Capital* (1867) were overwhelmingly concerned with this stage of social development, for which Maurer, Morgan, and the ample Russian literature which he devoured from 1873 on provided a far more solid base of study than had been available in 1857–8. Apart from the agrarian orientation of his work in *Capital* III, two reasons for this concentration of interests may be suggested. First, the development of a Russian revolutionary movement increasingly led Marx and Engels to place their hopes for a European revolution in Russia. (No misinterpretation of Marx is more grotesque than the one which suggests that he expected a revolution exclusively from the advanced industrial countries of the West.)[39] Since the position of the village community was a matter of fundamental theoretical disagreement among Russian revolutionaries, who consulted Marx on the point, it was natural for him to investigate the subject at greater length.

It is interesting that – somewhat unexpectedly – his views inclined towards those of the Narodniks, who believed that the Russian village community could provide the basis of a transition to socialism without prior disintegration through capitalist development. This view does not follow from the natural trend of Marx's earlier historical thought, was not accepted by the Russian Marxists (who were among the Narodniks' opponents on this point) or by subsequent Marxists, and in any case proved to be unfounded. Perhaps the difficulty Marx had in drafting a theoretical justification of it[40] reflects a certain feeling of awkwardness. It contrasts strikingly with Engels' lucid and brilliant return to the main Marxist tradition – and to support for the Russian Marxists – when discussing the same topic some years later.[41] Nevertheless, it may lead us to the second reason for Marx's increasing preoccupation with primitive communalism: his growing hatred of and contempt for capitalist society. (The view that the older Marx lost some of the revolutionary ardour of the younger is always popular among critics who wish to abandon the revolutionary practice of Marxism while retaining a fondness for his theory.) It seems probable that Marx, who had earlier welcomed the impact of Western capitalism as an inhuman but historically progressive force on the stagnant pre-capitalist economies, found himself increasingly appalled by this inhumanity. We know that he had always admired the positive social values embodied, in however backward a form, in the primitive community. And it is certain that after 1857–8 – both in *Capital* III[42] and in the subsequent Russian discussions[43] – he increasingly stressed the viability of the primitive commune, its powers of resistance to historical disintegration and even – though perhaps only in the context of the Narodnik discussion – its capacity to develop into a higher form of economy without prior destruction.[44] I will not here give a detailed account of Marx's outline of primitive evolution in general, as available in Engels' *Origin of the Family*,[45] and of the agrarian community in particular. However, two general observations about this body of work are relevant here. First, pre-class society forms a large and complex historical epoch of its own, with its own history and laws of development, and its own varieties of socio-economic organisation, which Marx tends now to call collectively 'the archaic Formation' or 'Type'.[46] This, it seems clear, includes the four basic variants of primitive communalism, as set out in the *Formen*. It probably also includes the 'Asiatic mode' (which we have seen to be the most primitive of the developed socio-economic formations), and may explain why this mode apparently disappears from Engels' systematic treatments of the subject in *Anti-Dühring* and *Origin of the Family*.[47] It is possible that Marx and Engels also had in mind some sort of intermediate historical phase of communal disintegration, out of which ruling classes of different types might emerge.

Second, the analysis of 'archaic' social evolution is in every way consistent with the analysis sketched in the *German Ideology* and the *Formen*. It merely elaborates them, as when the brief references to the crucial importance of human (sexual) reproduction and the family in the *Ideology*[48] are expanded, in the light of Morgan, into the *Origin of the Family*, or when the summary analysis of primitive communal property is filled out and modified (in the light of scholars like Kovalevsky, who, incidentally, was himself influenced by Marx), into the stages of disintegration of the agrarian community of the Zasulich drafts.

A second field in which the founders of Marxism continued their special studies was that of the feudal period. This was Engels' rather than Marx's favourite.[49] A good deal of his work, dealing as it did with the origins of feudalism, overlaps with Marx's studies of primitive communal forms. Nevertheless, Engels' interests appear to have been slightly different from Marx's. He was probably preoccupied rather less with the survival or disintegration of the primitive community, and rather more with the rise and decline of feudalism. His interest in the dynamics of serf agriculture was more marked than Marx's. In so far as we possess analyses of these problems from the later years of Marx's lifetime, they are in Engels' formulation. Moreover, the political and military element plays a rather prominent part in Engels' work. Lastly, he concentrated almost entirely on medieval Germany (with an excursus or two on Ireland, with which he had personal connections), and was undoubtedly more preoccupied than Marx with the rise of nationality and its function in historic development. Some of these differences in emphasis are due merely to the fact that Engels' analysis operates on a less general level than Marx's; which is one reason why it is often more accessible and stimulating to those who make their first acquaintance with Marxism. Some of them are not. However, while recognising both that the two men were not Siamese twins and that (as Engels recognised) Marx was much the greater thinker, we should beware of the modern tendency of contrasting Marx and Engels, generally to the latter's disadvantage. When two men collaborate as closely as Marx and Engels did over forty years, without any theoretical disagreement of substance, it is to be presumed that they know what is in each other's mind. Doubtless if Marx had written *Anti-Dühring* (published in his lifetime) it would have read differently, and perhaps contained some new and profound suggestions. But there is no reason at all to believe that he disagreed with its content. This also applies to the works Engels wrote after Marx's death.

Engels' analysis of feudal development (which is seen exclusively in European terms) attempts to fill several of the gaps left in the extremely global analysis of 1857–8. In the first place a logical connection between the decline of the ancient and the rise of the feudal mode is established, in spite of the fact that one was established by foreign barbarian invaders on the ruins of the other. In ancient times the only possible form of large-scale agriculture was that of the slave latifundium, but beyond a certain point this had to become uneconomic, and give way once again to small-scale agriculture as 'the only profitable [*lohnende*] form'.[50] Hence ancient agriculture was already halfway towards medieval. Small-scale cultivation was the dominant form in feudal agriculture, it being 'operationally' irrelevant that some of the peasantry were free, some owed various obligations to lords. The same type of small-scale production by petty owners of their own means of production predominated in the cities.[51] Though this was under the circumstances a more economic form of production, the general backwardness of economic life in the early feudal period – the predominance of local self-sufficiency, which left scope for the sale or diversion of only a marginal surplus – imposed its limitations. While it guaranteed that any system of lordship (which was necessarily based on the control of large estates or bodies of their cultivators) must 'necessarily produce large ruling landowners and dependent petty peasants', it also made it impossible to exploit such large estates either by the ancient methods of slavery or by modern large-scale serf agriculture; as proved by the failure of Charlemagne's imperial 'villas'. The only exception were the monasteries, which were 'abnormal social bodies', being founded on celibacy, and consequently their exceptional economic performance must remain exceptional.[52]

While this analysis plainly somewhat underestimates the role of large-scale lay demesne agriculture in the high Middle Ages, it is exceedingly acute, especially in its distinction between the large estate as a social, political and fiscal unit, and as a unit of *production*, and in its emphasis on the predominance of peasant agriculture rather than demesne agriculture in feudalism. However, it leaves the origin of villeinage and feudal lordship somewhat in the air. Engels' own explanation of it appears to be social, political and military rather than economic. The free Teutonic peasantry was impoverished by constant war, and (given the weakness of royal power) had to place itself under the protection of nobles or clergy.[53] At bottom this is due to the inability of a form of social organisation based on kinship to administer or control the large political structures created by its successful conquests: these therefore automatically implied both the origin of classes and of a state.[54] In its simple formulation this hypothesis is not very satisfactory, but the derivation of class origins from the contradictions of social structure (and not simply from a primitive economic determinism) is important. It continues the line of thought of the 1857–8 manuscripts, e.g. on slavery.

The decline of feudalism depends, once again, on the rise of crafts and trade, and the division and conflict between town and country. In terms of agrarian development it expressed itself in an increase in the feudal lords' demand for consumer goods (and arms or equipment) available only by purchase.[55] Up to a point – given stagnant technical conditions of agriculture – an increase in the surplus extracted from the peasants could be achieved only extensively – e.g. by bringing new land under cultivation, founding new villages. But this implied 'friendly agreement with the colonists, whether villeins or free men'. Hence – and also because the primitive form of lordship contained no incentive to intensify exploitation, but rather a tendency for fixed peasant burdens to become lighter as time went on – peasant freedom tended to increase markedly, especially after the thirteenth century. (Here again Engels' understandable ignorance of the development of demesne market agriculture in the high Middle Ages and the 'feudal crisis' of the fourteenth century somewhat over-simplifies and distorts his picture.)

But from the fifteenth century the opposite tendency prevailed, and lords reconverted free men into serfdom, and turned peasant land into their own estates. This was (in Germany at least) due not merely to the growing demands of the lords, which could henceforth be met only by growing sales from their own estates, but by the growing power of the princes, which deprived the nobility of other former sources of income such as highway robbery and other similar extortions.[56] Hence feudalism ends with a revival of large-scale agriculture on the basis of serfdom, and peasant expropriation corresponding to –and derived from –the growth of capitalism. 'The capitalist era in the countryside is ushered in by a period of large-scale agriculture [*landwirtschaftlichen Grossbetriebs*] on the basis of serf labour services.'

This picture of the decline of feudalism is not entirely satisfactory, though it marks an important advance in the original Marxist analysis of feudalism – namely, the attempt to establish, and take into account, the dynamics of feudal agriculture, and especially the relations between lords and dependent peasants. This is almost certainly due to Engels, for it is he who (in the letters relating to the composition of *The Mark*) lays special emphasis on the movements of labour services, and indeed points out that Marx was formerly mistaken in this matter.[57] It introduces (on the basis largely of Maurer) the line of analysis in medieval agrarian history which has since proved exceptionally fruitful. On the other hand it is still worth noting that this field of study appears to be marginal to Marx's and Engels' major interests. The writings in which Engels deals with the problem are short and cursory, compared with those in which he deals with the origin of feudal society.[58] The argument is by no means worked out. No adequate or direct explanation is given why large-scale agriculture, which was uneconomic in the early Middle Ages, once again became economic on a serf (or other) basis at their end. More surprisingly (in view of Engels' keen interest in the technological developments of the transition from antiquity to the Middle Ages, as recorded by archaeology),[59] technological changes in farming are not really discussed, and there are a number of other loose ends. No attempt to apply the analysis outside Western and Central Europe is made, except for a very suggestive remark about the existence of the primitive agrarian community under the form of direct and indirect villeinage (*Hörigkeit*), as in Russia and Ireland,[60] and a remark – which seems somewhat in advance of the rather later discussion in *The Mark* – that in Eastern Europe the second enserfment of the peasants was due to the rise of an export market in agricultural produce and grew in proportion to it.[61] Altogether it does not seem that Engels had any intention of altering the general picture of the transition from feudalism to capitalism which he and Marx had formulated many years earlier.

No other major excursions into the history of 'forms which precede the capitalist' occur in the last years of Marx and Engels, though important work on the period since the sixteenth century, and especially contemporary history, was done. It therefore remains only to discuss briefly two aspects of their later thoughts on the problem of the phases of social development. How far did they maintain the list of formations as set out in the Preface to the *Critique of Political Economy*? What other general factors about socio-economic development did they consider or reconsider?

As we have seen, in their later years Marx and Engels tended to distinguish or to imply sub-varieties, sub-phases and transitional forms within their larger social classifications, and notably within pre-class society. But no major changes in the general list of formations occur, unless we count the almost formal transfer of the 'Asiatic mode' to the 'archaic type' of society. There is – at least on Marx's part – no inclination to abandon the Asiatic mode (and even a tendency to rehabilitate the 'Slavonic' mode); and quite certainly a deliberate refusal to reclassify it as feudal. Arguing against Kovalevsky's view that three of the four main criteria of Germano-Roman feudalism were to be found in India, which ought therefore to be regarded as feudal, Marx points out that 'Kovalevsky forgets among other things serfdom, which is not of substantial importance in India. (Moreover, as for the *individual role* of feudal lords as *protectors* not only of unfree but of free peasants . . . this is unimportant in India except for the *wakuf* (estates devoted to religious purposes).) Nor do we find that "poetry of the soil" so characteristic of Romano-Germanic feudalism (cf. Maurer) in India, any more than in Rome. In India the land is nowhere *noble* in such a way as to be, e.g., inalienable to non-members of the noble class (roturiers).'[62] Engels, more interested in the possible combinations of lordship and the substratum of the primitive community, seems less categoric, though he specifically excludes the Orient from feudalism[63] and as we have seen makes no attempt to extend his analysis of agrarian feudalism beyond Europe. There is nothing to suggest that Marx and Engels regarded the special combination of agrarian feudalism and the medieval city as anything except peculiar to Europe.

On the other hand a very interesting elaboration of the concept of social relations of production is suggested by a number of passages in these later years. Here again it seems that Engels took the initiative. Thus of serfdom he writes (to Marx, on December 22, 1882 – possibly following a suggestion by Marx): 'It is certain that serfdom and villeinage are not a specifically medieval-feudal form, it occurs everywhere or almost everywhere, where conquerors have made the native inhabitants cultivate the soil for them.' And again, about wage-labour: 'The first capitalists already encountered wage-labour as a form. But they found it as something ancillary, exceptional or makeshift, or a point of passage.'[64] This distinction between modes of production characterised by certain relations, and the 'forms' of such relations which can exist in a variety of periods or socio-economic settings, is already implicit in earlier Marxian thought. Sometimes, as in the discussion of money and mercantile activities, it is explicit. It has considerable importance, for not only does it help us dismiss such primitive arguments as those which deny the novelty of capitalism because merchants existed in ancient Egypt, or medieval manors paid their harvest-labour in money, but it draws attention to the fact that the basic social relations which are necessarily limited in number are 'invented' and 'reinvented' by men on numerous occasions, and that all monetary modes of production (except perhaps capitalism) are complexes made up from all sorts of combinations of them.

V

Finally, it is worth surveying briefly the discussion on the main socio-economic formation among Marxists since the death of Marx and Engels. This has in many respects been unsatisfactory, though it has the advantage of never regarding Marx's and Engels' texts as embodying final truth. They have, in fact, been extensively revised. However, the process of this revision has been strangely unsystematic and unplanned, the theoretical level of much of the discussion disappointing, and the subject has, on the whole, been confused rather than clarified.

Two tendencies may be noted. The first, which implies a considerable simplification of Marx's and Engels' thought, reduces the chief socio-economic formations to a single ladder which all human societies climb rung by rung, but at different speeds, so that all eventually arrive at the top.[65] This has some advantages from the point of view of politics and diplomacy, because it eliminates the distinction between societies which have shown a greater and those with a lesser built-in tendency to rapid historical development in the past, and because it makes it difficult for particular countries to claim that they are exceptions to general historical laws,[66] but it has no obvious scientific advantages, and is also at variance with Marx's views. Moreover, it is quite unnecessary politically, since, whatever the differences in past historical development, Marxism has always firmly held the view that all peoples, of whatever race or historical background, are equally capable of all the achievements of modern civilisation once they are free to pursue them.

The unilinear approach also leads to the search for 'fundamental laws' of each formation, which explain their passing to the next-higher form. Such general mechanisms were already suggested by Marx and Engels (notably in *Origin of the Family*) for the passage from the admittedly universal primitive communal stage to class society, and for the very different development of capitalism. A number of attempts have been made to discover analogous 'general laws' of feudalism[67] and even of the slave-stage.[68] These have, by general consent, not been very successful, and even the formulae finally suggested for agreement seem to be little more than definitions. This failure to discover generally acceptable 'fundamental laws' applicable to feudalism and slave-society is in itself not insignificant.

The second tendency partly follows from the first, but is also partly in conflict with it. It led to a formal revision of Marx's list of socio-economic formations, by omitting the 'Asiatic mode', limiting the scope of the 'ancient', but correspondingly extending that of the 'feudal'. The omission of the 'Asiatic mode' occurred, broadly speaking, between the late 1920s and the late 1930s: it is no longer mentioned in Stalin's *Dialectical and Historical Materialism* (1938), though it continued to be used by some – mainly English-speaking – Marxists until much later.[69] Since the characteristic for Marx was resistance to historical evolution, its elimination produces a simpler scheme which lends itself more readily to universal and unilinear interpretations. But it also eliminates the error of regarding oriental societies as essentially 'unchanging' or ahistorical. It has been remarked that 'what Marx himself said about India cannot be taken as it stands', though also that 'the theoretical basis [of the history of India] remains Marxist'.[70] The restriction of the 'ancient' mode has posed no major political problems or (apparently) reflected political debates. It has been due simply to the failure of scholars to discover a slave-phase everywhere, and to find the rather simple model of the slave-economy which had become current (much simpler than Marx's own) adequate even for the classical societies of antiquity.[71] Official Soviet science ceased to be committed to a universal stage of slave-society.[72]

'Feudalism' has expanded its scope partly to fill the gap left by these changes – none of the societies affected could be reclassified as capitalist or were reclassified as primitive-communal or 'archaic' (as we remember Marx and Engels inclined to do) – and partly at the expense of societies hitherto classified as primitive communal, and of the earlier stages of capitalist development. For it is now clear that class differentiation in some societies formerly loosely called 'tribal' (e.g. in many parts of Africa) had made considerable progress. At the other end of the timescale the tendency to classify all societies as 'feudal' until a formal 'bourgeois revolution' had taken place made some headway, notably in Britain.[73] But 'feudalism' has not grown merely as a residual category. Since very early post-Marxist times there have been attempts to see a sort of primitive or proto-feudalism as the first general – though not necessarily universally occurring – form of class society growing out of the disintegration of primitive communalism.[74] (Such direct transition from primitive communalism to feudalism is of course provided for by Marx and Engels.) Out of this proto-feudalism, it is suggested, the various other formations developed, including the developed feudalism of the European (and Japanese) type. On the other hand a reversion to feudalism from formations which, while *potentially* less progressive, are in actual fact more highly developed – as from the Roman Empire to the tribal Teutonic kingdoms – has always been allowed for. Owen Lattimore goes so far as 'to suggest that we think, experimentally, in terms of evolutionary and relapse (or devolutionary) feudalism', and also asks us to bear in mind the possibility of the temporary feudalisation of tribal societies interacting with more developed ones.[75]

The net result of all these various tendencies has been to bring into currency a vast category of 'feudalism' which spans the continents and the millennia, and ranges from, say, the emirates of northern Nigeria to France in 1788, from the tendencies visible in Aztec society on the eve of the Spanish conquest to tsarist Russia in the nineteenth century. It is indeed likely that all these can be brought under one such general classification, and that this has analytical value. At the same time it is clear that without a good deal of sub-classification and the analysis of sub-types and individual historical phases, the general concept risks becoming much too unwieldy. Various such sub-classifications have been attempted, e.g. 'semi-feudal', but so far the Marxist clarification of feudalism has not made adequate progress.

The combination of the two tendencies noted here has produced one or two incidental difficulties. Thus the desire to classify every society or period firmly in one or another of the accepted pigeon-holes has produced demarcation disputes, as is natural when we insist on fitting dynamic concepts into static ones. Thus there has been much discussion in China about the date of the transition from slavery to feudalism, since 'the struggle was of a very protracted nature covering several centuries . . . Different social and economic modes of life had temporarily coexisted on the vast territory of China.'[76] In the West a similar difficulty has led to discussions about the character of the centuries from the fourteenth to the eighteenth.[77] These discussions have at least the merit of raising problems of the mixture and coexistence of different 'forms' of social relations of production, though otherwise their interest is not as great as that of some other Marxist discussions.[78]

However, with de-Stalinisation, and partly under the stimulus of the *Formen*, Marxist discussion began to show a welcome tendency to revive, and to question several of the views which had come to be accepted over the past few decades. This revival appeared to have begun independently, in a number of countries, both socialist and non-socialist. Contributions came from France, the German Democratic Republic, Hungary, Britain, India, Japan and Egypt.[79] These dealt partly with general problems of historical periodisation, such as were discussed in a debate in *Marxism Today*, 1962; partly with the problems of specific pre-capitalist socio-economic formations; partly with the vexed and now reopened question of the 'Asiatic mode'.[80]

All this indicated attempts to escape from the historic developments in the international Marxist movement in the generation before the middle 1950s, which had an unquestionably negative effect on the level of Marxist discussion in this as in many other fields. Marx's original approach to the problem of historical evolution had been in some respects simplified and changed, and such reminders of the profound and complex nature of his methods as the publication of the *Formen* had not been used to correct these tendencies. Marx's original list of socio-economic formations had been altered, but no satisfactory substitute had yet been provided. Some of the gaps in Marx's and Engels' brilliant but incomplete and tentative discussion had been discovered and filled, but some of the most fruitful parts of their analysis had also been allowed to sink from sight.

All the more reason why today the much-needed clarification of the Marxist view of historical evolution, and especially the main stages of development, should be undertaken. A careful study of the *Formen* – which does not mean the automatic acceptance of all Marx's conclusions – can only help in this task, and is indeed an indispensable part of it.

8

The Fortunes of Marx's and Engels' Writings

I

The writings of Marx and Engels have acquired the status of 'classics' in the socialist and communist parties deriving their inspiration from them, including, since 1917, a growing number of states in which they became the basis of official ideology, or even of a secular equivalent of theology. A great deal of Marxist discussion since the death of Engels – indeed, probably most of it – has taken the form of textual exegesis, speculation and interpretation, or of debates about the acceptability of, or the desirability for the revision of, the views of Marx and Engels as contained in the texts of their writings. Yet these writings did not, initially, form a complete published corpus of the works of the two classics. Indeed, no attempt to publish a complete edition of their work was made before the 1920s, when the celebrated *Gesamtausgabe* (usually known as MEGA) was initiated in Moscow under the editorship of David Ryazanov. It remained incomplete in the original German, though the work was continued in Russian, but in a less complete form than originally intended. Independent attempts to publish an edition intended to be complete were made elsewhere at the same time, notably in France by Alfred Costes Editeur. A full but not by any means complete edition of the works of Marx and Engels (usually known and cited as *Werke*) was published in the German Democratic Republic from 1956, and provided the basis for various similar editions in other languages. The most ambitious of these was the (much fuller) *Collected Works* of Marx and Engels published in fifty English-language volumes from 1975 to 2004.

After lengthy preparation a new *Gesamtausgabe* (known as the new MEGA) began publication in 1975 under the auspices of the Institutes of Marxism-Leninism of the USSR and the German Democratic Republic. The demise of both states shifted this publication from an ideological into an academic mode: overall responsibility for it was transferred to a foundation, the Internationale Marx-Engels Stiftung, at the Amsterdam International Institute for Social History, which has since 1933 held the actual archives of Marx and Engels; and practical work on the project moved to the Berlin and Brandenburg Academy of Sciences, and research centres in various countries. The plan provided for upwards of 120 volumes – almost certainly an underestimate, since reading extracts, rough notes and marginalia were to be included. Fifty-four volumes had been published by the start of the new century. It is hoped to complete publication by 2030.

For most of the history of Marxism, debate has therefore been based on a varying selection of Marx's and Engels' writings. To understand that history, a brief and necessarily cursory survey of the fortunes of these writings is therefore required.

If we omit a great body of journalistic work, mainly in the 1840s and 1850s, the actual body of writing published by Marx and Engels in Marx's lifetime was relatively modest. Before the 1848 revolution it comprises, *grosso modo*, various important essays by Marx (and to a lesser extent Engels) written before the start of their systematic collaboration (e.g. in the *Deutsch-Französische Jahrbücher*); Engels' *Condition of the Working Class in*

Englaand (1845); Marx's and Engels' *Die Heilige Familie* (1845); Marx's polemic with Proudhon *Misère de la Philosophie* (1847); the *Communist Manifesto* (1848); and some lectures and articles of the later 1840s. Except for the *Manifesto*, none of these was republished in Marx's lifetime in a form accessible to a wider public. After the defeat of 1848–9 Marx published the now celebrated analyses of the revolution and its aftermath in émigré reviews of sadly restricted circulation, i.e. the works now known as *Class Struggles in France* and – under that original title – *The 18th Brumaire of Louis Bonaparte*. The latter work he reprinted in 1869. Engels' work on the *German Peasant War* (1850), which also appeared in the émigré press – unlike the articles now known as *Revolution and Counterrevolution in Germany* which appeared under Marx's name in the *New York Tribune* – was also reprinted in Marx's lifetime. Marx's published works thereafter, omitting current journalism and political polemics, are virtually confined to the *Critique of Political Economy* (1859), not reprinted; *Das Kapital* (vol. I, 1867), whose history will be briefly referred to; and a number of works written for the International Workingmen's Association, of which the *Inaugural Address* (1864) and *The Civil War in France* (1871) are the most famous. The latter work was reprinted on several occasions. Engels published various pamphlets, mainly on military-political questions, but in the 1870s began, with his *Herr Eugen Dührings Umwälzung der Wissenschaft* (1878) (*Anti-Dühring*), the series of writings through which, in effect, the international socialist movement was to become familiar with Marx's thought on questions other than political economy. Most of these, however, belong to the period after Marx's death.

In, say, 1875, the known and available corpus of Marx's and Engels' work was therefore exiguous, since much of the early writing had long gone out of print. It consisted essentially of the *Communist Manifesto*, which began to be better known from the early 1870s on; *Capital*, which was translated into Russian and French; and *Civil War in France*, which gave Marx a good deal of publicity. Nevertheless, between 1867 and 1875 we can say that *a* corpus of work by Marx for the first time became available.

The period between Marx's death (1883) and Engels' (1895) saw a double transformation. In the first place interest in Marx's and Engels' work quickened with the rise of the international socialist movement. In these twelve years, according to Andréas, no fewer than seventy-five editions of the *Communist Manifesto* appeared in fifteen languages.[1] It is interesting that the editions in the languages of the Tsarist Empire already outnumbered those in the original German. Secondly, a large corpus of the work of the classics was now published systematically in the original language, mainly by Engels. This comprised (a) republications (generally with new introductions) of works long out-of-print whose permanent significance Engels thus wished to underline; (b) new publication of works left unpublished or incomplete by Marx; and (c) new writing by Engels, sometimes incorporating important unpublished texts by Marx such as the Theses on Feuerbach, in which he attempted to provide a coherent and rounded picture of the Marxian doctrine. Thus, under (a) Engels republished as a pamphlet Marx's articles on *Wage Labour and Capital*, *The Poverty of Philosophy*, *The 18th Brumaire*, *The Civil War in France*, and finally *Class Struggles in France*, as well as his own *Condition of the Working Class* and reprints of various writings of his from the 1870s. The main works made available under (b) were the second and third volumes of *Capital* and the *Critique of the Gotha Programme* (1891). The main works under (c) were the *Anti-Dühring*, the even more frequently reprinted *Socialism, Utopian and Scientific*, adapted from the larger work *The Origin of the Family, Private Property and the State* (1884), and *Ludwig Feuerbach* (1888), as well as numerous contributions to current political debate. These works were, perhaps with the exception of *Socialism, Utopian and Scientific*, not published in large editions. Nevertheless, they were and henceforth remained permanently available. They form the bulk of what Engels considered the corpus of his and Marx's writings, though, had he lived, he might have added some further texts – e.g. the *Theories on Surplus Value*, which eventually appeared under Kautsky's editorship, and a revised version of the *Peasant War*, which he himself had hoped to bring out.

With some exceptions, such as writings originally published in English (some of which were reissued by Eleanor Marx shortly after Engels' death), this was the material available for the international Marxist movement at the end of the nineteenth century, including for foreign translation. It consisted of a selection, and to some extent a compilation, made by Engels. Thus *Capital* has come down to us not as Marx intended it, but as Engels thought he would have intended it. The last three volumes, as is well known, were put together by Engels – and later Kautsky – from Marx's incomplete drafts. However, the first volume is also a text finalised by Engels and not by Marx, for the standard version (the German fourth edition of 1890) was modified by Engels in the light of the last (second) edition revised by Marx, the further changes made by Marx for the French edition of 1872–5, some manuscript notes, and minor technical considerations. (Indeed, Marx's own second edition of 1872 included substantial rewriting of sections of the first edition of 1867.) This, then, was the main corpus of the classic texts on which the Marxism of the Second International would have been built, had not many of its theoreticians and leaders, especially in Germany, had direct personal contact with Engels in his later years, both in conversation and through the bulky correspondence which was not published until after the First World War. The point to note is that it *was* a corpus of 'finished' theoretical writings, and intended as such by Engels, whose own writings attempted to fill the gaps left by Marx and to bring earlier publications up to date. Thus the object of his editorial labours on *Capital* was (naturally enough) not to reconstruct the flow and development of Marx's own economic thought, still in progress at the time of his death. Such a historical reconstruction of the genesis and development of *Capital* (including the changes between editions of the published volume) was only undertaken seriously after the Second World

War, and is even now not complete. Engels' object was to produce a 'final' text of his friend's major work, which would make the earlier drafts superfluous.

His own brief compendia of Marxism, and notably the very successful *Socialism, Utopian and Scientific*, were intended to make the contents of this corpus of theory accessible to the members of the new mass socialist parties. And indeed during this period a good deal of the attention of the theorists and leaders of socialist movements was also devoted to making such popular compendia of Marx's doctrine. Thus in France Deville, in Italy Cafiero and in Britain Aveling produced compendia of *Capital*, while Kautsky published his *Economic Doctrines of Karl Marx*. These are only some of the works of this type. Indeed, the main educational and propagandist effort of the new socialist movements appears to have concentrated on the production and diffusion of works of this kind, rather than those of Marx and Engels themselves. In Germany, for instance, the average number of copies printed per edition of the *Communist Manifesto* before 1905 was a mere 2,000 or at most 3,000 copies, though thereafter the size of the print runs increased (data taken from SPD *Parteitage*). For a comparison, Kautsky's *Social Revolution* (part I) was printed in an edition of 7,000 in 1903 and 21,500 in 1905; Bebel's *Christenthum und Sozialismus* sold 37,000 copies between 1898 and 1902, followed by another edition of 20,000 in 1903; and the party's *Erfurt Programme* (1891) was distributed in 120,000 copies.

This does not mean that the now available corpus of classic writings was not read by socialists of a theoretical bent. It was certainly translated rapidly into various languages. Thus in Italy, admittedly a country with an unusually lively interest in Marxism among intellectuals during the 1890s, virtually the whole corpus as selected by Engels was available by 1900 (except for the later volumes of *Capital*), and the *Scritti* of Marx, Engels and Lassalle edited by Ciccotti (from 1899) also included a number of further works.[2] Until the middle 1930s very little was added in the English language to the body of classic writings which had been translated by 1913 – albeit often rather badly – mainly by the firm of Charles H. Kerr, Chicago.

Among those with theoretical interests – that is to say among intellectuals in Central and Eastern Europe, and also partly in Italy, where Marxism appealed greatly – a demand for the rest of Marx's and Engels' writings was naturally lively. The German Social Democratic Party, which owned the literary *Nachlass* of the founders, made no attempt to publish their complete works, and may indeed have considered it inexpedient to publish or to republish some of their more tactless or offensive remarks, or their political writings of purely temporary interest. Nevertheless Marxist scholars, notably Kautsky and Franz Mehring in Germany and D. Ryazanov in Russia, set about issuing a more complete body of Marx's and Engels' *published* writings than Engels had evidently considered immediately necessary. Thus Mehring's *Aus dem literarischen Nachlass von Marx und Engels* republished writings of the 1840s, while Ryazanov reissued works dating from between 1852 and 1862 in several volumes.

Before 1914 at least one major breakthrough into the *unpublished* material was achieved with the publication of the correspondence between Marx and Engels in 1913. Kautsky had already from time to time published selected manuscript material in the *Neue Zeit*, the SPD's theoretical review, notably (in 1902) Marx's letters to Dr Kugelmann and (in 1903–4) a few fragments from what is now known as the *Grundrisse*, such as the incomplete Introduction to the *Critique of Political Economy*. Writings by Marx and Engels addressed to correspondents in specific countries, or published in the languages of those countries, or having special reference to them, were also published from time to time locally, though at the time they were rarely translated into other languages. The availability of the classic writings in 1914 is perhaps best indicated by the bibliography attached by Lenin to his encyclopaedia article on Karl Marx, written in that year and frequently republished under the title *The Teachings of Karl Marx*. If a text of Marx and Engels was not known to the Russian Marxists, the most assiduous students of the classic works, then it may be assumed that it was not effectively available to the international movement.

II

The Russian Revolution transformed the publication and popularisation of the classic works in several ways. First, it transferred the centre of Marxian textual scholarship to a generation of editors who had had no personal contact with Engels, let alone with Marx – men such as Bernstein, Kautsky and Mehring. This new group was therefore no longer directly influenced either by Engels' personal judgements on the classic writings or by the questions of tact and expediency – whether in relation to persons or to contemporary politics – which had so obviously influenced Marx's and Engels' immediate literary executors. The fact that the main centre of Marxian publication was now the communist movement underlined this break, for communist (and especially Russian) editors tended – sometimes quite correctly – to interpret the omissions and modifications of earlier texts by German social democracy as 'opportunist' distortions. Second, the Revolution opened the way for the Bolshevik Marxists, who now possessed the resources of the Soviet state, to achieve their aim of publishing the *entire* body of the classic writings – in short, a *Gesamtausgabe*.

This raised a number of technical problems, of which two may be mentioned. Marx's and to a lesser extent Engels' writings ranged from finished works published with varying degrees of care, through drafts of varying degrees of incompleteness and provisionality to mere reading notes and marginalia. The line between 'works' and preliminary notes and drafts was not easy to draw. The newly formed Marx-Engels Institute, under the direction of that formidable Marx scholar D. Ryazanov, excluded some writings from the actual 'works', though it set out to publish them in a parallel miscellaneous periodical, the *Marx-Engels Archiv*. They were not to be included in a collection of *all* writings until the new MEGA of the 1970s. Furthermore, while the bulk of the actual drafts was available in the Marx-Engels *Nachlass*, in the possession of the SPD (and after 1933 transferred to the International Institute for Social History in Amsterdam), the correspondence of the classics was widely dispersed, and a collected edition was therefore impossible, if only because the whereabouts of much of it was not known. In practice, a number of letters from Marx and Engels were published separately, sometimes by the recipients or their literary executors, from *c*. 1920 on, but for instance so large and important a corpus as the correspondence with Lafargue was not published until the 1950s. Since MEGA was never completed, these problems soon lost their urgency, but they ought to be noted. So also should the continued publication of Marxiana based on the surviving older centres of Marxian material, notably the SPD archives. For although the Moscow Institute sought to acquire all possible writings of the classics for their complete edition – the only one in preparation – in fact it was able to acquire only photocopies of the overwhelmingly largest archival collection, the originals remaining in the West.

The 1920s therefore saw a remarkable spurt in the publication of the classic writings. For the first time two classes of material became generally available: unpublished manuscripts and the correspondence of Marx and Engels with third parties. However, political events soon put obstacles in the way of both publication and interpretation, such as had not been thought of before 1914. The triumph of the Nazis in 1933 disrupted the Western (German) centre of Marxian studies, and largely postponed the repercussion of the interpretations based on them. To take merely one example, Gustav Mayer's monumental biography of Engels, a work of remarkable scholarship, had to appear in 1934 in a Dutch émigré edition and remained virtually unknown to younger Marxists in post-1945 West Germany until well into the 1970s. Many of the new publications of Marxian texts were not merely reproducing 'Marxist rarities' (to quote the title of a series published in the 1920s)[3] but inevitably themselves *became* rarities. In Russia the rise of Stalin disrupted the Marx-Engels Institute, particularly after the dismissal and subsequent murder of its director Ryazanov, and put an end to the publication of MEGA in German, though not – in spite of the tragic impact of the purges – to further editorial work. Furthermore, and in some ways more seriously, the growth of what might be called an ortho-dox Stalinist interpretation of Marxism, officially promulgated in the *History of the CPSU(b): Short Course* of 1938, made some of Marx's own writings appear heterodox, and therefore caused problems with regard to their publication. This was notably the case with the writings of the early 1840s.[4] Finally, the disruption of the Second World War had serious results for Marx's works. The splendid edition of the *Grundrisse* published in Moscow in 1939–41 remained virtually unknown (though one or two copies reached the USA) until the East Berlin reprint of 1953.

The third way in which the publication of the classic writ-ings was transformed after 1917 concerns their popularisation. As has been suggested, the mass social-democratic parties before 1914 made no serious attempt to get their members to read Marx and Engels themselves, with the possible exception of *Socialism, Utopian and Scientific*, and perhaps the *Manifesto. Capital* I was indeed frequently reprinted – in Germany ten times between 1903 and 1922 – but it may be doubted whether it lent itself to wide popular reading. Many of those who bought it were proba-bly content to have it on their shelf as a tangible demonstration that Marx had proved the inevitability of socialism scientifically. Small parties, whether composed of intellectuals, cadres or those unusually devoted militants who like to gather together in Marxist sects, certainly made greater demands on their members. Thus between 1848 and 1918 thirty-four editions of the *Manifesto* were published in English for the relatively minuscule Marxist groups and parties of the Anglo-Saxon world, as against twenty-six in French and fifty-five for the enormous parties of the German-speaking countries.

The international communist movement, on the other hand, paid enormous attention to the Marxist education of its members, and no longer relied primarily on doctrinal compendia for this purpose. Hence the selection and popularisation of the actual classic texts became a matter of major concern. The increasing tendency to back political argument by textual authority, which had long marked some parts of the Marxist tradition – notably in Russia – encouraged the diffusion of classic texts, though naturally within the communist movement in the course of time the textual appeals to Lenin and Stalin were considerably more frequent than those to Marx and Engels. The wide availability of such texts undoubtedly transformed the situation of those who wished to study Marxism everywhere they were allowed to appear, though the area in which Marx and Engels could be published contracted sharply between 1933 and 1944.

Of the major hitherto unpublished manuscripts, those of the 1840s began to make their impact before 1939. Both the *German Ideology* and the *Economic-Philosophical Manuscripts* of 1844 were published in 1932, though slow to be translated *in extenso*. This is not the place to discuss their significance. We merely note in passing that a great deal of Marxist discussion since 1945 turns on the interpretation of these early writings, and conversely, that most Marxist discussion before 1932 proceeded in ignorance of these works. The second large body of unpublished manuscripts concerned the preliminary work for *Capital*. One large body of writing, the *Grundrisse* of 1857–8, remained, as we have seen, unknown for even longer, since its first effective publication occurred in 1953 and its first (unsatisfactory) translations into foreign languages were only published in the late 1960s. It did not become a major basis for international Marxist debate until the 1960s, and even then initially not as a whole but chiefly in relation to the historical section of the manuscript, which was separately published under the title *Formen, die der kapitalistischen Produktion vorhergehen* (Berlin, 1952) and translated within a few years (into Italian 1953–4, into English 1964). Once again the appearance of this text forced upon the majority of Marxists who had hitherto been ignorant of it a major reconsideration of Marx's writings. Of the substantial body of Marx's drafts in connection with the writing of *Capital* which were not included in the final published versions, sections have filtered into circulation even later and more gradually – e.g. the projected part VII of vol. I (*Resultate des unmittelbaren Produktionsprozesses*) which, though published in the *Arkhiv K. Marksa i F. Engelsa* in 1933, did not come to be seriously discussed until the late 1960s and was not translated, at all events into English, until 1976. Some of this material remains unpublished.

The third major unpublished manuscript, Engels' *Dialectics of Nature*, was first issued somewhat earlier, together with other Engels drafts, in the *Arkhiv K. Marksa i F. Engelsa* (1925). That it was not included in, or perhaps destined for, publication in the *Gesamtausgabe* was probably due to the fact, noted by Ryazanov, that much of Engels' discussion of the natural sciences, written in the 1870s, had become factually obsolete. Nevertheless, the work fitted into the 'scientist' orientation of Marxism which, long popular in Russia, was reinforced in the Stalin era. The *Dialectics of Nature* was therefore quite rapidly diffused in the 1930s and indeed cited by Stalin in the *Short Course* of 1938.[5] The text had some influence among the then rapidly growing number of Marxist natural scientists.

Of the Marx–Engels correspondence with third parties, which constituted probably the largest single body of unpublished Marxian material other than notes, relatively little had been published before 1914, partly in periodicals, partly as collections or selections of letters to individual correspondents, such as the *Briefe und Auszüge aus Briefen von Joh. Phil. Becker, Jos. Dietzgen, Friedrich Engels, Karl Marx u. A. an F.A. Sorge und Andere* (Stuttgart, 1906). A number of similar collections were published after 1917, notably of letters to Bernstein (in Russian 1924, in German 1925), and correspondence with Bebel, Liebknecht, Kautsky and others (Russian 1932, German, Leningrad 1933), but no complete collection was published before the Russian edition (*Sochineniya* XXV–XXIX) of 1934–46, or, in the original German, the *Werke* of 1956–68. As already noted, some highly important collections did not become available until the late 1950s, and the publication of the correspondence can still not be considered complete. Nevertheless, the material available to the Moscow Institute by 1933 included a very substantial body of letters, which were popularised mainly through foreign translations and adaptations of the *Selected Correspondence* from the early 1930s.

However, a note about the 'official' publication of these letters is necessary. They were seen not so much as a correspondence (except for the exchanges between Marx and Engels), rather as part of the classic writings. The letters of Marx's and Engels' correspondents were therefore not usually included in the official communist collections, though some editions of special collections, mainly produced by Marx's and Engels' correspondents or their executors (e.g. Kautsky, Victor Adler) did contain both sides of the exchange. The Engels–Lafargue correspondence (1956–9) was perhaps the first issued under communist auspices which included both sides, thus opening a new phase in the study of this aspect of the Marx–Engels texts. Moreover, the practice of keeping the Marx–Engels letters and their correspondence with third parties separate in the various collected editions of their works until the 1970s made a strictly chronological study of the letters relatively inconvenient.

III

As we have seen, the publication and translation of the corpus of Marx's and Engels' works in a far more complete form made substantial progress after the Second World War, and especially in the post-Stalin era. By the early 1970s it could be said that, barring further discoveries of drafts and letters, the great bulk of the known works were in print in the original language, though not necessarily widely available. This increasingly included the highly incomplete preparatory material – reading notes, marginalia, etc. – which it became increasingly customary to treat as 'works' and to publish accordingly. What is perhaps more to the point, the attempt to analyse and interpret such materials with a view to discovering the lines of Marx's own thinking – especially on subjects on which he did not publish even drafts of texts – was increasingly made, as in the edition of Marx's *Ethnological Notebooks* (ed. L. Krader, Assen, 1972). This may be regarded as the beginning of a new and promising phase in Marxian textual scholarship. The same applies to the study of Marxian drafts and variants, such as the preparatory drafts for the *Civil War in France* and the famous letter to Vera Zasulich of 1881. Indeed, such a development was inevitable, since several of the more important new texts, such as the *Grundrisse*, were themselves drafts, not intended for publication in the surviving form. The study of textual variants also advanced substantially with the republication in Japan of the original first chapter of *Capital* I (1867 edition) which had been substantially rewritten by Marx for subsequent editions.

One might say that, particularly since the 1960s, Marxian scholarship has increasingly tended to seek in Marx and Engels not a definitive and 'final' set of texts expounding the Marxist theory, but a *process* of developing thought. It has also increasingly tended to abandon the view that the works of Marx and Engels are substantially indistinguishable components of the corpus of Marxism, and has investigated the differences and sometimes divergences between the two lifelong partners. That this has led to sometimes exaggerated interpretations of these differences does not concern us here. The gradual decline of Marxism as a formal dogmatic system since the middle 1950s has naturally encouraged these new tendencies in Marxian textual scholarship, though it has also led to the search for textual authority for alternative and sometimes dogmatic versions of 'Marxism' in the recently published or popularised and less familiar Marxian writings.

IV

The decline in dogmatic Marxism after 1956 produced a growing divergence between the countries under Marxist government, with their more or less monolithic official Marxist doctrines, and the rest of the world, in which a plurality of Marxist parties, groups and tendencies coexisted. Such a divergence had hardly existed before 1956. The Marxist parties of the pre-1914 Second International, though tending to develop an orthodox interpretation of doctrine as against 'revisionist' challengers on the right and anarcho-syndicalist challengers on the left, accepted a plurality of interpretations, and were hardly in a position to prevent it, had they wished. Nobody in the German SPD thought it odd that the arch-revisionist Eduard Bernstein should edit the correspondence of Marx and Engels in 1913, though Lenin detected 'opportunism' in his editorial judgements. Social-democratic and communist Marxism coexisted in the 1920s, yet with the foundation of the Marx-Engels Institute the centre of publication for the classic texts passed increasingly on to the communist side. It may be observed in passing that it remains there. In spite of attempts since the 1960s to publish rival editions of the classic works (e.g. by M. Rubel in France and by Benedikt Kautsky in Germany), the standard editions without which none of the others, including numerous translations, would be conceivable remain those based on Moscow (and, since 1945, East Berlin): the first and second MEGA and the *Werke*. After 1933 for practical purposes the vast majority of Marxists in and outside the USSR were associated with the communist parties, for the various schismatics and heretics of the communist movement gained no numerically significant body of supporters. Marxism in the social-democratic parties – even if we leave aside the virtual destruction of the German and Austrian parties after 1933–4 – grew increasingly attenuated and openly critical of classic orthodoxy. After 1945, with few exceptions, these parties no longer considered themselves Marxist, except perhaps in a historical sense. It is only in retrospect, and in the light of the Marxist pluralism of the 1960s and 1970s, that the plural character of the Marxist literature between the wars was recognised, and systematic efforts were made, notably in Germany since the middle 1960s, to publish or reprint the writings of that period.

For something like a quarter of a century, therefore, there was no substantial difference between the Marxism of communist parties abroad (which meant most of Marxism in quantitative terms) and that of the USSR; at least no such difference was allowed to emerge into the open. This situation changed gradually, but with increasing speed, after 1956. Not merely was one doctrinal orthodoxy replaced by at least two, with the split between the USSR and China, but the non-governmental communist parties increasingly faced competition from rival Marxist groups with more substantial support, at least among intellectuals – i.e. readers of Marxian texts – while within several Western communist parties a considerable freedom of internal theoretical discussion developed, at least on matters of Marxian doctrine. There was thus a marked divergence between the countries in which Marxism remained official doctrine, closely associated with government, and, at any given moment, with a single binding version of 'what Marxism teaches' on any and every subject; and those in which this was no longer the case. A convenient measure of this divergence is the treatment of the actual biography of the founders. In the first group of countries this remained, if not totally hagiographic, then at all events restricted by a reluctance to deal with aspects of their lives and activities which did not show them in a favourable light. (This tradition was not new: it is very noticeable in the first phase of orthodox Marx-biography in Germany before 1914, as exemplified in Mehring's quasi-official life, published in 1918, and perhaps even more in the omissions from the original Marx–Engels *Correspondence.*) In the second group of countries Marxists and Marx-biographers have publicly come to terms with the facts of the founders' lives, even when they do not show their subjects in an attractive light. Divergences of this kind have been increasingly characteristic of the history of Marxism, including the Marxian texts, since 1956.

It remains to survey briefly the diffusion of the works of the classics. Here again it is important to note the major significance of the period of 'monolithic' communist orthodoxy, which was also that of the systematic popularisation of actual texts by the founders. This popularisation took four forms: the publication of separate works by Marx and Engels, the publication of selected or collected works, the publication of anthologies on special topics, and finally, the compilation of compendia of Marxist theory based on, and containing quotations from, the classics. It need hardly be said that during this period 'the classics' included Lenin and, later, Stalin as well as Marx and Engels. However, with the exception of Plekhanov, no other Marxist writer maintained himself internationally in the company of the 'classics', at least after the 1920s.

Works published separately in the more modest series, under some such title as 'Les Eléments du Communisme' or 'Piccola Biblioteca Marxista' (probably on the model of the 'Elementarbücher des Kommunismus' pioneered in Germany before 1933), included the *Manifesto, Socialism, Utopian and Scientific, Value, Price and Profit, Wage Labour and Capital, Civil War in France,* and suitable topical selections, e.g. in the 1930s Marx's and Engels' polemics with anarchists. The longer works were also usually published in a standard format, under some such title as 'The Marxist-Leninist Library' or 'Classici del Marxismo'. The catalogue of this library in Britain on the eve of the Second World War may illustrate the content of such a series. It included (omitting works not by Marx or Engels) *Anti-Dühring, Feuerbach, Letters to Kugelmann, Class Struggles in France, Civil War in France, Germany, Revolution and Counter-revolution,* Engels' *The Housing Question, Poverty of Philosophy,* the *Selected Correspondence* of Marx and Engels, the *Critique of the Gotha Programme,* Engels' *Essays on 'Capital'* and a shortened edition of the *German Ideology. Capital* I was now usually published *in extenso,* and not in such abbreviated or digested forms as had been popular in the social-democratic era. Until the end of the 1930s no attempt seems to have been made to issue a *Selected Works* of Marx and Engels, but Moscow produced such a selection in two (later three) volumes which was distributed in various languages mainly after the war. No communist attempt to produce a *Collected Works* in languages other than Russian appears to have been made after the end of MEGA, until the appearance of the *Werke* (1956–68). The French edition did not get under way until the 1960s, the Italian edition until 1972, the English edition until 1975, doubtless because the task of translation was vast and difficult. The importance placed on the diffusion of Marxist texts is indicated by the fact that the leader of the Italian Communist Party, Palmiro Togliatti, himself figures as the translator of several of the Italian versions of these works.

Anthologies of Marxist texts on various themes seem to have become popular, both in Russian-based and locally based selections, during the 1930s: Marx and Engels on Britain, Marx and Engels on Art and Literature, on India, China, Spain etc. Of the compendia the most authoritative by far was section 2 of chapter 4 of the *History of the CPSU(b): Short Course,* associated with Stalin himself. This work became influential, especially in countries with few vernacular editions of the classics, not only because of the pressure on communists to study it, but also because its simple and lucid presentation made it a brilliantly effective teaching-manual. Its impact on the generation of

Marxists between 1938 and 1956, and perhaps especially in Eastern Europe after 1945, cannot be exaggerated.

In the 1960s, particularly with the rise of a large body of students and other intellectuals interested in Marxism, and of various Marxist or *Marxisant* movements outside the communist parties, the diffusion of the classic texts ceased to be something like a monopoly of the USSR and the communist parties associated with it. Increasingly, commercial publishers entered this market, with or without urging from Marxists or sympathisers on their staffs. The number and variety of left and 'progressive' publishers also multiplied. To some extent, of course, this was a reflection of the widespread acceptance of Marx as a 'classic' in the general rather than the political sense – as someone about whom the normally educated and cultured reader should know something, irrespective of his or her ideological views. It was for this reason that he was published in the Pléiade collection of French classics, as *Capital* had long since been published in the British Everyman's Library. The new interest in Marxism was no longer confined to the traditional corpus of popular works. Thus in the 1960s such works as the *Critique of Hegel's Philosophy of Law*, *Holy Family*, Marx's Doctoral Dissertation, the 1844 Manuscripts and *German Ideology* were available in countries not hitherto in the forefront of Marxian studies, such as Spain. Certain of these works were no longer primarily translated under communist auspices, e.g. the French, Spanish and English translations of the *Grundrisse* (1967–8, 1973 and 1973 respectively; the Italian translation appeared in 1968–70).

Finally, a few words about the geographical distribution of the Marxian classics. Some elementary texts were widely translated even before the October Revolution. Thus between 1848 and 1918 the *Communist Manifesto* appeared in something like thirty languages, including even three Japanese editions and one Chinese – though in practice Kautsky's *Economic Doctrines of Karl Marx* remained the main basis for Chinese Marxism. For a fuller analysis of the fortunes of the *Communist Manifesto*, see chapter 5. Meanwhile, *Capital* I had been translated into most major literary languages of Europe (German, Russian, French, Danish, Italian, English, Dutch and Polish) before the death of Engels, though only incompletely into Spanish. Before the October Revolution it was also translated into Bulgarian (1910), Czech (1913–15), Estonian (1910–14), Finnish (1913) and Yiddish (1917). In Western Europe a few stragglers brought up the rear much later: Norwegian (presumably delayed because familiarity with Danish as a literary language made translation less essential) in 1930–1, and the first incomplete Portuguese edition in 1962. Between the wars *Capital* penetrated southeastern Europe, though incompletely, with Hungarian (1921), Greek (1927) and Serbian (1933–4) editions. No major attempt seems to have been made to translate it into the languages of the USSR, except for Ukrainian (1925). A local version was published in independent Latvia (1920), a late echo of the major development of Marxism in the Tsarist Empire. In this period too for the first time *Capital* penetrated the non-European world (outside the USA) with editions in Argentina (1918), in Japanese (1920), Chinese (1930–3) and Arabic (1939). It is safe to say that this penetration was closely connected with the effects of the Russian Revolution.

The post-war decades brought a large-scale translation of *Capital* into the languages of countries under communist government (Romanian in 1947, Macedonian in 1953, Slovak in 1955, Korean in 1955–6, Slovene in 1961, Vietnamese in 1961–2, Spanish (Cuba) in 1962). Curiously enough the systematic effort to translate this work into the languages of the USSR did not occur until 1952 and thereafter (Byelorussian, Armenian, Georgian, Uzbek, Azerbaijani, Lithuanian, Ugrian, Turkmen and Kazakh). The only other major linguistic extension of *Capital* occurred in independent India, with editions in Marathi, Hindi and Bengali in the 1950s and 1960s.

The wide range of certain international languages (Spanish in Latin America, Arabic in the Islamic world, English and

French) conceals the actual geographic spread of Marxian texts; nevertheless, it may be suggested that even in the late 1970s the writings of Marx and Engels were not available in the spoken languages of a very substantial part of the non-socialist world outside Europe, with the exception of Latin America. How accessible or widely diffused the available texts were cannot be investigated here, though it may be suggested that, where not prohibited by governments, they were probably more widely available in schools and universities and for the educated public than ever before, in all parts of the world. How far they were read or even bought outside these circles is unclear. To answer this question would require very considerable research, which has not at present been undertaken.

II

MARXISM

9

Dr Marx and the Victorian Critics

Since the appearance of Marxism as an intellectual force hardly a year – in the Anglo-Saxon world since 1945, hardly a week – has passed without some attempt to refute it. The resulting literature of refutation and defence has become increasingly uninteresting, because increasingly repetitive. Marx's works, though voluminous, are limited in size; it is technically impossible for more than a certain number of original criticisms to be made of them, and most of them have been made long ago. Conversely, the defender of Marx finds himself increasingly saying the same things over and over again, and though he may try hard to do so in novel terms, even this becomes impossible. An effect of novelty may be achieved in only two ways: by commenting not on Marx himself but on later Marxists, and by checking Marx's thought against such facts as have come to light since the last critic wrote. But even here the possibilities are limited.

Why then does the debate continue among scholars – for it is natural that it does so among propagandists on both sides, who are not primarily concerned with originality? Ideas do not become forces until they seize hold of the masses and this, as advertising agents have recognised, requires much repetition or even incantation. This applies both to those of us who think Marx a great man and his teachings politically desirable, and to those who take the opposite view. However, another reason is sheer ignorance. It is a melancholy illusion of those who write books and articles that the printed word survives. Alas, it rarely does. The vast majority of printed works enter a state of suspended animation within a few weeks or years of publication, from which they are occasionally awakened, for equally short periods, by research students. Many of them appear in languages beyond the reach of most English commentators. But even when they do not, they are often as forgotten as the original bourgeois critics of Marx in Britain. And yet their work throws light not only on the intellectual history of our country in the late Victorian period, but on the general evolution of Marx-criticism.

They strike us chiefly by their *tone*, which differs very considerably from what has since become usual. Thus, Professor Trevor-Roper, who wrote an essay on *Marxism and the Study of History*[1] some years ago, was far from untypical of the tone of anti-Marxism in that discouraging decade. He spent a good deal of space propounding the very implausible proposition that Marx made no original contribution to history except 'to sweep up the ideas already advanced by other thinkers and annex them to a crude philosophical dogma', that his historical interpretation was useless for the past and wholly discredited as the basis of prediction about the future, and that he had been without significant influence on serious historians, while those who claimed to be Marxists either wrote 'what Marx and Lenin would have called "bourgeois" social history' or were 'an army of dim scholiasts busily commenting on each other's scholia'. In brief, the argument was widely accepted that Marx's intellectual reputation had been grossly inflated, for, 'disproved by all intellectual tests, the Marxist interpretation of history is sustained and irrationally justified by Soviet power alone'.

The writings of the Victorian Marx-critics are mostly and justly forgotten; a warning to those of us who engage in this discussion. But when we dip into them we find a wholly different tone. Admittedly British writers found it abnormally easy to maintain their calm. No anti-capitalist movement challenged them, few doubts about the permanence of capitalism nagged them, and between 1850 and 1880 it would have been hard to find a British-born citizen who called himself a socialist in our sense, let alone a Marxist. The task of disproving Marx was therefore neither urgent nor of great practical importance. Happily, as the Rev. M. Kaufmann, perhaps our earliest non-Marxist 'expert' on Marxism, put it, Marx was a pure theorist who had not tried to put his doctrines into practice.[2] By revolutionary standards he seemed to be even less dangerous than the anarchists and was therefore sometimes contrasted with those fire-eaters; to his advantage by Broderick,[3] to his disadvantage by W. Graham of Queens College, Belfast, who observed that the anarchists had 'a method and logic . . . wanting in the rival revolutionists of the school of Karl Marx and Mr Hyndman'[4] Consequently, bourgeois readers approached him in a spirit of tranquillity or – in the case of the Rev. Kaufmann – Christian forbearance, which our generation has lost: 'Marx is a Hegelian in philosophy and a rather bitter opponent of ministers of religion. But in forming an opinion of his writings we must not allow ourselves to be prejudiced against the man.'[5] Marx evidently returned the compliment, for he revised Kaufmann's account of himself in a later book at the instigation of an unidentified 'mutual acquaintance'.[6]

English literature on Marxism, as Bonar[7] observed, not without smugness, thus showed a calm and judicial spirit already lacking from German discussions of this subject. There were few attacks on Marx's motives, his originality or scientific integrity. The treatment of his life and works was mainly expository, and where one disagrees with it, it is because the authors have not read or understood enough, rather than because they mix prosecution with exposition. Admittedly their expositions were often defective. I doubt whether anything even approximating to a usable non-socialist summary of the main tenets of Marxism, as they would be understood today, exists before Kirkup's *History of Socialism* (1900). But the reader could expect to find, as far as it went, a factual account of who Marx was and what the author thought he was at.

He could expect to find, above all, an almost universal admission of his stature. Milner, in his 1882 Whitechapel lectures[8] plainly admired him. Balfour in 1885 thought it absurd to compare Henry George's ideas with his 'either in respect of [their] intellectual force, [their] consistency, [their] command of reasoning in general or of [their] economic reasoning in particular'.[9] John Rae, the acutest of our early 'experts'[10] treated him with equal seriousness. Richard Ely, an American professor of vaguely progressive leanings whose *French and German Socialism* was published here in 1883, observed that good judges placed *Capital* 'on a par with Ricardo' and that 'about the ability of Marx there is unanimity of opinion'. W.H. Dawson[11] summed up what was almost certainly the opinion of all except, as he notes, the miserable Dühring, whom recent Marx-critics have been vainly trying to rehabilitate: 'However its teaching may be viewed, no one will venture to dispute the masterly ingenuity, the rare acumen, the close argumentation and, let it be added, the incisive polemic which are displayed in . . . the pages [of *Capital*].'*

This chorus of praise is less surprising when we recall that the early commentators were far from wishing to reject Marx *in toto*. Partly because some of them found him a useful ally in their fight against laissez-faire theory, partly because they did not appreciate the revolutionary implications of all his theory, partly

---

*Readers may find a few of these opinions in Dona Torr's Appendix to the 1938 reprint of *Capital*, vol. I; but she had obviously consulted only a small fraction of the available literature.

because, being tranquil, they were genuinely prepared to look at him on his merits; they were even prepared, in principle, to learn from him. With one exception: the labour theory of value, or, to be more precise, Marx's attacks on current justifications of profit and interest. Perhaps the critical fire was concentrated against these because the moral accusation implied in the phrase 'labour is the source of all value' affected confident believers in capitalism more than the prediction of the decline and fall of capitalism. If so, they criticised Marx precisely for one of the less 'Marxist' elements in his thought, and one which, though in a cruder form, the pre-Marxian socialists, not to mention Ricardo, had already propounded. At all events the theory of value was regarded as 'the central pillar of German and all modern Socialism'[12] and once it fell, the main critical job was done.

However, beyond this it seemed clear that Marx had a good deal to contribute, notably a theory of unemployment critical of the crude Malthusianism which was still in vogue. His views on population and the 'reserve army of labour' were not only normally presented without criticism (as in Rae), but were sometimes quoted with approval, or even partly adopted, as by the pioneer economic historian Archdeacon Cunningham[13] – he had read *Capital* as early as 1879[14] – and William Smart of Glasgow, another economist whose fame rests on his work in economic history (*Factory Industry and Socialism*, Glasgow, 1887). Similarly Marx's views on the division of labour and machinery met with general approval, e.g. from the reviewer of *Capital* in the *Athenaeum*, 1887. J.A. Hobson (*Evolution of Modern Capitalism*, 1894) was clearly very struck with them: all his references to Marx deal with this topic. But even more orthodox and hostile writers, like J. Shield Nicholson of Edinburgh[15] observed that his treatment of this and allied topics 'is both learned and exhaustive, and is well worth reading'. Furthermore, his views on wages and economic concentration could not be brushed aside. Indeed, so anxious were some commentators to avoid a total rejection of Marx that William Smart wrote his 1887 review of *Capital* specifically to encourage readers who might have been put off by the critique of the value theory from studying the book, which contained much 'of very great value both to the historian and the economist'.[16]

In an elementary textbook designed for Indian university students M. Prothero sums up reasonably well what non-Marxists saw in Marx; all the better for being slightly ignorant and thus reflecting current views rather than individual study. Three things were singled out: the theory of value, the theory of unemployment, and Marx's achievement as a historian, the first to point out that 'the economic structure of the present capitalist society has grown out of the economic structure of the feudal society'.[17] Indeed Marx made his greatest impact as a historian, and among economists with a historical approach to their subject. (As yet, he hardly influenced the professional non-economic historians in England, who were still sunk in the routine of purely constitutional, political, diplomatic and military history.) In spite of recent writers, there was really no dispute among those who read him about his influence. Foxwell, as bitter an academic anti-Marxist as was to be found in the 1880s, mentioned him as a matter of course among the economists who 'have most influenced serious students in this country' and among those who had produced the marked advance in 'historic feeling' at this period.[18] Even those who rejected the 'peculiar, and in my opinion erroneous, theory of value given in *Capital*' felt that the historical chapters must be judged differently.[19] Few doubted that, thanks to Marx's stimulus 'we are now beginning to see that large sections of history will have to be rewritten in this new light',[20] apparently ignoring Professor Trevor-Roper's demonstration that the stimulus was not Marx's, but Adam Smith's, Hume's, de Tocqueville's or Fustel de Coulanges'. Bosanquet[21] has no doubt that the 'economic or materialist view of history' is 'primarily connected with the name of Marx', though 'it may also be illustrated by many contentions of Buckle and Le Play'. Bonar, though specifically denying that Marx invented historical materialism – he very properly instances the seventeenth-century thinker Harrington as a pioneer[22] – has nevertheless not previously heard of the following Marxist historical contentions, which amaze him: that 'the very Reformation is ascribed to an economical cause, that the length of the Thirty Years' War was due to economic causes, the Crusades to feudal land-hunger, the evolution of the family to economic causes, and that Descartes' view of animals as machines could be brought into relation with the growth of the Manufacturing system'.[23]

Naturally his influence was most marked among our economic historians, of whom only Thorold Rogers can be regarded as wholly insular in inspiration. Cunningham in Cambridge, as we have seen, had read him with sympathy since the late 1870s. The Oxford men – perhaps owing to the much stronger Germanic tradition among local Hegelians – knew him before there were English Marxist groups, though Toynbee's only incidental criticism of his history (*The Industrial Revolution*) happens to be mistaken.[24] George Unwin, perhaps the most impressive English economic historian of his generation, took to his subject through Marx, or at any rate to confute Marx. But he had no doubt that 'Marx was trying to get at the right kinds of history. The orthodox historians ignore all the most significant factors in human devdopment'.[25]

Nor was there much disagreement about his achievement as a historian of capitalism. (His views on earlier periods the reviewer in the *Athenaeum* found 'unsatisfactory and quite superficial', but they were normally neglected, and indeed, most of his and Engels' most brilliant *aperçus* were not as yet available to a wide public.) Even the most extended and hostile British critique of his thought – Flint's *Socialism* (1895, written mainly in 1890–1) – admits: 'Where alone Marx did memorable work as a historical theorist, was in his analysis and interpretation of the capitalist era, and here he must be admitted to have rendered eminent service, even by those who think his analysis more subtle than accurate, and his interpretations more ingenious than true'.[26]

Flint was alone neither in his British distrust of 'a tendency to overrefinement in reasoning'[27] nor in his admission of Marx's merits as a historian of capitalism; more especially of nineteenth-century capitalism. It is the modern practice to throw doubts on his and Engels' scholarship, integrity and use of sources,[28] but contemporaries hardly explored this avenue of criticism, since it seemed patent to them that the evils which Marx attacked were only too real. Kaufmann spoke for many when he observed that 'though he presents us exclusively with the dismal side of contemporary social life, he cannot be accused of wilful mis-representation.[29] Llewellyn-Smith felt that 'though Marx has coloured his picture too darkly, he has rendered great service in calling attention to the more gloomy features of modern indus-try, to which it is useless to shut our eyes'.[30] Shield Nicholson[31] thought his treatment in some respects exaggerated, but also that 'some of the evils are so great that exaggeration seems impossible'.[31] And even the most ferocious attack on his *bona fides* as a scholar did not dare maintain that Marx had coloured a white, or even a grey picture black, but at best that, black as the facts were, they sometimes contained 'silvery streaks' of evi-dence which Marx had paid no attention to.[32]

Was the modern tone of hysterical anxiety completely absent from the early bourgeois criticism of Marx? No. From the moment that a Marxist-inspired socialist movement appeared in Britain, Marx-criticism of the modern stamp, seeking to discredit and refute to the exclusion of understanding, also begins to appear. Some of it was in continental works translated into English: notably from the mid-eighties. Hostile continental work was now translated – Laveleye's *Socialism of Today* (1885), Schäffle's *Quintessence of Socialism* (1889). But home-grown anti-Marxism also began to sprout, notably in Cambridge, the leading centre of academic economics. The first serious attack on Marx's scholarship, as we have seen, came from two Cambridge dons in 1885 (Tanner and Carey), though Llewellyn-Smith of Oxford – a far less 'anti-Marxist' place in those days – did not take the criticism too tragically, merely observing, a few years later, that Marx's 'quotations from blue books are very important and instructive, though not always trustworthy'.[33] It is the tone of denigration rather than the content of the Cambridge critics which is interesting: phrases like 'the mongrel algebraical expressions' of *Capital* or 'an almost criminal recklessness in the use of authorities which warrants us in regarding other parts of Marx's work with suspicion'[34] indicate – at least in economic subjects – something more than scholarly disapproval. In fact, what made Tanner and Carey mad was not simply his treatment of the evidence – they shied away from 'the charge of deliberate falsification . . . especially since falsification seems so unnecessary' (i.e., since the facts were black enough anyway) – but 'the unfairness of his whole attitude towards Capital'.[35] Capitalists are kinder than Marx gives them credit for; he is unfair to them; we must be unfair to him. Such, broadly, appears to be the basis of the critics' attitude.

At about the same time Foxwell of Cambridge developed the now familiar line that Marx was a crank with a gift of the gab, who could only appeal to the immature, notably among intellectuals; a man – in spite of Balfour's warning – to be bracketed with Henry George: '*Capital* was well calculated to appeal to the somewhat dilettante enthusiasm of those who were educated enough to realise, and to be revolted by the painful condition of the poor, but not patient or hard-headed enough to find out the real causes of this misery, nor, sufficiently trained to perceive the utter hollowness of the quack remedies so rhetorically and effectively put forward'.[36] Dilettante, not patient or hard-headed, utter hollowness, quack, rhetorical: the emotional load on the critic's vocabulary piles up. To Foxwell we also owe (through the Austrian Menger) the popularisation of the German parlour-game of attacking Marx's originality and

regarding him as a pillager of Thompson, Hodgskin, Proudhon, Rodbertus, or any other early writers who took the critic's fancy. Marshall's *Principles* (1890) took this over in a footnote, though the pointed reference to Menger's demonstration of Marx's lack of originality was dropped after the fourth edition (1898). The view that Rodbertus and Marx – the two were often bracketed together – made 'mainly exaggerations of, or inferences from, doctrines of earlier economists'[37] or that some other earlier thinker – Rodbertus[38] or Comte[39] – had said what Marx wanted to say about history earlier and vastly better, already brings us into a familiar universe. Marshall himself, the greatest of the Cambridge economists, showed his usual combination of marked emotional hostility to Marx and equally marked circuitousness.*
But on the whole the root-and-branch anti-Marxists remained in a minority in the nineteenth century, and for a generation thereafter tended to follow the Marshallian line of tangential sneering rather than full-scale attack. For Marxism rapidly lost that influence which provokes discussion.

Oddly enough the calm type of Marx-criticism proved much more effective than the hysterical type. Few critiques of Marx have been more effective than Philip Wicksteed's '*Das Kapital* – a criticism' which appeared in the socialist *To-Day* in October 1884. It was written with sympathy and courtesy, and with full appreciation of 'that great work', 'that remarkable section' in which Marx discusses value, 'that great logician' and even of the 'contributions of extreme importance' which Wicksteed believed Marx to have made in the latter part of volume I. But, whatever we may now think of the pure marginalist approach to value-theory, Wicksteed's article did more to create the mistaken feeling among socialists that Marx value theory was somehow irrelevant to the economic justification of socialism than the emotional diatribes of a Foxwell or a Flint ('the greatest failure in the history of economics'). It was in a Hampstead

---

*His views are discussed at greater length in a special *Note* below.

discussion group in which Wicksteed, Edgeworth* – another marginalist who avoided emotionalism – Shaw, Webb, Wallas, Olivier and some others discussed *Capital*, that much of *Fabian Essays* was matured. And if, a few years later, Sidgwick could talk of Marx's 'fundamental muddle . . . which the English reader, I think, need hardly spend time in examining, as the more able and influential among English socialists are now careful to give it a wide berth',[40] it was not because of Sidgwickian jeers that they did so, but because of Wicksteedian argument – and perhaps, we might add, because of the inability of British Marxists to defend Marxian political economy against its critics. Workers still insisted on Marxism, and revolted against the early WEA because they did not teach it; but not until events had demonstrated that the confidence of the Marx-critics in their own theories was misplaced, or excessive, did Marxism revive as an academic force. It is unlikely that it will disappear from the academic scene again.

Note

Marshall and Marx

Marshall appears to have begun without any marked views about Marx. The only reference in the *Economics of Industry* (1879) is neutral, and even in the first edition of the *Principles* there are signs (p.138) that at one time the danger to capitalism from Henry George worried him more than that from Marx. The references to Marx in the *Principles* are as follows: (1) A criticism of his 'arbitrary doctrine' that capital is only that which 'give(s) its owners the opportunity of plundering and

---

*Edgeworth, who had never troubled to study Marx seriously, seems to have shared the Cambridge economists' total rejection of and dislike for Marx (*Collected Papers*, III, p.273ff, in a review written in 1920). However, there is no evidence that he expressed this view publicly in the old century.*

exploiting others' (p.138). (From the third edition –1895 – this is transposed and elaborated.) (2) That economists ought to avoid the term 'abstinence', choosing rather something like 'waiting', because – at least so I interpret the addition of a footnote at this point – 'Karl Marx and his followers have found much amusement in contemplating the accumulations of wealth which result from the abstinence of Baron Rothschild' (p.290). (This reference is dropped from the Index from the third edition, though not from the text.) (3) That Rodbertus and Marx were not original in their views, which claim that 'the payment of interest is a robbery of labour', and are criticised as a circular argument, though one 'shrouded by the mysterious Hegelian phrases in which Marx delighted' (pp.619–20). (In the second edition an attempt is made to substitute a summary of Marx's doctrine of exploitation for the earlier caricature of it (1891).) (4) A defence of Ricardo against the charge of being a labour theorist of value, as falsely claimed not only by Marx but by ill-informed non-Marxists. (This defence is progressively elaborated in subsequent editions.) It will be remembered that Marshall had too great an admiration for Ricardo to wish to throw him overboard as an ancestor of socialist theorists, as many other economists – Foxwell for instance – were prepared to do. But the task of showing that Ricardo was not a labour theorist is complex, as he seems to have appreciated. Thus we note not only that all Marshall's references to Marx are critical or polemical – the only merit he allows him, since he lived in pre-Freudian days, is a good heart – but also that his critique seems to be based on a much less detailed study of Marx's writings than one might expect, or than was undertaken by reputable contemporary academic economists.

10

The Influence of Marxism 1880–1914

I

Histories of Marxism have generally defined their subject by exclusion. Their territory is delimited by those who are not Marxists, a category which doctrinaire Marxists and committed anti-Marxists have both tended to make as large as possible, on ideological and political grounds. Even the most comprehensive and ecumenical historians have maintained a sharp separation between 'Marxists' and 'non-Marxists', confining their attentions to the former, though ready to include as wide a range of them as possible. And indeed they must, because if there was not such separation a special history of Marxism would not need to, and perhaps could not, be written. Yet they have also been tempted to write the history of Marxism exclusively as that of the development of and the debates within the body of specifically Marxist theory, and therefore to neglect an important, though not easily definable, area of Marxist radiation. Yet this cannot be neglected by the historian of the modern world, as distinct from the Marxist movements. The history of 'Darwinism' cannot be confined to that of Darwinians or even biologists in general. It cannot but consider, even if only marginally, the use of Darwinian ideas, metaphors or even phrases which became part of the intellectual universe of people who never gave a thought to the fauna of the Galapagos islands or the precise modifications required in the theory of natural selection by modern genetics. Similarly the influence of Freud extends far beyond the diverging and conflicting schools of psychoanalysis, and even beyond those who have ever read a line written by its founder. Marx, like Darwin and Freud, belongs to the small class of thinkers whose names and ideas have, in one form or another, entered the general culture of the modern world. This influence of Marxism on general culture began to make itself felt, speaking very broadly, in the period of the Second International. The present chapter is an attempt to survey it.

The dramatic expansion of labour and socialist movements associated with the name of Karl Marx in the 1880s and 1890s inevitably spread the influence of his theories (or what were considered to be his theories) both inside these movements and outside them. Within them 'Marxism' competed with, and in several countries superseded, other ideologies of the left, at least officially. Outside them, the impact of 'the social problem' and the growing challenge of socialist movements attracted attention to the ideas of the thinker whose name was increasingly identified with them, and whose originality and impressive intellectual stature were obvious. In spite of polemical attempts to prove that Marx was easily discredited, and that he said little more than earlier socialists and critics of capitalism had done – or even that he had largely plagiarised them – serious non-Marxists were unlikely to make so elementary a mistake.[1] To some extent his analysis was used to supplement non-Marxist analyses, as when some British economists in the 1880s, aware of the insufficiencies of the orthodox Malthusian theory of unemployment, took a generally positive interest in Marx's views on the 'reserve army of labour'.[2] Such a dispassionate approach was, of course, less likely in countries in which Marxist-inspired labour movements were less negligible than they were at that time in Britain. There the need to mobilise the heavy artillery of the academic intellect to confute him, or at least to understand the nature of his appeal, was more urgently felt. Hence, especially in Germany and Austria, the appearance in the middle and late 1890s of works of great learning and substantial weight, devoted to this purpose: Böhm-Bawerk's *Das Ende des Marxschen Systems* (1896), Rudolf Stammler's *Wirtschaft und Recht nach materialistischer Geschichts-auffassung* and Heinrich Herkner's *Die Arbeiterfrage* (1896).[3]

Another form of Marxist influence outside the labour and socialist movements was exercised through the semi-Marxists and ex-Marxists who became increasingly numerous from the time of the 'crisis of Marxism' in the late 1890s. This was the period when we see the birth of the familiar phenomenon of Marxism as a temporary stage in the political and intellectual development of men and women; and as we know it is rare that those who have passed through such a stage are not in some way marked by this experience. One has merely to mention such names as Croce in Italy, Struve, Berdyayev and Tugan-Baranowsky in Russia, Sombart and Michels in Germany or – in a less academic field – Bernard Shaw in Britain to appreciate the weight of this first generation of the ex-Marxists of the 1880s and 1890s in the general culture and intellectual life of the period. To the ex-Marxists one must add the growing number of those who, while reluctant to break their links with Marxism, increasingly moved away from what was now becoming a more sharply defined orthodoxy – such as many German 'revisionist' intellectuals – and those who, while not Marxists, were, mainly because they took the side of a socialist left, attracted by some aspects of Marx's ideas.

These forms of the radiation of Marxism were found, to a greater or lesser extent, wherever labour and socialist movements developed in this period, that is to say in most of Europe and some areas settled primarily or largely by European emigrants overseas. Beyond the range of such movements it hardly existed at this period, with the possible, but in any case marginal exception of Japan. There is no evidence of Marxist influence in the pre-1914 revolutionary movements in India, although these were open not only (obviously) to British intellectual influences but also to Russian, and although the constituency from which, for example, the Bengal terrorists of the pre-1914 period were drawn was later to show itself highly receptive to Marxism. There is none in the Islamic world, in sub-Saharan Africa, or, with the exception of the heavily immigrant 'southern cone', in Latin America. We can neglect all these areas.

On the other hand the radiation of Marxism was particularly important and general in some countries of Europe in which virtually all social thought, irrespective of its political connections with socialist and labour movements, was marked by the influence of Marx, who in this context was not so much a challenger of accepted bourgeois orthodoxies (which hardly existed) but rather one of the main founding fathers of any kind of analysis of society and its transformations. This was the case in parts of Eastern Europe and especially in tsarist Russia. In such countries there was even then no way of avoiding Marx, since he already formed part of the general fabric of intellectual life. This does not mean that all those who underwent his influence saw themselves, or can be seen, as Marxists in any specific sense.

II

Though the period with which this chapter is concerned is not much longer than thirty years, nevertheless it cannot be treated as a single unit. Three main sub-periods must be distinguished. The first is that of the emergence of more or less Marxist-oriented socialist and labour parties at various times in the 1880s and early 1890s, and especially the enormous leap forward of such movements in the five or six first years of the International. What is important in this period is not so much the organisational, electoral or trade unionist strength of these movements, though this was often revealed as very great, but their sudden irruption on to the political scene of their countries and (through such initiatives as May Day) internationally, as well as the remarkable and sometimes utopian wave of working-class hope on which they seemed to be carried upward. Capitalism was in crisis: its end, though not always conceived in any specific form, seemed to be in sight. Both the penetration of Marxism within labour movements – the German Social Democratic Party became officially committed to it in 1891 – and its positive and negative radiation beyond the range of these movements therefore made striking progress in a number of countries.

The second sub-period begins in the middle 1890s when the revival of global capitalist expansion became evident. In spite of fluctuations, the mass socialist labour movements, where they existed, continued to grow rapidly, and indeed in some countries mass movements or even more or less permanently organised movements came into existence during this phase; though it became increasingly clear in the areas where they were legal that revolution or total social transformation was not their immediate objective. The 'crisis in Marxism'[4] which outside observers noted from 1898 was not only a debate about the significance for Marxist theory of this demonstration that capitalism still flourished – the 'revisionist' debate – but also due to the emergence of groups with very different interests within what had until recently appeared to be a single forward surge of socialism, e.g. national splits within such movements as the Austrian, Polish and Russian. This clearly transformed the nature both of the debates within Marxism and the socialist movements, and the impact of Marxism outside them.

The Russian Revolution introduces the third sub-period, which may be taken to end in 1914. It was dominated on the one hand by the revival of major mass actions, both in the wake of the 1905 revolution and, a few years later, in the labour unrest which filled the last years before World War One; and on the other hand by the corresponding revival of a revolutionary left both within the Marxist movements and outside them (revolutionary syndicalism). At the same time the scale of the organised mass labour movements continued to grow. Between 1905 and 1913 the membership of the social-democratic unions in the countries covered by the Amsterdam trade union International had doubled, from just under three million to just under six million,[5] while the social democrats were the largest single party – with between 30% and 40% of the votes – in Germany, Finland and Sweden.

The preoccupation with Marxism outside the socialist movements naturally grew. Thus Max Weber's *Archiv für Sozialwissenschaft und Sozialpolitik* published only four articles on the subject between 1900 and 1904, but fifteen between 1905 and 1908, while the number of German academic theses on socialism, the working class and similar themes grew from an average of between two and three a year in the 1890s to an annual average of four in 1900–5, 10.2 in 1905–9 and 19.7 in 1909–12.[6] Since the revolutionary movement was at this time not identified simply with Marxism – revolutionary syndicalism and other even less defined forms of rebellion competed with it in the last pre-war years – the impact of Marxism both on potential sympathisers and on critics was complex and difficult to define. Yet it was probably by this time more widely distributed in one form or another than ever before, not least through the works of the now substantial number of ex-Marxists, or those who felt they had to establish their position in relation to Marxism.

III

If we are to trace the influence of Marxism more precisely, we have to consider two major variables in addition to the sheer size (and therefore political presence) of labour and socialist parties: the extent to which these were themselves Marxist and the extent to which Marxism appealed to the stratum more likely than any other to be concerned with theories, the intellectuals.

The labour movements were either officially identified with Marxism or became so; or were associated with other revolutionary or analogous ideologies of a socialist type; or were essentially non-socialist. Broadly speaking, most member-parties of the Second International, led by the German SPD, were of the first type, though the hegemony of Marxism within them obscured the presence of numerous other ideological influences. Nevertheless, there were some, like the French, which were predominantly imbued with older and indigenous revolutionary traditions, some barely tinged with Marx's influence. While there were countries in which the socialist left was to be found overwhelmingly in such parties, in other countries rival ideologies and movements competed with it.

However, among the rival ideologies of the left, apart from some that were predominantly nationalist, Marxist influence had some scope for penetration, partly because (unless there were special reasons to the contrary) association with the greatest theorist of socialism had a certain symbolic value, but mainly because their theoretical analysis of what was wrong with society was poorly developed in comparison with their ideas about the way to achieve revolution and their ideas, vague though these were, about the post-revolutionary future. The main ideologies which concern us here, in addition to primarily nationalist ones (which in turn infiltrated Marxism), are anarchism and its partial derivative revolutionary syndicalism, Narodnik tendencies and, of course, the radical-Jacobin tradition, particularly in its revolutionary form. From the middle 1890s on, some attention must also be paid to a deliberately non-Marxist socialist reformism whose main intellectual centre was the British Fabian Society. Small though this was, it exercised some international influence not only through temporary foreign residents who were influenced by it – most notably Eduard

Bernstein – but also through the cultural links between Britain and such regions as the Netherlands and Scandinavia. However, interesting though this radiation of Fabianism is, the phenomenon is too small to detain us.[7]

The radical-Jacobin tradition remained largely impervious to the penetration of Marxism even when – or perhaps just because – its more revolutionary members were only too willing to pay their respects to a great revolutionary name and to identify themselves with causes associated with him. Marxism remained unusually undeveloped in France. Until the 1930s numerous distinguished intellectuals of the French Communist Party cannot be seriously described as theoretical Marxists, though at that time many of them, but not all, began to describe themselves as such. The party's intellectual review, *La Pensée*, founded in 1938, is still entitled 'a review of modern rationalism'. Conversely anarchism, in spite of the notorious hostility between Marx and Bakunin, borrowed extensively from the Marxian analysis, except on the specific points in dispute between the two movements. This was not particularly surprising since, until anarchists were excluded from the International in 1896 – and in some countries even later – often no sharp line could be drawn between them and the Marxists within the revolutionary movement, part of the same milieu of rebellion and hope.

The theoretical divergences between orthodox Marxism and revolutionary syndicalism were greater, if only because what these revolutionaries rejected in Marxism was not merely its views on organisation and the state, but the entire system of historical analysis identified with Kautsky, which they regarded as historical determinism – even fatalism – in theory, and reformism in practice. Indeed, revolutionary syndicalism had some attraction for leftwing intellectuals given to ideological debate, but let us not forget that even those who had not come from Marxism, especially those too young for the 1890s, breathed an air saturated by Marxist argument. Thus G.D.H.

Cole, a rebellious but quite uncontinental young British socialist, naturally thought of Georges Sorel's writings as 'neo-Marxist'.[8] Actually the revolutionary syndicalist intellectuals protested not so much against the Marxist analysis per se, but rather against the automatic evolutionism of official social democracy and what the young Gramsci called suffocating revolutionary thought under 'positivist and scientist [*naturalistiche*] incrustations';[9] that is to say against the odd blend of Marx with Darwin, Spencer and other positivist thinkers that so often passed for Marxism, especially in Italy. Indeed, in the West the first generation converted to Marxism, by and large those born round 1860, quite naturally combined Marx with the prevalent intellectual influences of the time. For many of them Marxism, however novel and original as a theory, belonged to the general sphere of progressive thought, albeit politically more radical, and specifically linked to the proletariat.

By contrast, in socially explosive Eastern Europe no other explanations of the nineteenth-century transformation to modernity could compete with Marxism, and its influence became correspondingly profound, even before those countries had developed a working class let alone labour movements, or bourgeois ideologies of any significance other than some local nationalisms. That is why Russia, home of a socially ill-fitting stratum, the critical 'intelligentsia', produced passionate readers of *Capital* before any other country and why, even later, Eastern Europe was to be the essential home of passionate Marxist erudition and analysis. Politically, Marx's first Russian admirers were likely to sympathise with the Narodniks (until their conversion to Marxist groups in the 1880s), but they also included a number of clearly non-radical academic economists who accepted the Marxist method of analysis and even its terminology.[10] Specifically Russia was conquered by an ideology that announced that the progress of capitalism was historically irreversible, and could not be overcome by the resistance of forces external to it (such as that of the peasantry), however hostile, but only by the forces it had itself generated and which were destined to take over from it. What this meant was that Russia had to pass through the stage of capitalism.

Hence the paradox of Russian Marxism: it was both an alternative to the peasant-based revolutionary anti-capitalism of the Narodniks (who had in any case taken over parts of Marx's analysis of capitalism), and a justification of bourgeois capitalist development in a country deeply unsympathetic to it. It produced both revolutionaries and the curious phenomenon of the 'legal Marxists', who put their faith in the advance of economic growth though capitalism but saw the prospect of its overthrow as irrelevant. No such reconciliation beween Marx and the bourgeoisie was needed in central and western Europe, where such thinkers would almost certainly have seen themselves as some kind of liberal. Whatever the disagreements among all these sectors of the educated Russian left, except for a marginal fringe (Tolstoi), the influence of Marx was pervasive.

By the 1890s labour movements not linked to socialism were as common in the Anglo-Saxon regions – Britain, Australia, the USA – as they were rare outside it. Nonetheless in those countries too Marxism was of some significance, though less so than in continental Europe. Nor, especially in the USA, should we underestimate the importance of a mass of immigrants from Germany, tsarist Russia and elsewhere, who often brought Marxist-influenced ideologies with them to the new world as part of their intellectual baggage.[11] And nor should we underestimate the movement of resistance to 'big business' during this period of acute social tension and ferment in the USA, which made a number of radical thinkers receptive to, or at least interested in socialist critiques of capitalism. One thinks not only of Thorstein Veblen but of progressive, centrally placed economists like Richard Ely (1854–1943) who 'probably exerted a greater influence upon American economics during its vital formative period than any other individual'.[12] For these reasons the USA, though developing little independent Marxist thinking itself, became, rather surprisingly, a significant centre for the diffusion of Marxist writings and influence. This affected not only the Pacific countries (Australia, New Zealand, Japan) but also Britain, where the small but growing groups of Marxist labour activists in the 1900s received much of their literature – including not only Marx and Engels but also Dietzgen – from the Chicago publishing house of Charles H. Kerr.[13]

However, since the non-socialist labour movements appeared to pose no serious challenge to the intellectual hegemony of the dominant groups, their intellectuals did not as yet feel a need to meet this challenge with any urgency. During the 1880s and 1890s they debated Marx and socialism very much more than during the 1900s. Thus, among the elite group of Cambridge intellectuals associated with the (secret) discussion club generally known as 'The Apostles' (H. Sidgwick, Bertrand Russell, G.E. Moore, Lytton Strachey, E.M. Forster, J.M. Keynes, Rupert Brooke, et al.), the early twentieth century was a notably non-political period. Whereas Sidgwick had criticised Marx, and Bertrand Russell, close to the Fabians in the 1890s, had written a book on German social democracy (1896); and even as the last pre-1914 student generations began to turn to socialism (though in a non-Marxist form), the most eminent and, as it turned out, politically active economist to emerge from this circle, J.M. Keynes, shows no sign of any interest in or even knowledge of either Marx or any of the economic debates about Marx.[14]

IV

The second factor which could be expected to determine Marxist influence was the appeal of Marxism to middle-class intellectuals as a group, irrespective of the size of the local working-class movement. There were strong labour movements which at that time contained or attracted practically no intellectuals, as in

Australia (where a labour government was actually in being as early as 1904). Perhaps this was because there were few intellectuals in that continent. Similarly, the strong, mainly anarchist, labour movement of Spain held little attraction for Spanish intellectuals. Conversely, we are all familiar with revolutionary Marxist organisations essentially confined to university students, though in the heyday of the Second International such a phenomenon would have been rather unusual. However, it is evident that some socialist movements such as the Russian were predominantly composed of intellectuals, if only because the obstacles to the legal emergence of mass labour movements were so great. Similarly there were other countries where the appeal of socialism to intellectuals and academics was notably great, at least for a time, as in Italy.

We need not, in this connection, delve too deeply into the sociology of intellectuals as a group, or into the question whether or not they formed a separate stratum ('intelligentsia'), though this much preoccupied Marxist discussion at times. All countries contained a body of men, and to a much smaller extent women, who had undergone some sort of higher academic education, and it is the appeal of socialism/Marxism to these which is at issue.[15] In the debates of the SPD, what we would today call 'intellectuals' were typically and habitually referred to as *Akademiker* – people with diplomas. However, two observations must be made. In many countries a fairly clear distinction must be made between the practitioners of what German conveniently expresses as *Kunst* (all the arts) and practitioners of *Wissenschaft* (all the world of learning and science), in spite of the largely common recruitment of both from the middle classes. Thus in France, anarchism, which attracted 'artists' (in this wider sense) in considerable numbers in the 1890s, had no significant appeal to *universitaires*. The difference can only be noted and not explained in this context. The relations between Marxism and the arts will be separately considered below. Secondly, a distinction must be made between countries in which a minority of intellectuals were prominent in socialist parties and movements while the majority remained outside them (as in, say, Germany and Belgium), and those in which the terms 'intellectual' and 'left-wing intellectual' were, at least in youth, almost interchangeable (as in Russia). Most socialist movements, of course, gave a prominent place to intellectuals in their leadership. (Victor Adler, Troelstra, Turati, Jaurès, Branting, Vandervelde, Luxemburg, Plekhanov, Lenin, etc.) as well as drawing their theorists almost exclusively from among them.

There are no adequate comparative studies of the political attitude of European students and academics in the period, still less of the wider professional strata which would have included most adult intellectuals. Our assessment of the attraction of socialism/Marxism for them must therefore be impressionist.[16] On the whole, however, it is safe to say that this attraction was unusually great in only a few countries, mainly on the periphery of the developed zone of capitalism.

In the Iberian peninsula the bulk of intellectuals remained anticlerical liberals and radicals. This is perhaps why the 'generation of 98' which called for a renewal of Spain after the defeats of war – Unamuno, Baroja, Maeztu, Ganivet, Valle-Inclán, Machado, et al. – were hardly liberal; but neither were they socialist. In Britain intellectuals were overwhelmingly liberals of some kind or other, and very little attracted to socialism, though this attraction may have been more felt by the more marginal sector of young educated middle-class women, who formed a large proportion of the Fabian Society's membership and the model for the journalists' stereotype of 'the New Woman' of the 1880s and 1890s. A significant socialist student movement hardly began to emerge until the last years before 1914. Most of the male intellectuals in the Fabian Society came from a new stratum of self-made professionals whose background was working class and lower middle class (Shaw, Webb, H.G. Wells, Arnold Bennett).[17] Indeed, the most interesting left-wing theorist in

England, and a man so close to continental tendencies as to be both influenced by Marx (in his *Development of Modern Capitalism*) and an influence on Marxists (through his *Imperialism*), was, characteristically, not even a Fabian socialist but a progressive Liberal: J.A. Hobson. The native middle-class Marxist intellectuals were numerically and intellectually negligible, with the exception of William Morris (see below).

The French revolutionary tradition naturally exercised a major influence on the intellectuals of that country and, since it included a native socialist component, the influence of socialism also made itself felt, though often as no more than a temporary badge of left-wing opinions. (Michels observes, in contrast to the permanence of loyalties in other countries, that five out of the six deputies elected as socialists in France in 1893 had by 1907 become not merely non-socialists but anti-socialists.')[18] Similarly, a youthful ultra-radicalism was part of bourgeois tradition. There is thus no difficulty in discovering socialism among French intellectuals, and certain prestigious institutions such as the Ecole Normale Supérieure became veritable nurseries of socialist or socialising intellectuals from the 1890s, particularly during the Dreyfus period., Yet since the influence of Marx – or even the attraction to the socialist party claiming allegiance to Marx, the Guesdistes – was small,[19] little more need be said about its appeal to French intellectuals in this period. Indeed, before 1914 the works of Marx and Engels available in French were a distinctly more modest selection than those available – if we include the American editions – in English, let alone in German, Italian or Russian.[20]

The German intellectual and academic community, whatever its liberalism in 1848, was by the 1890s profoundly committed to the Wilhelmine empire and militantly opposed to socialism rather than attracted by it; with the possible exception of the Jews, among whom, according to Michels' undocumented estimate of 1907, 20–30% of intellectuals supported social democracy.[21] While between 1889 and 1909 the French universities produced thirty-one dissertations in the general field of social-ism, social democracy and Marx, the much larger German academic community produced only eleven dissertations on these subjects in the same period.[22] Marxism and social democracy preoccupied German intellectuals and academics; they did not attract many of them. Moreover, there is some evidence that those who were attracted to social democracy were, at least until the last years before 1914, much more likely to be on its moderate and revisionist wing than on its left; certainly the Socialist Students organisation in Germany was among the first champions of revisionism. The German party was, of course, overwhelmingly proletarian in its composition; perhaps more so even than other mass socialist parties.[23] However, even within these limits the relatively modest appeal of Marxism to German intellectuals is suggested by the fact that the party itself had to import several of its own prominent Marxist theo-rists from abroad: Rosa Luxemburg from Poland, Kautsky and Hilferding from Austro-Hungary, 'Parvus' from Russia.

Of the smaller countries in northwestern Europe, Belgium and the Scandinavian nations developed relatively enormous and strongly working-class mass parties, officially identified with Marxism, though in Belgium the broad-based Parti Ouvrier also embodied earlier native traditions of the left. Among the Scandinavians the Danes seem to have shown a somewhat stronger interest in Marx than the Swedes and Norwegians. Apart from an occasional doctor or pastor, the leading figures in Norway were mainly workers. The Swedish movement, like the rest of the Scandinavians (including also the strongly organised Finns), produced no theorists of note and took no significant part in the debates of the International. In the world of the arts the attraction of socialism (or anarchism) may have been stronger, but on the whole it seems likely that what socialism there was among Scandinavian intellectuals was a sort of left-ward extension of the democratic and progressive radicalism so characteristic of that part of Europe; perhaps with special emphasis on cultural and sexual-moral reform. If any figure represents the theoretical left of Swedish intellectuals at this period, it is probably the economist Knut Wicksell, radical republican, atheist, feminist and neo-Malthusian: he remained apart from socialism.

The role of the Low Countries in European culture was probably greater in this period than at any time since the seventeenth century. In the overwhelmingly proletarian Belgian Labour Party intellectuals and academics, mainly drawn from the rationalist academic milieu of Brussels, played a notably prominent part: Vandervelde, Huysmans, Destrée, Hector Denis, Edmond Picard, and on the left De Brouckère. Nevertheless it may be noted that both the party and its intellectual spokesmen tended to stand on the right wing of the international movement, and could, by international standards, be regarded as only approximate Marxists.[24] It is doubtful whether Vandervelde would have called himself a Marxist, but for time and place. As G.D.H. Cole says: 'He came into the Socialist movement at a time when Marxism, in its German Social-Democratic form, had made itself so much the pivotal factor in Socialist development in Western Europe that it was not only almost necessary but also natural for any continental Socialist who aspired to political leadership, especially at an international level, to accept the prevailing Marxist framework and to adapt his thinking to it.'[25] Especially one in the mass workers' party of a small country. Certainly the influence of Marxism on Belgian intellectuals was not notable.

The Netherlands, where no national labour movement of comparable political weight developed, was the only Western European country in which the influence of socialism among intellectuals seems to have been culturally crucial, and conversely, the role of intellectuals in the movement unusually marked.[26] The Social Democratic Party was indeed sometimes sarcastically described as the party of students, pastors and lawyers. It eventually became, as elsewhere, largely a party of skilled manual workers; but the dominant and traditional division of the country into confessional groups (Calvinist, Catholic and secular), each forming a political block cutting across class lines, initially left less scope than elsewhere for the formation of a class party. This seems to have been associated with a marked enlargement of the secular sector of culture. Initially the new party rested largely on two somewhat untypical sectors: the farm labourers of Frisia (both territorially marginal and nationally specific) and the Jewish diamond-workers of Amsterdam. In this small movement intellectuals like Troelstra (1860–1930), a Frisian who became the party's main moderate leader, and Herman Gorter, a leading literary figure who, with the poetess Henrietta Roland-Holst and the astronomer A. Pannekoek, was to be the chief figure on the revolutionary left, played a disproportionately visible role. One is struck not only by the role of intellectuals in the party and the appearance of some Marxist social scientists of interest, such as the criminologist W. Bonger, but above all by the international prominence of the home-grown intellectual ultra-left. In spite of its similarities and links with Rosa Luxemburg, it was independent of East European influence. The Dutch were an anomalous case in Western Europe, though a small one.

The powerful Austrian Social Democratic Party was both notably militant and notably identified with Marxism, if only through the close personal friendship between its leader Victor Adler (1852–1918) and the old Engels. Indeed, Austria was the only country to produce a school of Marxism identified specifically with it: Austro-Marxism. In the Habsburg monarchy we enter, for the first time, a region in which the presence of Marxism in the general culture is undeniable, and the appeal of social democracy to intellectuals more than marginal. However, their ideology was, inevitably and profoundly, marked by that 'national problem' which determined the fate of the monarchy. Characteristically, Austrian Marxists were the first to analyse it systematically.[27]

The intellectuals of those nations which possessed no autonomy, such as the Czechs, were largely drawn to their own linguistic nationalism or, if parts of some *irredenta*, to that of the state they aspired to join (Romania, Italy). Even when influenced by the socialists the national element was likely to prevail – as in the Narodní-Socialists who split from the Austrian party in the later 1890s to become essentially a Czech petty-bourgeois radical party. Though keenly aware of Marxism, they remained largely immune to it: the most eminent Czech intellectual, Tomáš Masaryk, made his name internationally with a study of Russia and a critique of Marxism. There remained the intellectuals of the two dominant cultures, the German and Magyar – and the Jews. The influence of Marxism on general culture in the dual monarchy cannot be understood without some consideration of this anomalous minority.

The common tendency of middle-class Jewish minorities in Western Europe had been to assimilate culturally and politically, as they were largely allowed to do: to become Jewish Englishmen like Disraeli or Jewish Frenchmen like Durkheim, Jewish Italians and, above all, Jewish Germans. In Austria virtually all German-speaking Jews in the 1860s and 1870s regarded themselves as Germans, i.e. believers in a united liberal greater Germany. The exclusion of Austria from Germany, the rise of political anti-semitism from the late 1870s, the increasingly massive westward migration of culturally unassimilated Jews and the sheer size of the Jewish community made this position impossible. Unlike in France, Britain, Italy and Germany, Jews formed not a small component of the population but a large sector of the middle classes: 8–10% of the total population of Vienna, 20–25% of that of Budapest (1890–1910). The situation of the Jewish intellectuals – and Jews were certainly the most enthusiastic beneficiaries of the education system[28] – was thus *sui generis*.

In Hungary the assimilation of Jews continued to be actively welcomed as part of the policy of magyarisation, and therefore enthusiastically pursued by the Jews. And yet they could not be completely integrated. In a sense their situation was similar to that of South African Jews later in the twentieth century: accepted as part of the ruling nation as against non-Magyars (or non-whites), but by their very concentration and social specialisation precluded from complete identification. It is true that their role in Hungarian social democracy, which showed little interest in theoretical matters and operated under conditions of moderate repression, was not outstanding. However, in the 1900s strong social-revolutionary currents became influential in the student movement, which were to lead to the marked Jewish role in the Hungarian left after the 1917 revolution. Nevertheless, the case of the Hungarian Marxist most widely known abroad is significant. Georg Lukacs (1885–1971), though a socialist from at least 1902 and in contact with the leading Marxist/anarcho-syndicalist intellectual of the country, Erwin Szabo (1877–1918), showed no sign of serious Marxist theoretical interests before 1914.

The Austrian half of the monarchy marginalised the Jews earlier and more obviously. Unlike the Magyars, it possessed an ample reservoir of non-Jewish intellectuals speaking German from which to staff its senior public service and its academic apparatus, two overlapping areas. The 'Austrian school' of economists which emerged after 1870 consisted essentially of such men, among whom (with the exception of the Mises brothers) few Jews were to be found: Menger, Wieser, Böhm-Bawerk, and the somewhat younger Schumpeter and Hayek. Moreover, the great-German nationalism to which most Jews adhered came to be particularly, though not exclusively,[29] associated with antisemitism. This left the Jews without an obvious focus for their loyalties and political aspirations. Socialism was one possible alternative, which was taken by Victor Adler, though almost certainly only by a minority even of his younger contemporaries. Austrian social democracy remained passionately attached to great-German unity until 1938. Zionism (the invention of an ultra-assimilated Viennese intellectual) was later to be another, though then with much smaller appeal. The rise of a notably powerful, devoted and militant labour movement, primarily among German-speaking workers, no doubt made some appeal to intellectuals; and the fact that in Vienna as elsewhere it was the only mass movement which opposed the dominant antisemitic mass parties is not to be overlooked. Nevertheless, the majority of Austrian Jewish intellectuals were certainly not drawn to socialism, rather to an intensive life of culture and personal relations, a largely non-political evasion or introspective analysis of the crisis of their civilisation. (The appeal of socialism to Christian intellectuals was even smaller.) The names which come to mind when Austrian (i.e largely Viennese) culture in this period is mentioned are not primarily socialist: Freud, Schnitzler, Karl Kraus, Schoenberg, Mahler, Rilke, Mach, Hofmannsthal, Klimt, Loos, Musil.

On the other hand in the main cities, particularly Vienna and Prague, social democracy (i.e. in intellectual terms, Marxism) became an unavoidable part of the experience of young intellectuals, as may be seen from the most vivid portrait of the (predominantly Jewish) cultured Viennese middle-class milieu in Arthur Schnitzler's novel *Der Weg ins Freie* (1908). It is therefore not surprising that Austrian social democracy became a nursery of Marxist intellectuals and developed an 'Austro-Marxist' group: Karl Renner, Otto Bauer, Max Adler, Gustav Eckstein, Rudolf Hilferding, as well as the founder of Marxist orthodoxy Karl Kautsky and a flourishing collection of Marxist academics. (Austrian universities did not discriminate as systematically against them as German ones.) Among these, Carl Grünberg, Ludo M. Hartmann and Stefan Bauer are notable for founding in 1893 the journal which, under its later name of *Vierteljahrschrift für Sozial- und Wirtschaftsgeschichte*, was to become the main organ of economic and social history in the German-speaking world, but eventually ceased to reflect its socialist origins. Grünberg, from his chair in Vienna, founded the Archiv für die Geschichte des Sozialismus und der Arbeiterbewegung (commonly known as Grünberg's Archiv) in 1910, which pioneered the academic study of the socialist, and particularly the Marxist, movement. Conversely, Austrian social democracy was distinguished by a particularly brilliant press and an unusual breadth of cultural interest: if it did not appreciate Schoenberg, at least it was one of the few institutions to help the musical revolutionary to survive as the director of workers' choirs.

'Probably in no other country are so many socialists to be found among scientists, scholars and eminent writers,' observed an American writer of Italy.[30] The strikingly large and prominent role of intellectuals in the Italian socialist movement and – at least in the 1890s – the enormous temporary appeal of Marxism among them have often been noted. They did not form a numerically large section of it – less than 4% in 1904[31] – and there is little doubt that socialists were not a majority even among the (masculine) bourgeois youth and students of the early 1890s. Nevertheless, unlike the overwhelmingly conservative students and professors of German and Austrian universities, Italian socialism was often propagated – as in Turin – from progressive as well as academically and politically influential milieus of Italian universities (French academic socialism followed rather than initiated). Unlike the overwhelmingly non-Marxist socialism of the French *universitaires* at this time, Italian academic intellectuals were so strongly attracted to Marxism that much of Italian Marxism was little more than a dressing poured over the basic positivist, evolutionist and anticlerical salad of Italian middle-class male culture. Moreover, it was not only a movement of youthful revolt. The converts to Italian socialism/Marxism included established and mature men: Labriola was born in 1843, Lombroso in 1836, the writer De Amicis in 1846, though the typical generation of the leaders of the International was that of *c.* 1856–66. Whatever we may think of the kind of Marxism or *Marxisant* socialism which prevailed among Italian intellectuals, there is no doubt about their intense preoccupation with Marxism. Even the polemical anti-Marxists (some, like

Croce, themselves ex-Marxists) bear witness to it: Pareto himself introduced a volume of extracts from *Capital* selected by Lafargue (Paris, 1894).

We can legitimately speak of Italian intellectuals as a whole, since, in spite of the country's notable localism and the difference between North and South, the intellectual community was national, even in its general readiness to accept foreign (French and German) intellectual influences. It is less legitimate to think of the relations between the socialism of the intellectuals and the labour movement in national terms, since regional differences play an enormous part in this respect. In some ways the interactions between intellectuals and the socialist labour movement in the industrial North – Milan and Turin – are comparable to those in, say, Belgium and Austria, but this was clearly not so in Naples or Sicily. The peculiarity of Italy was that it fitted the pattern neither of Western Marxist social democracy nor of Eastern Europe. Its intellectuals were not a dissident revolutionary intelligentsia. This is suggested not so much by the fact that the wave of their enthusiasm for Marxism, at its height in the early 1890s, subsided fairly rapidly, as by the rapid transfer of most of the Socialist Party's intellectuals to its reformist and revisionist wing after 1901, and by the failure of that party to develop a Marxist left opposition of any size within it, as happened in Germany and Austria.

Italian intellectuals as a group conformed to the basic West European pattern of the period: they were members in good standing of their national middle class, and after 1898 accepted as part of the system even when they were socialist politicians. There were no doubt good reasons why many of them should become socialists in the 1890s; probably, given the political development of Italy since the Risorgimento, the miserable poverty of Italian workers and peasants and the great mass rebellions of the 1880s and 1890s, stronger reasons even than in Belgium. The generosity and rebelliousness of youth reinforced these. At the same time, not only were socialist middle-class intellectuals not discriminated against as such, their socialism being, with a few exceptions, accepted as a comprehensible extension of progressive and republican views, but the pattern of their lives and careers was not substantially different from that of non-socialist intellectuals. Felice Momigliano (1866–1924) had a somewhat troubled career as a secondary school teacher for a few years after his militant adhesion to the Socialist Party in 1893, but thereafter there seems to have been little in his professional life as a teacher and university professor, or even (apart from the contents) in his literary activities, to distinguish him from non-socialist teachers in *licei* with a Mazzinian background and strong intellectual interests. We can at most guess that, had he not been a socialist, he might have reached the university rather earlier.

In short, most Western socialist intellectuals enjoyed at the very least what Max Adler described as 'personal immunity and the possibility of the free development of their spiritual (*geistige*) interests'.[32] This was not the case of the intelligentsia of the Russian type, which, though initially and primarily sprung from 'the well-to-do classes of the population' was sharply distinguished from them by its essentially revolutionary definition. The gentry and officials 'in their majority cannot be classed in the category of intellectuals', as Pešehonov stated firmly in 1906.[33] Their very vocation and the reaction of the regime and society they opposed precluded the Western type of integration, whether the intelligentsia was defined subjectively and idealistically, as by the Narodniks, or as a separate social stratum – a question much debated on the Russian left in the early 1900s. As it happened, the growth of both a proletariat and an increasingly self-confident bourgeoisie in the 1900s complicated their situation. Since an increasingly visible part of the intelligentsia now seemed to belong to the bourgeoisie ('In Russia also, as in Western Europe, the intelligentsia is breaking up, and one of its fractions, the bourgeois fraction, places itself at the disposal of the bourgeoisie and merges itself definitively in it', as Trotsky argued),[34] the nature, or even the separate existence of this stratum, no longer seemed clear. However, the very nature of these debates indicates the profound differences between Western Europe and the countries of which Russia was then the major example. In Western Europe it would hardly have been possible to argue, like the Russo-Polish revolutionary Machajski (1866–1926) and some of his commentators, that the intellectuals as such were a social group seeking, by means of a revolutionary ideology, to substitute themselves for the bourgeoisie with the aid of the proletariat before exploiting the proletariat in their turn.[35]

Given the central role of Marx as the inspirer of the analysis of modern society in Russia, the pervasiveness of Marxist influence among the intelligentsia hardly needs much comment. All positions on the left, whatever their nature and inspiration, had also to be defined in relation to it. Indeed, it was so central that even nationalist movements underwent its influence. In Georgia the Mensheviks were to become, in effect, the local 'national' party; the Bund – the nearest thing at this time to a national political organisation of the Jews – was strongly Marxist; and even the then relatively modest Zionist movement clearly shows this influence. The founding fathers of Israel, who largely came to Palestine in the 'second Aliyah' from Russia in the aftermath of the 1905 revolution, brought with them the revolutionary ideologies of Russia, which were to inspire the structure and ideology of the Zionist community there. But even peoples less likely to be influenced by Marxism than the Jews demonstrate its influence. What became the main champion of Polish nationalism was, nominally, the Polish Socialist Party of the Second International – to some extent a genuine workers' party – so much so that the older Marxist tradition had to reconstitute itself as a rival, and more truly Marxist, Social Democracy of the Kingdom of Poland and Lithuania (under Rosa Luxemburg and Leo Jogiches). A similar division developed in Armenia, with the rise of the Dashnaks (who nevertheless saw themselves as part of the Second International). In short, in Russia intellectuals who broke with the older traditions of their people were quite unable to escape the influence of Marxism in some form or another.

This is not to suggest that they were all Marxists, or remained so, or that, when they regarded themselves as such, they agreed with one another about the right interpretation of Marxism – especially not the latter. In Russia, as elsewhere, after the great wave of the early 1890s, which saw a sharp decline in Narodism and the temporary convergence of most revolutionary and progressive ideologies towards a generic Marxism, the divergence and divisions became particularly marked in the next century, and – perhaps for the first time – a distinctly anti-Marxist, perhaps even in some ways a non-political intelligentsia emerged. But it emerged from a melting-pot in which it had, inevitably, come into contact with Marxism and undergone its influence.

The appeal of Marxism to intellectuals in southeastern Europe was limited chiefly by the scarcity of any kind of intellectuals in some of the more backward countries (as in parts of the Balkans): by their resistance to German and Russian influences – as in Greece and to some extent Romania, which tended to look to Paris;[36] by the failure of significant labour and peasant movements to emerge (as in Romania, where the socialism of an isolated group of intellectuals soon collapsed after the 1890s); and by the rival appeal of nationalist ideologies, as perhaps in Croatia. Marxism penetrated parts of this area in the wake of Narodnik influence (as notably in Bulgaria), and through the Swiss universities, foci of revolutionary mobilisation, where politically dissident students from Eastern Europe concentrated and mixed. *Capital* had not been translated into any southeastern European language except Bulgarian before 1914. Perhaps it is more significant that some Marxism did penetrate these backward regions – even, in a way, the remote valleys of Macedonia – rather than that its impact (outside Russian-influenced Bulgaria) remained relatively modest.

V

What, then, was the influence of Marxism on the educated culture of the period, allowing for these national and regional variations? Perhaps it would be useful to remind ourselves that the question itself is biased. What we are considering is an interaction between Marxism and non-Marxist (or non-social-ist) culture rather than the extent to which the second shows the influence of the first. It is impossible to separate this from the corresponding influence of non-Marxist ideas within Marxism. These were regretted and condemned as corrupting by the more rigorous Marxists, as witness Lenin's polemics against the Kantianisation of Marxist philosophy and the penetration of Mach's 'empirio-criticism'. One can understand these objections: after all, if Marx had wished to be a Kantian he could perfectly easily have become one. Moreover, there is also no doubt that the tendency to substitute Kant for Hegel in Marxian philosophy was sometimes, though by no means always, associated with revisionism. However, in the first place it is not the task of the historian in the present context to decide between 'correct'; and 'incorrect', pure and corrupt Marxism, and in the second place, and more importantly, this tendency for Marxist and non-Marxist ideas to interpenetrate is one of the strongest pieces of evidence for the presence of Marxism in the general culture of the educated. For it is precisely when Marxism is strongly present on the intellectual scene that the rigid and mutually exclusive separation of Marxist and non-Marxist ideas is most difficult to maintain, since both Marxists and non-Marxists function in a cultural universe which contains both. Thus in the 1960s the tendency in parts of the left to combine Marx with structuralism, with psycho-analysis, academic econometrics etc. provides, among other things, evidence of the strong attraction of Marxism on university intellectuals at that time. Conversely it was in Britain, where academic economists in the 1900s wrote as though Marx had not existed, that Marxist economics, confined to small groups of militants, existed in total separation, and without any overlap, with non-Marxist economics.

It is, of course, true that the large Marxist parties of the International, in spite of their tendency to formulate an orthodox Marxist doctrine in opposition to revisionism and other heresies, were careful not to exclude heterodox interpretations from the legitimate range of debate within the socialist movement. They were not merely anxious, as practical political bodies, to maintain party unity, which in mass parties implied accepting a considerable variety of theoretical opinions, but they were also faced with the task of formulating Marxist analyses in fields and on topics to which the classic texts provided no adequate guide, or no guide at all, e.g. on 'the national question', on imperialism, and numerous other matters. No a priori judgement on 'what Marxism taught' about these was possible, and still less the appeal to authoritative texts. The range of Marxist debate was therefore unusually wide. However, a rigid and mutually exclusive separation of Marxism from non-Marxism would have been possible only by a draconian restriction of Marxist orthodoxy, and – as the event proved – the virtual prohibition of heterodoxy by state power or party authority. The first was not available, the second either not applied or relatively ineffective. The growing influence of Marxist ideas outside the movement was therefore accompanied by some influence of ideas drawn from non-Marxist culture within the movement. They were the two sides of the same coin.

Without judging its nature or political significance, can we assess the presence of Marxism in the general educated culture of the period 1880–1914? It was almost certainly small in the field of the natural sciences, though Marxism itself was very powerfully influenced by these, and especially by (Darwinian) evolutionary biology. Marx's own writings hardly touched the natural sciences and Engels' writings were significant, if at all, only for the scientific popularisation and workers' education of the labour movement. His *Dialectics of Nature* was considered so little in tune with scientific developments since 1895 that Ryazanov excluded it from the collected edition of Marx's and Engels' works and later published it (for the first time) only in the marginal *Marx-Engels-Archiv*. There is nothing comparable in the period of the Second International to the intense interest of brilliant natural scientists in Marxism in the 1930s. Moreover, there is no evidence of great political radicalism among the natural scientists of the period, admittedly, outside (largely German) chemistry and medicine, then a numerically exiguous group. No doubt a socialist can be found among them here and there in the West, as among the products of left-wing institutions such as the Ecole Normale Supérieure (e.g. the young Paul Langevin). The occasional scientist had been in contact with Marxism, like the biological statistician Karl Pearson,[37] who was to move in a very different ideological direction. Marxists anxious to discover socialist Darwinians did not succeed in discovering many.[38] The major political trend among (largely Anglo-Saxon) biologists, neo-Malthusian eugenics, was at this time regarded at least in part as on the political left, but could hardly be other than independent of, if not hostile to, Marxist socialism.

The most that can be said is that scientists brought up in Eastern Europe like Marie Sklodkowska-Curie, and perhaps those trained or working in the Swiss universities, heavily colonised by the radical eastern intelligentsia, were clearly cognisant of Marx and debates about Marxism. The young Einstein, who as is known married a Yugoslav fellow-student from Zürich, was therefore in touch with this milieu. But for practical purposes these contacts between the natural sciences and Marxism must be regarded as biographical and marginal. The subject can be neglected.

This was naturally far from the case in philosophy, and even more in the social sciences. Marxism could not but raise profound philosophical questions which called for some discussion. Where the influence of Hegel was powerful, as in Italy and Russia, this discussion was intense. (In the absence of a strong Marxist movement the British philosophical Hegelians, mainly an Oxford group, showed little interest in Marx, though several were drawn towards social reform.) Germany, the home of philosophers, was at this time notably non-Hegelian, and not only because of the family connection between Hegel and Marx.[39] *Neue Zeit* had to rely on Russians like Plekhanov for its discussions of Hegelian themes, in the absence of German social democrats with this philosophical expertise.

Conversely, the far more influential neo-Kantian school not only, as already suggested, influenced some German Marxists substantially (e.g. among the revisionists and Austro-Marxists), but also developed some sympathetic interest in social democracy; as e.g. in Vorländer, *Kant und des Sozialismus* (Berlin, 1900). Among the philosophers, therefore, the Marxist presence is undeniable.

Of the social sciences, economics remained fairly solidly hostile to Marx, and the marginalist neo-classicism of the dominant schools (the Austrian, Anglo-Scandinavian and Italo-Swiss) clearly had few points of contact with his kind of political economy. While the Austrians spent much time refuting him (Menger, Böhm-Bawerk), the Anglo-Scandinavians did not even bother to do so after the 1880s, when several of them had satisfied themselves that Marxian political economy was wrong.[40] This does not mean that the Marxian presence was not felt. The most brilliant younger member of the Austrian school, Josef Schumpeter (1883–1950), was from the start of his scientific career (1908) preoccupied with the historic fate of capitalism and the problem of providing an alternative interpretation of economic development to Marx's (see his *Theorie der wirtschaftlichen Entwicklung*, 1912). However, the deliberate restriction of the field of economics by the new orthodoxies made it difficult for it to contribute to such major macro-economic problems as growth and economic crises. Curiously enough, the Italians' interest (from a strictly non-Marxist or anti-Marxist point of view) in socialism led to the demonstration – against the Austrian Mises, who had argued the contrary – that a socialist economy was theoretically feasible. Pareto had already argued that its impracticability could not be theoretically proved, before Barone (1908) produced his fundamental paper on 'Il ministro della produzione nello stato collettivo', which was to make its impact on economic debate after our period. Some Marxist influence, or stimulus, may perhaps be detected in the 'institutional' school or current of American economics then popular in the USA where, as already mentioned, the strong sympathy of many economists for 'progressivism' and social reform inclined them to look favourably on economic theories critical of big business (R.T. Ely, the Wisconsin school; above all Thorstein Veblen).

Economics as a discipline separate from the rest of the social sciences hardly existed in Germany, where the influence of the 'historical school' and the concept of the *Staatswissenschaften* (best translated as 'policy sciences') was dominant. The impact of Marxism, i.e. of the massive fact of German social democracy, on economics cannot be treated in isolation. It need hardly be said that the official social sciences of Wilhelmine Germany were strongly anti-Marxist, though the old liberals, who had engaged in polemics with Marx himself (Lujo Brentano, Schäffle)[41] seem to have been more eager to plunge into controversy than the more Prussian-oriented school of Schmoller. *Schmoller's Jahrbuch* abstained from printing any article about Marx before 1898, while Schäffle's *Zeitschrift für die gesamte Staatswissenschaft* reacted to the rise of social democracy with a salvo of articles (seven between 1890 and 1894) before falling silent on the subject. In general, as suggested earlier, the concern of German social science with Marxism increased with the strength of the SPD.

If German social sciences kept its distance from a specialised economics, it also distrusted a specialised sociology, which it identified with France and Britain, and – as in other countries – with too sympathetic an interest in the left.[42] And indeed sociology as a special field only began to emerge in Germany in the last years before the First World War (1909). Still, if we survey sociological thought, whatever it chose to call itself, the influence of Marx was, then as later, strongly felt. Gothein had no doubt that Marx and Engels, whose approach to social science was more convincing than Quetelet's and 'even more logical and coherent' than Comte's, had provided the most powerful single impetus.[43] And at the end of our period a quotation from one of the most influential American sociologists may indicate the standing of Marxism. 'Marx', wrote Albion Small in 1912, 'was one of the few really great thinkers in the history of social science . . . I do not think that Marx added to social science a single formula which will be final in the terms in which he expressed it. In spite of that I confidently predict that in the ultimate judgment of history Marx will have a place in social science analogous to Galileo in physical science.'[44]

The influence of Marxism was evidently promoted by the political radicalism of many sociologists who, Marxists or not, found themselves close to the social-democratic movements, as in Belgium. Thus Leon Winiarski, whose now forgotten theories can hardly be called Marxist in any sense, is found contributing an article on 'Socialism in Russian Poland' to *Neue Zeit* (1, 1891). The direct influence of Marx on non-Marxists may be illustrated by the founders of the German Sociological Society who included Max Weber and Ernst Troeltsch, Georg Simmel and Ferdinand Tönnies, of whom it has been said that 'it seems clear that Marx's resolute exposure of the seamier side of competition exerted an influence . . . second only to that of Thomas

Hobbes'.[45] Weber's *Archiv für Sozialwissenschaft und Sozialpolitik* was perhaps the only organ of German social science which opened itself to the collaboration of writers close to, influenced by, or even identified with socialism.

Little need be said about the mixture of eclectic borrowings from Marx with positivism and anti-Marxism polemic in Italian, Russian, Polish or even Austrian sociology, except that they also demonstrate the presence of Marx; there is even less to say of remoter countries in which sociology and Marxism were virtually identified, as among the few Serbian practitioners of the subject. However, the notable weakness of the Marxist presence in France, though not expected, may be noted, as in Durkheim. Though the strongly Republican and Dreyfusard milieu of French sociology inclined it to the left, and several of the younger members of the *Année Sociologique* group became socialists, some Marxist influence has only been claimed in the case of Halbwachs (1977–1945) and is doubtful, at any rate before 1914.

Whether we read intellectual history backwards, singling out the thinkers who have since come to be accepted as the ancestors of modern sociology, or whether we look at what was accepted as the influential sociology in the 1880s–1900s (Gumplowicz, Tatzenhofer, Loria, Winiarski, etc.), the presence of Marxism is both strong and undeniable. The same is true in the field of what today would be called political science. The traditional political theory of 'the state', developed in this period, perhaps chiefly by philosophers and jurists, was certainly not Marxist, yet, as we have already seen, the philosophical challenge of historical materialism was strongly felt and answered. The concrete investigation of how politics operated in practice, including such novel subjects for study as social movements and political parties, was likely to be more directly influenced. We need not claim that, at a time when the emergence of democratic politics and mass popular parties made the class struggle and the political management of the masses (or their resistance to such management) a matter of acute practical concern, theorists needed Marx to discover them. Ostrogorski (1854–1921), exceptionally for a Russian, shows no more signs of Marx's influence than de Tocqueville, Bagehot or Bryce. Nevertheless, Gumplowicz's doctrine that the state is always the tool of the minority holding the majority in subjection, which may have even had some effect on Pareto and Mosca, was certainly in part influenced by Marx, and the Marxist influence on Sorel and Michels is obvious. Little more need be said about a field which was then little developed in comparison with more recent periods.

If sociology was obviously influenced by Marx, the fortress of official academic history defended itself passionately against any such incursions, especially in the West. It was a defence not only against social democracy and revolution, but against all the social sciences. It denied historical laws, the primacy of forces other than politics and ideas, evolution through a series of pre-determined stages; indeed it doubted the legitimacy of any historical generalisation. 'The basic issue', argued the young Otto Hintze, 'is the old controversial question about whether historic phenomena have the regularity of law'.[46] Or, as a less cautious review of Labriola put it, 'History will and should be a descriptive discipline.'[47]

The enemy was thus not only Marx but any encroachment by social scientists on the historian's field. In the acrimonious German debates of the mid-90s, which had some international echoes, the main adversary was not Marx but the polemically minded Karl Lamprecht; all historians inspired by Comte; or – the tone of suspicion is clear – any economic history which tended to derive political history from socio-economic evolution, or even any economic history.[48] And yet in Germany at least it was evident that Marxism was much in the minds of those who attacked all 'collectivist' history as essentially a 'materialist conception of history'.[49] Conversely, Lamprecht (supported by younger historians like R. Ehrenberg, whose *Zeitalter der Fugger* came under similar attack) claimed that he was accused of materialism in order to identify him with Marxism. Since the *Neue Zeit*, while criticising him, also thought that among bourgeois historians he 'had come closest to historical materialism' his disclaimers carried little conviction among the orthodox, who hinted that he 'has perhaps learned more from Marx than his school is willing to admit to itself.[50]

It would therefore be mistaken to look for the influence of Marxism only among frankly Marxist historians, of whom there were few; some of whom could, very properly, be dismissed as historically unqualified propagandists.[51] As in the field of sociology, it is to be looked for among writers who attempted to answer similar questions to Marx's, whether or not they arrived at similar answers. That is to say it was felt among historians who sought to integrate the field of narrative, political, institutional and cultural history into a wider framework of social and economic transformations. Few of these were orthodox academic historians, though the influence of Lamprecht was clearly dominant in the Belgian Henri Pirenne, who was very far from any kind of socialism.[52] He wrote a determined defence of Lamprecht in the *Revue Historique* (1897).[53] Economic and social history – largely separate from ordinary history – was the most receptive ground, and indeed younger historians, repelled by the aridity of official conservatism, began to feel themselves more at home in this specialised field. As we have seen, even in Germany itself the first journal of economic and social history was a (largely Austrian) Marxist initiative. The most brilliant economic historian of his generation in England, George Unwin, who took to his subject in order to refute Marx, was nevertheless convinced that 'Marx was trying to get at the right kinds of history. The orthodox historians ignore all the most significant factors in human development.[54] Nor should the influence of the Narodnik-Marxist-saturated Russian historians be underestimated: Kareiev and Loutchisky in France, Vinogradov in Britain.

To sum up: Marxism was part of a general tendency to integrate history into the social sciences, and in particular to stress the fundamental role of social and economic factors even in political and intellectual developments.[55] Since it was admittedly the most comprehensive, powerful and consistent theory attempting to do so, its influence, though not rigidly separable from others, was substantial. Just as Marx recognisably provided a more serious base for a science of society than Comte, if only because he also included a sociology of knowledge which already exercised 'a great if subterranean influence' on non-Marxists such as Max Weber, so there were already good observers who knew that the real challenge to traditional history came from him rather than from, say, a Lamprecht.

Still, the actual Marxist influence on non-Marxist thought is not always clearly specifiable or definable. There is a large grey zone in which it was obviously, and increasingly, present, though disclaimed on political grounds by both Marxists and non-Marxists. Were the reviewers in the *Historische Zeitschrift* converging with Marxism when they claimed that Labriola 'gets closer to the conceptions of bourgeois historians than other younger representatives of socialist theory' or that he 'as is known, represents a moderate materialism'?[56] Plainly they did not think so, since they rejected both him and Marx. Yet it is in this grey zone in which non-Marxists recognised that they could not totally disagree with what Marxists said, that we must look for most of the Marxist influence upon them and upon the culture of non-Marxists in general. At the time of Marx's death it had been small, if only because Marx was little known or read outside the intelligentsia of Eastern Europe. By 1914 it had become very large. Few educated persons, in large areas of Europe, were now unaware of his existence, and some aspects of his theory had entered the public domain.

VI

We are left with the even more general problem of the relations between Marxism and the arts, and especially the cultural avantgarde which played an increasingly important role in the arts during this period. There is no necessary or logical connection between the two phenomena, since the assumption that what is revolutionary in the arts must also be revolutionary in politics is based on a semantic muddle. On the other hand there is or was frequently an existential connection, since social democrats and the artistic and cultural avantgarde were both outsiders, opposed to and by bourgeois orthodoxy; not to mention the youth and, quite often, the relative poverty of many members of the avantgarde and bohème. Both were to some extent pressed into a not unfriendly coexistence, with each other and with other dissidents from the morals and value systems of bourgeois society. Politically revolutionary or 'progressive' minority movements attracted not only the usual fringe of cultural heterodoxy and alternative lifestyles – vegetarians, spiritualists, theosophists, etc. – but independent and emancipated women, challengers of sexual orthodoxy, and young people of both sexes who had not yet made their way into bourgeois society, or rebelled against it in whatever way they thought most demonstrative, or felt excluded from it. Heterodoxies overlapped. Such milieus are familiar to every cultural historian. The small British socialist movement of the 1880s provides several examples. Eleanor Marx was not only a Marxian militant but a free professional woman who rejected official marriage, a translator of Ibsen and an amateur actress. Bernard Shaw was a Marxist-influenced socialist activist, a self-made literary man, a hammer of conventional orthodoxy as a critic of music and drama, and a champion of the avantgarde in arts and thought (Wagner, Ibsen). The avantgarde Arts and Crafts movement (William Morris, Walter Crane) was drawn into (Marxian) socialism, while the avantgarde of sexual liberation – the homosexual Edward Carpenter and the champion of general sexual liberation Havelock Ellis – operated in the same milieu. Oscar Wilde, though political action was hardly his field, was much attracted to socialism and wrote a book on the subject.

Fortunately for this coexistence of the avantgardes and Marxism, Marx and Engels had written very little specifically about the arts and published even less. The early Marxists were therefore not seriously constrained in their tastes by a classical doctrine: Marx and Engels had shown no fondness for any contemporary avantgarde after the 1840s. At the same time the absence of a body of aesthetic doctrine in the founding fathers obliged them to evolve one. The most obvious criterion of contemporary arts acceptable to social democracy (there was never any doubt about the founding fathers) was that they should present the realities of capitalist society frankly and critically, preferably with special emphasis on the workers, and ideally with a commitment to their struggles. This did not in itself imply a preference for the avantgarde. Traditional and established writers and painters could just as easily extend their subject-matter or their social sympathies, and indeed among the painters the turn to the depiction of industrial scenes, workers or peasants and sometimes even scenes of labour struggles (as in H. Herkomer's *Strike*) was most usually found in mildly progressive but far from avantgarde figures (Liebermann, Leibl). However, these require no special discussion.

This kind of socialist aesthetics raised no special problems for the relations between Marxism and the avantgardes in the 1880s and 1890s, an era dominated, at least in prose literature, by realistic writers with strong social and political interests, or those which could be interpreted in this way. Some were increasingly influenced by the rise of labour to take a specific interest in the workers. Marxists had no difficulty in welcoming, on these grounds, the great Russian novelists whose discovery in the West was largely due to the 'progressives', the drama of Ibsen as well as other Scandinavian literature (Hamsun and, for modern eyes more surprisingly, Strindberg), but above all the writers of schools described as 'naturalist', who were so patently preoccupied with those aspects of capitalist reality from which conventional artists turned aside (Zola and Maupassant in France, Hauptmann and Sudermann in Germany, Verga in Italy). That so many naturalists were political and social campaigners or even, like Hauptmann, attracted to social democracy[57] made naturalism even more acceptable. Of course the ideologists were careful to distinguish between socialist consciousness and mere muck-racking. Mehring, surveying naturalism in 1892–3, welcomed it as a sign that 'art begins to feel capitalism in its own body', drawing a parallel, then less unexpected than it would be today, between it and impressionism: 'Indeed in this manner we can easily explain the otherwise inexplicable pleasure which the Impressionists . . . and the Naturalists . . . take in all the unclean refuse of capitalist society; they live and work amid such rubbish, and, moved by obscure instinct, can find no more tormenting protest to throw at the faces of those who torment them'.[58] But, he argued, this was at best a first step toward a 'true' art. Nevertheless, *Neue Zeit*, which opened its columns to 'modernists',[59] reviewed or published Hauptmann, Maupassant, Korolenko, Dostoyevsky, Strindberg, Hamsun, Zola, Ibsen, Björnson, Tolstoi and Gorki. And Mehring himself did not deny that German naturalism was drawn to social democracy, even if he believed that 'bourgeois naturalists are socialist-minded, as feudal socialists were bourgeois-minded, no more and no less'.[60]

A second significant point of contact between Marxism and the arts was visual. On the one hand a number of socially conscious visual artists discovered the working class as a subject and were therefore drawn towards the labour movement. Here are elsewhere in the avantgarde culture, the role of the Low Countries, situated at the intersection of French, British and to some extent German influences, and with a particularly exploited and brutalised labouring population (in Belgium), was significant. Indeed the international cultural role of these countries – especially Belgium – was at this period, as already mentioned, more central than for some centuries past: neither symbolism nor art nouveau and later modernist architecture and avantgarde painting after the Impressionists can be understood without their contribution. Specifically, in the 1880s the Belgian Constantin Meunier (1831–1905), one of a group of artists close to the Belgian Labour Party, pioneered what later became the standard socialist iconography of 'the worker' – the muscular bare-chested labouring man, the emaciated and suffering proletarian wife and mother. (Van Gogh's explorations in the world of the poor only became known later.) Marxist critics like Plekhanov treated this extension of the subject-matter of painting into the world of capitalism's victims with the usual reticence, even when it went beyond mere documentation or the expression of social pity. Nevertheless, for those artists primarily interested in their subject-matter, it built a bridge between their world and the milieu in which Marxism was debated.

A more powerful and direct link with socialism came through the applied and decorative arts. The link was direct and conscious, especially in the British Arts and Crafts movement, whose great master William Morris (1834–96) became a sort of Marxist and made both a powerful theoretical as well as an outstanding practical contribution to the social transformation of the arts. These branches of the arts took as their point of departure not the individual and isolated artist but the artisan. They protested against the reduction of the creative worker-craftsman into a mere 'operative' by capitalist industry, and their main object was not to create individual works of art, ideally designed to be contemplated in isolation, but the framework of human daily life, such as villages and towns, houses and their interior furnishings. As it happened, for economic reasons the main market for their products was found among the culturally adventurous bourgeoisie and the professional middle classes – a fate also familiar to champions of a 'people's theatre' then and later.[61] Indeed, the Arts and Crafts movement and its development, 'art nouveau', pioneered the first genuinely comfortable bourgeois lifestyle of the nineteenth century, the suburban or semi-rural 'cottage' or 'villa', and the style, in various versions, also found a particular welcome in young or provincial bourgeois communities anxious to express their cultural identity – in Brussels and Barcelona, Glasgow, Helsinki and Prague. Nevertheless, the social ambitions of the artist-craftsmen and architects of this avantgarde were not confined to supplying middle-class needs. They pioneered modern architecture and town-planning in which the social-utopian element is evident – and these 'pioneers of the modern movement' often, as in the case of W.R. Lethaby (1857–1931), Patrick Geddes and the champions of garden cities, came from the British progressive-socialist milieu. On the continent its champions were closely associated with social democracy. Victor Horta (1861–1947), the great architect of the Belgian art nouveau, designed the Maison du Peuple of Brussels (1897), at whose 'art section' H. Van de Velde, later a key figure in the development of the modern movement in Germany, gave lectures on William Morris. The socialist pioneer of Dutch modern architecture, H.P. Berlage (1856–1934), designed the offices of the Amsterdam Diamond Workers' Union (1899).

The crucial fact is that the new politics and the new arts converged at this point. Even more significantly, the original (mainly British) artists who pioneered this revolution in the applied arts were not merely directly influenced by Marxism, as for instance Morris, but also – with Walter Crane – provided much of the internationally current iconographical vocabulary of the social-democratic movement. Indeed, William Morris developed a powerful analysis of the relations between art and society which he certainly consid ered Marxist, even though we can also detect the earlier influences of the Pre-Raphaelites and Ruskin. Curiously enough, orthodox Marxist thinking about the arts remained almost completely unaffected by these developments. William Morris's writings have not, to this day, made their way into the mainstream of Marxist aesthetic debates, though after 1945 they became much better known and found powerful Marxist champions.[62]

No equally obvious links brought together the Marxists and the other main group of avantgardists of the 1880s and 1890s, whom we may roughly call the symbolists. Yet it remains a fact that most symbolist poets had revolutionary or socialist sympathies. In France they were chiefly attracted to anarchism in the early 1890s, like most of the newer painters of the period (the older Impressionists were, with odd exceptions like Pissarro, rather apolitical). Presumably this was not because they had any objection in principle to Marx – 'the majority of young poets' who were converted 'to the doctrines of revolt, whether those of Bakunin or Karl Marx'[63] probably would have welcomed any suitably rebellious banner – but because the French socialist leaders (until the rise of Jaurès) did not inspire them. The schoolmasterly philistinism of the Guesdistes in particular would hardly attract them, while the anarchists not only took a much greater interest in the arts but certainly included significant painters and critics among their early militants, e.g. Félix Fénéon.[64] Conversely, in Belgium it was the Parti Ouvrier Belge which attracted symbolists, not only because it included the anarchising rebels, but also because the group of its leaders or spokesmen who came from the cultured middle class were visibly and actively interested in the arts. Jules Destrée wrote extensively about socialism and art and published a catalogue of Odilon Redon's lithographs; Vandervelde frequented poets; Maeterlinck remained associated with the party until almost 1914; Verhaeren almost became its official poet; the painters Eekhoud and Khnopff were active in the Maison du Peuple. It is true that symbolism flourished in countries where Marxist theorists keen to condemn it (like Plekhanov) were hardly present. Relations between artistic and political revolt were thus amicable enough.

Hence, until the end of the century, a good deal of common

ground existed between the cultural avantgardes and the arts admired by discriminating minorities on the one hand and the increasingly Marxist-influenced social democracy on the other. The socialist intellectuals who became leaders in the new parties – characteristically born around 1860 – were still young enough not to have lost contact with the tastes of 'the advanced': even the oldest, Victor Adler (b.1852) and Kautsky (b.1854), were still well below forty in 1890. Adler, a frequenter of the Café Griensteidl, main centre of Viennese artists and intellectuals, was thus not only deeply impregnated with classical literature and music, but also a passionate Wagnerian (like Plekhanov and Shaw, he stressed the revolutionary and 'socialist' implications of Wagner more than is usual today), an enthusiast for his friend Gustav Mahler, an early champion of Bruckner, an admirer, in common with almost all socialists of this generation, of Ibsen and Dostoyevsky, and profoundly moved by Verhaeren, whose poems he translated.[65] Conversely, as we have seen, a large part of the naturalists, symbolists and other 'advanced' schools of the time were drawn towards the labour movement and (outside France) social democracy. The attraction was not always lasting: the Austrian *littérateur* Hermann Bahr, who fancied himself as a spokesman of 'the moderns', veered away from Marxism at the end of the 1880s, and the great naturalist Hauptmann moved in a symbolist direction which confirmed the theoretical reservations of Marxist commentators. The split between socialists and anarchists also had its effects, since it is clear that some (particularly in the visual arts) had always been attracted by the pure rebellion of the latter. Still, 'the moderns' felt at home in the neighbourhood of the labour movements, and the Marxists, at least the cultured intellectuals among them, with 'the moderns'.

For reasons which have not been adequately investigated these links were broken for a time. Some reasons may be suggested. In the first place, as the 'crisis in Marxism' demonstrated in the late 1890s, the belief that capitalism was on the verge of breakdown, the socialist movement on the verge of revolutionary triumph, could no longer be maintained in Western Europe. Intellectuals and artists who had been drawn to a broad, vaguely defined movement of workers by the general air of hope, confidence, even utopian expectation which it generated round itself now faced a movement uncertain of its future prospects and riven by internal and increasingly sectarian debates. This ideological fragmentation was also present in Eastern Europe: it was one thing to sympathise with a movement all of whose currents appeared to converge in a generally Marxist direction, as in the early 1890s, or with Polish socialism before the split between nationalists and anti-nationalists, and quite another to make a selection between rival and mutually hostile bodies of revolutionaries and ex-revolutionaries.

In the West, however, there was the additional fact that the new movements became increasingly institutionalised, involved in the daily politics which were unlikely to excite artists and writers, while they became in practice reformist, leaving the future revolution to some version of historical inevitability. Moreover, institutionalised mass parties, often developing their own cultural world, were less likely to favour arts which a working-class public would not readily understand or approve. It is true that the subscribers to German workers' libraries increasingly abandoned political books for fiction, while also reading less poetry and classical literature; but their most popular writer, almost certainly Friedrich Gerstaecker, an author of adventure tales, would not inspire the avantgarde.[66] It is hardly surprising that in Vienna Karl Kraus, though initially much drawn towards the social democrats by his own cultural and political dissidence, moved away from them in the 1900s. He blamed them for not fostering a sufficiently serious cultural level among the workers, and was not inspired by the party's major – and eventually victorious – campaign for universal suffrage.[67]

The revolutionary left of social democracy, initially somewhat marginal in the West, and the revolutionary syndicalist or
anarchist tendencies were more likely to attract avantgarde culture of a radical turn of mind. After 1900 the anarchists in
particular increasingly found their social base, outside some
Latin countries, in a milieu composed of bohemians and some
self-educated workers, shading over into the *Lumpenproletariat* – in
the various Montmartres of the Western world – and settled
down into a general subculture of those who rejected, or were
not assimilable by, 'bourgeois' lifestyles or organised mass movements.[68] This essentially individualist and antinomian rebellion
was not opposed to social revolution. It often merely waited for
a suitable movement of revolt and revolution to which it could
attach itself, and was once again mobilised en masse against the
war and for the Russian Revolution. The Munich soviet of 1919
gave it perhaps its major moment of political assertion. Yet
both in reality and in theory it turned away from Marxism.
Nietzsche, a thinker who was for fairly obvious reasons deeply
unattractive to Marxists or other social democrats, in spite of his
hatred of 'the bourgeois', became a characteristic guru of anarchist and anarchising rebels, as of non-political middle-class
cultural dissidence.

Conversely, the very cultural radicalism of avantgarde developments in the new century cut them off from workers'
movements whose members remained traditional in their tastes,
inasmuch as they (and the movement) remained attached to the
understood languages and symbolic codes of communication
which expressed the contents of works of art. The avantgardes
of the last quarter of the century had not yet broken with these
languages, though they had stretched them. With a little adjust-
ment it was perfectly possible to discern what Wagner and the
Impressionists, or even a good many of the symbolists, 'were
about'. From the early twentieth century – perhaps the Paris
Salon d'Automne of 1905 marks the break in the visual arts –
this was no longer so.

Moreover, the socialist leaders, even the younger generation born after 1870, were no longer 'in touch'. Rosa Luxemburg had to defend herself against the charge of not liking 'the modern writers'; but though she had been much moved by the avantgarde of the 1890s, such as the German naturalist poets, she admitted that she did not understand Hofmannsthal and had never heard of Stefan George.[69] And even Trotsky, who prided himself on much closer contact with new cultural fashions – he wrote a lengthy analysis of Frank Wedekind for *Neue Zeit* in 1908 and reviewed art exhibitions – does not appear to show any specific familiarity with what the adventurous young in 1905–14 would have regarded as the avantgarde – except, of course, in Russian literature. Like Rosa Luxemburg, he noted and disapproved of its extreme subjectivism – its capacity, in Luxemburg's words, to express 'a state of mind' – but nothing else ('but one cannot make human beings with states of mind'.[70] Unlike her, he attempted a Marxist interpretation of the new trends of subjectivist rebellion and the 'purely aesthetic logic' which 'naturally transformed the revolt against academicism into a revolt of self-sufficient artistic form against content, considered as an indifferent fact'.[71] He ascribed it to the novelty of life in the environment of the modern giant city, and more specifically the expression of this experience by the intellectuals who lived in these modern Babylons. No doubt both Luxemburg and Trotsky echoed the particularly strong social preconceptions of Russian aesthetic theory, but at bottom they reflected a very general attitude of Marxists, eastern or western. Someone particularly interested in the arts and anxious to maintain contact with the latest trends might develop a taste for some of these innovations as a private individual, but how exactly was such an interest to be linked to his or her socialist activities and convictions?

It was not simply a matter of age, though few of the established names in the International were below thirty in 1910, and most were well into middle age. What Marxists understandably failed to appreciate was what they saw as a retreat (rather than, as the avantgarde saw it, an advance) into formal virtuosity and experiment, an abandonment of the content of the arts, including their overt and recognisable social and political content. What they could not accept was the avantgarde's choice of a pure subjectivism, almost solipsism, such as Plekhanov detected in the Cubists.[72] It was already regrettable, if explicable, that 'among the bourgeois ideologists who go over to the side of the proletariat there are very few practitioners of the arts' (Künstler); and in the years before 1914 there seemed to be even fewer who were drawn towards the workers' movement than before 1900. The avantgarde of French painters was 'à l'écart de toute agitation intellectuelle et sociale, confinés dans les conflits de technique' ('removed from any intellectual and social agitation, confining itself to arguments about technique').[73] But more than this, in 1912–13 Plekhanov could state as something evident that 'the majority of today's artists occupy the bourgeois standpoint and are totally impervious to the great ideas of freedom of our time.'[74] It was not easy, among the mass of artists who claimed to be 'anti-bourgeois', to find more than a few who were close to the organised socialist movements – even the anarchists found fewer devoted enthusiasts among the painters than they had done in the 1890s – but it was a good deal easier to discover those who complained about the philistinism of the workers, frank elitists like the Stefan George circle in Germany or the Russian acmeists, searchers for (preferably female) aristocratic company, and even – especially in literature – potential and actual reactionaries. Moreover, it must not be forgotten that the new experimental avantgardes rebelled not so much against academicism as against precisely those avantgardes of the 1880s and 1890s which had been relatively close to the labour and socialist movements at that time.

In short, what could Marxists see in these new avantgardes except yet another symptom of the crisis of bourgeois culture, and the avantgardes in Marxism except yet another proof that the past could not understand the future? No doubt there were some among the few dozen individuals on whose patronage (as collectors or dealers) the new painters depended who were also Marxist sympathisers (e.g. Morozov and Shchukin). The amateurs of rebellious art were unlikely to be politically conservative at this time. The occasional Marxist theorist – Lunacharski, Bogdanov – might even rationalise his sympathy for the innovators, but was likely to meet with resistance. Yet the cultural world of the socialist and labour movements had no obvious place for the new avantgardes, and the orthodox aesthetic theorists of Marxism (de facto a Central and Eastern European species) condemned them.

However, if some of the new avantgardes certainly remained remote from socialism or any other politics – and some were to become frankly reactionary or even fascist – a great part of the rebels in the arts were merely waiting for a historic conjuncture when artistic and political revolt could once again merge. They found it after 1914 in the movement against the war and in the Russian Revolution. After 1917 the junction between Marxism (in the shape of Lenin's Bolshevism) and the avantgarde was once again made, initially mainly in Russia and Germany. The era of what the Nazis called (not incorrectly) *Kulturbolschewismus* does not fall within the scope of this chapter: the history of Marxism in the period of the Second International. Nevertheless the post-1917 developments must be mentioned, because they led to the bifurcation of Marxist aesthetic theory between the 'realists' and the 'avangardistes' – the conflicts between Lukacs and Brecht, the admirers of Tolstoi and those of James Joyce. And as we have seen, this division had its roots in the period before 1914.

If we look back on the period of the Second International as a whole, we must conclude that the relation between Marxism and the arts was never comfortable, even before 1900 – when it became so noticeably difficult. Marxist theorists had never felt completely happy about any of the 'modern' movements of the 1880s and 1890s, leaving their enthusiastic championship to intellectuals on the fringes of Marxism (as in Belgium) or to non-Marxist revolutionaries and socialists. The leading ortho-dox Marxist critics saw themselves as commentators or referees rather than supporters or players in the football match of cul-ture. This did no harm to their historical analysis of artistic developments as symptoms of the decay of bourgeois society – an impressive analysis. And yet we cannot but be struck by the externality of their observations. Every Marxist intellectual saw himself or herself as a participant in the labours of philosophy and the sciences, however amateur; hardly any saw themselves as participants in the creative arts. They analysed the relation of art to society and the movement and gave good or bad marks to schools, artists and works. At most they cherished such few artists as actually joined their movements, and made allowances for their personal and ideological vagaries, as bourgeois society also did. The influence of Marxism on the arts was therefore likely to be peripheral. Even naturalism and symbolism, which were close to the socialist movements of their time, would have evolved very much in the way they did if Marxists had taken no interest at all in them. In fact, Marxists found it difficult to see any role for the artist under capitalism except as a propagandist, a sociological symptom or a 'classic'. One is tempted to say that the Marxism of the Second International really had no ade-quate theory of the arts and, unlike in the case of the 'national question', was not obliged by political urgency to discover its theoretical inadequacy.

But within the Marxism of the Second International there was a genuine theory of the arts in society, though the official corpus of Marxist doctrine was not aware of it: the theory most fully developed by William Morris. If there was a major and lasting Marxist influence on the arts, it came through this cur-rent of thought, which looked beyond the structure of the arts in the bourgeois era (the individual 'artist') to the element of artistic creation in all labour and the (traditional) arts of popu-lar life, and beyond the equivalent of commodity production in art (the individual 'work of art') to the environment of everyday life. Characteristically, it was the only branch of Marxist aesthetic theory which paid attention to architecture, and indeed regarded it as the key to and crown of the arts.[75] If Marxist criticism was the fly on the wheel of naturalism or 'realism', it was the engine of the Arts and Crafts movement, whose historic impact on modern architecture and design was and remains fundamental.

It was neglected because Morris, who was one of the earliest British Marxists,[76] was seen merely as a famous artist but a political lightweight, and no doubt also because the British tradition of theorising about art and society (neo-romantic medievalism, Ruskin), which he merged with Marxism, had little contact with the mainstream of Marxist thought. Yet it came from within the arts, it was Marxist – at least Morris declared that it was – and it converted and influenced practitioners in the arts, designers, architects and town-planners, and not least the organisers of museums and art schools, over a large part of Europe. Nor was it accidental that this major Marxist influence on the arts came from Britain, though in that country Marxism was of negligible importance. For at this period Britain was the only European country sufficiently transformed by capitalism for industrial production to have transformed artisan production. On reflection, it is not surprising that Marx's 'classic' country of capitalist development produced the only major critique of what capitalism did to the arts. Nor was it surprising that the Marxist element in this significant movement within the arts has been forgotten. Morris himself was sufficiently realistic to know that while capitalism lasted, art could not become socialist.[77] As capitalism emerged from its crisis to flourish and expand, it appropriated and absorbed the arts of the revolutionaries. The comfortable and cultured middle class, the industrial designers, took it over. The greatest work of H.P. Berlage, the Dutch socialist architect, is not the building of the Diamond Workers' Union but the

Amsterdam Stock Exchange. The nearest Morrisian town-planners got to their people's cities were 'garden suburbs', eventually occupied by the middle class, and 'garden cities' remote from industry. In this manner the arts reflect the hopes and the disappointments of the socialism of the Second International.

11

In the Era of Anti-fascism 1929–45

I

The 1930s is the decade in which Marxism became a serious force among the intellectuals of Western Europe and the English-speaking world. It had long been such a force in Eastern and parts of Central Europe and the Russian Revolution had naturally attracted numerous Western socialists and other rebels and revolutionaries. However, contrary to common belief, after the revolutionary wave of 1917–20 subsided, the type of Marxism which became overwhelmingly predominant – that of the Communist International – did not demonstrate any very strong attraction for Western intellectuals, especially those of bourgeois origin. Some dissident Marxist groups were more attractive to them, notably Trotskyism, but such groups were numerically so small compared with the main communist parties that this is quantitatively negligible. Most communist parties in the West were predominantly proletarian, and the situation of the 'bourgeois' intellectual in them was often anomalous and not always comfortable.[1,2] Moreover, particularly after the period of 'bolshevisation', the role of workers in the leadership of such parties had been deliberately stressed. Unlike the parties of the Second International, few of the prominent leaders of communist parties were intellectuals (except in some of the under-developed and colonial countries), nor did such parties usually take pride in having intellectuals at their head, though they liked having prominent ones associated with them in other capacities. The influx of intellectuals into Communist parties in the 1930s was therefore a new phenomenon: in Britain almost 15% of the delegates to the CP Congress of 1938 were students or members of the professions.[3]

The penetration of intellectual Marxism into these Western countries was not only novel but autochthonous. The significance of political refugees for the diffusion of socialism, and notably Marxism, in the era of the Second International has attracted some attention,[4] and the 1930s was, alas, a period of massive political emigration. Moreover, the impact of such emigrants on the intellectual life of the receiving countries was profound, both in Britain and even more in the USA, though probably not so much in France. But on the Marxism of the native generations which now turned in this direction in the West it had no major impact.

This was perhaps due to the fact that the version which overwhelmingly attracted them was that associated with the communist parties and the USSR, which was made available through the publication of 'the classics' (now including Lenin and Stalin as well as Plekhanov) in translation. A standardised international version of Marxism now existed, most systematically exemplified by the section on 'Dialectical and Historical Materialism' in the *History of the CPSU(b): Short Course* of 1938. Orthodox communist refugees would not therefore bring with them, or care to propagate in public, anything they knew to be at variance with this standard version. Heterodox Marxists or *Marxisants* would be relatively isolated by the known fact of their heterodoxy, even if contact with them was not actually prohibited for loyal communists, as it was with the followers of Trotsky.

Two further factors diminished the influence of the Marxist diaspora. The first was linguistic. The two major languages of earlier Marxist discourse, German and Russian, were not widely known in the West, or not known at all.[5] Outside the USA there was no major public of Russian or German origin capable of reading works in those languages and likely to be interested in left-wing literature. Thus even writers acceptable to orthodox communists were inaccessible unless translated. But they rarely were. The first collection of Lukacs' studies published in English in book form dates from 1950, and even so basic a text as Marx's *Frühschriften*, available since 1932, made its impact in France only through the two or three individuals who could read it in German, and then not immediately. Conversely, of course, the works that were translated acquired a disproportionate significance, as witness the revolutionary impact on British scientists of B. Hessen's paper on Newton (see page 294 below). The second factor was the growing closure of native societies against the influx of immigrants. The political or other emigrants from Hitler's Germany were reluctantly accepted in the West, but with the partial exception of the USA they were neither welcomed nor, except in special cases, integrated. They remained marginal and often unknown.[6] The Western Marxists thus developed independently of the central Marxist tradition or traditions. It is perhaps no accident that the first, and still in many ways the best, account of Marxist economic theory in English which embodied the debates and developments of the period of the Second International was published in the USA, that is to say in a country where the separation between the Marxism (or knowledge of Marxism) of the emigrants and the native 'new left' of the period was least marked.[7]

The penetration of Marxism was therefore a paradoxical phenomenon. It was home-grown and not imported, inasmuch as it took place in each country independent of outside influences other than official communism. At the same time it overwhelmingly took a uniform and standardised form for this very reason. And yet this uniformity cannot conceal a distinct tendency towards national intellectual segregation, which contrasts both with the period of the Second International and with the international character of intellectual Marxism since about 1960. This was due in part to the very centralised and disciplined structure of the Communist International and the increasingly 'official' character of the writings which emanated from it and the USSR, but which – until about 1948 – operated rather selectively (see below). International communist journals, published in various languages, with some regional variations in content, such as the *International Press Correspondence* and the *Communist International*, were overwhelmingly concerned with current politics and mainly written by political leaders and what might be called the international staff writers of the movement. There was in the 1930s no equivalent to the *Neue Zeit* in any language.[8] Conversely, the theoretical, intellectual and cultural Marxist or *Marxisant* journals which began to appear in various Western countries in the later 1930s were left mainly to intellectuals lacking political authority, and had no significant international resonance beyond the native speakers of the languages in which they were written, though some established international connections. So, paradoxically, there was scope for local variation and development insofar as there was no international 'line' on a subject, or insofar as that 'line' was not adequately advertised as mandatory. There was thus, as we shall see, a good deal of independent Marxist theorising, e.g. about the natural sciences and about literature in Britain, some of which eventually fell victim to the imposition of a more all-embracing orthodoxy in the Zhdanov period. However, basically, each country or cultural area in which Marxism was not officially prohibited adapted the standard international model in its own way and in the light of its local conditions – a development facilitated by the change in the Comintern's international line after 1934.

In one field only can we speak of a genuine non-centralised

internationalism of intellectuals on the left. Characteristically it was in the field of literature and the arts. These were linked to the politics of the left not so much through theoretical reflection as through an emotional commitment of their practitioners and admirers to the struggles of the period. Art and the left re-established strong links in the First World War, but not through orthodox Marxist theory. In the field of culture alone do we encounter a genuine resistance, even among communist intellectuals, to the imposition of orthodoxy. Few communists openly challenged 'socialist realism', which became official in the USSR from 1934, though it is significant that the debate about what might be called 'modernism' never quite ceased, and the unorthodox side never actually surrendered. Brecht did not give in to Lukacs. Sincere efforts were made to admire what came out of the USSR in the 1930s and to pass over in silence those of its productions which could not be admired (notably in painting and sculpture), but most of the genuine admiration went to what still survived of the Soviet art and literature of the 1920s. Few were prepared to disagree publicly with the official critique of the most celebrated international figures of the 'modern' movement in the arts, but even fewer were prepared, at least in private, to cease their admiration for Joyce, Matisse or Picasso, even when sincerely propagating styles closer to 'socialist realism'.[9] Jazz did not meet with the approval of the official orthodoxy, but its most passionate and active admirers, champions and practical supporters in the Anglo-Saxon world included a disproportionately large number of communists and their sympathisers.

Marxist intellectuals not cut off from the rest of the world therefore tended, whatever their country of origin, to share an international left-wing culture. It included writers and artists who identified themselves with communism or at least with commitment to the anti-fascist struggle, of whom there was fortunately a great number: Malraux, Silone, Brecht (insofar as he was then known), García Lorca, Dos Passos, Eisenstein, Picasso, etc.[10] For members of the communist parties it might include the corpus of writers more or less officially approved as communist or 'progressive': Barbusse, Rolland, Gorki, Andersen Nexö, Dreiser et al. It would almost certainly include the names which formed part of the international dramatis personae of educated culture, unless they were known to be identified with reaction and fascism: writers like Joyce and Proust, the famous (mainly French) painters of the early twentieth century, the celebrated architects of the 'modern movement' and, not least, the famous Russian filmmakers and Charlie Chaplin. The novelty of the 1930s lay not in the existence of such an international culture whose names were indifferently drawn from a variety of countries – in fact, mainly from France, America, the British Isles, Russia, Germany and Spain – but in its close association with political commitment to the left.[11] It was certainly not a specifically Marxist culture, but the role of a minority of committed Marxists (i.e., for practical purposes, of communists) in crystallising it was undoubtedly crucial.[12]

II

The radicalisation of intellectuals in the 1930s was rooted in a response to the traumatic crisis of capitalism in the early years of this decade. Its immediate origins, at least for the younger generations, are to be found in the Great Depression of 1929–33. Thus in Britain the first serious signs of the growth of an interest in Marxism and the Communist Party among intellectuals are to be found in 1931, when dialectical and historical materialism became a topic of debate among a small number of academics and a student communist group established itself here and there – e.g. in the University of Cambridge – after an absence of some years. What impressed these small bodies of potential or actual communist intellectuals, as well as very much wider strata, was not only the global catastrophe of the capitalist economy, dramatised in mass unemployment and the destruction of surplus stocks of wheat and coffee while men and women cried out for them, but the apparent immunity of the Soviet Union to it. This phase of the process is illustrated by the spectacular conversion of the oldest champions of social-democratic gradualism, the fathers of Fabianism, Sidney and Beatrice Webb, to 'the Marxian theory of the historical development of profit-making capitalism'.[13] The Webbs, though unimpressed by the British Communist Party, devoted the remainder of their lives to the admiring exposition of the Soviet Union.

If the contrast between capitalist breakdown and planned socialist industrialisation turned some intellectuals towards Marxism, the triumph of Hitler, an evident political consequence of the crisis, turned very many more into anti-fascists. With the establishment of the National Socialist regime anti-fascism became the central political issue for three main reasons. First, fascism itself, hitherto primarily seen as a movement identified with Italy, became the major international vehicle of the political right. Fascist political movements, or those wishing to associate themselves with the prestige and power of the two major European states now under fascist rule, multiplied and grew in a number of countries. Other movements of militant reaction found themselves associated with domestic or foreign fascism, or seeking support from foreign fascism, or at least considering the rise of international and especially German fascism to be a bulwark against their domestic left: as the phrase went, 'Better Hitler than Léon Blum'. The left naturally inclined to assimilate all such movements to fascism or philo-fascism, and to stress their links with Berlin and Rome. Like communism for the right, fascism for the left in each country was now not merely a problem for foreigners, but a domestic danger made all the more ominous by its international character and the sympathy and possibly the support of two great powers. It is impossible to understand the international wave of support for the Spanish Republic in 1936 without this sense that the battles fought in that barely known and marginal country of Europe were, in the most specific sense, battles for the future of France, Britain, the USA, Italy, etc.

Second, the threat of fascism was far more than merely political. What was at issue – and nobody was more aware of this than intellectuals – was the future of an entire civilisation. If fascism stamped out Marx, it equally stamped out Voltaire and John Stuart Mill. It rejected liberalism in all its forms as implacably as socialism and communism. It rejected the entire heritage of the eighteenth-century Enlightenment together with all regimes sprung from the American and the French Revolutions as well as the Russian Revolution. Communists and liberals, confronted by the same enemy and the same threat of annihilation, were inevitably pressed into the same camp. It is impossible to understand the reluctance of men and women on the left to criticise, or even often to admit to themselves, what was happening in the USSR in those years, or the isolation of the USSR's critics on the left, without this sense that in the fight against fascism, communism and liberalism were, in a profound sense, fighting for the same cause. Not to mention the more obvious fact that each needed the other and that, in the conditions of the 1930s, what Stalin did was a Russian problem, however shocking, whereas what Hitler did was a threat everywhere. This threat was immediately dramatised by the abolition of constitutional and democratic government, the concentration camps, the burnings of books, and the massive expulsion or emigration of political dissidents and Jews, including the flower of German intellectual life. What the history of Italian fascism had hitherto only hinted at now became explicit and visible to even the most short-sighted.

The significance of this aspect of the menace of fascism is indicated by the inability of Nazi Germany to make any significant political capital out of its undoubted and rapid economic success. To have liquidated unemployment served Hitler's propaganda less well in the 1930s than the claim to have 'made the trains run on time' had served Mussolini's propaganda in the 1920s. Nazi Germany, it was clear, was a regime to be judged by other criteria than its success in recovering from economic depression.

Third, and most crucially, 'fascism meant war'. Every year after 1933 made this dramatically clear as the Nazi putsch in Austria (1934) was followed by the Ethiopian war (1935), Hitler's reoccupation of the Rhineland and the Spanish Civil War (1936), the Japanese invasion of China (1937) and the German occupation of Austria and the subjugation of Czechoslovakia after Munich (1938). The generations after 1918 lived in the shadow and in the fear of another world war. Few believed after 1933 that it could be permanently avoided, and yet none but fascists and fascist governments regarded it without horror. The line between aggressors and defenders was never more clearly drawn than in this period; but so, increasingly, was the line between those in the non-fascist countries who were prepared to resist, if necessary with arms, and those who, for whatever reason, were not. It did not simply divide right from left: there were resisters among traditional conservatives and patriots, and appeasers or pacifists on the non-communist left, particularly in France and Britain; and even the resisters did not call for war, but rather believed (not without plausibility until after Munich) that there was a good chance of avoiding the catastrophe by constructing a powerful and broad front of states and peoples willing to resist the aggressors and capable of overawing them, because capable if necessary of defeating them. Yet as aggression advanced and succeeded, the necessity of resistance became increasingly obvious, and drew politically conscious opinion into the anti-fascist camp. And indeed eventually war and resistance clarified the issue beyond any doubt. And as it became so clarified anti-fascism came increasingly closer to the communists, who had not merely pioneered the policy of the broad anti-fascist alliance and of resistance in theory, but visibly played a leading role in the struggle in practice. So long as the fascist danger, represented after May 1940 by the actual conquest of vast areas of Europe, remained acute, even the absurd temporary reversal of international communist policy in 1939 could not halt this trend.[14]

Nevertheless, the process by which intellectuals and others were drawn into anti-fascism and therefore towards the left, and often the Marxist left, was neither as linear nor as unproblematical as might appear at first sight. The zig-zags and turns of Comintern and Soviet policy have already been mentioned, and need not detain us: the delay in liquidating the sectarian strategy of the 'Third Period' and the about-turn of 1939–41. However, some other complicating factors must be briefly discussed.

Globally speaking, the most important of these concerned the dependent and colonial countries. In these anti-fascism was not an overriding issue, either because the phenomenon of European fascism was remote and had little bearing on their domestic situations, as in large parts of Latin America, or because fascism could not realistically be identified with the main enemy or danger; or both. It is true that in Latin America the traditional right (especially where it relied on the Church) was likely to sympathise with the relevant European right which was increasingly drawn into alliance with fascism – as notably in the Spanish Civil War. Some ultra-right movements on the fascist model also developed here and there, such as the Synarchists in Mexico and Plinio Salgado's Integralistas in Brazil. To this extent the left would also have identified with anti-fascism, even if it had not already been tempted to do so on other grounds, such as a sympathy for Marxist anti-imperialism and the very powerful European cultural influence on Latin American intellectuals, and their personal experiences. The Spanish Civil War evidently played a crucial part here, particularly in Mexico, Chile and Cuba. On the other hand, in large parts of Latin America the readiness in the 1930s to adopt ideas and phraseology from fascism – a prestigious, successful and fashionable movement in that Europe to which Latin America had long looked for its ideological fashions – did not necessarily have the connotations it had in the continent of its origin. There it would have been unthinkable for politicians or politically minded young officers who were attracted by such ideas to make their major impact on national life by mobilising the working class as a trade-unionist and electoral force (as in Argentina) or to join with the trade unions to make a social revolution (as in Bolivia). Perhaps this did not greatly affect the bulk of the continent's intellectuals, but it should warn us against too facile an application of the European political alignments in Latin America. Moreover, that continent was not effectively involved in World War Two.

The situation was more complex in Asia and (insofar as it was politically mobilised), Africa, where there was no local fascism[15] – though Japan, a militantly anti-communist power, was allied with Germany and Italy – and where Britain, France and the Netherlands were the obvious main adversaries for anti-imperialists. The bulk of secular intellectuals were certainly opposed to European fascism, given its racialist attitude to peoples of yellow, brown and black skins. Moreover, movements in these countries were often strongly influenced by those of the metropoles, i.e. by the liberal and democratic traditions of Western Europe, as notably in the Indian National Congress. Nevertheless it was logical for anti-imperialists to take the view long held among Irish rebels, namely that 'England's difficulty is Ireland's opportunity'. Indeed, the tradition of seeking support from the enemies of local colonialists went back to the First World War, when both Irish and Indian revolutionaries (including some who later became Marxists) had looked to Germany for help against Britain. Therefore anti-fascism, based on the priority of defeating Germany, Italy and Japan over immediate colonial liberation, conflicted with the instincts and the political calculation of local anti-imperialism, except in special cases such as Ethiopia and China. The question ceased to be academic with the outbreak of war – and had begun to complicate local political life some years earlier (e.g.

in Indochina). Orthodox communists[16] who put global anti-fascism first, risked and generally achieved political isolation as soon as the war moved sufficiently close – as it did in the Middle East from 1940, and in South and Southeast Asia in 1942. Intellectuals of the left identified with theoretical anti-fascism or even some sort of Marxism might, like Jawaharlal Nehru and the bulk of the Indian National Congress, launch themselves directly into a confrontation with British imperialism, or, like Subhas Bose of Bengal, actually organise an Indian Army of Liberation under the aegis of the Japanese. There is no doubt that the overwhelming bulk of anti-imperialism in the Muslim Middle East, whatever its ideology, was pro-German. In short, the relation between intellectuals and anti-fascists outside Europe did not, and could not, conform to the European pattern.

European anti-fascism had its own complexities. In the first place, as the 1930s advanced it became increasingly clear that the anti-fascist alliance would have to embrace not only the political centre and left, but any persons, tendencies, organisations and states who, for whatever reasons, were prepared to resist fascism and the fascist powers. Popular fronts inevitably tended to become 'national fronts'. The logical recognition of this situation by the communists shocked the traditional susceptibilities of the left, including its intellectuals, as Thorez held out his hand to the Catholics, the French party appealed to Joan of Arc (long a symbol of the extreme right), and the British party called for an alliance with Winston Churchill, equally symbolic of all that was reactionary and opposed to the labour movement. This probably caused relatively little difficulty, at least until liberation or victory. The danger of Nazi Germany was such that a coalition with yesterday's and tomorrow's enemy against the greater danger made sense, especially as it did not imply an ideological rapprochement. The ultra-leftists who opposed assistance for Ethiopia against Italy on the (quite correct) ground that Haile Selassie was a feudal emperor won little support. On the other hand, for the revolutionary socialist left the question whether the broad anti-fascist strategy must be pursued at the expense (at least in the short term) of the socialist revolution which was their real objective raised more profound uncertainties. What sacrifices ought revolutionaries to make in the necessary cause of rolling back fascism? Was it not conceivable that victory over fascism would be won – but at the cost of postponing the revolution, or even reinforcing non-fascist capitalism? Insofar as revolutionaries were moved by such considerations, they had something in common with anti-fascism in the colonial and semi-colonial world.

But even intellectuals, though perhaps more inclined to raise such questions than other militants, were not much troubled by them. The defeat of fascism was, after all, a matter of life or death even for committed revolutionaries. Neither communists nor dissident Marxists claimed to see any incompatibility between anti-fascism and revolution. Within the ambit of the Comintern it was argued, though cautiously, intermittently, and not in a very public manner, that the broad anti-fascist front might provide a strategy for the transition to socialism. Of course publicly the limited democratic and defensive aspects of anti-fascism were stressed above all, in order not to frighten away non-socialist anti-fascists including some bourgeois governments. The resulting ambiguities will be considered below. Conversely, the radical element took the utopian road of denying any contradiction between anti-fascism and immediate proletarian revolution. Even those who did not reject the broad anti-fascist front altogether as an unnecessary betrayal of revolution (as Trotsky did, misled by his hostility to the Stalinist Comintern which was the main advocate of such a front), called for its conversion into insurrection at any suitable moment – 1936 in France, 1944–5 in France and Italy – and hailed it in Spain in 1936. As we shall see, at the time these utopian arguments carried little weight. They may even account for the isolation and lack of influence of those who propounded them, such as the Trotskyite and other dissident

Marxist groups. People who fought with their backs to the wall against the encroaching forces of fascism gave priority to the immediate struggle. If it was lost then the revolution of tomorrow – even, in Spain, the revolution of today – had no chance.

The logic of the struggle also clarified another complexity of the anti-fascist left: pacifism. As a specific ideology this was largely confined to the Anglo-Saxon world, where it flourished both within the labour movement[17] and, at least temporarily in the 1930s, among a substantial body of liberal intellectuals and a much wider movement in favour of general disarmament, international understanding and the League of Nations. In the form of a deep-rooted emotional revulsion against war, a fear of another mass holocaust like the First World War or – as in the USA – a refusal to be involved in the wars of Europe, it was very widespread. In the nature of things, the hatred of war and militarism was primarily a phenomenon of the political left. Yet fascism faced men and women who held such beliefs with a dilemma which could not be surmounted except by the conviction (generally backed by references to Gandhi and non-violent resistance in India) that in some way passive non-cooperation on its own could stop Hitler. Few, even among intellectuals, seriously believed this. Refusal to fight therefore implied a readiness to see fascism win; and several of the most passionate pacifists in France logically enough became collaborators.[18] The alternative was to abandon pacifism and to conclude that resistance to fascism justified taking up arms. This was in fact the view taken by the bulk of anti-fascist peace-lovers, other than those committed to pacifism by their religion, such as the Quakers. After June 1940 many young British intellectuals who had registered as 'conscientious objectors' at the outbreak of war put on uniform. The refusal to wage any war, even a war against fascism, remained a serious political force only in the form of 'isolationism', i.e. in countries like the USA which were sufficiently remote from Nazi Germany not to take the threat of their conquest by Hitler too seriously.

In short, anti-fascism prevailed over all other considerations on the European left. Just as even the fight for proletarian insurrection found its immediate practical expression in the armed levies of the Spanish Republic against Franco, and the armed partisans resisting Hitler and Mussolini, so the fight against war paradoxically led to the mobilisation of intellectuals for anti-fascist war. The British scientists, many of them radicalised in and through the Cambridge Scientists' Anti-War Group, and who spent much of the 1930s warning the people that there was no effective protection against the horrors of air-raids and poison-gas which haunted the imagination of the post-1918 generations, turned into the scientific war-makers. Leading radical and communist figures – Bernal, Haldane, Blackett – in fact became involved in the war effort through their original investigations of the ways in which the civilian population could be protected against aerial bombardment. This was what initially brought them into contact with government planners.[19]

III

We have spoken of 'intellectuals' in general. And indeed the mobilisation of what may be called the 'public intellectuals' against fascism was extremely striking. In most non-fascist countries a few well-known figures in the world of the creative arts – notably in literature – were attracted to the political right, sometimes even to fascism, though few in the visual arts[20] and hardly any in the sciences. However, these formed small and untypical minorities. Indeed at this time even some whose traditionalist ideology might have been expected to draw them to the right, like the most influential of British literary critics, F.R. Leavis, found themselves not only surrounded by anti-fascist and even some Marxist disciples, but hesitated on the brink of expressing cautious and qualified sympathy with their cause, before withdrawing from the political arena.[21]

In Britain, France and the USA those mobilised in favour of the Spanish Republic and more generally for anti-fascism comprised a majority of talent and intellect. The American writers who declared their support for the Spanish Republicans included Sherwood Anderson, Stephen Vincent Benét, Dos Passos, Dreiser, Faulkner, Hemingway, Archibald MacLeish, Upton Sinclair, John Steinbeck and Thornton Wilder, to name but a few. In the Hispanic world the poets supported the Republic almost without exception. Since the publicity value of such well-known names was obvious, and was exploited by various forms of collective gatherings, public statements and other manifestations, this part of the intellectuals' anti-fascism is particularly well recorded. Indeed, some accounts of the subject are virtually confined to the discussion of the public, i.e. essentially the literary, intelligentsia.[22]

The anti-fascism of persons of unusual talent, intelligence and established or future intellectual achievement, is historically significant, and so is their attraction in this period to Marxism, which was particularly marked among the generations which reached adult maturity in the 1930s and 1940s. This phenomenon was particularly striking in countries where Marxism had no established intellectual tradition such as Britain and the USA. (In the latter country dissident Marxism, mainly of the Trotskyite kind, attracted a larger number of intellectuals than elsewhere.) This selective recruitment of the unusually gifted at particular periods is difficult to explain satisfactorily at present, but the facts are not in doubt. However, this cannot exhaust the question of anti-fascism and the intellectuals, and in some respects it makes its analysis more difficult by obscuring the problem of the social identity of the anti-fascist intellectuals.

Socially speaking – and abstracting for the moment from national variations – the Western intellectuals of the 1930s were, in the main, either the children of the established bourgeoisie (which might or might not contain a recognised stratum of the *Bildungsbürgertum*, which owed its status to a tradition of higher education), or they represented an upwardly mobile stratum drawn from the poorer classes. In the most simplified terms, they belonged to those for whose children a non-vocational higher education was already taken for granted, or to those for whom it was not. Since the old-established institutions for education past the age of, say, fifteen or sixteen years were still largely confined to the children of the established upper strata, the two types often had a different educational formation as well as social background. There was no equally clear distinction between the professions they eventually followed, though the older and more prestigious professions of 'traditional intellectuals' and the higher technical professions of the 'organic intellectuals' of the bourgeoisie were considerably more likely to be recruited from the established bourgeoisie, whose members were even more likely to dominate the older generations of these professions. On the other hand, the bulk of intellectuals from poorer backgrounds were no longer confined, for practical purposes, to the subaltern branches of teaching, bureaucracy and the priesthood, though both teaching and government employment probably still provided the largest secular outlet for them. A number of other non-manual occupations were now expanding in which first-generation intellectuals could find a lodging – e.g. in the rapidly growing field of mass communications, as well as in general white-collar or subaltern technical and design work.

How sharp the line between the two groups was depended on national conditions. National traditions also largely determined the political sympathies of both intellectuals in general and particular professions: French secondary teachers and academics were predominantly on the left, their German equivalents leaned distinctly to the right. A further distinction, in most countries, between those engaged in the strictly intellectual disciplines and those in the creative arts or entertainments must be noted. Their political behaviour was by no means the same. Finally, the differences of age, sex and national or historical origins must be taken account of. Other things being equal, the young were more likely to be radical than their elders, though this did not necessarily commit them to radicalism of the left. Women intellectuals were almost by definition much more likely to be on the left, not only because the right was almost uniformly hostile to women's emancipation, but also because the families likely to give their daughters an intellectual education were very much more likely to belong to the liberal or 'progressive' wing of the established bourgeoisie. National origins could determine the over-representation of intellectuals in general and those of the left in particular among such groups as the Jews (with both a strong tradition of cherishing learning and the experience of discrimination) or the Welsh in Britain (a people virtually without a native bourgeoisie, but with a status system which set a high value on intellectual and cultural achievement – literature, teaching and preaching). Conversely, intellectuals were likely to be under-represented in certain other groups, e.g. Slavic and Italian immigrants into the USA, largely drawn from backward strata and confined to subordinate manual work, or African Americans, as distinct from Afro-Caribbeans.

Finally, the specific national or regional political situation and tradition could be decisive. Thus university students in Western and Central Europe remained predominantly unaffected by anti-fascism, and were indeed – as in Germany, Austria and France – much more likely to be mobilised on the right, while in some Balkan countries (notably Yugoslavia) their enthusiasm for communism was proverbial. British and American students were probably mainly non-political, but the organised right was not prominent among them and the organised left was almost certainly stronger than ever before, and in some universities dominant. Indian students were likely to be predominantly anti-imperialist, but nationalist intellectuals from Bengal were likely to be closer to the revolutionary left (i.e. in the 1930s to Marxism) than any others. It is therefore impossible to generalise about the intellectuals and anti-fascism *en bloc*.

The politics of intellectuals from the established bourgeoisie have attracted most attention, as is legitimate in countries where entry to the intellectual professions was mainly confined to children of this stratum, and transfer from subaltern to higher intellectual activities was difficult. When the illegal Italian CP began to attract a new generation of intellectuals, they naturally came from this milieu. Amendola, Sereni and Rossi-Doria, who came to the PCI in the late 1920s via the University of Naples, may have come from exceptionally distinguished backgrounds, but it is clear that sympathisers were also to be found among young men from the upper Milanese bourgeoisie, and in the largely bourgeois student milieu elsewhere.[23]

Similarly in Britain the young members of the upper bourgeoisie, products of the so-called 'public schools' and the ancient universities, have attracted a quite disproportionate amount of public attention, partly because of their high cultural visibility (e.g. the group of left-wing poets including W.H. Auden, Stephen Spender, Cecil Day-Lewis), partly because several young communist intellectuals took their commitment so far as to become Soviet secret agents in the 1930s (Burgess, Maclean, Philby, Blunt). This is not the place to speculate about the causes of the conversion to communism of a significant, though numerically tiny, minority of the children of a ruling class as self-confident and unshaken as the British. Nor has it been systematically investigated yet, except in the somewhat untypical context of the search for Soviet agents.[24] Probably most of the young rebels moved 'forward from liberalism' (to cite the title of a book by one of them).[25] There are several examples of traditionally liberal or 'progressive' families of the upper middle class in which the generations of the 1920s and 1930s thus became communist, for longer or shorter periods.[26] However, there were breakaways even from traditionally conservative and imperialist families (Philby).[27] There were even signs of political polarisation within part of the traditionalist aristocracy: of the children of Lord Redesdale two daughters and probably one son became fascists, and one daughter became a communist, marrying a nephew of Winston Churchill who went to fight in Spain.

In the USA there is also evidence that some younger members of the elite of Eastern millionaire families (e.g. Lamonts and Whitney Straights) were attracted by communism, though almost certainly on a smaller scale. It is possible that research on this aspect of the social history of other European countries may reveal – and help to explain – similar phenomena elsewhere. Outside Europe, where Western education was largely confined to a very restricted elite, it is perhaps less surprising that communism in the 1930s, like Western liberalism and movements to modernise local cultures, was largely confined to the strata, or even the families, which also played a leading role in local government and high society as officials of the colonial order or otherwise. Cadres of all kinds were most easily drawn from the same small reservoir. Of the four children of one such Indian family – all educated in England, the boys at Eton – three became communists, two of them subsequently government minister and businessman, the fourth commander-in-chief of the Indian army.

Nevertheless, such elite recruits to communism should not obscure the numerically very substantial proportion – in Britain and the USA a majority – of the anti-fascist and communist students who did not come from the British 'public schools' or the elite US 'prep schools' and 'Ivy League' universities, and those intellectuals who did not come from universities at all. In the history of 1930s Marxism institutions like the London School of Economics and City College, New York played a role as important or more important than did Oxford and Yale. Among the British Marxist historians of the generation of the 1930s and 1940s, the majority of those who later became well known came from grammar schools, and indeed often from provincial non-conformist Liberal or Labour back-grounds, though several of them converged with the elite in the ancient universities of Oxford and Cambridge. In France, the narrow ladder of meritocratic promotion brought sons of Republican lower officials and primary school-teachers to the higher levels of left-wing intellectualism as well as the sons of professional families with a long tradition of higher academic education.[28] In short, in the countries of established liberal democracy, where fascism made little mass appeal to the middle and lower middle classes, the recruitment of anti-fascist intellectuals was relatively broad.

This is particularly obvious among the large number of non-university intellectuals. We know that 75% of the members of the British Left Book Club (which at its peak reached 57,000 members and a readership of a quarter of a million) were white-collar workers, lower professionals and other non-academic intellectuals.[29] This public was certainly similar to the mass public for cheap and intellectually demanding paperbacks which was also discovered in Britain in the middle 1930s by Penguin Books, whose main intellectual series was edited by men of the left. The bulk of the passionate champions of folk-music and jazz in both Britain and America – they contained a dispropor-tionate percentage of young communists in Britain – were also to be found on the borders of the skilled class of workers, subal-tern technicians and professions and the middle class, as well as among students.[30] The growing field of journalism, advertising and entertainment provided employment for both non-univer-sity intellectuals and such university intellectuals as did not choose to make a career in one of the traditional public or pri-vate professions – particularly in countries like Britain and the USA, where entry into these new fields was comparatively easy. New centres of organised anti-fascist and left-wing activity there-fore developed in such centres of the film industry (which was then the major mass medium) as Hollywood, and in mass jour-nalism of a non-political or not specifically reactionary kind.[31]

Anti-fascism was therefore not confined to an intellectual elite. It included those librarians and social workers in the USA to whom communism made a particularly strong appeal. It included those whom the elite despised: 'the discontented magazine-writer, the guilty Hollywood scenarist, the unpaid high school teacher, the politically inexperienced scientist, the intelligent clerk, the culturally aspiring dentist'.[32] It thus reflected the democratisation of the intelligentsia.

IV

Since anti-fascism was a much wider movement than communism, communist parties made no attempt to convert intellectuals to Marxism *en masse*, though among the growing number politically mobilised through anti-fascism the parties naturally found their potential and actual intellectual recruits. The major task was to mobilise the widest range of intellectuals, and especially prominent ones, and associate them with the cause of anti-fascism and peace in its various forms. Ideological criteria could hardly be stressed in an appeal signed by such diverse figures as Aragon, Bernanos, Chamson, Colette, Guéhenno, Malraux, Maritain, Montherlant, Jules Romains and Schlumberger after Hitler's occupation of Prague.[33]

In countries with a long tradition of the intellectuals' commitment to the left, even those who actually joined the Communist Party were unlikely to be asked to change their ideology dramatically, especially if their names were sufficiently prominent to lend lustre to the party. This was very much the case in the French Communist Party, where the tradition of revolution was strong but Marxism was weak. 'It wasn't until the years of the Popular Front, the Resistance, and the Liberation' that such traditional French academic intellectuals of the left, often socialists, believers 'in goodness, progress, justice, work, truth [. . .] gradually and unobtrusively adopted the kindred allegiance [of Communism], not because they had changed their former rationalist, positivist opinions but, on the contrary, because they had remained true to themselves'.[34] Even in the late 1940s there were professors who denied being Marxists, having joined the Communist Party because of its record in anti-fascism and resistance. Intellectuals of this kind must be distinguished from those (mainly of a younger generation) who were also attracted to communism by Marxist theory, and who were systematically educated in Marxism within and on the outskirts of the party. It must not be forgotten that the 1930s saw the most systematic international effort made up to that date to publish, popularise and study the 'classics' of Marxism. It was made by the communists.

Nevertheless, no clear line separated 'old' and 'new' left. As the communists after 1933 came to insist on the progressive traditions of the bourgeois revolutions as well as the anti-fascism they shared with socialists and liberals, the 'old' left also discovered the need for common ground. Was not the bourgeoisie itself abandoning the old verities of rationalism, science and progress? Who were their most determined defenders today? Georges Friedmann's influential *La Crise du Progrès,* published in 1936 under the prestigious auspices of the *Nouvelle Revue Française,* argued persuasively that the common ground was dialectical materialism, long dismissed by its opponents as the enemy of all the higher aspirations of humanity by virtue of its materialism. The USSR now represented both the traditions and aspirations abandoned by the bourgeoisie.

All this not only made it easier to attract anti-fascist intellectuals into the neighbourhood of Marxism, it also significantly affected the development of Marxism itself. It reinforced those elements within it which were closest to the rationalist, positivist, scientist tradition of the Enlightenment and its belief in man's unlimited capacity for progress. Consciously or not, in drawing nearer to each other Marxists tended to modify their theory more substantially than non-Marxists.

But of course they did so not only, or perhaps not even primarily, because they wanted to establish a common front against fascism with non-Marxist intellectuals. To overcome what Dimitrov called 'the isolation of the revolutionary vanguard' implied the reconstruction 'of our policies and tactics in accordance with the changing situation', but not any modifications in Marxist theory and ideology. It was, paradoxically, the internal development of the USSR more than the requirements of resistance to Hitler which led to the reinforcement of the tendencies in Marxism which brought it closer to the old ideology of nineteenth-century progress. And indeed, in the experience of the anti-fascist era the impact of Hitler and that of the USSR cannot be clearly separated.

Thus, the interpretation of 'dialectical and historical materialism' which prevailed in this period – with Stalin's authority it became canonical for communists – owed nothing to the need to construct an anti-fascist front, though it almost certainly facilitated it. It derived from the Marxist orthodoxy of the Second International period, whose spokesman was Karl Kautsky, and which in turn was based on the late Engels' codification of his and Marx's teachings: a version of Marxism which both gave it the authority of science, the certainty of scientific method and prediction, and the claim to interpret all phenomena in the universe by means of dialectical materialism – the dialectics being indeed of Hegelian derivation, but the materialism essentially in the line of the eighteenth-century French *philosophes*. It was an interpretation which (as in Engels' *Feuerbach*) married the triumphant natural sciences of the nineteenth century with Marxism – once they abandoned the superficial, static, mechanical materialism of the eighteenth century, as indeed (in Engels' view) the progress of these sciences themselves led them to abandon it, in consequence of the three decisive discoveries of the cell, the transformation of energy, and the Darwinian theory of evolution.

There was nothing very surprising in this. The marriage between 'progress' and 'revolution', eighteenth-century materialism and Marxism, combining as it did the certainties of the natural sciences and historical inevitability, had long made a deep appeal to working-class movements. In this the Russian movement was not exceptional. Moreover, the situation of post-revolutionary Russia was likely to encourage an even more emphatic scientism. Once the Revolution failed to achieve what both Marx and Lenin had regarded as its primary aim, namely to 'give the signal for a workers' revolution in the West, so that both complement each other',[35] the major, the dominant tasks of the Bolsheviks were and had to be the economic and cultural development of a backward and impoverished country, in order to create the conditions both for survival against foreign attack and for the construction of socialism in an isolated, if gigantic country. In material terms, production and technology (Lenin's 'electrification') had to take precedence. In cultural terms priority was given to mass enlightenment, seen both as mass education and the struggle against religion and superstition. The battle against backwardness and for 'development' was no doubt conducted in a different way from similar battles in the nineteenth century. Nevertheless, the themes of science, reason and progress as forces of liberation were to a great extent recognisably the same. 'Dialectical materialism' in such a society derived its force not simply from tradition and authority, but also from its usefulness as a weapon in this battle, and its appeal to party militants and future cadres, themselves workers and peasants, to whom it gave confidence, certainty and instruction in what was both scientifically true and destined to triumph.

As already observed, it was the combination of the 'crisis of progress' in bourgeois society with a confident reassertion of its traditional values in the USSR that attracted intellectuals to Marxism. They came to it as the bearer of the banner of reason and science which the bourgeoisie had dropped, the defender of the values of the Enlightenment against fascism which was dedicated to its destruction. And in doing so they not only accepted but welcomed and developed 'dialectical materialism' as now formulated in the Soviet and international orthodoxy, especially if they were new Marxists; and the great majority of Marxist intellectuals in this period were new Marxists, for whom Marxism itself was as much of a novelty as, say, jazz, sound films and private-eye novels.

V

The context of Marxism in the late twentieth century, and therefore the experience of most readers of this history, is so different that the specific historical character of the Marxism of the anti-fascist era must be underlined, if anachronistic and therefore mistaken interpretations of it are to be avoided. Intellectual Marxists since the 1960s have been submerged in a flood of Marxist literature and debate. They have access to something like a giant supermarket of Marxisms and Marxist authors, and the fact that at any time the choice of the majority in any country may be dictated by history, political situation and fashion does not prevent them from being conscious of the theoretical range of their options. This is all the more wide since Marxism, again mainly from the 1960s, has been increasingly integrated into the content of formal higher education, at least in the humanities and social sciences. The new Marxists of the 1930s in most Western countries had access only to a relatively exiguous literature, almost entirely excluded from official culture and education, except as a target for hostile criticism. Even their own contributions to Marxist literature were as yet quite small in quantity. Thus before 1946 the sum-total of works on history in English which could be described as 'Marxist or near-Marxist' – omitting the writings of the 'classics' – consisted of some thirty books and at most a couple of dozen articles.[36]

Insofar as older Marxist traditions existed, the new Marxists were largely cut off from them for four reasons. The split between social democracy and communism made them suspicious of most pre-1914 social-democratic Marxism and its later developments. The formation of a standard communist version of Marxism (Leninism) largely buried such native traditions of revolutionary Marxism as had survived into the early years of communism (e.g. in Britain those associated with the 'Plebs League').[37] It also marginalised certain tendencies within communist Marxism, even when these were not condemned. The elimination of Stalin's opponents and other 'deviationists' removed a section of Bolshevik Marxist writings from effective circulation (e.g. Bogdanov and eventually Bukharin, not to mention Trotsky). To this extent the 'Bolshevisation' of the later 1920s was not only political and organisational, but intellectual. Lastly, as already suggested, technical reasons – both linguistic and political (e.g. the effects of Hitler's triumph) – simply made much existing work unavailable. Thus, as we have seen, Gustav Mayer's monumental biography of Engels, published in an *émigrant* edition in the Netherlands in 1934, remained virtually unknown in Germany long after the war and was accessible in English only in a ruthlessly abbreviated translation.

As has already been suggested, ignorance – and in particular linguistic ignorance – did not necessarily narrow the horizons of contemporary Marxists. Even in the conditions of monolithic theoretical orthodoxy which were progressively being imposed on the communist movements, it might have the opposite effect. Contemporary Western Marxists were largely ignorant of the Soviet orthodoxy which became more clearly defined, specific and binding in the USSR in the early 1930s on a variety of matters ranging from literature and the arts through economic theory, history and philosophy, and amounting to the creation of a 'dialectical materialism' which, as is now evident, included major revisions of Marx himself.[38] However, as already suggested, this orthodoxy was not yet formally imposed on communists outside the USSR. At all events, while no communist was unaware of the duty of denouncing directly political heresies stigmatised as such (and notably 'Trotskyism'), the imposition of a new orthodoxy in matters more remote from political practice was not specifically publicised outside Russia, the major discussions (except for those on art and literature) remaining untranslated and therefore virtually unknown.

They therefore hardly affected Western communists. British, American, Chinese and other writers continued throughout the 1930s – and in English-speaking countries even later – to operate with the 'Asiatic Mode of Production', while Russian ones were already careful to avoid doing so.[39] A Soviet philosophical textbook adapted for British use (and published by a non-communist publisher) contained the now standard denunciations of Deborin and Luppol, but a work by Luppol was still happily published by the official publishing house of the French CP in 1936.[40] Marxists who knew German and had access to the *Frühschriften* enthusiastically embodied the Marx of the Paris Manuscripts in their analysis, apparently unaware of the Soviet reservations about these early writings. And indeed, even the famous fourth chapter of the *History of the CPSU(b): Short Course*, which embodied the new dogmas of dialectical and historical materialism, was read not as a call to criticise those who deviated from them, but in most cases simply as a lucid and powerful formulation of basic Marxist beliefs. Had they been asked to, Western communists would no doubt have denounced those whose views were implicitly or explicitly condemned in the Soviet debates with as much loyalty and conviction as they denounced Trotskyism, but they were not specifically asked to at this time, and few were as yet aware that Russian communists were.

To this extent the new Marxists of the 1930s were largely ignorant or unaware of alternative interpretations of Marxist theory – even those of what has since been called 'Western Marxism'[41] which were or had been identified with Bolshevism, or sympathetic to it. Moreover, unlike the late twentieth-century

Marxists, they were not particularly interested in intra-Marxist controversies on theory (except insofar as these were embodied in the authoritative corpus of Lenin and Stalin or made mandatory by Soviet or Comintern decisions). Such debates have tended to emerge in periods of uncertainty about the validity of past Marxist analysis as at the end of the nineteenth century (the revisionist 'crisis of Marxism') or in the era of global capitalist triumph and post-Stalinism. But the new Marxists of the 1930s saw no reason to doubt the Marxist prognosis in the years of the great capitalist crisis, and no reason to scrutinise the classic texts for alternative meanings. They rather saw Marxism as the key to understanding vast ranges of phenomena which had hitherto remained obscure and puzzling. As a young Marxist mathematician and militant put it: 'In the midst of much that is still under detailed investigation, a Marxist cannot help feeling that here vast realms of thought await dialectical understanding.'[42] They saw their intellectual task as the exploration of that vast realm, and the writings of the classics and of older Marxists not so much as an enigma awaiting intellectual clarification, but as a collective store-house of illuminating ideas. Possible gaps and internal inconsistencies seemed far less important than the enormous advances it made possible. The most obvious of these advances, for intellectuals, was the critique of the non-Marxist views which surrounded them. They naturally concentrated on this rather than on the critique of other Marxists, unless their political commitment brought such criticism with it. One suspects that, left to themselves, they might well have regarded even the Marxists they disagreed with as interesting rather than diabolical. Henri Lefebvre, in his interesting reflections on the national problem (1937), considered Otto Bauer's definition of the national to differ from Stalin's in being less precise, rather than in being dangerously wrong.[43]

Yet it must be noted that the new Marxists accepted the orthodox interpretation not only because they knew no other, and because they were not particularly bothered about fine doctrinal distinctions within Marxism, but also because it fitted in with their own approach to Marxism. Karl Korsch's *Karl Marx* (published in English in 1938) made a negligible impact not so much because he was recognised as a dissident – few except a handful of German emigrants knew who he was – but rather because it somehow seemed tangential to this approach. The official view of Marx's early philosophical writings was that they 'contain the writings of Marx's youth. They reflect his evolution from Hegelian idealism to a consistent materialism.'[44] But while there were enough *agrégés* of philosophy in the French CP to recognise, as Henri Lefebvre pointed out, that this hardly exhausted the problem of Marx's relation to Hegel, there is no echo of the Hegelian Marx in Georges Politzer's *Principes Elémentaires de la Philosophie* (based on a course of lectures given in 1935–6) or, in spite of his knowledge and appreciation of Lenin's Philosophical Notebooks, in the contemporary *Textbook of Dialectical Materialism* by the Englishman David Guest.[45] Neither of these able and independent thinkers can be regarded as a mere populariser.

The specific character of the Western Marxism of the anti-fascist period is perhaps best illustrated by the fact that this was the first, and probably to date the only era when natural scientists were attracted to Marxism in significant numbers, as well as mobilised for more general anti-fascist purposes. In the 1960s and 1970s it became the fashion to dismiss the idea that Marxism was a comprehensive world view embracing the natural cosmos as well as human history, following lines of criticism already suggested much earlier by Korsch and others. But in the 1930s it was precisely this omni-comprehensiveness of Marxism which attracted the new Marxists as well as older and younger natural scientists to the theory as expounded by Engels.[46]

The phenomenon was particularly marked in Britain, the USA and France, the main Western centres of research in the natural sciences after the German catastrophe. At the highest level the number of scientists of present or future eminence who were communists, sympathisers or closely identified with the radical left was extremely impressive. In Britain alone it included at least five future Nobel laureates. At a lower level, the radicalism of scientists in Cambridge, by far the most important scientific centre in Britain, was proverbial. The Cambridge Scientists' Anti-War Group launched itself with some eighty members among research workers, a restricted group in those days.[47] And if activists were in a minority, the majority was at least passively sympathetic to the left. It has been estimated that of the 200 best British scientists under the age of forty, in 1936 fifteen were Communist Party members or fellow-travellers, fifty actively left of centre, a hundred passively sympathetic to the left, and the rest neutral, apart from perhaps five or six on the eccentric wings of the right.[48]

The anti-fascism of scientists was natural, given the mass expulsion and emigration of scientists from the countries of fascism. Yet their attraction to Marxism was not equally natural, given the difficulty of reconciling much of twentieth-century science with the nineteenth-century models on which Engels had based his view, and for which Lenin battled philosophically.[49] Both Engels' *Dialectics of Nature* and Lenin's *Materialism and Empiriocriticism* were of course available. Engels' manuscript, as Ryazanov noted with scholarly integrity in his introduction to it, had actually been submitted in 1924 to Einstein for a scientific assessment, and the great scientist had stated that 'the content is of no particular interest either from the point of view of current physics or for the history of physics', but might be worth publishing 'insofar as it is an interesting contribution to the process of illuminating Engels' intellectual significance'.[50] Yet it was read not as a contribution to Engels' intellectual biography but, by at least some young scientists who were the present author's contemporaries in Cambridge, as a stimulating contribution to the formation of their ideas about science.[51] It must also be said that even then there were communist scientists who privately admitted that dialectical materialism did not seem directly relevant to their research.

Since this is not the place to investigate the history of the Marxist interpretation of the natural sciences, little can be said here about the various attempts to apply dialectics to them at this period.[52] However, three observations about the appeal of Marxism to natural scientists may be made.

First, it reflected the dissatisfaction of scientists with the determinist mechanical materialism of the nineteenth century, which had produced results plainly difficult to reconcile with this explanatory principle. This produced not merely considerable difficulties within each science, but a general fragmentation of science, and a growing contradiction between the revolutionary advances of scientific knowledge and the increasingly chaotic and incoherent image of the total reality it purported to explain. As a brilliant young Marxist (soon to be killed in Spain) put it:

> A point is reached where practice with its specialised theory has in each department so contradicted the general unformulated theory of science as a whole that in fact the whole philosophy of mechanism explodes. Biology, physics, psychology, anthropology and chemistry, find their empirical discoveries too great a strain for the general unconscious theory of science, and science dissolves into fragments. Scientists despair of a general theory of science and take refuge in empiricism, in which all attempts at a general world view are given up; or in eclecticism, in which all the specialised theories are lumped together to make a patchwork world view without an attempt to integrate them; or in specialisation, in which all the world is reduced to the particular specialised theory of science with which the theorist is practically concerned. In any case, science dissolves in anarchy; and man for the first time despairs of gaining from it any positive knowledge of reality.[53]

To those who felt the world view of science to be thus breaking down by virtue of the very revolutionary advances of the past decades, whether in the 'crisis of physics' about which Christopher

Caudwell wrote, or in the difficulties which genetics created for Darwinian evolutionary theory, which J.B.S. Haldane tried to overcome,[54] or in more general terms, dialectical materialism had three major attractions. In the first place it claimed to unify and integrate *all* fields of knowledge, and therefore counteracted its fragmentation. It is probably no accident that the most prominent Marxist scientists, like Haldane, J.D. Bernal or Joseph Needham, were particularly encyclopedic in their range of knowledge and interests. It also firmly maintained the belief in a single objectively existing and rationally knowable universe as against an indeterminate, unknowable one, in the face of philosophical agnosticism, positivism or mathematical games. In this sense they were on the side of 'materialism' against 'idealism', and prepared to overlook the philosophical and other weaknesses of such defences of it as Lenin's *Empiriocriticism*.

In the second place Marxism had always been a critique of the mechanical, determinist materialism which was the basis of nineteenth-century science, and therefore claimed to provide an alternative to it. Indeed, its own scientific affiliations had been non-Galilean and non-Newtonian, for Engels himself maintained a lifelong tenderness for the German 'natural philosophy' in which German students of his youth had no doubt been brought up. He sympathised with Kepler rather than Galileo. It is possible that this aspect of the Marxist tradition helped to attract scientists whose field (biology) or whose cast of mind made the mechanical-reductionist models of a science whose greatest triumph was physics, and the analytical method of isolating the experimental subject from its context ('keeping other things equal'), seem particularly inapposite. Such men (Joseph Needham, C.H. Waddington) were interested in wholes rather than parts, in general systems theory – the phrase was not yet familiar – in ensembles which integrate, in a living reality, phenomena which conventional 'scientific method' separated; for instance, 'bombed yet still functioning cities' (to use an illustration by Needham suitable to the age of anti-fascism).[55]

Thirdly, dialectical materialism appeared to provide a way out of the inconsistencies of science by embodying the concept of contradiction in its approach. ('The discoveries of different workers seem to contradict each other flatly. And here a dialectical approach is essential' – J.B.S. Haldane.)

What scientists found in Marxism was therefore not a better way of formulating hypotheses in a falsifiable manner, or even a heuristically fertile way of looking at their fields. Nor were they necessarily troubled by the errors and obsolescence of Engels' *Dialectics of Nature*. They found in it a comprehensive and integrated approach to the universe and all it contained at a time when this appeared to have disintegrated, and nothing seemed, for the time being, to replace it. Without this sense of science in disarray, in the early 1930s, divided (as in physics) between the new generation (Heisenberg, Schrödinger, Dirac) pushing forward into new territory without bothering about its coherence, and 'Einstein and Planck . . . the last of the "Old Guard" of Newtonian physics' conducting a 'kind of stonewalling [defence] . . . unable to lead any counterattack on the enemy positions',[56] the search for a new way through dialectical materialism cannot be understood.

However, Marxism made another major contribution to science. Its application to the history of science struck many scientists with the force of a revelation: hence the enormous significance in the development of the scientists' Marxism of B. Hessen's paper on 'The social and economic roots of Newton's *Principia*', first presented at a conference in Britain in 1931.[57] It integrated scientific progress into the movements of society, and in doing so showed that the 'paradigms' of scientific explanation (to use a term invented much later) were not derived exclusively from the internal progress of intellectual investigation. Here, once again, the actual validity of concrete Marxist analyses was not the main issue. Hessen's own paper was even then open to justified criticism. It was the novelty and fertility of the approach which made its impact.

And it did so in part because it was linked with the third major contribution, not so much of Marxism as of Marxist scientists and the USSR, to the world of science: the insistence on the social significance of science, the need to plan its development, and the role of the scientist in doing so. It is no accident that Marxism first entered the discussions of the influential British club of scientists and other intellectuals the 'Tots and Quots' early in 1932 in the form of a paper by the Marxist mathematician H. Levy (supported by Haldane, Hogben and Bernal) on the need to plan science 'in accordance with the trends of social development'.[58] Nor that, in a society like France, where scientific research lacked systematic support, scientists of the left should have made themselves its champions and the Popular Front government should have been convinced by them of its necessity: the socialist Jean Perrin and the communist sympathiser (and later communist) Paul Langevin were the main movers behind the Caisse Nationale de la Recherche Scientifique, which later became the Centre National de la Recherche Scientifique, and Irène Joliot-Curie became Undersecretary of State for Science. In this sense perhaps the most significant, and certainly by far the most influential publication of Marxist science was J.D. Bernal's *The Social Function of Science* (London, 1939), simply because it was a Marxist who in it formulated sentiments and opinions which were shared by a wide range of scientists who otherwise had no particular sympathy for Marxism: the claim of scientists to be treated as a fourth or fifth 'estate' and the critique of states and societies which failed to recognise the fundamental role of science in production (and war) and for planning the resources of society with its help. The call met with so wide a response at this time because scientists felt that only they knew what the theoretical and practical implications of the new scientific revolution were (e.g. nuclear physics). It is an irony of history that the first and greatest success of scientists in persuading governments of the indispensability of modern scientific theory to society was in the war against fascism. It is an even greater and more tragic irony that it was anti-fascist scientists who convinced the American government of the feasibility and necessity of manufacturing nuclear arms, which were then constructed by an international team of largely anti-fascist scientists.

The appeal of Marxism to a number of significant natural scientists proved to be short-lived. It would probably not have lasted even if internal developments in the USSR (notably the Lysenko affair) had not antagonised scientists in general and made the position of communist ones almost impossible after 1948. It has almost been forgotten in historiography and Marxist discussion, at least in the period when it became the fashion to deny that Marx had anything to say – or even intended to say anything – about the natural sciences, and Engels' own writings on the subject were dismissed as the work of merely another nineteenth-century evolutionist and a scientific and philosophical amateur. Yet it is not only a reminder that the relations of Marxism to the natural sciences cannot be so dismissed, but an essential element of the Marxism of intellectuals in the era of anti-fascism. It reflects both the continuity with the pre-Marxist tradition of rationalism and progress and the recognition that this tradition could be carried forward only through a revolution in practice and theory. And it helps to esplain why dialectical and historical materialism in the orthodox Soviet version was genuinely and sincerely hailed by contemporary Marxist intellectuals, and not merely accepted (with more or less rationalisation) because it came from the USSR.

For the Marxists, Marxism implied both continuity with the old bourgeois (and indeed proletarian) tradition of reason, science and progress and its revolutionary transformation in both theory and practice. For non-Marxist intellectuals who found themselves converging with the communists by whose side they fought against the common enemy, it had no such major theoretical implications. They found themselves on the same side as the Marxists. They recognised, or thought they could recognise, familiar attitudes and aspirations even when they found the arguments strange, or at the very least they admired and respected the hope, the confidence, the *élan* and moral force, and very often the heroism and self-sacrifice, of the young zealots, as J.M. Keynes – in no sense a sympathiser with Marxism or even with socialism of any kind – did.

> There is no one in politics today worth sixpence outside the ranks of the liberals, except the post-war generation of intellectual Communists under thirty-five. Them, too, I like and respect. Perhaps in their feelings and instincts they are the nearest thing we now have to the typical nervous nonconformist English gentlemen who went to the Crusades, made the Reformation, fought the Great Rebellion, won us our civil and religious liberties and humanised the working classes last century.[59]

The various intellectual 'fellow-travellers' whose history has been written with retrospective scepticism and derision[60] belonged essentially to this milieu. The term itself is ambiguous, since by means of it Cold War anti-communism has sought to conflate the widespread political consensus between liberal and communist intellectuals on fascism and the practical necessities of anti-fascism, with the much smaller group of those who could be relied on to adorn the 'broad' platforms at congresses organised by communists, to sign their manifestos, and the even smaller group who became regular defenders of or apologists for Soviet policies. The line between these groups was vague and shifting, but it must nevertheless be drawn. The imperatives of anti-fascism discouraged criticism of its most active and effective forces, just as the imperatives of war were to discourage anything which might weaken the unity of the forces fighting Hitler and the Axis. But this implied no 'fellow-travelling'.

The literary fortunes of George Orwell in Britain illustrate this. The difficulties of this writer, critical of Stalinism, the communist policy in the Spanish Civil War and various tendencies on the British left, came not so much from the communists (with whom he had little to do) or from their sympathisers, but rather from quite non-communist and non-Marxist editors and publishers who were sincerely reluctant to publish writings likely to give aid and comfort to 'the other side'.[61] Indeed, until the post-war era, which gave Orwell a mass audience, the public was quite unreceptive to such writings. His *Homage to Catalonia* (1938) did not sell more than a few hundred copies.

The intellectual 'fellow-travellers' who – with all due qualifications – deserve the name were a very miscellaneous group by intellectual origins and sympathies, though for almost all of them the experience of the First World War, which they had detested almost without exception, had been traumatic and decisive. Most of them were, or had become, men of the liberal and rationalist left. They were rarely attracted by Marxism, or by communist parties. Indeed their own, generally elevated image of the role of the intellectual precluded constant activism and submission to party discipline. Men like Romain Rolland, Heinrich Mann and Lion Feuchtwanger, while sometimes (like Zola) prepared to intervene in public affairs and always expecting to be listened to with attention, saw themselves, in Rolland's phrase, as standing '*au dessus de la mêlée*' – above the turmoil of struggle.

They were not even greatly attracted by the drama of the Russian or any other revolution, and indeed, like Rolland, Mann and Arnold Zweig, had been alienated by the repressive and terrorist aspects of internal Soviet policy. Before Hitler's triumph they had even protested against it.[62] In the 1930s antifascism alone would have led them to support and defend the USSR. As Thomas Mann was to put it in 1951, 'If nothing else were to command me to respect the Russian Revolution, it would be its immutable opposition to fascism.'[63] Yet basically it was the heritage of the Enlightenment, of rationalism, science and progress, which they believed they recognised in the USSR.

They did so at the very moment when the reality of the USSR might have been expected to repel Western liberal intellectuals: at the time of the Stalinist terror and among the advancing glaciers of the ice-age of Russian culture. But it was also the time of earthquakes for the bourgeois-liberal societies of the West, of the triple trauma of slump, fascist triumph and approaching world war. The backwardness and barbarism long associated with Russia seemed less relevant than its passionate public commitment to the values and aspirations of the Enlightenment amid the twilight of liberalism in the West, its planned industrialisation which contrasted dramatically with the crisis of the liberal economy, not to mention its anti-fascist role. 'USSR in Construction' (to use the phrase which became the title of an opulently illustrated periodical for foreign propaganda) could appear as a society built in the image of reason, science and progress, the lineal descendant of the Enlightenment and the great French Revolution. It became the exemplification of social engineering for human purposes – of the force of human hope for a better society. It was this phase of Soviet history which appealed to writers who had been unmoved by the utopian hopes, the social eruption of the revolution itself, by the mixture of poverty and high hope, of ideals and absurdity, and the cultural effervescence of the 1920s.

Moreover, whereas Soviet Russia in its revolutionary phase and the early communist parties had rejected their liberal humanism, they now underlined what they had in common with it. George Lukacs argued, against the avantgardists, that it was precisely the great bourgeois classics and their successors – Gorki, Rolland, the two Manns – who produced not only the best literature but the politically most positive literature. The judgement fitted in not only with his taste and critical principles (not to mention the political inclinations he could no longer express freely since the 'Blum Theses' of 1928–9), but with the

principles of a broad anti-fascist front which now became official communist policy. The 1936 Constitution of the USSR
was far more acceptable to Western 'bourgeois democrats' than
its predecessor(s). If it remained entirely on paper, that paper at
least represented aspirations which they could sincerely welcome.

What drew Marxists and non-Marxists together was thus
more than the practical need to unite against a common enemy.
It was a profound sense, both underlined and catalysed by the
slump and Hitler's triumph, that both belonged together in the
tradition of the French Revolution, of reason, science, progress
and humanist values. The identification was made easier for
both sides by the version of Marxist philosophy which became
official in this period and by the transfer of the centres of
Western Marxism to France and the Anglo-Saxon countries, in
which both Marxist and non-Marxist intellectuals had been
formed in a culture penetrated by this tradition.

VI

Yet anti-fascism was not primarily a gateway to academic
theory. It was in the first instance a matter of political action,
policy and strategy. As such it faced both Marxists who were
intellectuals and those who were not, those who entered politics
in the anti-fascist period and those with longer political memories, with problems of political analysis and decision which
cannot be omitted from this chapter.

It is impossible in the present state of research to quantify the
mobilisation of intellectuals in the anti-fascist cause, but it can
confidently be said that, like the Dreyfus affair, it made a special
appeal to them as a group, that it mobilised a large number of
them for political action, and above all that it provided far
greater opportunities for them to serve the cause *as intellectuals*
than had been at all usual in the past. It is not surprising that

some should have gone to fight in Spain, though no particular effort was made to encourage them to do so; indeed in Britain students were tacitly dissuaded from volunteering.[64] However, they joined the International Brigades not as intellectuals but as soldiers. That they should join wartime resistance movements is not surprising either; nor even that they joined, and sometimes became prominent, in the armed partisan struggle. Neither of these activities was confined to intellectuals. What was new in this period – and probably recognised earlier by the communist movement than elsewhere – was the scope of specific intellectuals' contributions to the anti-fascist movement: not only, if prominent, as propagandist symbols, but by their work in the media (publishing, the press, the cinema, theatre, etc.), as scientists, or in other ways which required people of their qualifications. There is no precedent, for instance, for the voluntary and spontaneous mobilisation of scientists *as such* against war, and subsequently for war.

And indeed, the career of a figure like J. Robert Oppenheimer, the scientist chiefly responsible for the construction of the first atomic bombs, becomes comprehensible only in the context of the specific historical circumstances which determined it. Naturally an intellectual of his kind became an anti-fascist, attracted to communism in the 1930s. But anti-fascist scientists were the only ones who could have drawn the attention of their governments to the possibility of nuclear weapons, since only scientists could recognise this possibility and only politically conscious scientists would have felt with such urgency the need to acquire such weapons before the fascists did. Inevitably such men became indispensable to their governments and privy to the most vital secrets of the state: no one else could have discovered and constructed what necessarily became secret. Equally inevitably, their position was complex and became difficult. Not only did they themselves hold moral and political positions at variance with those of the state apparatus which employed them (if only on the matter of free scientific communication), but that state apparatus increasingly distrusted them as intellectuals and, when Russia became the major enemy after the war, as people with an anti-fascist and philo-communist past. Inevitably their opinions on military-technical matters and on moral and political issues could not be clearly separated. However, while this had caused little difficulty when the struggle against fascism dominated all minds, the issues of post-war nuclear policy – e.g. whether hydrogen bombs should be constructed – left room for far greater moral and political divergences.

Oppenheimer became the most spectacular victim of the Cold War: the most eminent and influential of official scientific advisers of the US government baselessly accused of espionage for Russia and deprived of access to information as a 'security risk'. The predicament of such men as he and of his government could not have arisen in any earlier war, since no weapon relying so exclusively on the initiative and expertise of pure university scientists had then existed. It was less likely to arise for the scientists of subsequent generations, because they lacked the politically equivocal past of their seniors, even when they did not belong to the now substantial regiment of scientific functionaries or people who served the cause of destruction professionally as non-political experts. It was characteristically a predicament of the intellectuals of the period of anti-fascism and the governments who found themselves involved with them.

Anti-fascism thus faced intellectuals, the Marxists among them, not only with new tasks and possibilities but also with new problems of political and public action. These were particularly acute for the communists and communist sympathisers. This is not the place to consider their reaction to developments after the defeat of fascism. Nor need we spend much time on the effects of particular policy changes in the communist movement during the period of anti-fascism, though some of them – notably the reversal of Soviet policy in 1939–41 and the temporary dissolution of some communist parties in the Americas ('Browderism') – produced significant shock-waves among communists. Broadly speaking, the international line of the communist movement remained unchanged between 1934 and 1947, and reverted to its main course after such temporary deviations. Nor need we be much concerned with the specific frictions within communist parties between their leadership and intellectuals, though, as already mentioned, these existed. In the anti-fascist period they were almost certainly more than offset by the influx of intellectuals into the movement, the parties' appreciation of their political value (indicated by the multiplication of more or less 'broad' or at any rate not specifically party-identified journals and associations,[65] and the relatively wide scope for their autonomous activities. Individuals no doubt tended to leave or be expelled for various reasons, and the most articulate critics of communist policy and the USSR were no doubt to be found among intellectuals, but since, on the whole, there were in this period no major splits in the communist movement, and no significant secessions of *groups* of intellectuals (except to some extent in the USA), and since dissident Marxist groups were at this time insignificant, the tension between parties regarding themselves as representing essentially 'loyal' proletarians and intellectuals regarded as fundamentally 'petty-bourgeois' and 'unreliable' were on the whole kept under control.

The major difficulties arose out of the very adoption of the anti-fascist policy by the international communist movement. The impact of the change from the 'class-against-class' line to the support of anti-fascism and popular fronts is discussed elsewhere, but it is nevertheless worth underlining the dramatic change it represented in what most communists had learned to believe about politics. Their beliefs had been formulated precisely in opposition to liberalism and social democracy, in order to protect Bolshevism, devoted to world revolution, from contamination by any kind of reformism and compromise with the status quo.

The difficulties this caused were psychological rather than theoretical. It was not hard to find Marxist justifications and precedents for the line of the Seventh World Congress of the

Comintern, and these seemed all the more persuasive because they visibly coincided with common sense. What was difficult for communists brought up in the period of 'Bolshevisation' and 'class-against-class' was to envisage the new line in other than purely tactical terms, as a temporary concession to a temporary situation, after which the old struggles would resume; or as other than a sort of disguise. The Seventh World Congress itself bears witness to the novelty (for communists) of the new line, by its very insistence that it was not a break with the old, but simply its adaptation to a specific political conjuncture, as well as, of course, the correction of avoidable 'errors' in the past. At the same time the novelty of the new perspectives was obscured by the reluctance to discuss them freely and clearly for tactical reasons, as well as – presumably – in order not to foreclose the options of USSR state policy. Nor is it at all clear how far their implications were clearly recognised by or accepted by communists, old and new, who were still officially committed to Soviet power as the only conclusive form of the overthrow of 'the class rule of the exploiters'.[66]

Yet, however cautiously and provisionally formulated, the new line was clearly intended to be more than a tactical interim. It envisaged a model of transition to socialism other than by the insurrectionary seizure of power – even, in Ercoli's report, a possible peaceful transition. It envisaged transitional forms of regime which would not be identical with the 'dictatorship of the proletariat', as in the concept of a 'new democracy' or 'people's democracy'. Moreover, it implied a communist politics which would not be substantially an extension of the class struggle between proletarians and capitalists, with such 'class alliances' as might be necessary and possible, and which was therefore directly derivable from the economic structure of capitalism. It rather envisaged or implied a politics that was both autonomous and designed to achieve working-class leadership or hegemony over the entire nation. No doubt fascism was presented as the extreme and logical version of capitalism, though it was not argued that all capitalists were fascist. The minority of philo-fascists among them could be identified with the 'monopoly-capitalists' (such as the '200 families' in France) who could be represented as the exploiters of 'the peasants, artisans and petty-bourgeois masses' as well as of the workers. However, the test of anti-fascism was not class position or ideology, but exclusively the readiness to join the anti-fascist front, or, more precisely, to join in opposing German fascism as the principal instigator of war. Capitalists were expropriated after victory not as capitalists, but as fascists and traitors.

Retrospectively the implications of the new line are clearer than they were seen to be at the time. If we re-read an official communist analysis of the Spanish Civil War – written by Palmiro Togliatti at its outset under the significant title *The Spanish Revolution* (December 1936) – its tenor is not in doubt. The struggle of the Spanish people 'is the greatest event in the struggle of the masses of the people in capitalist countries for their emancipation, second only to the October Socialist Revolution of 1917'. It was a revolution. While it was 'solving the tasks of the bourgeois-democratic revolution', it was 'solving [them] . . . in a new way which is in accordance with the deepest interests of the vast mass of the people' – i.e. it was not *merely* a bourgeois-democratic revolution (as Togliatti also suggested by arguing that it was not entirely comparable either to 1905 or 1917). It did so in conditions of armed struggle, brought on by the military rising; it was forced to confiscate the property of the insurgent section of landlords and employers; it could draw on the experience of the Russian Revolution; and finally 'the Spanish working class is striving to accomplish its leading role in the revolution, and place upon it a proletarian imprint by the sweeping range and form of its struggle'. At the same time this was not a classic struggle conducted by workers and peasants only, for the Spanish Popular Front had a much broader basis. Nor did it merely represent the equivalent of the 'democratic dictatorship of the proletariat and the peasantry' which Lenin had envisaged in 1905, for 'under the pressure of the civil war it is adopting a series of measures which go somewhat further than the programme of revolutionary-democratic dictatorship'. It would be forced to go further in the direction 'of the strict regulation of the whole economic life of the country' by the necessities of war. Consequently, 'should the people be victorious, this new democracy cannot but be alien to all conservatism; for it possesses all the conditions for its own further development, it provides the guarantees for further economic and political achievements by the working people of Spain'.

In short, what Togliatti – acting as a spokesman of the Comintern – presented was a strategy of transition to socialism growing out of the specific conditions of anti-fascist struggle, in this instance in the form of civil war, and different from the Russian revolutionary process of 1905–17. There could be room for argument about the forms of this struggle, i.e. about the policies of the Republican government and the best ways of winning the war. There was indeed argument, and the debate still continues. But there can be no room for argument about the revolutionary perspectives of this analysis, even though it must be said that later communist statements about Spain tended to play down the revolutionary character of events in that country. Yet the studied vagueness and allusiveness of Togliatti's formulations ('in accordance with the deepest interests of the vast mass of the people', 'go somewhat further', 'all the conditions for its own further development', etc.), clear though their implications were for old Bolsheviks, contained an element of deliberate ambiguity. It was hardly expedient either to remind non-socialist anti-fascists that communists saw 'the final victory of the People's Front over fascism' as a preparation for the victory of the proletariat, or to spell out too clearly to communists how great a break with their past assumptions about revolutionary strategy was implied in the new line. For both it was best to concentrate on the immediate tasks of the anti-fascist struggle.

This did not affect the great mass of those who passionately supported the Spanish Republic in 1936–9. The Spanish Civil War provoked the greatest spontaneous international mobilisation of anti-fascism, particularly among intellectuals – a relatively even greater one than the wartime resistance movements, since it was independent of governments, and neither imposed by the response to conquest of one's own country, nor divided about the nature of the main enemy. It divided the international right, for sections of it – even among Catholics – were sympathetic to the Republic or hostile to its enemies. It united the left, from liberal democrats to anarchists, in spite of the mutual hostilities between its sections. The left disagreed about many things, including the best ways of fighting Franco, but not about the necessity of fighting him. And it is safe to say that for most Republican sympathisers abroad what counted above all was the defeat of Franco, rather than the nature of the Spanish regime which might follow. It is even possible to go further. Most Republican sympathisers, like most supporters of wartime resistance, looked to post-fascist regimes which would be, in a more or less vague sense, 'new', even 'revolutionary' – freer and more just societies, or at any rate not simply a restoration of the former status quo.

Yet for the Marxists the problem of the relation between anti-fascism and socialism was more concrete and acute, and for the communists among them the mist which surrounded the debate about it was never dissipated. As communists they were confident that the broad anti-fascist line would bring them closer to a transfer of power. Communist parties were dramatically strengthened as a consequence of applying it, the resistance movements – the logical products of the anti-fascist line – actually transformed the political struggle into an armed struggle, and indeed not only did communist parties emerge from the anti-fascist period stronger than they had ever been before – except in Spain and parts of Germany – and as participants in many governments of anti-fascist unity, but power had actually been transferred in a number of countries.

Hence few communists were seriously troubled by the criticism of dissident Marxists and others who argued that in strengthening anti-fascist unity the class struggle and the revolution were being betrayed, and that the USSR was not interested in revolutions abroad (except perhaps those imposed by the Red Army). No doubt some of the more extreme applications of national and international unity against the main enemy shocked the militants, because they conflicted with their instincts, traditions and even experience. Nevertheless, in general the communist line, insofar as it represented the logic of anti-fascism, seemed convincing and realistic. What alternative to the communist policy of fighting the Spanish Civil War was there? Then as now the answer must be: none.[67] Was Thorez wrong in 1936 to proclaim against Marceau Pivert: 'The Popular Front is not the Revolution'? Historians and leftists have argued about this, but at the time it seemed a reasonable rather than an outrageous statement. The communist parties of Italy and France have been bitterly criticised for their failure to pursue a more radical policy in 1943–5, or even to attempt a seizure of power, but the mass of their members and sympathisers, mainly recruits of the period of resistance and liberation, seem to have accepted the parties' line without major difficulty. As for the USSR, the very idea that it could *not* be in favour of socialism abroad seemed absurd to communists whose political analysis was based on the assumption that, whatever the variations of the international state policy of the USSR, the interests of the first and only socialist state in the world and those who wished to construct socialism on its model elsewhere could not but be fundamentally identical.

Indeed debates on the validity of the communist line in its anti-fascist phase were of comparative insignificance at the time, except on the then isolated dissident Marxist fringes. They gained a wider audience not only with the disintegration of the monolithic Moscow-centred communist movement in the period after Stalin's death, but above all with the discovery that the anti-fascist strategy, with all its extraordinary triumphs, had not in fact solved the problem of the further advance to social-ism, except in those countries in which for one reason or another the war led communist parties to power.[68] However, there is no doubt that the studied ambiguity which surrounded the ulterior perspectives of the anti-fascist line postponed and indeed discouraged clear analysis of this problem.

For this reason a discussion of the attitude of Marxist intel-lectuals (or of any communist Marxists) to it is unusually difficult, and perhaps impossible. It hardly arose as a problem until the moment when victory over fascism appeared certain – say around 1943, though, as we have seen, it had been envis-aged in the context of the Spanish revolution. Until fascism faced evident defeat, the problem of what would succeed it seemed, and was, entirely academic. When victory seemed cer-tain, the new perspective appeared for the communists in the form of 'people's democracy' or 'new democracy', but, given the disappearance of the Communist International and the conditions of war, they were neither formally promulgated (as anti-fascism had been by the Seventh World Congress) nor in effect systematically diffused and discussed throughout the com-munist parties. They appeared rather in the form of a series of documents emanating from various Soviet or other communist quarters, or of apparently ad hoc party decisions, some of them subsequently rescinded.[69]

The sidelong manner in which 'people's democracy' made its entry on the political stage did nothing to disperse the ambigu-ity which surrounded the term. It could be regarded in purely short-range terms, as a necessary concession in the interests of maintaining maximum unity internationally and within each nation among the forces fighting for victory against the Axis. Any suggestion that the communists were preparing for a resumption of hostilities against their present domestic or for-eign allies might tempt these in turn to prepare for the fight against future enemies rather than concentrate wholeheartedly on fighting the present ones. This, and perhaps no more, was clearly implied in the 'new line' which was recognised in the Comintern from October 1942.[70] The regimes of liberated countries would be 'democracies' – popularly oriented or 'new' democracies – but the project to establish these was 'no social-ist programme', as the Austrian communists observed realistically, and its immediate task was 'neither the realisation of socialism nor the introduction of a soviet system', as Dimitrov stated, but 'the consolidation of the democratic and parliamentary regime'.[71] The line between the formally similar governments of national anti-fascist unity with communist participation in post-liberation Eastern and Western Europe was thus left extremely hazy.

But it could also be regarded as the logical development of the kind of transition adumbrated in the line of the Seventh World Congress. The 'government of the anti-fascist united front' widened into the national anti-fascist front could be envisaged as transforming themselves into organs for the grad-ual and peaceful transition to socialism, by means of the establishment of working-class hegemony over the coalition of anti-fascist forces, that hegemony in turn being due to the recognition of the leading role of the working class in the fight against fascism and the positions consequently acquired by the communist parties. In this sense it was an alternative road to socialism to the one taken by Russia in 1917, and – as Dimitrov and his then spokesman Chervenkov put it as late as the inau-gural meeting of the Cominform in September 1947 – an alternative to the 'dictatorship of the proletariat'.[72] However, since very little about it was publicly discussed, the political conditions making such a road possible or impossible remained in obscurity, as also did the unprecedented problems of pluri-party politics during such a transition period. They were not publicly raised in the communist movement until after this perspective, in East or West, had been de facto abandoned officially.

Thirdly, the new line might also be interpreted in terms of post-war international relations. The continuation of the wartime alliance was envisaged together with the long-term peaceful coexistence of non-fascist capitalist and socialist states which it implied. Indeed, insofar as the post-war situation was systematically discussed by communists in a position to do so publicly, it was primarily in these terms, particularly in the light of the Teheran Conference between Stalin, Roosevelt and Churchill in late 1943. It created some uneasiness among at least some communist intellectuals. However, while the Teheran perspective did not exclude the 'people's democracy' perspective of a transition to socialism,[73] it also implied that in some countries the struggle for socialism should be deliberately subordinated to the greater requirements of peaceful coexistence, and perhaps to the possibilities of advance elsewhere. To put it brutally, 'British and American ruling circles had to be convinced that their joint war together with the Soviet Union . . . would not result in the Soviet socialist system being extended to western Europe under the stimulus of the victorious Red Armies'.[74] In the USA it was reasonable to assume that, since there was no realistic chance of socialism, the maintenance of capitalism (a capitalism ready to cooperate with the USSR) would be the basis of communist policy in that country, but the foreclosing of left-wing options elsewhere could hardly be welcomed; which is perhaps why 'Browderism' was denounced in 1945 in France. Nevertheless, the 'Teheran perspective' implied that *some* communist parties outside the expected zone of influence of the USSR might accept a lengthy capitalist future for their countries, though it left entirely unclear which countries these were, and for how long or short a period they would abandon the struggle for a socialist transformation, or what the future perspectives of their communists were in these circumstances. The questions remained unanswered because, with the exception of the shortlived Browder episode in the USA, they remained unasked.

These were uncertainties and obscurities of a specific and relatively brief period, when the era of anti-fascism was coming to an end. Yet they illustrate ambiguities implicit in the anti-fascist strategy from the start. It implied, as Trotskyites and other leftists rightly pointed out, an approach to the struggle for socialist power difficult to reconcile with that of 'proletarian revolution' as hitherto conceived by Bolsheviks and other social revolutionaries. In this they were right, though they condemned themselves to isolation by rejecting policies which for most intellectuals, Marxist or not, were necessary if fascism was to be defeated, and because they themselves produced no plausible alternative. Yet this strategy only hovered on the edge of explicitness, it was never clearly formulated, and indeed the discussions on the post-fascist future, other than in the vaguest of terms, were muted and discouraged for most of the period. It was perfectly possible for equally loyal communists – say, Togliatti and Tito – to read into the anti-fascist line very different implications for political action unless possible choice was eliminated by a decision from higher authority.

The theoretical fog which thus swirled around the future troubled most communist intellectuals less than it might or perhaps ought to have done, chiefly because the tasks of the present were so clear and, until victory over fascism seemed certain, communist strategy – omitting temporary episodes such as 1939–41 – provided so lucid and convincing a guide to what had to be done *now*. For, in the final analysis, for most of them the fight against fascism came first. If it were lost, arguments about the future became academic. For Marxist intellectuals, old or young, anti-fascism was obviously not an end in itself. It was justified by its contribution to the eventual overthrow of world capitalism, or at least capitalism in a large part of the world. Yet in a real sense it needed no such justification. Whatever the future might bring, fascism was evil and had to be resisted, A generation of intellectuals came to Marxism in and mainly through the slump and the struggle against fascism, in times of falling darkness. Those who survived have often been disappointed. They have delved into their past to discover whether they were mistaken, what their errors might have been, or what went wrong with their high hopes. Many have ceased to be Marxists. But it is safe to say that very few, if any of them, reject their participation in the fight against and the defeat of fascism. It is hard to find a man or woman who regrets their support of the Spanish Republic or their share, however small, in the war against fascism, whether as civilians, uniformed soldiers or resisters. It is a part of their past on which they look back with modest pride. For some it is the only part of their political past on which the survivors of that time look back with unqualified satisfaction.

12

Gramsci

Antonio Gramsci died in 1937. For the first ten of the subsequent seventy-five years he was virtually unknown except to his old comrades from the 1920s, since very little of his writings was published or available. This does not mean that he lacked influence, for Palmiro Togliatti may be said to have led the Italian Communist Party on Gramscian lines, or at least on his interpretation of Gramscian lines. Nevertheless, for most people anywhere until the end of the Second World War, even for communists, Gramsci was little more than a name. During the second decade after his death he became extremely well known in Italy, and was admired far beyond communist circles. His works were extensively published by the CP, but above all by the house of Einaudi. Whatever criticisms were subsequently made of these early editions, they made Gramsci widely available and allowed Italians to judge his stature as a major Marxist thinker, and more generally, a major figure in twentieth-century Italian culture.

But only Italians. For during this decade Gramsci remained for practical purposes quite unknown outside his own country, since he was virtually untranslated. Indeed, attempts to get even his moving prison letters published in Britain and the USA failed. Except for a handful of people with personal contacts in Italy and who could read Italian – mostly communists – he might as well not have existed this side of the Alps.

During the third decade, there were the first serious stirrings of interest in Gramsci abroad. They were no doubt stimulated by de-Stalinisation and even more by the independent attitude of which Togliatti made himself the spokesman after 1956. At all events in this period we find the first English selections from his work and the first discussions of his ideas outside communist parties. Outside Italy, the English-speaking countries seem to have been the first to develop a sustained interest in Gramsci. Paradoxically in Italy itself, during the same decade, criticism of Gramsci became articulate and sometimes shrill, and arguments about the interpretation of his work by the Italian CP developed.

Finally, in the 1970s Gramsci came fully into his own. In Italy itself the publication of his works was for the first time put on a satisfactory scholarly basis by the complete edition of the *Prison Letters* (1965), the publication of various early and political writings, and above all by Gerratana's monument of scholarship, the chronologically ordered edition of the *Prison Notebooks* (1975). Both Gramsci's biography and his role in the history of the Communist Party now became much clearer, thanks largely to the systematic historical work on its own records promoted and encouraged by the Communist Party. The discussion continues, and this is not the place to survey the Italian Gramsci debate since the middle 1960s. Abroad, translations of Gramsci's writings for the first time became available in adequate selections, notably in the two Lawrence & Wishart volumes edited by Hoare and Nowell Smith. So have translations of important secondary works such as Fiori's *Life* (1970).[1] Here again, without attempting to survey the growing literature about him in our language – representing different but universally respectful points of view – it is enough to say that on the fortieth anniversary of his death there was no longer any excuse for not knowing about Gramsci. What is more to the point, he *is* now known, even by people who have not actually read his writings. Such typically Gramscian terms as 'hegemony' occur in Marxist, and even in non-Marxist discussions of politics and history as casually, and sometimes as loosely, as Freudian terms did between the wars. Gramsci has become part of our intellectual universe. His stature as an original Marxist thinker – in my view the most original thinker produced in the West since 1917 – is pretty generally admitted. Yet what he said and why it is important is still not as widely known as the simple fact that he *is* important. I shall here single out one reason for his importance: his theory of politics.

It is an elementary observation of Marxism that thinkers do not invent their ideas in the abstract, but can only be understood in the historical and political context of their times. If Marx always stressed that men make their own history – or, if you like, think out their own ideas – he also stressed that they can only do so (to quote a famous passage from *The 18th Brumaire*) under the conditions in which they find themselves immediately, under conditions which are given and inherited. Gramsci's thought is quite original. He is a Marxist, and indeed a Leninist, and I don't propose to waste any time by defending him against the accusations of various sectarians who claim to know exactly what is and what is not Marxist and to have a copyright in their own version of Marxism. Yet for those of us brought up in the classical tradition of Marxism, both pre-1914 and post-1917, he is often a rather surprising Marxist. For instance, he wrote relatively little about economic development, and a great deal about politics, including about and in terms of theorists like Croce, Sorel and Machiavelli, who don't usually figure much or at all in the classical writings. So it is important to discover how far his background and historical experience explain this originality. I need not add that this does not in any way diminish his intellectual stature.

When Gramsci entered Mussolini's jail, he was the leader of the Italian Communist Party. Now Italy in Gramsci's day had a number of historical peculiarities which encouraged original departures in Marxist thinking. I shall mention several of them briefly.

(1) Italy was, as it were, a microcosm of world capitalism inasmuch as it contained in a single country both metropolis and colonies, advanced and backward regions. Sardinia, from where Gramsci came, typified the backward, not to say archaic, and semi-colonial side of Italy; Turin with its Fiat works, where he became a working-class leader, then as now typifies the most advanced stage of industrial capitalism and the mass transformation of immigrant peasants into workers. In other words, an intelligent Italian Marxist was in an unusually good position to grasp the nature both of the developed capitalist world and the 'Third World' and their interactions, unlike Marxists from countries belonging entirely to one or the other. Incidentally it is therefore a mistake to consider Gramsci simply as a theorist of 'Western communism'. His thought was neither designed exclusively for industrially advanced countries nor is it exclusively applicable to them.

(2) One important consequence of Italy's historical peculiarity was that even before 1914 the Italian labour movement was both industrial and agrarian, both proletarian and peasant-based. In this respect it stood more or less alone in Europe before 1914, though this is not the place to elaborate the point. Still, two simple illustrations will suggest its relevance. The regions of the strongest communist influence (Emilia, Tuscany, Umbria) are not industrial regions, and the great post-war leader of the Italian trade union movement, Di Vittorio, was a southerner and a farm-worker. Italy did not stand quite so alone in the unusually important role played by intellectuals in its labour movement – largely intellectuals from the backward and semi-colonial South. However, the phenomenon is worth noting, as it plays an important part in Gramsci's thinking.

(3) The third peculiarity is the very special character of Italy's history as a nation and a bourgeois society. Here again, I don't want to go into details. Let us merely recall three things: (a) that Italy pioneered modern civilisation and capitalism several centuries before other countries, but was unable to maintain its achievement and drifted into a sort of backwater between Renaissance and Risorgimento; (b) that unlike France the bourgeoisie did not establish its society by a triumphant revolution, and unlike Germany it did not accept a compromise solution offered it by an old ruling class from above. It made a partial revolution: Italian unity was achieved partly from above – by Cavour – partly from below – by Garibaldi; (c) so, in a sense the Italian bourgeoisie failed – or partly failed – to achieve its historic mission to create the Italian nation. Its revolution was incomplete and Italian socialists like Gramsci would therefore be especially conscious of the possible role of their movement, as the potential leader of the nation, the carrier of national history.

(4) Italy was (and is) not merely a Catholic country, like many others, but a country in which the Church was a specifically Italian institution, a mode of maintaining the rule of the ruling classes without, and separate from, the state apparatus. It was also a country in which a national elite culture preceded a national state. So an Italian Marxist would be more aware than others of what Gramsci called 'hegemony', i.e. the ways in which authority is maintained which are not simply based on coercive force.

(5) For a variety of reasons – I have suggested some just now – Italy was therefore a sort of laboratory of political experiences. It is no accident that the country has long had a powerful tradition of political thought, from Machiavelli in the sixteenth century to Pareto and Mosca in the early twentieth; for even foreign pioneers of what we would now call political sociology also tended to be linked with Italy or to derive their ideas from Italian experience – I am thinking of people like Sorel and

Michels. So it is not surprising that Italian Marxists should be particularly aware of political theory as a problem.

(6) Finally, a very significant fact. Italy was a country in which, after 1917, several of the objective and even the subjective conditions of social revolution appeared to exist – more so than in Britain and France and even, I suggest, than in Germany. Yet this revolution did not come off. On the contrary, fascism came to power. It was only natural that Italian Marxists should pioneer the analysis of why the Russian October Revolution had failed to spread to Western countries, and what the alternative strategy and tactics of the transition to socialism ought to be in such countries. That, of course, is what Gramsci set out to do.

And this brings me to my main point, namely that Gramsci's major contribution to Marxism is to have pioneered a Marxist theory of politics. For though Marx and Engels wrote an immense amount about politics, they were rather reluctant to develop a general theory in this field, largely since – as Engels pointed out in the famous late letters glossing the materialist conception of history – they thought it more important to point out that 'legal relations as well as forms of State could not be understood from themselves, but are rooted in the material conditions of life' (Preface to *Critique of Political Economy*). And so they stressed above all 'the derivation of political, juridical and other ideological conceptions from the basic economic facts.' (Engels to Mehring). So Marx's and Engels' own discussion of such matters as the nature and structure of rule, the constitution and organisation of the state, and the nature and organisation of political movements, is mostly in the form of observations arising out of current commentary, generally incidental to other arguments – except perhaps for their theory of the origin and historic character of the state. Lenin felt the need for a more systematic theory of the state and revolution, logically enough on the eve of taking power, but as we all know the October Revolution supervened before he could complete it. And I would point out that the intensive discussion about the structure, organisation and leadership of socialist movements which developed in the era of the Second International was about practical questions. Its theoretical generalisations were incidental and ad hoc, except perhaps in the field of the national question, where the successors of Marx and Engels had practically to start from scratch. I am not saying that this did not lead to important theoretical innovations, as it clearly did with Lenin, though these were, paradoxically, pragmatic rather than theoretical, though underpinned with Marxist analysis. If we read the discussions about Lenin's new concept of the party, for instance, it is surprising how little Marxist *theory* enters the debate, even though Marxists as celebrated as Kautsky, Luxemburg, Plekhanov, Trotsky, Martov and Ryazanov took part in them. A theory of politics was indeed implicit in them, but it only partly emerged.

There are various reasons for this gap. In any case it did not seem to matter much until the early 1920s. But then, I would suggest, it became an increasingly serious weakness. Outside Russia the revolution had failed or never taken place, and a systematic reconsideration became necessary, not only of the movement's strategy for winning power, but also of the technical problems of a transition to socialism, which had never been seriously considered before 1917 as a concrete and immediate problem. Within the USSR the problem of what a socialist society would and should be like, in terms of its political structure and institutions, and as a 'civil society', emerged, as Soviet power emerged from its desperate struggles to maintain itself to become permanent. Essentially this is the problem which has troubled Marxists in recent years, and which was to be at issue between Soviet communists, Maoists and 'Eurocommunists', not to mention those outside the communist movement.

I stress the fact that we are here talking about two *different* sets of political problems: strategy and the nature of socialist societies.

Gramsci tried to get to grips with both, though some commentators seem to me to have concentrated excessively on only one of them, namely the strategic. But, whatever the nature of these problems, pretty soon it became, and for a long time remained, impossible to discuss them within the communist movement. In fact, one might well say that it was only possible for Gramsci to grapple with them in his writings because he was in prison, cut off from politics outside, and writing not for the present but for the future.

This does not mean that he was not writing politically in terms of the current situation of the 1920s and early 1930s. In fact one of the difficulties in understanding his work is that he took for granted a familiarity with situations and discussions which are now unknown to most of us or forgotten. Thus Perry Anderson has recently reminded us that some of his most characteristic thinking derives from and develops themes which appeared in the Comintern debates of the early 1920s. At all events, he was led to develop the elements of a full political theory within Marxism, and he was probably the first Marxist to do so. I shall not try to summarise his ideas: instead I shall pick out a few strands and underline what seems to me to be their importance.

Gramsci is a political theorist inasmuch as he regards politics as 'an autonomous activity' (*Prison Notebooks*), within the context and limits set by historical development, and because he specifically sets about investigating 'the place that political science occupies or should occupy in a systematic (coherent and logical) conception of the world in Marxism' (ibid). Yet that meant more than that he introduced into Marxism the sort of discussions found in the works of his hero, Machiavelli – a man who does not occur very often in the writings of Marx and Engels. Politics for him is the core not only of the strategy of winning socialism, but of socialism itself. It is for him, as Hoare and Nowell Smith rightly point out, 'the central human activity, the means by which the single consciousness is brought into contact with the social and natural world in all its forms' (*Prison Notebooks*). In short, it is much wider than the term as commonly used. Wider even than the 'science and art of politics' in Gramsci's own narrower sense, which he defines as 'a body of practical rules for research and of detailed observations useful for awakening an interest in effective reality and for stimulating more rigorous and more vigorous political insights'. It is partly implicit in the concept of praxis itself: that understanding the world and changing it are one. And praxis, the history that men make themselves, though in given – and developing – historical conditions, is what they *do*, and not simply the ideological forms in which men become conscious of the contradictions of society. It is, to quote Marx, how they 'fight it out'. In short, it is what can be called political action. But it is also partly a recognition of the fact that political action itself is an autonomous activity, even though it is 'born on the "permanent" and "organic" terrain of economic life'.

This applies to the construction of socialism as well as – perhaps more than – anywhere else. You might say that for Gramsci what is the basis for socialism is not socialisation in the economic sense – i.e. the socially owned and planned economy (though this is obviously its basis and framework) – but socialisation in the political and sociological sense, i.e. what has been called the process of forming habits in collective man which will make social behaviour automatic, and eliminate the need for an external apparatus to impose norms; automatic but also conscious. When Gramsci speaks of the role of production in socialism it is not simply as a means of creating the society of material plenty, though we may note in passing that he had no doubt about the priority of maximising production. It was because man's place in production was central to his consciousness under capitalism; because it was the experience of workers in the large factory which was the natural school of this consciousness. Gramsci tended to see, perhaps in the light of his experience in Turin, the large modern factory not so much as a place of alienation, more as a school for socialism.

But the point was that production in socialism could therefore not simply be treated as a separate technical and economic problem; it had to be treated simultaneously, and from his point of view primarily, as a problem of political education and political structure. Even in bourgeois society, which was in this respect progressive, the concept of work was educationally central, since 'the discovery that the social and natural orders are mediated by work, by man's theoretical and practical activity, creates the first elements of an intuition of the world free from all magic and superstition. It provides a basis for the subsequent development of an historical, dialectical conception of the world, which understands movement and change . . . which conceives the contemporary world as a synthesis of the past, of all past generations, that projects itself into the future. That was the real basis of the primary school'. And we may note in passing a constant theme in Gramsci: the future.

The main themes of Gramsci's political theory are outlined in the famous letter of September 1931:

My study of the intellectuals is a vast project . . . I greatly extend the notion of intellectuals beyond the current meaning of the word, which refers chiefly to great intellectuals. This study also leads me to certain determinations of the State. Usually this is understood as political society (i.e. the dictatorship of coercive apparatus to bring the mass of the people into conformity with the type of production and economy dominant at any given moment) and not as an equilibrium between political society and civil society (i.e. the hegemony of a social group over the entire national society exercised through the so-called private organisations such as the Church, the trade unions, the schools, etc.) Civil society is precisely the special field of action of the intellectuals.[2]

Now the conception of the state as an equilibrium between coercive and hegemonic institutions (or if you prefer, a unity of both) is not in itself novel, at least for those who look realistically at the world. It is obvious that a ruling class relies not only on coercive power and authority but on consent deriving from hegemony – what Gramsci calls 'the intellectual and moral leadership' exercised by the ruling group and 'the general direction imposed upon social life by the dominant fundamental group'. What is new in Gramsci is the observation that even bourgeois hegemony is not automatic but achieved through conscious political action and organisation. The Italian Renaissance city bourgeoisie could have become nationally hegemonic only, as Machiavelli proposed, through such action – in fact through a kind of Jacobinism. A class must transcend what Gramsci calls 'economic-corporative' organisation to become politically hegemonic; which is, incidentally, why even the most militant trade unionism remains a subaltern part of capitalist society. It follows that the distinction between 'dominant' or 'hegemonic' and 'subaltern' classes is fundamental. It is another Gramscian innovation, and crucial to his thought. For the basic problem of the revolution is how to make a hitherto subaltern class capable of hegemony, believe in itself as a potential ruling class and be credible as such to other classes.

Here lies the significance for Gramsci of the *party* – 'the modern Prince'. For quite apart from the historic significance of the development of the party in general in the bourgeois period – and Gramsci has some brilliant things to say about this – he recognises that it is only through its movement and its organisation, i.e. in his view through the party, that the working class develops its consciousness and transcends the spontaneous 'ecconomic-corporative' or trade unionist phase. In fact, as we know, where socialism has been victorious it has led to and been achieved by the transformation of parties into states. Gramsci is profoundly Leninist in his general view of the role of the party, though not necessarily in his views about what the party organisation should be at any given time or about the nature of party life. However, in my view, his discussion of the nature and functions of parties advances beyond Lenin's.

Of course, as we know, considerable practical problems arise from the fact that party and class, however historically identified, are not the same thing, and may diverge – particularly in socialist societies. Gramsci was well aware of these, as well as of the dangers of bureaucratisation etc. Indeed, his hostility to Stalinist developments in the USSR caused him trouble even in prison. I wish I could say that he proposes adequate solutions to these problems, but I am not sure that he does, any more than, so far, anyone else. Nevertheless, Gramsci's remarks on the bureaucratic centralism, though concentrated and difficult (e.g. in *Prison Notebooks*) are well worth serious study.

What is also new is Gramsci's insistence that the apparatus of rule, both in its hegemonic and to some extent in its authoritarian form, consists essentially of 'intellectuals'. He defines these not as a special elite or as a special social category or categories, but as a sort of functional specialisation of society for these purposes. In other words, for Gramsci all people are intellectual, but not all exercise the social function of intellectuals. Now this is important, in the sense that it underlines the autonomous role of the superstructure in the social process, or even the simple fact that a politician of working-class origin is not necessarily the same as a worker at the bench. However, though it often makes for brilliant historical passages in Gramsci, I cannot myself see that the observation is as important for Gramsci's political theory as he himself evidently thought. In particular, I think that his distinction between the so-called 'traditional' intellectuals and the 'organic' intellectuals produced by a new class itself is, at least in some countries, less significant than he suggests. It may be, of course, that I have not entirely grasped his difficult and complex thought here, and I ought certainly to stress that the question is of great importance to Gramsci himself, to judge by the amount of space he devoted to it.

On the other hand, Gramsci's *strategic* thought is not only – as always – full of quite brilliant historical insights, but of major practical significance. I think we ought to keep three things quite separate in this connection: Gramsci's general analysis, his ideas about communist strategy in specific historical periods, and lastly, the Italian Communist Party's actual ideas about strategy at any given time, which have certainly been inspired by Togliatti's reading of Gramsci's theory, and by that of Togliatti's successors. I don't want to go into the third of these, because such discussions are irrelevant for the purposes of the present essay. Nor do I want to discuss the second at length, because our judgement of Gramsci does not depend on his assessment of particular situations in the 1920s and 1930s. It is perfectly possible to hold that, say, Marx's *18th Brumaire* is a profound and basic work, even though Marx's own attitude to Napoleon III in 1852–70 and his estimate of the political stability of his regime were often unrealistic. This does not, however, imply any criticism of either Gramsci's own or Togliatti's strategy. Both are defensible. Leaving aside these matters, I would like to single out three elements in Gramsci's strategic theory.

The first is not *that* Gramsci opted for a strategy of protracted or 'positional' warfare in the West, as against what he called 'frontal attack' or a war of manoeuvre, but *how* he analysed these options. Granted that in Italy and most of the West there was not going to be an October Revolution from the early 1920s on – and there was no realistic prospect of one – he obviously had to consider a strategy of the long haul. But he did not in fact commit himself in principle to any particular outcome of the lengthy 'war of position' which he predicted and recommended. It might lead directly into a transition to socialism, or into another phase of the war of manoeuvre and attack, or to some other strategic phase. What would happen, must depend on the changes in the concrete situation. However, he did consider one possibility which few other Marxists have faced as clearly, namely that the failure of the revolution in the West might produce a much more dangerous long-term weakening of the forces of progress by means of what he called a 'passive revolution'. On the one hand the ruling class might grant certain demands to forestall and avoid revolution, on the other the revolutionary movement might find itself in practice (though not necessarily in theory) accepting its impotence and might be eroded and politically integrated into the system (see *Prison Notebooks*). In short, the 'war of position' had to be systematically thought out as a fighting strategy rather than simply as something for revolutionaries to do when there was no prospect of building barricades. Gramsci had of course learned from the experience of social democracy before 1914 that Marxism was not a historical determinism. It was not enough to wait for history somehow to bring the workers to power automatically.

The second is Gramsci's insistence that the struggle to turn the working class into a potential ruling class, the struggle for hegemony, must be waged *before* the transition of power, as well as during and after it. But this struggle is not merely an aspect of a 'war of position', it is a crucial aspect of the strategy of revolutionaries in all circumstances. Naturally the winning of hegemony, so far as possible, before the transfer of power is particularly important in countries where the core of ruling-class power lies in the subalternity of the masses rather than in coercion. This is the case in most 'Western' countries, whatever the ultra-left says, and however unquestioned the fact that *in the last analysis*, coercion is there to be used. As we may see in, say, Chile and Uruguay, beyond a certain point the use of coercion to maintain rule becomes frankly incompatible with the use of apparent or real consent, and the rulers have to choose between the alternatives of hegemony and force, the velvet glove and the iron fist. Where they choose force, the results have not usually been favourable to the working-class movement.

However, as we may see even in countries in which there has been a revolutionary overthrow of the old rulers, such as Portugal, in the absence of *hegemonic* force even revolutions can run into the sand. They must still win enough support and consent from strata not yet detached from the old regimes. The basic problem of hegemony, considered strategically, is not *how* revolutionaries come to power, though this question is very important. It is how they come to be accepted, not only as the politically existing or unavoidable rulers, but as guides and leaders. There are obviously two aspects to this: how to win assent, and whether the revolutionaries are ready to exercise leadership. There is also the concrete political situation, both national and international, which may make their efforts more effective or more difficult. The Polish communists in 1945 were probably not accepted as a hegemonic force, though they were ready to be one; but they established their power thanks to the international situation. The German social democrats in 1918 would probably have been accepted as a hegemonic force, but they did not want to act as one. Therein lies the tragedy of the German revolution. The Czech communists might have been accepted as a hegemonic force both in 1945 and in 1968, and were ready to play this role, but were not allowed to do so. The struggle for hegemony before, during and after the transition (whatever its nature or speed) remains crucial.

The third is that Gramsci's strategy has as its core a permanent organised class movement. In this sense his idea of the 'party' returns to Marx's own conception, at least in later life, of the party as, as it were, the organised class, though he devoted more attention than Marx and Engels, and even than Lenin, not so much to formal organisation as to the forms of political leadership and structure, and to the nature of what he called the 'organic' relationship between class and party. At the time of the October Revolution most mass parties of the working class were social-democratic. Most revolutionary theorists, including the Bolsheviks before 1917, were obliged to think only in terms of cadre parties or groups of activists mobilising the spontaneous discontent of the masses as and when they could, because mass movements were either not allowed to exist or were, usually, reformist. They could not yet think in terms of permanent and rooted, but at the same time revolutionary, mass working-class movements playing a major part on the political scene of their countries. The Turin movement, in which Gramsci formed his ideas, was a relatively rare exception. And though it was one of the main achievements of the Communist International to create some communist mass parties, there are signs, for instance in the sectarianism of the so-called 'Third Period', that the international communist leadership (as distinct from communists in some countries with mass labour movements) was unfamiliar with the problems of mass labour movements which had developed in the old way.

Here Gramsci's insistence on the 'organic' relationship of revolutionaries and mass movements is important. Italian historical experience had familiarised him with revolutionary minorities which had no such 'organic' relation, but were groups of 'volunteers' mobilising as and when they could, 'not really mass parties at all . . . but the political equivalent of gypsy bands or nomads' (*Prison Notebooks*). A great deal of leftist policy even today – perhaps especially today – is based in this way, and for similar reasons, not on the real working class with its mass organisation but on a notional working class, on a sort of external view of the working class or any other mobilisable group. The originality of Gramsci is that he was a revolutionary who never succumbed to this temptation. The organised working class as it is and not as in theory it ought to be was the basis of his analysis and strategy.

But, as I have repeatedly stressed, Gramsci's political thought was not only strategic, instrumental or operational. Its aim was not simply victory, after which a different order and type of analysis begins. It is very noticeable that time and again he takes some historical problem or incident as his starting-point and then generalises from it, not just about the politics of the ruling class or of some similar situations, but about politics *in general*. That is because he is constantly aware that there is something in common between political relations among men in all, or at least in a historically very wide range of societies – for instance, as he liked to recall, the difference between leaders and led. He never forgot that societies are more than structures of economic domination and political power, that they have a certain cohesion even when riven by class struggles (a point made long before by Engels), and that liberation from exploitation provides the possibility of constituting them as real communities of free men. He never forgot that taking responsibility for a society – actual or potential – is more than looking after immediate class or sectional or even state interests: that, for instance, it presupposes continuity 'with the past, with tradition or with the future'. Hence Gramsci insists on the revolution not simply as the expropriation of the expropriators, but also, in Italy, as the creation of a people, the realisation of a nation – as both the negation and the fulfilment of the past. Indeed, Gramsci's writing poses the very important problem – which has been seldom discussed – of what exactly in the past is revolutionised in a revolution, and what is preserved and why, and how; the problem of the dialectic between continuity and revolution.

But of course for Gramsci this is important not in itself, but as a means of both popular mobilisation and self-transformation, of intellectual and moral change, of collective self-development as part of the process by which, in its struggles, a people changes and makes itself under the leadership of the new hegemonic class and its movement. And though Gramsci shares the usual

Marxist suspicion of speculations about the socialist future, unlike most others he does seek a clue to it in the nature of the movement itself. If he analyses its nature and structure and development as a political movement, as a party, so elaborately and microscopically; if he traces, for instance, the emergence of a permanent and organised movement – as distinct from a rapid 'explosion' – down to its smallest capillary and molecular elements (as he calls them); then it is because he sees the future society as resting on what he calls 'the formation of a collective will' through such a movement, and *only* through such a move-ment. Because only this way can a hitherto subaltern class turn itself into a potentially hegemonic one – if you like, become fit to build socialism. Only in this way can it, through its party, actually become the 'modern Prince', the political engine of transformation. And in building itself it will in some sense already establish some of the bases on which the new society will be built, and some of its outlines will appear in and through it.

Let me ask, in conclusion, why I have chosen in this chapter to concentrate on Gramsci as a political theorist. Not simply because he is an unusually interesting and exciting one. And certainly not because he has a recipe for how parties or states should be organised. Like Machiavelli, he is a theorist of how societies should be founded or transformed, not of constitutional details, let alone of the trivialities which pre-occupy lobby correspondents. It is because among Marxist theorists he is the one who most clearly appreciated the importance of politics as a special dimension of society, and because he recognised that in politics more is involved than power. This is of major practical importance, not least for socialists.

Bourgeois society, at least in developed countries, has always paid primary attention to its political framework and mecha-nisms, for historical reasons into which this is not the place to go.

That is why political arrangements have become a powerful means for reinforcing bourgeois hegemony, so that slogans such as the defence of the republic, the defence of democracy, or the defence of civil rights and freedoms bind rulers and ruled together for the primary benefit of the rulers; but this does not mean that they are irrelevant to the ruled. They are thus far more than mere cosmetics on the face of coercion, or even than simple trickery.

Socialist societies, also for comprehensible historical reasons, have concentrated on other tasks, notably those of planning the economy, and (with the exception of the crucial question of power, and perhaps, in multinational countries, of the relation between their component nations) have paid very much less attention to their actual political and legal institutions, and processes. These have been left to operate informally, as best they can, sometimes even in breach of accepted constitutions or party statutes – e.g. the regular calling of Congresses – and often in a sort of obscurity. In extreme cases, as in China in recent years, the major political decisions affecting the future of the country appear to emerge suddenly from the struggles of a small group of rulers at the top, and their very nature is unclear, since they have never been publicly discussed. In such cases something is clearly wrong. Quite apart from the other disadvantages of this neglect of politics, how can we expect to transform human life, to create a socialist *society* (as distinct from a socially owned and managed economy), when the mass of the people are excluded from the political process, and may even be allowed to drift into depoliticisation and apathy about public matters? It is becoming clear that the neglect of their political arrangements by most socialist societies is leading to serious weaknesses, which must be remedied. The future of socialism, both in countries which are not yet socialist and in those which are, may depend on paying much more attention to them.

In insisting on the crucial importance of politics, Gramsci

drew attention to a crucial aspect of the construction of social-ism as well as of the winning of socialism. It is a reminder that we should heed. And a major Marxist thinker who made politics the core of his analysis is therefore particularly worth reading, marking and inwardly digesting today.

13

*The Reception of Gramsci**

Gramsci in Europe and America

Probably all who read a book about Gramsci's international impact in 1994 will agree with the statement of his first Spanish champion, quoted by Professor Fernández Buey: 'Gramsci es un clásico, o sea un autor que tiene derecho a no estar de moda nunca y a ser leído siempre.' ('Gramsci is a classic, that is to say an author who is never fashionable yet is read at all times.') And yet, every chapter of this book testifies to the paradox that the international fortunes of this classic writer have fluctuated with the changes of fashion on the intellectual left. Thus in the 1960s the vogue for Althusser in Latin America largely blocked the way for Gramsci, although in France itself Althusser's prominence also gave publicity to the then barely known Italian, whom he both praised and criticised. The element of fashion was particularly evident inasmuch as the reception of Gramsci coincided largely with the heyday of the 'new lefts' of the 1960s and 1970s, whose

*This chapter was originally written as an introduction to the collective work *Gramsci in Europa e America*, Antonio A. Santucci (ed), (Rome and Bari, 1996).

capacity to consume what Carlos Nelson Coutinho calls the 'zuppa eclectica' ('eclectic soup') of mutually incompatible intellectual ingredients was considerable. The element of fashion is even more evident in the 1990s, when former leftists transformed into neo-liberals no longer cared to be reminded of anything that recalled old enthusiasms. As Irina Grigor'eva notes of post-1991 Russia: 'Today everything connected with the heritage of ideas related to Marxism is condemned'. Hence Russia in 1993 was 'perhaps the least "Gramscian" country in the world'.

It is equally evident that Gramsci could not have become a major figure on the world intellectual scene but for a complex concatenation of circumstances in the forty years after his death. He would not have been known at all but for the determination of his comrade and admirer Palmiro Togliatti to preserve and publish his writings and to give them a central place in Italian communism. Under the conditions of Stalinism this was by no means an inevitable choice, especially given the known heterodoxy of Gramsci, even though the line of the Seventh World Congress of the International made it a little less risky. Whatever the subsequent criticisms of Togliatti's own views on Gramsci, his concern after Gramsci's death to 'sottrarli alle traversie del presente e garantirli per "la vita avvenire del partito"' (remove him from the troubles of the present and safeguard him for "the future life of the party"')[1] and his insistence on Gramsci's centrality from the moment of his return to Italy were the foundations of Gramsci's subsequent fortunes. The editorial deficiencies and omissions of the early post-war years were the price paid for making Gramsci known; in retrospect a price worth paying. Thanks to Togliatti's determination, and the new prestige of the PCI, at least the *Lettere* were published in a number of countries, including some 'people's democracies', before the death of Stalin. Where the local communist parties failed to do so, no one else did. Though excellent English translations were almost immediately made, it took decades actually to find publishers for the *Lettere* in Britain and the USA.

Even so, apart from a few foreigners with personal memories of the Italian Resistance and personal friendships on the postwar Italian left, the *Rezeptionsgeschichte* of Gramsci begins with the Twentieth Congress of the CPSU. For two decades it was part of the attempt by the international communist movement to emancipate itself from the heritage both of Stalin and the Communist International. Within the 'socialist camp' this was reflected in the almost immediate official acknowledgement of Gramsci as a political thinker as well as a martyr – as witness the publication of a three-volume selection from his works in the USSR in 1957–9, the Soviet presence at the first Gramsci Convegno in 1958 and the substantial and implicitly reformist Soviet delegation to the second (1967). Indeed, very few of the non-Italian authors who wrote about Gramsci in the twenty years after 1956 did not have some kind of committed Marxist past or present. Indeed it is hard to think of any non-Marxists in this field, before the end of the 1970s, except the American historian H. Stuart Hughes (who had a particular interest in Italy) and the British historian James Joll (who specialised in the history of the left). Eventually, of course, Gramsci was to make his way into the academic literature.

More precisely, Gramsci attracted attention outside Italy primarily as a communist thinker who provided a Marxist strategy for countries in which the October Revolution might have been an inspiration, but could not be a model – that is to say for socialist movements in non-revolutionary environments and situations. The prestige and success of the Italian Communist Party in the years between the Yalta Memorandum and the death of Enrico Berlinguer naturally spread the influence of a thinker generally considered as the inspirer of its strategies. Gramsci undoubtedly reached the peak of his international prominence in the years of 'eurocommunism' of the 1970s, and receded somewhat in the 1980s – except perhaps in the German Federal Republic, where he was discovered rather late, and interest in him was at its height in the first half of the

1980s. Where the left had not yet abandoned the hope of more classical strategies of insurrection and armed struggle, it preferred other intellectual gurus. Hence the curious two-stage history of Gramsci's penetration into Latin America: as part of the opening of CP Marxism after 1956–60, and after the collapse of the armed struggle strategies in the 1970s.

The international discussion on Gramsci, it seems, remained largely separate from and independent of the vigorous Italian debate on the country's greatest Marxist thinker. The major Italian books on Gramsci have not been translated, at all events into English – except for Fiore's biography – although introductions to the Italian literature are available, as in the works authored and edited by Showstack Sassoon and Mouffe. This is not surprising. Foreigners inevitably read some national thinkers, however universal his or her interests, in a different manner from readers in his or her own culture, and when the thinker is, like Gramsci, so closely concerned with his national reality foreign and national readings are even more likely to diverge. In any case, several of the issues most hotly debated in Italy were not so much arguments about Gramsci as arguments for or (more usually) against some phase of the policy of the PCI. These were not always of major interest to non-specialists outside. Nevertheless, it is relevant to note that what has influenced foreign readers is the text of Gramsci's writings rather than the literature of criticism and interpretation that has accumulated around them in his own country. That is to say, it is the Gramsci of the era when the first major selections of his work became available in the local languages or, at the earliest, when the first important local Gramscians appeared on the intellectual scene to introduce the as yet untranslated thinker. Essentially, we may say that the non-Italian Gramsci reception was that of the Gramsci as available in 1960–7.

The international reception of Gramsci has therefore been, and remains, subject to the fluctuating fortunes of the political left. And it will, and must, continue to be so to some extent. For

Gramsci was par excellence the philosopher of political praxis. Most of the luminaries of what has been called 'Western Marxism' can be read, as it were, as academics, which many of them were or could have been: Lukacs, Korsch, Benjamin, Althusser, Marcuse and others. They wrote at one or two removes from the concrete political realities even when, like Henri Lefebvre, they were at one time or another plunged into them as political organisers. Gramsci cannot be separated from these realities, since even his widest generalisations are invariably concerned with the investigation of the practical conditions for transforming the world by politics in the *specific* circumstances in which he wrote. Like Lenin, he was not designed for the academic life, though unlike Lenin he was a born intellectual, a man almost physically excited by the sheer attraction of ideas. Not for nothing was he the only genuine Marxist theorist who was also the leader of a Marxist mass party (if we leave aside the much less original Otto Bauer). One of the reasons why historians, Marxist and even non-Marxist, have found him so rewarding is precisely his refusal to leave the terrain of concrete historical, social and cultural realities for abstraction and reductionist theoretical models.

It is therefore likely that Gramsci will continue to be read mainly for the light his writings throw on politics, in his own words, the 'body of practical rules for research and of detailed observations useful for awakening an interest in effective reality and for stimulating more rigorous and more vigorous political insights'. I do not believe that those looking for such insights will only be found on the left, although for evident reasons those who share Gramsci's objectives are most likely to look to him for guidance. As Joseph Buttigieg notes, American anti-communists are worried because Gramsci can still inspire the post-Soviet left, even when Lenin, Stalin, Trotsky and Mao no longer can. Yet, while one hopes that Gramsci may still be a guide to successful political action for the left, it is already clear that his international influence has penetrated beyond the left, and indeed beyond the sphere of instrumental politics.[2]

It may seem trivial that an Anglo-Saxon reference work can – I quote the entry in its entirety – reduce him to a single word: 'Antonio Gramsci (Italian political thinker, 1891–1937), see under HEGEMONY'.[3] It may be absurd that an American journalist quoted by Buttigieg believes that the concept of 'civil society' was introduced into modern political discourse by Gramsci alone.[4] Yet the acceptance of a thinker as a permanent classic is often indicated by just such superficial references to him by people who patently know little more about him than that he is 'important'.

Fifty years after his death Gramsci had become 'important' in this manner even outside Italy, where his stature in national history and national culture was recognised almost from the beginning. It is now recognised in most parts of the globe. Indeed, the flourishing historical school of 'subaltern studies' centred in Calcutta suggests that Gramsci's influence is still expanding. He has survived the political conjunctures which first gave him international prominence. He has survived the European communist movement itself. He has demonstrated his independence of the fluctuations of ideological fashion. Who now expects another vogue for Althusser, any more than for Spengler? He has survived the enclosure in academic ghettos which looks like being the fate of so many other thinkers of 'Western Marxism'. He has even avoided becoming an 'ism'.

What the future fortunes of his writings will be, we cannot know. However, his permanence is already sufficiently sure, and justifies the historical study of his international reception.

Gramsci in English

The list of the world's authors whose works are most frequently cited in international literature on the humanities and arts[5] contains few Italians, and only five born since the sixteenth century. It does not, for instance, include either Vico or Machiavelli.

But it does contain the name of Antonio Gramsci. Citation does not guarantee either knowledge or understanding, but it does indicate that the author cited has an intellectual presence. Gramsci's presence in the world fifty years after his death was undeniable. It was particularly notable among historians in the English-speaking regions.

Gramsci became known in this area soon after the war, which had brought numerous anti-fascist intellectuals of English speech to Italy. His work was discussed sympathetically in the *Times Literary Supplement* as early as 1948, i.e. shortly after the publication of *Il Materialismo Storico*. Historians played a significant part in his discovery outside Italy. A young British historian compiled what is probably the first selection of his writings in a non-Italian language (Louis Marks, *The Modern Prince*, London, 1956), and as early as 1958 an established American historian discussed him under the heading 'Gramsci and Marxist Humanism' in what has remained the best-known work in the language on the general intellectual history of early twentieth-century Europe (H. Stuart Hughes, *Consciousness and Society*). Another British historian, Gwyn A. Williams, produced the first non-Italian discussion of 'The concept of *egemonia* in the thought of Antonio Gramsci' in 1960 (in the *Journal of the History of Ideas*). At the same time an American doctoral dissertation was completed by yet another historian, which a few years later became the first book about Gramsci outside Italy: John M. Cammett's *Antonio Gramsci and the Origins of Italian Communism* (Stanford, 1967). In short, by 1960 more was known about Gramsci in the English-speaking world than anywhere else outside Italy, though it was little enough. The exceptionally well-chosen selections of Gramsci's writings edited by Hoare and Nowell Smith from 1971 on reinforced the advantage enjoyed by English readers.[6]

Gramsci's major influence has, naturally, been on Marxist historians, who have been in some ways more active and influential in the English-speaking world than elsewhere in the West. Nevertheless, there is no 'Gramscian school' of history, nor can Gramsci's influence on historians be clearly distinguished from his influence on Marxism in general. Gramsci's writings and example have helped, above all, to crack open the hard shell of doctrine which had grown up round the living body of Marxist thought, concealing even strategies and observations as original as Lenin's behind appeals to textual orthodoxy. Gramsci has helped Marxists to liberate themselves from vulgar Marxism, and in turn made it more difficult for opponents of the left to dismiss Marxism as a variant of determinist positivism.

In this sense the main lessons of Gramsci are not Gramscian but Marxian. They are a set of variations on Marx's own theme that 'men make their own history, but they do not make it . . . under circumstances chosen by themselves, but under circumstances directly found, given and transmitted by the past' (*18th Brumaire*) (or, as Gwyn A. Williams puts it, 'The human will was central to Gramsci's Marxism, but it was an historic will, geared to the objective realities of history').[7] Even Gramsci's insistence, rare among his Marxist contemporaries, on the autonomy of the spheres of politics and culture can be seen as a reminder of Marx, as so acute a Marx-scholar as the late George Lichtheim did not fail to observe.[8]

It is therefore natural that an authoritative survey of developments in historiography sees Gramsci exclusively in this context.[9] And that a Marxist historian could state: 'The Gramscian influence on Marxist history is not particularly new. I don't think myself that Gramsci has much of a specific approach to history other than Marx's own approach.'[10] This does not make his influence less important. Historians anxious to break with the rigidities of the inherited communist tradition found themselves enormously encouraged, and inspired, by discovering that this 'theoretician of uncommon ability' (Lichtheim) was on their side. Moreover, few of the Marxist theorists who emerged, or were rediscovered, from the 1950s on were as steeped in history as he, and therefore as profitable to study or as likely to be read by historians.

Yet there is also a specifically Gramscian influence on historians, and not merely a Gramscian encouragement to turn (or return) to Marx. For not only are certain concepts in Gramsci's own theoretical work extremely fertile, adding, as it were, new dimensions to historical analysis, but he himself wrote extensively on problems which are essentially historical as well as political.

His reflections on Italian history, though much discussed in his own country, have not had much echo elsewhere, except in the restricted community of Italianists. On the other hand in one specific field, or complex of fields, of historical studies Gramsci's direct influence is strong, or even dominant. This is the history of ideology and culture, chiefly as it affects the 'common people', especially in pre-industrial society. Gramsci's influence in this field goes back a long way. As long ago as 1960 I noted that 'One of the most stimulating suggestions in the work of Antonio Gramsci is the call to pay far greater attention than in the past to the study of the world of the "subaltern classes".'[11].

The history and study of the world of the subaltern classes has since become one of the most rapidly growing and flourishing fields of historiography. It is practised not only by Marxists and a considerable number of what can best be described as left-wing populists, but by historians of other ideologies. The field has not grown because Gramsci called for such study; but anyone entering it seriously could not but take notice of one of the rare thinkers of any kind (and the only one in Western Marxism, not excluding Mar himself) who had given serious thought to it. For while there is a long tradition on which the historian of high culture and the ideas expressed in books can call, the historians in the new field of popular culture were virtually without guidance. Hence the intellectual void at the heart of such vapid concepts as the 'histoire des mentalités'. It is therefore natural that even non-Marxists who are drawn into this area, like the distinguished Cambridge historian Peter Burke, find themselves turning, if only incidentally, to Gramsci's writings, as in his path-breaking *Popular Culture in Early Modern Europe* (London, 1978). Indeed, it may today be difficult or impossible to discuss the problems of popular culture, or any culture, without moving closer to Gramsci, or making a more explicit use of his ideas; as Burke suggests that E.P. Thompson and Raymond Williams were to do.[12]

But the strength of Gramsci's intellectual engagement in this field, as in all the others he thought and wrote about, lies in the fact that it is not purely academic. Praxis stimulated and fertilised his theory and was the end of his theory. The reason why his influence on students of ideology and culture has been unusually marked is that for all those concerned with popular culture, the field is not purely academic either. The object of almost all who enter these studies is not primarily to write dissertations and books. They are passionately concerned, as Gramsci was, with the future as well as with the past: with the future of the ordinary people who form the bulk of humanity, including the working class and its movements, with the future of nations and civilisation. Seventy years after his death we are grateful to Gramsci not only for intellectual stimulation, but for teaching us that the effort to transform the world is not only compatible with original, subtle, open-eyed historical thinking, but impossible without it.

14

The Influence of Marxism 1945–83

No thinker has ever lived up more successfully to his own injunction: 'The philosophers have hitherto only interpreted the world: the point is to change it' (*Theses on Feuerbach*). Marx's ideas became the doctrines inspiring the labour and socialist movements of most of Europe. Mainly via Lenin and the Russian Revolution they became the quintessential international doctrine of twentieth-century social revolution, equally welcome as such from China to Peru. Through the triumph of parties and governments identified with these doctrines, versions of these ideas became the official ideology of the states in which, at their peak, something like a third of the human race lived, not to mention political movements of varying size and importance in the rest of the world. The only individually identifiable thinkers who have achieved comparable status are the founders of the great religions in the past, and with the possible exception of Muhammad none has triumphed on a comparable scale with such rapidity. No secular thinker can be named beside him in this respect.

How far Marx himself would have approved of what has been done in his name, and what he would have thought of the doctrines, often transformed into the secular equivalent of theologies, which are officially accepted as unchallengeable truth, is a matter for interesting but academic speculation. The fact remains that, however remote they may be from his own ideas, insofar as we can document or infer them, they derive historically from them, and the derivation, in thought and action, can be directly established. They belong to the history of Marxism. Whether these developments are logically implicit in Marx's ideas is a different and separate question. It has been much discussed, mainly because the regimes and governments successfully established in the name of Marx (so far usually in combination with some revolutionary leader claiming to be his disciple – Lenin, Stalin, Mao, etc.) have so far all had a certain family resemblance; or rather because they have all shared the negative characteristic of being unlike liberal democracy.

To answer this question is not part of the present chapter, but two comments may be made. Insofar as any set of ideas survives its originator, it ceases to be confined to its original intentions and content. Within the very wide limits set by the human capacity of exegesis, or even the human readiness to assert association with a desirable or cherished predecessor, it is subject to an unpredictably wide range of modifications and transformations in practice, and a very wide range in theory. Regimes claiming to be Christian, and deriving their authority from a particular body of written texts, have ranged from the feudal kingdom of Jerusalem to the Shakers, from the empire of the Russian tsars to the Dutch Republic, from Calvin's Geneva to Georgian England. Christian theology has at different times absorbed Aristotle and Marx. All could claim to be derived from the teachings of Jesus – though not usually to the satisfaction of other equally convinced Christians. Just such a wide range of ideas and practices have claimed to be derived from and compatible with the texts of Marx, directly or through his successors. If we did not know that they all claimed this derivation, we might well consider the differences between, say, Zionist *kibbutzim* and Pol Pot's Kampuchea, between Hilferding and Mao, between Stalin and Gramsci, Rosa Luxemburg and Kim Il-sung, to be more evident than their similarities. There is no theoretical reason why Marxist regimes should take a certain form, though there are good historical reasons why those which established themselves in the course of the historically brief period since 1917 by autochthonous revolution, imitation and conquest in a number of countries on the margins of or outside the industrialised world should have developed common negative or positive characteristics.[1] The argument that Marxian theory necessarily implies Leninism and only Leninism (or any other school claiming Marxist orthodoxy) therefore falls to the ground.

What can, however, be said is that any corpus of ideas, including those of Marx, is necessarily transformed by becoming a significant political force mobilising masses, whether this is done through parties and movements, through governments, or in other ways. Just so, any body of ideas is transformed, if only by formalisation, stabilisation and pedagogic simplification, if it comes to be taught in primary and secondary schools, and often enough in universities. Interpreting the world and changing the world, however organically linked, are not the same thing. Whether this happens through the formation of an informal set of beliefs such as that which distinguished nineteenth-century businessmen and their journalists from the actual writings of Adam Smith, on which they purported to be based, or – in extreme cases – by formal dogmas, dissent from which is not tolerated, is secondary. The fact of transformation remains. Indeed, much of the academic history of the ideas of past thinkers, particularly the history of political ideas, consists in rediscovering the original meaning and intention of thinkers and the original contexts and references of their thought, behind the posthumous reinterpretation. The only writings which escape this fate are the ones nobody ever took seriously, or those so closely identified with a particular time and place as to be forgotten immediately afterwards. The Adam Smith of today is not the Adam Smith of 1776, except for a handful of specialist scholars. The same is inevitably true of Marx.

The political impact of Marxism is no doubt the most important achievement of Marx from the point of view of history. Yet the intellectual impact has been almost as striking, though it cannot be separated from the political impact, least of all by Marxists. There are not many thinkers whose name alone suggests major transformations of the human intellectual universe. Marx is among them, together with such figures as Newton, Darwin and Freud. As this list of names implies, the intellectual transformations with which such names are identified are not comparable, except insofar as they have all penetrated far beyond the ranks of specialists in their respective fields into general educated culture. It is not suggested that Freud, or even Darwin, was of the same intellectual calibre as Newton. Nevertheless, whatever their abilities and the nature of their intellectual achievement, the names on such a list are few. Marx's position on it is hardly to be questioned, but it is peculiar in two ways. First, as this book shows, it is for practical purposes posthumous. Very few indeed would have predicated such fame in Marx's lifetime. Second, it was achieved in the face of a century of persistent, massive, passionate and intellectually very far from negligible criticism. Many of the best minds have devoted intensive efforts to the attempt to demonstrate Marx's errors and inadequacies, including many who, having once been Marxists, later became critics. This is not uncommonly encountered by thinkers who transform the intellectual universe. Nevertheless, the course of other such figures seems on the whole to have been less stormy, and intellectually serious criticism to have been confined to their specialist fields. At the time of the centenary of his death Marx had survived a century of concentrated fire directed against his ideas by anyone within reach of a pen, typewriter, public platform or – in suitable cases – a censor's blue pencil and detachments of police. His own intellectual stature was not in serious question. What is more, his global ideological presence was almost certainly greater than ever before or since; his writings and those he inspired more widely influential, read and discussed. And this was in spite of the increasingly evident facts that the formerly Marxist social-democratic parties disclaimed his influence, and that the Soviet Union was visibly losing both its attraction for the global left and, with de-Stalinisation, its supremacy among the revolutionary branches of the Marxist tradition.

There are three possible reasons for this remarkable record. Marxism has been persistently attacked because, since shortly after Marx's death, it has always been identified somewhere or other with powerful political movements threatening the status quo, and since 1917 with state-regimes regarded as internationally subversive, dangerous and threatening. Until the 1990s it never ceased to represent formidable political forces. Moreover, it always remained in theory international, thus presenting its critics with potentially universal danger or error. In this respect it differed from doctrines identified with particular nations or races and therefore unlikely to convert others, or from theoretically universal doctrines which are in practice confined to particular regions, such as Orthodox Christianity or Shi'ite Islam.

Moreover, Marxism had always been a revolutionary critique of the status quo with serious intellectual pretensions, and very soon established itself as by far the most influential and dominant among such critiques. By the 1970s virtually all opponents of the status quo who wished to replace it by a better 'new' society, and even some who wished to replace it by returning to an idealised 'old' society, described their aim as 'socialism'. But the position of Marxist analysis in socialist theory was such that a critique of socialism inevitably implied a criticism of Marx. One year after his death a well-informed survey of contemporary socialism,[2] while noting the extinction of the original pre-Marxian 'utopian' or 'mutualist' schools, could still devote only one of its nine chapters to Karl Marx. In the second half of the twentieth century discussions[3] were more likely to consider all variants of socialist doctrines essentially in terms of their relation to the doctrines of Marxism, which was tacitly assumed to be the central tradition of socialism.

By the same token, those who wished to criticise existing society were as attracted to the theory which dominated such critiques as on the other hand those who wished to defend it, or were sceptical of the proposals of revolutionaries, were impelled to attack Marx. Only under regimes in which Marxist doctrine was identified with the official ideology of the status quo was this not so. However, states ruled by Marxist regimes were in a minority. In any case, except for the USSR, all such states were no older than thirty to forty years, and the social-critical element in the Marxism of the first post-revolutionary generation or generations retained some significance, though perhaps a diminishing one.

There is a third reason for the centrality of Marxism and debate about Marxism in the intellectual universe of the late twentieth century: its disproportionate attractiveness to intellectuals. Thanks to the explosion of secondary and university education their number multiplied in this period as never before. Admittedly only sometimes have intellectuals been attracted to Marxism *en masse* and, even then, most of them not permanently. Moreover, there have been times, places and intellectual occupations which have been notably immune to Marxism or repelled by it. Nevertheless it remains true that of all ideologies associated with modern social movements, Marxism has, as a theory, been by far the most interesting. It has therefore provided maximum scope not only for political commitment and activity but for discussion and theoretical elaboration. It was neither accident nor the mere reflection of intellectual fashion that the number of entries under 'Marx' and 'Marxism' in the index of the *International Encyclopaedia of the Social Sciences* (1968) should greatly exceed that under the names of any other thinker, even if we omit the additional entries under 'Leninism'.

Three complexes of events were of primary importance in shaping Marxist discussion in the quarter-century after 1945: developments in the USSR and the other socialist countries since 1956, those connected with what in the 1950s had already come to be (misleadingly) called the 'Third World', and in particular

Latin America, and the striking and unexpected outburst of political radicalisation, especially of students, in the countries of
industrial capitalism at the end of the 1960s. In terms of their
actual political significance, direct or indirect, they are of very
unequal weight, though not in their impact on Marxist discussion.
Nor can they be clearly separated from one another, especially
after 1960.

The 'Soviet' complex influenced developments in Marxism in
three ways. First, because de-Stalinisation in the USSR and the
other East European states had both practical and theoretical
effects. It led to the recognition that the actual organisation of
these societies and their operation – not least that of their
economies – required reforms, a recognition which made itself
particularly felt in the years following the Twentieth Congress
and in the late 1960s. It also led to a certain intellectual thaw
which permitted rethinking, or sometimes even encouraged the
reopening of questions firmly closed in the Stalin era.

Second, it influenced Marxism through the breakdown of a
single monolithic and monocentric international communist
movement dominated by one 'leading party', that of the USSR.
This monolithic unity, already weakened by the secession of
Yugoslavia since 1948, virtually ceased to exist with the split
between China and the USSR around 1960. All communist
parties, and therefore Marxist discussion within them, were in
varying degrees affected by this breakdown, or more precisely
by the recognition de jure or de facto that a variety of 'national
roads to socialism' or within socialism were now possible, and
sometimes desirable. Moreover, even for those who still han-
kered after a single international orthodoxy of theory, the
existence of rival orthodoxies now raised acute problems of
readjustment.

Third, the Soviet complex affected developments within
Marxism through the often dramatic political events within the
socialist world – or more precisely in the states within the Soviet
sphere of influence and in China: the early East European

reactions to the Twentieth Congress in 1956 (Poland, Hungary), the crises of the late 1960s of which the 'Prague Spring' (of 1968) was the most traumatic, the series of Polish cataclysms between 1968 and 1981, and the political earthquakes which shook China in the late fifties, in the mid-sixties (the 'Cultural Revolution') and after the death of Mao.

Finally, the growth of direct communication between the socialist sector of the globe and the rest, if only in the form of journalism, tourism, cultural interchange and the creation of significant bodies of emigrants from socialist countries, influenced developments in Marxism inasmuch as it swelled the body of information about them accessible to Western Marxists, which could only be overlooked with increasing difficulty. If such countries were nevertheless still turned into models, sometimes almost utopian, of what Western revolutionaries aspired to, it was largely because Western revolutionaries knew little about them, and sometimes were in no position, or did not care, to learn more. The idealisation of the Chinese 'Cultural Revolution' by many Western revolutionaries had about as little to do with China as Montesquieu's *Lettres Persanes* had to do with Iran, or the eighteenth-century 'Noble Savage' with Tahiti. All used what purported to be the experience of a remote country for the social critique of another part of the world. Nevertheless, with the growth of communication and information, the tendency to seek utopia under some already fluttering red state flag diminished markedly. The period since 1956 is one in which most Western Marxists were forced to conclude that existing socialist regimes, from the USSR to Cuba and Vietnam, were far from what they would themselves have wished a socialist society, or a society in the process of constructing socialism, to be like. The bulk of Marxists were forced to revert to the position of socialists everywhere before 1917. Once again they had to argue for socialism as a necessary solution for the problems created by capitalist society, as a hope for the future, but one only very inadequately supported by practical experience.

Conversely, the migration from socialist countries of 'dissidents' reinforced the old temptation to identify Marx and Marxism exclusively with such regimes, and especially with the USSR. It had once served to exclude from the Marxist community anyone who failed to give total and uncritical support to whatever came from Moscow. It now served those who wanted to reject all of Marx, since they claimed that the only road which led forward from the *Communist Manifesto*, or *could* lead forward, was that which ended in the gulags of Stalin's Russia or their equivalent in some other state governed by Marx's disciples. This reaction was psychologically comprehensible among disillusioned communists contemplating 'the god that failed'. It was even more comprehensible among intellectual dissidents in and from socialist countries, whose rejection of anything to do with their official regimes was total – starting with the thinker to whose theory these regimes appealed. Intellectually, it has about as much justification as the thesis that all Christianity must logically and necessarily always lead to papal absolutism, or all Darwinism to the glorification of free capitalist competition.

The 'Third World' complex of events affected developments in Marxism in two main ways.

In the first place it concentrated attention on the liberation struggles of peoples in Asia, Africa and Latin America, and on the fact that many such movements and some of the new regimes which emerged from decolonisation were attracted to Marxist slogans, and to state structures and strategies associated (at least by them) with Marxism. Such movements and regimes found inspiration in the experiences of socialist countries, most of them initially backward, for their own efforts at escaping from backwardness. A large number of movements and regimes in the 'Third World' claimed, at least from time to time, to have socialism as their aim (often qualified as African socialism, Islamic socialism, etc.) If these socialisms had a model, it was derived from regimes ruled by Marxists. Naturally the quantity of Marxist as of other writing about formerly colonial or semi-colonial countries grew enormously.

During the decades of the great global capitalist boom, it increasingly seemed that social revolutions would be hoped for primarily in the dependent and 'under-developed' world. Hence the second point to note is that 'Third World' experience concentrated the attention of Marxists on the relations between the dominant and the developed countries, on the specific character and problems of the possible transition to socialism in such regions, and on the social and cultural peculiarities which affected their future development. These matters raised issues not only of current political strategy, but of Marxist theory. Moreover, the opinions of Marxists both as political practitioners and (one is tempted to say 'consequently') as theorists diverged widely.

A striking example of this interaction between 'Third World' experience and Marxist theory may be found in the field of historiography. The nature of the transition from feudalism to capitalism had long preoccupied Marxist scholars, not without interventions by Marxist politicians, for, in Russia at least, it raised issues of current interest. There 'feudalism' was a recent phenomenon, the 'absolutism' of the tsars whose class nature was open to debate had only recently been overthrown, and furthermore the holders of various interpretations on these matters were (like M.N. Pokrovsky) identified by their opponents, rightly or wrongly, with political opposition or with theories which encouraged it. It was also a matter of political judgement in Japan. We need not follow these arguments back beyond the publication of Maurice Dobb's ambitious attempt to provide a systematic survey of the problem in his modestly named *Studies in the Development of Capitalism* (1946), which led to a lively international debate mainly in the 1950s.[4]

Several questions were at issue. Was there a basic internal contradiction in feudalism (a 'general law') which disintegrated it and eventually led to its replacement by capitalism? If so (and most orthodox Marxists believed that there was), what was it? If there was not – i.e. if feudalism seemed to be a self-stabilising economic system – how could its supersession by capitalism be explained? If there was such a mechanism of disintegration, did it operate in all feudal systems, in which case the failure of capitalism to develop outside the European region had to be explained, or only in that one region, in which case the specific characteristics which distinguished it from the rest of the world required analysis? The crux of Paul M. Sweezy's critique of Dobb, which launched the debate, was that Sweezy was dissatisfied with the attempts to explain the disintegration of feudalism by mechanisms implicit in the main 'relation of production' within that system, namely that between lords and serfs. Instead, Sweezy chose to emphasise – or to re-emphasise, since there were plenty of non-Marxist as well as Marxist precedents for it – the role of *trade* in the undermining and transformation of the feudal economy. 'The growth of trade was the decisive factor in bringing about the decline of western European feudalism'.[5]

The debate, though it has continued intermittently up to the present, subsided. However, some time in the 1960s the question of the historic genesis of the modern capitalist economy was raised afresh, in a completely different manner – though apparently deriving from Sweezy's side of the older controversy. The new thesis was put forward polemically by A. Gunder Frank (*Capitalism and Underdevelopment in Latin America*, 1967) and subsequently in a more elaborate and historically documented form by I. Wallerstein,[6] who had begun his academic career as a political scientist specialising in contemporary Africa and had moved into history from that starting-point. Three major propositions formed the core of this interpretation. First, that capitalism could be essentially equated with *market* relations, and on a world scale with the development of a 'world system' consisting of a world market in which a number of developed 'core' countries established domination over the 'periphery' and exploited it. Second, that the establishment of this 'world market', which could be traced back to the first era of colonial conquests in the sixteenth century, created an essentially capitalist world, which must be analysed in terms of a capitalist economy. Third, that the development of the metropolitan 'core' capitalist countries by the domination and exploitation of the rest produced both the progressive 'development' of the core and the progressive 'under-development' of the 'Third World', i.e. the widening, and under capitalism unbridgeable gap between the two sectors of the world.

Interest in these historical problems revived spectacularly in the 1970s. In its origins it reflects the specific political disputes on the left in that zone of the world, and particularly in the Latin America of the 1950s and 1960s.

The issue which divided the left in that continent was the nature of the main domestic enemy for the revolutionaries. The international enemy was obviously 'imperialism', primarily seen as the USA. But was the main fire at home to be directed against the landowners, dominating vast backward tracts and agrarian economies specialising in exports to the world market in return for the importation of manufactured goods from the industrial world, or against the local bourgeoisie? Both the local bourgeois groups interested in industrialisation (by import substitution backed by state support) and the orthodox communist parties favoured the view that the major task of Latin Americans was to destroy the agrarian interests and 'latifundism' (often loosely identified with 'feudalism' or its relics). For the 'national' bourgeoisie – and in a continent full of Marxist intellectuals there were even businessmen who themselves accepted this label – this meant removing the major political obstacle to industrialisation, as well as the major economic obstacle to the formation of large national markets for national manufactures: the virtual exclusion of impoverished and marginalised peasant masses from the modern economy. For the orthodox communists it meant the creation of a common national front against US imperialism and the local 'oligarchy'. This implied that the struggle for an immediate socialist transformation of these countries was not on the agenda, as indeed it was not. It also implied that communist parties would, in most cases, refrain from the more dramatic forms of insurrection and armed struggle. For the ultra-left, on the other hand, the communist policy was a betrayal of the class struggle. Latin America, they held, was not a feudal economy, or even a set of 'dual' economies, but plainly capitalist. The main enemy was the bourgeoisie which, so far from having interests opposed to US imperialism, was basically identified with it and functioned as the local agent of American and international monopoly capital. Moreover, the objective conditions for a successful revolution were present, and socialism, rather than the current equivalent of the 'bourgeois-democratic stage', was its immediate objective. The divisions of the left were dramatised by the almost simultaneous split between the USSR and China – the latter apparently at this stage dedicated to peasant revolution which would eventually encircle and capture the cities – and by the victory of Fidel Castro in Cuba.

The merits of the arguments on both sides are not our concern here. They simply projected current politics backwards into history. If the Spanish and Portuguese colonies had *always* been essentially part of a capitalist economy since the sixteenth century, then the transformation of 'feudal' or backward countries into flourishing bourgeois capitalist ones had always been a diversionary issue. If the 'obstacles to development', which were so zealously analysed in the 1950s and 1960s, consisted not of feudal survivals or the like at home, but of the simple fact that the dependence of colonial or neo-colonial countries on the international core of capitalism created and reinforced their under-development, then the conflicts between agrarians and industrialists were not significant, and could not produce the conditions for liquidating under-development, which only social revolution and socialism could do.

Clearly the nature of the relationship between the industrial world and the rest was not merely a question of history. It raised both the problems hitherto discussed under the general heading of 'imperialism', but in a historically new context; but it also raised the problem of how the two sectors of the world should be defined, or re-defined. The virtual disappearance of formal *colonies* (i.e. areas under the direct administration of a foreign power and therefore unable to take their own policy decisions as sovereign governments) threw into doubt the necessary connection between imperialism and 'colonialism'. Political decolonisation by itself hardly changed the economic relations between the areas concerned and the metropolitan countries, though it might affect the specific position of the country formerly ruling over the colony. In itself decolonisation made little difference to the Marxist analysis, since the existence of areas which were de facto parts of an imperial economy though ormally sovereign, and of nominally independent states subordinate to a foreign power, had long been recognised. On the other hand the fashion for such terms as 'the Third World' indicated a more comprehensive reclassification.

There is no Marxist precedent for the concept of the 'Third World', and indeed, though Marxists, like others, tended to use this vague but convenient term, it has no clear relation to any Marxist analysis. Nevertheless Marxists did not often resist the temptation of operating with it because it appeared to fit into a modified model of the imperialist exploitation of a colonial or neo-colonial world kept poor and essentially non-industrial by the nature of the operations of capitalism, and because the prospects of social revolution, which seemed increasingly distant in the countries of developed capitalism, seemed to survive only in Asia, Africa and Latin America. To this extent the difference between the 'Second' and the 'Third' worlds was, as it were, chronological. The Chinese revolution concluded a phase of socialist advance which had increased the number of states under Marxist leadership from one (or perhaps two, if Mongolia is included) to eleven. As it happened, several of these had, at least initially, most of the characteristics of 'Third World' countries (e.g. Albania and much of Yugoslavia). The subsequent additions to the number of such states all occurred

outside Europe: Vietnam (1954–75), Cuba (1959), the former
Portuguese colonies in Africa, Ethiopia, Somalia, South Yemen,
Kampuchea, Nicaragua in the 1960s and 1970s. Moreover the
states which, in many cases implausibly or temporarily, declared
themselves to be socialist or to aim at socialism without necessarily possessing or accepting a Marxist leadership were all to
be found in the 'Third World' zone. All these states, Marxist or
otherwise, continued to face the problems of poverty and backwardness as well as (where Marxist) the active hostility of the
USA and states aligned with it. In this respect the differences
between the political systems and aspirations of 'Third World'
countries appeared to be less significant than the common
situation in which they all found themselves.

In fact, in the course of the 1960s and 1970s the concept of
a single, all-embracing, 'under-developed' 'Third World'
became increasingly implausible and it was to be largely abandoned. Nevertheless, while the period of 'Third-Worldism'
lasted, Marxist thinking was powerfully influenced by it. Since
the movements in that world did not appear to rest on the working class – which hardly existed in many of the countries
concerned – Marxists turned their attention to the revolutionary
potential, and consequently the analysis, of other classes,
notably the peasantry. A considerable amount of Marxist as
well as non-Marxist theory has been devoted to agrarian and
peasant problems since the early 1960s. The Marxist literature
in this field, which was also stimulated by reflections on the
experience in socialist countries and the rediscovery of the
Russian Narodnik theorist Chayanov, is large and impressive.[7]
Interest in the 'Third World' probably also contributed to the
marked development of Marxist social anthropology, notably in
France (Godelier, Meillassoux), in this period.

Finally, the radical wave of the late 1960s affected Marxism
in two main ways. First, it multiplied the number of those who
produced, read and bought Marxist writings, in a spectacular
manner, and thus increased the sheer volume of Marxist

discussion and theory. Second, its scale was so vast – at least in some countries – its appearance so sudden and unexpected, and its character so unprecedented, that it appeared to require a far-reaching reconsideration of much that most Marxists had long taken for granted. Like the 1848 revolution, some aspects of which it recalled in the minds of the historically minded, it rose and fell with great rapidity. Like the 1848 revolution it left more behind than appeared at first sight.

The radical wave was peculiar in several respects. It began as a movement of young intellectuals, who were, specifically, students, whose numbers had multiplied enormously in the course of the 1960s in almost all countries of the globe, or more generally, were the sons and daughters of middle-class families. In some countries it remained confined to students or potential students, but in others – notably in France and Italy – it provided the spark for industrial movements of the working class on a scale not seen for many years. It was an extraordinarily international movement, crossing the boundaries between developed and dependent countries and between capitalist and socialist societies: 1968 is a date in the history of Yugoslavia, Poland and Czechoslovakia as well as Mexico, France and the USA. However, it attracted attention chiefly because it swept through countries which formed part of the core of developed capitalist society, at the peak of its economic prosperity. Lastly, its impact on the political system and institutions of several of the countries in which it occurred, however short-lived, was disproportionately dramatic.

So far as Marxism is concerned, it produced a 'new left' which, whatever its desire to identify itself with the name of Marx or some other figure in the Marxist pantheon, looked far beyond the limits of traditional Marxism. Thus we observe a rebirth of anarchist tendencies, both as a self-conscious phenomenon, or disguised by some apparently Marxist label (e.g. a great deal of Western 'Maoism'), or in the form of apolitical or anti-political cultural dissidence. We also observe the emergence of political groups whose enthusiasm for advertising their connection with Marx does not conceal that they were pursuing strategies and policies which Marxist revolutionaries had traditionally rejected or distrusted. 'Red Army Fractions' or 'Red Brigades' fit the pattern of Russian Narodnik terrorism rather than that of Lenin, while movements of national separatism in Western Europe, often with a historical ancestry on the political right, or even extreme right, now came to use the vocabulary of Marxist revolution, sometimes quite sincerely. One of the by-products of this development was a marked revival of the Marxist debate on what used to be called 'the national question' in the 1970s and 1980s.

Among the long-term factors influencing the development of Marxism since the 1950s, two interconnected ones stand out: the change in the social basis of Marxism as a political ideology and the transformations in world capitalism.

Unlike the periods of the Second and Third Internationals, the growth of Marxism since the 1950s took place primarily, and in some cases overwhelmingly, among intellectuals who now formed an increasingly large and important social stratum. Indeed, it reflected the radicalisation of important parts of this stratum, especially of its young members. Formerly Marxism's social roots had been primarily, and often overwhelmingly, in movements and parties of manual workers. This did not mean that many books or even pamphlets on Marxist theory were written, or even read, by workers, though the self-educated working-class militant (Brecht's 'lesender Arbeiter') formed an important sector of the public for such Marxist literature as was studied in the discussion circles, educational classes, libraries and institutes associated with the labour movement. Thus in the coalfields of South Wales a network of over a hundred miners' libraries grew up between 1890 and the 1930s, in which the union and political activists of this area – notoriously radical since before 1914 – acquired their intellectual formation.[8] What it meant was that organised workers in such movements accepted, applauded and imbibed a form of Marxist doctrine ('a proletarian science') as part of their political consciousness, and that the great majority of Marxist intellectuals, or indeed of any intellectuals associated with the movement, saw themselves essentially as serving the working class, or more generally, a movement for the emancipation of humanity through the historically inevitable rise and triumph of the proletariat.

From the early 1950s on it became clear that in most parts of the world where socialist labour parties had been established on a mass basis, they were no longer advancing but, if anything, tending to lose ground, whether in their social-democratic or communist form.[9] Moreover, in the industrialised countries, the manual working class, which had formed the core of labour movements, lost ground relatively and sometimes absolutely to other sectors of the occupied population. Moreover, its internal coherence and strength were weakened. The striking improvement in the working-class standard of living, the massive concentration of commercial publicity and the media on the desires (real or induced) of the consumer as individual or household, the consequent privatisation of working-class life, undoubtedly weakened the cohesion of working-class communities, which had formed so large an element of the strength of proletarian mass parties and movements. Meanwhile the growth of non-manual employment and the expansion of secondary and higher education drained off a much higher percentage than ever before of the sons and daughters of the better-paid and skilled working class – and of the potential proletarian cadres and leaders of labour movements, as well as those workers most likely to study and read. As the survey of South Wales miners' libraries sadly noted in 1973, when only thirty-four were still in existence, 'by the 1960s, unlike the 1930s, reading was not one of the major recreational pursuits in the coalfield'.[10] Those who left did not necessarily cease to believe in the cause of their parents, or to be politically active. But they were acutely conscious of the gap between the world of their parents and their own, especially in Britain where this experience produced a powerful literature combining autobiography, reportage and ideological reflection, some of whose authors – Raymond Williams – became important stars of the firmament of the left.

Such developments could not but profoundly affect both the working-class movements and Marxism, for both had grown up essentially on the basis of a belief that capitalism created its grave-diggers in the form of a proletariat (seen as a class of manual industrial workers) growing in numbers, self-conscious-ness and force, represented by its parties or movements, and which was historically destined both to become more socialist (i.e. revolutionary, though opinions differed as to what precisely this implied) and, as the vehicle of an inevitable historical process, to triumph. Yet the development of Western capitalism since World War Two and of the labour movements within it seemed to make this perspective increasingly doubtful.

On the one hand, manual workers lost that confidence in history which the socialist movements had given them (and which they had given these movements). A leading British Conservative statesman recalls an able and dynamic British Labour MP of working-class origins telling him, in the 1930s, 'Your class is a class in decline: my class is the class of the future.'[11] It is difficult to envisage such an exchange in the 1980s. On the other hand, Marxist parties, though long aware that predictions of the historically inevitable triumph of social-ism were far from a sufficient guide to political strategy, were nevertheless disorientated by the uncertainty of what so many of their members and leaders had regarded as the compass by which they charted their historical course. Their disorientation was intensified by developments in the USSR and other socialist countries, increasingly difficult, since 1956, not to admit or disapprove. A very fundamental rethinking of much of what Marxists had hitherto taken for granted, from the basic analysis of Marx and other 'classics' to the long- and short-term politi-cal strategy and tactics, became unavoidable.

Such rethinking had become increasingly difficult within the main tradition of post-1917 Marxism, that associated with the USSR and the international communist movement – until this increasingly dogmatic orthodoxy began to break up. The main tradition of Marxism had therefore been marked by immobility and ossification, and the process of revising the Marxist analysis had been artificially delayed, if only because for most Marxists since 1900, and certainly for all who had been formed in the communist movements,[12] the very words 'revision' and 'revisionism' suggested the abandonment, or even the betrayal of Marxism. When the movement to revise the Marxist analysis occurred, it was therefore all the more sudden, and the confrontation between the old and the new Marxisms was correspondingly dramatic. Thus it would have been possible to observe the changed character of post-war capitalism quite soon after the war. Non-Marxists like Galbraith and ex-Marxists like Strachey and Schonfield began to do so early in the 1950s. Yet while both committed Marxists and sympathetic critics agreed that in the 1930s Marxism 'still contributed a coherent though inadequate explanation of the world economic crisis and the fascist challenge' (Lichtheim), or that 'the Great Depression of the 1930s accorded admirably with Marxian theory' (Baran and Sweezy),[13] both also agreed that 'it has not been more successful than liberalism in formulating a theory of post-capitalist society' (Lichtheim) or 'contributed significantly to our understanding of some of the major characteristics of the "affluent society"' (Baran and Sweezy). For the best part of a generation most Marxists had failed, or hesitated, to confront the realities of the world they wished to transform.

The suddenness of the phenomenon of renovation within Marxism was reinforced by the massive radicalisation of young intellectuals, mainly in the course of their education, for as we have seen this largely transformed the social basis of support for Marxist theories. Marxist parties and organisations – mainly small – emerged whose membership, and certainly whose leadership, consisted mainly of people with educational diplomas.[14] For, as the development of trade unions shows, as the weight of organised manual labour in industry diminished, the numbers and weight of trade unionism increased among non-manual employees, especially in the growing public sector, in corporately organised professions and occupations, in the media, and in what might be called occupations directly concerned with social responsibility – education, health, social security and the like. And in such occupations non-manual workers were increasingly recruited from men and women who had undergone some form of higher schooling.

Moreover, the radicalisation of young intellectuals not only brought about a large growth in the public's desire for Marxist literature and in the Marxist intellectual presence, but also provided a mechanism for their reproduction.

Marxist elements came to permeate the language of public discourse of students, and as men and women emerging from student radicalism – which was sometimes endemic as in Latin America, sometimes epidemic, as in several European countries in the late 1960s – became teachers and communicators. And indeed – not only in the emerging countries – decision-makers in politics, state service and the media, areas in which recruitment was increasingly from among university students of the radical generations. Marxism acquired a firmer lodgement than before in the institutions concerned with education and communication. This stabilised its influence. The young products of the 1960s embarked on what would (but for systematic political purges) be for many of them long careers. While many of them might in time moderate or abandon their youthful convictions, they were not themselves subject to the violent fluctuations of student radicalism.

This development was not unpredicted. Some time before it became dramatically visible, one of the ablest observers of Marxism had already noted that in the 'developed' countries it seemed to have been 'turned into a critique of modern society as such', largely 'for the purpose of underpinning the intelligentsia's rejection of the world created by modern industry, and scientific technology; and the principal battleground of this debate has been furnished by the universities'.[15] What was new was the unexpected scale of the conversion of intellectuals to Marxism, largely because of the dramatic expansion of the number of institutions of higher education and their students all over the world in the 1960s, an expansion for which there was no historic precedent.

The radicalisation of (mainly youthful) intellectuals had a number of characteristics which were reflected in the Marxist thought produced in and for this milieu. In the first place, it was not initially a function of economic discontent and crisis. Indeed, it emerged in its most spectacular form in the late 1960s, i.e. at the peak of the era of 'economic miracles', capitalist expansion and prosperity, and at a time when the education and career prospects of students were excellent in most countries. The main direction of its critique was therefore not economics, but social or cultural. If any academic discipline represented this search for a critique of society as a whole, it was *sociology*, and this subject therefore attracted radical students in disproportionate numbers, and often became virtually identified with the radicalism of the 'new left'. In the second place, in spite of the traditional link of Marxism with the working class (and, in its 'Third World' versions, the peasantry), the radicalised young intellectuals were, by virtue of their life-patterns or their social origins, separated from both workers and peasants, however passionately they identified with them in theory. If they were the children of the established bourgeoisie they could at best seek to 'go to the people' like latter-day Narodniks, or glory in the relatively few proletarians, peasants or blacks who actually joined their groups. If they themselves came from a proletarian, peasant, or more usually a lower-middle-class background, their situation and future careers automatically took them away from their original social environment. They were no longer workers or peasants, or seen as such by their parents and neighbours. Moreover, their political views tended to be very much more radical than those of most workers, even when (as in France in May 1968) both were simultaneously engaged in militant action.

The intellectual 'new left' therefore sometimes tended to dismiss the workers as a class as no longer revolutionary, because integrated into capitalism – perhaps even 'reactionary' – the *locus classicus* for this analysis being Herbert Marcuse's *One Dimensional Man* (London, 1964). Or they tended at least to dismiss the existing mass labour movements and parties, whether social-democratic or communist, as reformed betrayers of socialist aspirations. Conversely, in virtually all countries of developed capitalism, and even to some extent outside, the mobilised students were by no means popular among the masses, at least insofar as they were regarded as privileged children of the middle classes or as a potential privileged ruling class. Marxist theory in the 'new left' milieu therefore developed in a certain isolation, and its links with Marxist practice were unusually problematical.

In the third place, this milieu tended to produce Marxist thinking which was academic in two senses: because it was primarily addressed to a public of past, present and future students and expressed in relatively esoteric language not easily accessible to non-academics, and because, to quote Lichtheim again, it 'fastened upon those elements of the Marxian system which were furthest removed from political action'.[16] It showed a marked preference for pure theory, and notably for that most general and abstract of disciplines, philosophy. The bibliography of Marxist philosophical publications multiplied after 1960, and indeed the national and international debates among Marxists which attracted most attention among radical intellectuals were those associated with philosophers: Lukacs and the Frankfurt School, the Gramscians, and Della Volpe, Sartre, Althusser and their various followers, critics and opponents. This was perhaps not surprising in countries where nobody who completed secondary school could escape some philosophical formation, e.g. in

Germany, France or Italy, but the taste for such philosophical discussions also became very marked where philosophy was not a part of general humanist higher education, as in the Anglo-Saxon countries.

Philosophy tended to encroach upon other disciplines, as when Althusserians seemed to consider Marx's *Capital* as though it were primarily a work of epistemology. It even replaced practice, as in the brief fashion (in the same quarters) for something described as 'theoretical practice'. The investigation and the analysis of the actual world retreated behind the generalised consideration of its structures and mechanism, or even behind the still more general enquiry how it was to be apprehended at all. Theorists were tempted to slide from a consideration of the actual problems and prospects of real societies into a debate on the 'articulation' of 'modes of production' in general.[17] The late Nicos Poulantzas defended himself against the criticism that he did not undertake concrete analyses or refer much to 'concrete empirical and historical facts' by arguing that such criticism is a sign of empiricism and neo-positivism, though he admitted that his work suffered from 'a certain *theoreticism*'.[18] Admittedly, the extremes of such theoretical abstraction were associated with the influence of the very able French Marxist philosopher Louis Althusser which was at its height *c.* 1965–75 – the extent of this international vogue was itself significant – but the general attraction of pure theorising was nevertheless notable. It baffled a number of older Marxists, and not only from countries given to empiricism.[19]

Such Marxists did not dismiss the concentration on abstract theory, especially when it grappled with problems to which Marx himself had devoted his energies – as in economic theory. Quite apart from the intellectual interest of these writings in themselves, and the intellectual merits of those who pursued such matters, the rethinking of the bases of Marxist theory was an essential element in the necessary critical scrutiny of Marx's own work and of Marxism as a coherent and consistent body of thought. Yet the distance which separated such theorising from the concrete analysis of the world was large, and the relation between such theorising and most of Marx's own work often seemed analogous to that between philosophers of science and working scientists. The latter have often admired the former, but they have not so often been helped by them in their actual researches, especially when the philosophy of science demonstrated that they could not satisfactorily prove what they had spent their life trying to establish.

However, the consequences of radicalisation among intellectuals were more than theoretical, if only because they could no longer be considered or consider themselves as individuals who crossed class lines to join the workers, and because, as we have seen, there was a widening gap between intellectuals and workers as social strata. In extreme cases (as in the USA) the ones provided the anti-war activists during the Vietnam War, whereas the others provided the pro-war demonstrators. But even when both stood on the left, the focus of their political interests tended to be different. Thus it was very much easier to rouse passionate concern for environmental and ecological questions on the intellectual left than in purely proletarian organisations. The combination of both groups was politically most powerful – where it still occurred: under left-wing auspices in Brazil, under anti-communist ones in Poland, both in the 1980s. The gap, or the lack of coordination between them, whether permanent or not, was therefore likely to affect the practical prospects of transforming society by the action of Marxist movements. At the same time experience suggested that political movements based primarily on intellectuals were unlikely to produce mass parties like the traditional socialist or communist parties of labour, held together by the solid bonds of class consciousness and class loyalty; or indeed any mass parties. This was also likely to affect the political possibilities and prospects of groups so based, and indeed of the Marxist doctrines they elaborated.

On the other hand the growing prominence of intellectuals

on the Marxist scene, especially when young or academic or both, facilitated extremely rapid communication between centres of them, even across national boundaries. Members of this stratum are exceptionally mobile and exceptionally used to rapid communication; moreover their links and networks are unusually immune to disruption, except by systematic and ruthless state action. The speed with which student movements spread from university to university illustrates this. The new phase therefore facilitated, both in practice and in theory, a rather effective informal internationalism, at the moment when the organised internationalism of Marxist movements, for the first time since 1889, was virtually ceasing to exist. In fact what emerged was an informal, if quarrelsome, cosmopolitan Marxist culture. Certainly national and regional patterns persisted, and there were Marxist authors who were little known outside their native territory. On the other hand there were few countries containing Marxist intellectuals in which certain names were not familiar to all who took an interest in such matters, whether they originally wrote in English, French or any of the other readily understood or translated world languages. The major obstacles to joining this international universe of Marxist discourse were linguistic (e.g. for works originally written in Japanese) or economic (as for the poverty-stricken stratum of Indian intellectuals, unable to afford the price of unsubsidised books or – because of a lack of foreign currency – to import more than a few copies of foreign publications). Yet, compared with any earlier period in the history of Marxism, this universe was geographically more extensive and the number of 'theorists' or other Marxist writers who debated within it was almost certainly larger – and more heterogeneous – than ever before.

How, finally, are we to summarise the trends and developments within Marxism as it existed on the centenary of Marx's death in 1983?

In the first place it had lost the cement of any dominant or binding international orthodoxy such as that de facto exercised by the German Social Democratic Party before 1914 and by Soviet communism in the period of its hegemony over world Marxism. It had become more difficult to treat heterodox interpretations as effectively not Marxist, and conversely the strategy of other parties and movements aiming at drastic change was now to tend to pin the badge of Marx on their ideological lapels. There were rival and conflicting Marxist orthodoxies, such as those of the Soviet bloc and China. The debate between Marxist interpretations within Marxist parties developed to the point where in some communist parties no single interpretation of Marxism could be said to prevail. This also produced rival trends or factions within such parties, and a multiplicity of groups and organisations, mainly on the left of the old communist parties, each combating these and each other in the name of Marxism or, where they themselves were divided, apt to generate further ideologically justified scissions. Marxism was now readily combined with other ideologies – Catholic, Islamic, and often nationalist – while others were content with appealing to Marx or some other Marxist (e.g. Mao) in the name of whatever ideology they happened to hold. The changing social composition of the Marxist population reinforced the tendency to pluralism, but also (through the new intellectual constituency for Marxism) tended to extend Marxism beyond the strictly political field into the general academic and cultural sphere.

The new pluralism must be distinguished from the toleration of divergence in the period before 1914. Bernstein's revisionism was tolerated within the German SPD, but at the same time it was rejected as a theory both by the party and by the bulk of Marxists as undesirable and unorthodox. Now, while some theories put forward by some Marxists aroused the suspicion and hostility of others, there was rarely a recognised consensus, nationally or internationally, on what constituted a legitimate interpretation and what had in effect ceased to be 'Marxist'. This was very marked in such fields as philosophy, history and economics.

One consequence of this ill-defined pluralisation of Marxism, and of the decline of authoritative interpretation, was the reappearance of the 'theorist' within Marxism. However, unlike the period before 1914, the 'theorist' was no longer closely linked to a particular political organisation or even policy, let alone occupying an important, if sometimes informal, political function, as Kautsky did in his time. The automatic identification of party leaders with theorists died with Stalinism, outside some socialist states where it produced some curious aberrations (e.g. North Korea), although in small movements led by intellectuals, leaders did still sometimes double as theorists. Even when the names which carry prestige and influence in the international Marxist debate, and around which 'schools' gather, were known as members of a party (e.g. L. Althusser as a member of the French CP), they were not usually regarded as 'representing' the party. In short, they tended to be influential as unattached private persons who wrote articles and books. Such, at various times and for various periods and purposes since the 1950s, has been the position of figures like Althusser, Marcuse, Sartre, Sweezy and Baran, Colletti, Habermas, A. Gunder Frank – to name but a few around whom Marxist debate has swirled. It is typical of the pluralism of this period that not only the nature of their Marxism but their actual relation to Marxism was sometimes unclear. And since print remains alive, it did not always matter that its authors were dead, except insofar as they were no longer able to comment on the interpretations made of their works. The disintegration of orthodoxy restored a large number of eminent Marxist figures of the past to the public domain of Marxist debate, ready once again to be admired and to inspire followers: Lukacs and Benjamin, Korsch and Otto Bauer, Gramsci and Mariategui, Bukharin and Luxemburg.

In the second place, as already suggested, the line between what was Marxist and what was not grew increasingly hazy. This was to be expected, since so much of Marxism, including intellectuals with Marxist roots, had penetrated into the mainstream of academic teaching and debate, in spite of the Cold War. It was also a natural by-product of the demand of a vast new public of radical students, and of the discovery that much of what had hitherto been accepted as essential to Marxism called for serious reconsideration. A (non-Marxist) survey of European historiography observed in 1978 that 'in recent decades Marxist historians have succeeded in entering the professional guild' – so much so that the index of this survey contains more entries for Marx than for any other names except Leopold von Ranke and Max Weber.[20] The most influential economic textbooks decided in the 1970s to include a special section on Marxist economics.[21] In France, for example, Marxism thus became just one component of an intellectual universe which also contained others – de Saussure, Lévi-Strauss, Lacan, Merleau-Ponty, or whoever else was influential in the senior classes of French *lycées* or discussed in the fifth and sixth *arrondissements* of Paris. Marxist intellectuals who grew up and acquired their Marxism in such a culture might find it desirable to translate Marxism into whatever was the prevalent theoretical idiom, both to make it comprehensible to readers unused to Marxist terminology and to demonstrate to critics that even in terms of their own theories, Marxism had something valid to say. A typical product of such a period is G.A. Cohen's reformulation of the materialist conception of history in the terminology of, and applying 'those standards of clarity and rigour which distinguish twentieth-century analytic philosophy'.[22] Or else they might simply produce some combination of Marxism with other influential theories – structuralism, existentialism, psychoanalysis or the like.

New Marxists were often attracted to Marx at a time when they had already acquired knowledge and theoretical positions of some other kind, at school or university, which coloured their subsequent Marxism. Thus it is no discredit to Althusser, who became a communist as an adult after the war (1948), to point out that his intellectual background was far from Marxist, and that he was almost certainly much better informed about the works of Spinoza than those of Marx when he began to write about the latter. If sufficiently young, such new Marxists might now sit at the feet of teachers who themselves sometimes combined elements of Marxism, perhaps acquired in their own youthful phase as revolutionaries, with other intellectual influences and developments. In principle, this was not new. Marxists with a higher education had in the past tried to bridge gaps, which the orthodoxy deliberately emphasised, between Marxism and university culture. This was clearly the case among Austro-Marxists and in the Frankfurt School. The novelty lay in the mass radicalisation of academically educated intellectuals at a time of crisis and uncertainty for the older strongholds of institutionalised and separatist Marxism.

At the same time Marxists were increasingly obliged to look outside Marxism, because the self-isolation and self-restriction of Marxist thought which had been so striking a feature of the communist phase of its development (both among the orthodox and among such heretics as the Trotskyites) had created vast areas about which Marxists had thought very little, but non-Marxists a great deal. Marxian economics is a good example of this. As soon as Marxist governments, administering centrally planned economies, became aware of the defects of their planning and management, it became impossible to dismiss bourgeois academic economics simply as a form of capitalist apologetics, and conversely, Marxist economics could not confine itself to modified restatements of the orthodoxies of 'political economy', designed primarily to prove that capitalism could not solve its problems and had not 'essentially' changed its character, while observations on socialist economies were restricted to meaningless generalities.[23] Whatever the theoretical orthodoxy, in practice economists in socialist societies (even if they were not formally described as economists) had to consider operations research and programming, and in doing so converge with, and utilise, the work of economists in capitalist societies, including work on the economies of socialism.[24] It does not greatly matter that some important developments in economics could be traced back to East European Marxists or others attempting to solve the novel problems of the Soviet economy in the 1920s, and could thus be given a Marxist pedigree, even though they had for long been excluded from the official Marxist canon.

Thus Marxists who did not treat their theory simply as an ideology legitimising their exclusive claim to truth and the error ('anti-Marxism') of all others could no longer afford not to know what non-Marxists in their field had been doing. Indeed, the new generation of academically formed Marxist intellectuals could hardly avoid their knowledge. Conversely, the pressure of student radicals also resulted in the introduction of special courses on Marxism or in such subjects as Marxist economics into universities, where ignorance in these matters had often been profound. They became quite common in the English-speaking world in the 1970s. However, even without such pressure the penetration of Marxist influence into the academic institutions and disciplines increased notably, partly because Marxist intellectuals of the older generation advanced in their careers while younger ones of the 1960s vintage entered them, but largely because in many fields the contributions of Marxism had been integrated even by those who had no special sympathy for it. This was notably the case in history and the social sciences. Neither the *Annales* school of historians in France nor its chief, Fernand Braudel, showed any significant Marxist influence in their early days. Yet there are more references to Marx in Braudel's important late work *Capitalism and Material Life* than to any other single writer, French or foreign. This eminent historian was far from being a Marxist, but a major work on this subject could hardly not refer back to Marx. Given this convergence, there were large fields of research tilled by both Marxists and non-Marxists in much the same way, so that it became difficult to decide whether a particular work was

Marxist or not, unless the author specifically advertised or disclaimed, defended or attacked, Marxism. The growing readiness of Marxists to abandon ancient canonical interpretations made it even more difficult, and sometimes pointless, to assign all works firmly to one camp or another.

This readiness of Marxists to reconsider not only Marxist traditions but the theory of Marx himself constitutes the third characteristic of development since the 1950s. This, of course, is not in itself new. The debate within Marxist economics, which revived spectacularly from 1960,[25] had always been lively, when not stifled by dogma imposed by superior authority. Attempts to modify part of Marx's analysis on various grounds were familiar in the 1900s, and not only in connection with Bernsteinian 'revisionism'. Indeed, the practice of valuing Marxism primarily as a 'method' rather than a body of doctrine, which seems to have originated with the early Austro-Marxists, was in part a polite form of expressing disagreement with what Marx had actually written.

Thus in the 1960s and 1970s Marxists were increasingly found who eliminated the labour theory of value or the declining rate of profit from Marxism, who rejected the proposition that 'it is not the consciousness of men that determines their social existence, but, on the contrary, it is their social existence that determines their consciousness' (i.e. Marx's views on 'basis' and 'superstructure'), who found all writings of Marx before 1882 insufficiently Marxist, who would (in traditional Marxist terms) be described as philosophic idealists rather than materialists – or who rejected the difference between the two positions – who dismissed Engels *en bloc*, or who held that 'the study of history is not only scientifically but politically valueless'.[26] I do not think that at any previous period of the history of Marxism these and other similar propositions flatly at variance with what most Marxists had hitherto accepted had ever been so widely put forward and positively received by people who regarded themselves as Marxists.

It is not the function of the historian to assess the validity of these often wholesale revisions of what had hitherto been considered as essential to their theory by most schools and tendencies of Marxism, though he can confidently affirm that many of their reconsiderations would have enraged the notoriously short-tempered Marx himself. What can be said from a, as it were, neutral position is that such challenges to Marx's own expressed views (not to mention those of Engels and subsequent 'classics') represented the most profound break so far recorded in the continuity of the Marxist intellectual tradition. At the same time, misguided or not, they represented an extraordinary effort to strengthen Marxism by renovating it, and to develop Marxist thinking further, and as such they are evidence for the remarkable vigour and attraction of Marx. For they indicated two things: the recognition of the need for a drastic *aggiornamento* of Marxism, which did not stop short of investigating the possible errors and inconsistencies in the founder's own thinking, and at the same time the conviction that the thought of Marx himself, taken as a whole, provides an essential guide to understanding and changing the world.

No doubt time will clear away some of this jungle of theoretical undergrowth, partly because some of the theoretical reformulators will follow the logic of their arguments out of Marxism, while others will drop out of sight, to await the occasional Ph.D. student in search of a thesis subject or future volumes of a history of Marxism. It is also possible that a certain consensus will once again emerge on what developments of the theory can be legitimately derived from or made consistent with Marx's own thought, and – a more controversial matter – on what parts of Marx's theory can be abandoned without depriving his analysis as a whole of its coherence. In that case the continuity of the Marxian tradition might be re-established, though not in the form of a single 'correct' Marxism, but rather in the form of re-establishing the limits of the territory within which debate and disagreement can reasonably claim intellectual filiation from Marx. But even if such intellectual continuity were to be re-established, what might be called Marxisms of the mainstream would continue to coexist with what might be called the fringe Marxisms of those who, for whatever reason, claimed a Marxist paternity for their ideas, though intellectual DNA tests did not confirm their claim. Insofar as they claim to be Marxist they are part of the history of Marxism, and indeed incomprehensible outside it, as much as fringe or syncretic religions and cults which claim to be Christian are part of the history of that religion, however remote their doctrines may have become from those which form the common stock of Christianity.[27] Lastly, both mainstream and fringe Marxisms would coexist, as they do not, with the growing (and largely, but not exclusively, academic) zone in which no sharp distinction is drawn between what is Marxist and what is not.

One thing, however, seems clear. Even if a consensus about what constitutes the Marxist mainstream (or streams) re-emerges, it is likely to operate at a greater distance from the original texts of 'the classics' than in the past. It is unlikely that they will often be referred to again, as they so often were, as a coherent corpus of internally consistent theory and doctrine, as an immediately usable analytic description of present economies and societies, or as a direct guide to current action by Marxists. The break in the continuity of the Marxist tradition is probably not completely reparable.

The 'classic' texts cannot easily be used as handbooks to political action, because Marxist movements today, and presumably in the future, find themselves in situations which have little in common (except by an occasional and temporary historical accident) with those in which Marx, Engels and the socialist and communist movements of the first half of this century elaborated their strategies and tactics. It is significant that half a century after Lenin's death, most of the old communist parties were still engaged in the struggle to supplant capitalism in their countries, looked for new strategies, and therefore (in spite of the nostalgia for ancient certainties among many of their older members) abandoned the Marxist equivalent of biblical fundamentalism. Conversely, where the thirst for old certainty still prevailed and Marxism taught 'lessons' which had only to be formulated and applied 'correctly' – though one group's 'correctness' was another group's 'error' – this type of Marxism atrophied theoretically. It tended to be reduced to a few simple elements, almost to slogans: the fundamental importance of the class struggle, the exploitation of workers, peasants or the Third World, the rejection of capitalism or imperialism, the necessity of revolution and revolutionary (including armed) struggle, the condemnation of 'reformism' and 'revisionism', the indispensability of a 'vanguard' and the like. Such simplifications made it possible to liberate Marxism from any contact with the complexities of the real world, since analysis was merely designed to demonstrate the already announced truths in their pure form. They could therefore be combined with strategies of pure voluntarism or whatever else the militants favoured. Essentially this residual form of fundamentalist Marxism used as a guide to action consisted of simplified elements taken from classical Leninism, unless (as among neo-anarchists) these too were effectively dissolved into rhetoric. There was clearly much to be learned from the experience of past struggles and from so brilliant a practitioner of revolutionary politics as Lenin, but not by literal reference to the past and its texts.

Again, while Marx's general economic theory and analysis of capitalist development must, presumably, remain the starting-point for later Marxists, 'classic' texts of one period cannot be used as descriptions of later phases of capitalism. With his usual realism, Lenin recognised this. His *Imperialism*, unlike some other Marxist works attempting to analyse the new phase of capitalism after 1900,[28] contains no reference whatsoever to the text of Marx and Engels except to two relevant passages from the *Correspondence* dealing with the effect of the British Empire on the British working class. However, in the period since 1917 a vast amount of Marxist writing about current developments in capitalism failed to heed this precedent, and devoted much time and effort to proving that Lenin's (or, much more rarely, some other Marxist) text still constituted an essentially valid analysis of a phase of capitalist development which he had incautiously described as 'the last'; or to making critical comments on it; or – when it was plainly out of date – to elaborating a casual phrase of his in 1917 into a theory of 'state monopoly capitalism' for the period since the Second World War.[29] Outside the diminishing range of the old dogmatic orthodoxies, by 1983 most Marxists no longer felt the obligation to express their analysis of the current phase of capitalism in terms of texts which described phases which now belonged predominantly to the past.

Finally, it was now widely recognised that Marx's own theory, insofar as he formulated it in a systematic manner, lacked homogeneity in at least one important respect. Thus, it might be held that it consisted both of an analysis of capitalism and its tendencies, and simultaneously of a historic hope, expressed with enormous prophetic passion and in terms of a philosophy derived from Hegel, of the perennial human desire for a perfect society, which is to be achieved through the proletariat. In Marx's own intellectual development, the second of these preceded the first, and cannot be intellectually derived from it. In other words there is a qualitative difference between e.g. the proposition that capitalism by its nature generates insuperable contradictions which must inevitably produce the conditions of its supersession as soon as 'centralisation of the means of production and socialisation of labour at last reach a point where they become incompatible with capitalist development', and the proposition that the post-capitalist society will lead to the end of human alienation and the full development of all individuals' human faculties. They belong to different forms of discourse, though both may eventually prove to be true.[30]

Moreover, it has never been denied that Marx did not leave behind a finished body of systematic theory (only one volume of *Capital* was actually completed), and it is difficult to deny that he did not always succeed in translating 'the grandeur of his vision'[31] into satisfactory theoretical analysis. Thus in Marxian economics there were 'theoretical problems which have long been the subject of controversy' among Marxists, and 'interpretations of Marxist theories have differed widely'[32] among them. This certainly led theorists to study the mass of Marx's texts with close attention, but their attempts to form them into a coherent, consistent and realistic whole had little in common with the use of such texts as authoritative statements of 'what Marxism teaches'. Few if any trained Marxist economists have ever regarded the popular expositions of Marxian political economy (such as part II of Engels' *Anti-Dühring* or Lenin's *Teachings of Karl Marx*) as adequate. Such expositions, or basic texts of Marx treated as such (e.g. *Value, Price and Profit*), played a prominent role in the period when the Marxist education of militants and members of mass socialist workers' parties was a major function of such parties. With the transformation, and sometimes the weakening, of such parties, and the decline of the orthodoxies of a single 'correct' Marxism, their role diminished. In any case, Marxist theory addressed de facto largely to intellectuals, whether militant, academic or both, tended to treat the classic texts in a less uncritical manner.[33]

A fourth characteristic of Marxist thought since the 1950s may be finally mentioned. Marxists concentrated their efforts overwhelmingly in the fields of the humanities and social sciences, as well as, naturally, on matters directly bearing upon political activity. The vast and crucial field of the natural sciences and technology is one into which few Marxists ventured *as Marxists* after 1947, and it even became fashionable in some quarters to deny that Marxism had any relevance in this field, or even that it was basically concerned with 'nature' except as 'human nature'.[34] This contrasts not only with Marx and Engels themselves, both of whom were plainly very interested in the natural sciences and thought they had something to say about them (even though Engels devoted more attention than Marx to this field), but with such periods as the 1930s, when a number of natural scientists, at all events in Britain and France, were attracted to Marxism and anxious to apply it to their subjects. Science, social affairs and politics are more closely enmeshed with each other than ever before today, and certainly many scientists are aware of their social role and responsibility. There are radical and even revolutionary scientists, and scientists who are Marxists, even though a certain hostility to science and technology as such (often under the disguise of a rejection of 'positivism' in philosophy) was notable in the radicalised youthful 'new left' from the 1960s. This probably diminished the attraction of the radical left to those who pursue such professions, except in such branches of the life-sciences as are plainly impossible to divorce from arguments about the nature of man and society (e.g. in and around genetics, such as the best known scientist of the period to describe himself as a Marxist, the American Stephen Jay Gould). However, the Marxism of radical scientists has little relation to their professional theory and practice.

One may hazard the guess that most natural scientists and technologists active in socialist states in 1983 would also take the view that Marxism was irrelevant to their professional activities, though they might be reluctant to express it in public, and although they, like all serious scientists, would necessarily have views about the relation between the natural sciences and the present and future of society.

This state of affairs represents a distinct narrowing of the scope of Marxism, one of whose most powerful appeals to past generations has been precisely that it seemed to constitute a comprehensive, all-embracing and illuminating view of the world, of which human society and its development form only one part. Is it likely to continue? It is impossible to tell. One might merely note some signs of a reaction against the complete extrusion of the non-human cosmos from Marxism.[35] One might also note that the philosophical fashions for denying the objective existence or accessibility of the world on the grounds that all 'facts' exist only by virtue of the prior structuring of concepts in the human mind have lost some of their popularity. (It is indeed difficult to combine with praxis, whether that of scientists or those who wish to change the world by political action.)

Given all that has been outlined in the past pages, it is not surprising that observers of the period since the 1950s could once again speak of a crisis of Marxism. The old certainties – or the competing versions of these certainties – about the future of capitalism, about the social and political forces which might be expected to bring about the transition to a new system of society, about the nature of the socialism that was to be brought about, and about the nature and prospects of the societies which already claimed to have achieved this transformation: all these were thrown into doubt. Indeed, they no longer existed. The basic theory of Marxism, including that of Marx himself, was subject to profound critical scrutiny, and a number of competing, but generally far-reaching reformulations. Much of what the majority of Marxists would have accepted in the past was seriously questioned. If we except the official ideologies of socialist states, and some generally small fundamentalist sects, all the intellectual efforts of Marxists assumed that the traditional theory and doctrines of Marxism required substantial rethinking, modification and revision. On the other hand, a hundred years after Marx's death, no single version of such rethought or modified Marxism could be said to have established itself as predominant.

And yet, as we have seen, the questioning of traditional Marxism went hand in hand with a marked global growth in the intellectual appeal and influence of Marxism. This was plainly not due to the attraction exercised by lively and growing Marxist political parties (as in the 1890s), for the record of most such parties was not inspiring during this period. Still less was it due to the attraction exercised by countries claiming to represent, in various ways, 'really existing socialism'. On the contrary, while before 1956 identification with the USSR – seen, rightly or wrongly, as the first workers' state, child of the first workers' revolution and building the first socialist society – was a genuine inspiration to militants in the world communist movement (and before 1945 to others besides), it increasingly alienated intellectuals, and the wider public. Indeed, the mainstream of anti-Marxism since the 1950s had tended to pursue a simple line of political argument, rejecting even the variously revised and broadened 'neo-Marxisms' essentially on the ground that, unless they specifically abandoned Marx, they must *inevitably* lead to Stalinism or its equivalent. The traditional attempts to demonstrate that Marx's theories were intellectually invalid, while they were not abandoned, became less prominent, and the attempts to dismiss Marx and Marxists as intellectually negligible were now rarely encountered.

The increase in Marxist influence was due to other factors. No doubt it was assisted by a certain clearing of the ideological ground in the 1950s. The defeat of fascism virtually eliminated right-wing radicalism as an idiom of quasi-revolutionary discourse for a period, because of its associations with Hitlerism, and the abdication of liberal social criticism, which in the 1950s often became a self-satisfied ideology celebrating the capacity of existing Western society to solve all its problems, left the field free for Marx. It was indeed the felt need for a fundamental critique of bourgeois society and the most obvious forms of inequality and injustice within it (e.g. in the 'Third World'), as well as the existence of patently unacceptable regimes, which made men and women Marxists.

*

The global intellectual tide of Marx and Marxism was probably at its peak in the 1970s, in the world where print was free and even in countries where authoritarian and militarist governments were on the brink of retreat or overthrow, such as Spain, Portugal and Greece. Marxist texts old and new poured out, from the illegal *Raubdrucke* (pirated republications) by the German radicals to the catalogues of otherwise politically unsullied publishing houses such as Penguin in Britain and Suhrkamp in the German Federal Republic. OUP published a (hostile) history of Marxism in three volumes, Macmillan a (friendly) Marx biography. Marxists themselves founded publishing houses (e.g. New Left Books) or planned ambitious 'collected works' of Marx and Engels (in Britain) or histories of Marxism (in Italy). As the centenary of Marx's death approached, Marxists might well look back on a half-century of extraordinary advancement.

There were some indications that the winds were no longer in Marx's favour, but few observers predicted the speed and scale of the reversal. Certainly I did not, as I took my part in the launch of the first volume of Edizioni Einaudi's collective *Storia del marxismo*, the most ambitious project of its kind, at the national festival of the Italian Communist Party in the decade of its greatest electoral success. The twenty-five years following the centenary of Marx's death were to be the darkest years in the history of his heritage.

15

Marxism in Recession 1983–2000

A century after Marx's death it became obvious that Marxism was in rapid retreat both politically and intellectually, and it continued to be for the next twenty-five years or so, in spite of some signs of potential revival at the very end of the century, paradoxically most evident among observers of the business world like John Cassidy of the *New Yorker*, who recalled his predictions of an increasingly uncontrollable globalisation of the capitalist economy. Nevertheless, there can be no doubt that for a quarter of a century Marx ceased to be regarded as a thinker relevant to the times, and in the greater part of the world Marxism was reduced to little more than the set of ideas of a slowly eroding corps of middle-aged and elderly survivors. Silence greeted the last instalment of the fifty-volume English translation of the *Collected Works* of Marx and Engels, in progress since the 1970s, when it was finally published in 2004. The majestic progress of another project of the 1970s, the 122 volumes of the new MEGA, the complete edition of every word written by Marx and Engels, proceeded and even accelerated. It attracted no attention, except perhaps as a case-study in intellectual continuity from an enterprise planned and financed by communist regimes to a multinational academic undertaking whose political and ideological implications, if any, were left in limbo.

At first sight the reasons for this dramatic setback for Marx and Marxism seem obvious. The political regimes officially identified with both were patently in crisis in the 1980s in Europe, and had changed course dramatically in China. The collapse of the USSR and its European satellites inevitably swept away the 'Marxism-Leninism' that had become their state religion whose dogmas were promulgated by a political authority that officially claimed authority over theory and fact. In itself this need not have affected Marxist thinking outside the region self-described as 'really existing socialism', since the days were long past when Stalin's *Short Course* was generally accepted as a standard compendium of 'dialectical and historical materialism', if not of the history of the Bolshevik party. In any case the dogmatic Soviet orthodoxy precluded any real Marxist analysis of what had happened and was happening in Soviet society. As previous chapters have shown, most Marxist thinking in non-state communist parties since 1956 criticised this orthodoxy, overtly or (within Moscow-line communist parties) by implication, and the leading political trends among post-1956 Marxists, the Trotskyites and Maoists, were defined by their hostility to the Soviet ideology as well as the Soviet regime.

Nevertheless, the fall of the USSR and the Soviet model was traumatic not only for communists but for socialists everywhere, if only because, with all its patent defects, it had been the only attempt actually to construct a socialist society. It had also produced a superpower which for almost half a century acted as a global counterbalance to the capitalism of the old capitalist countries. In both these respects its failure, not to mention its patent inferiority in most respects to Western liberal capitalism, was manifest, even to those who did not share the post-1989 triumphalism of Washington ideologists. Capitalism had lost its *memento mori*. Socialists saw that the end of the Soviet Union foreclosed any hope that somehow a different and better socialism ('with a human face' as the Prague Spring put it) could emerge from the heritage of the October Revolution. After eighty years of practice, those who still held to the original socialist hope of a society built in the name of co-operation instead of competition had to retreat again into speculation and theory. The Marxists among them could not escape from the evident failure of their theory's predictions of the historical future.

All this left non-state socialists bereft and discouraged. Within the states of 'really existing socialism' it simply swept away all of Marxism-Leninism not anchored to such Asian government parties as survived. In those countries communism (the 'vanguard party') had been designed as the doctrine for a select minority of leaders and activists, not a faith for universal conversion like Roman Catholicism and Islam. This alone tended to depoliticise those outside the sphere where ideology was required. What held the bulk of the population together, when available, were the traditional bonds tying peoples to states – historic continuity, patriotism, a sense of ethnic or other collective identity, even the habit of formal obedience to established power – but not a belief in Marxism-Leninism, except as a residuum of the moral/political education all children necessarily passed through. When the system collapsed, it left behind continuities, memories and symbols, but not loyalty to a civic religion.

By the 1980s a large and probably growing majority of its intellectuals probably had little time for the system or, if they had become enthusiastic supporters of their new regimes in the days of liberation – as many had – moved into silent or overt dissidence, like the university communists who became the brains-trust of Solidarity in Poland. If still committed to socialism, at the very least they had become critical of the defects of the 'really existing' version and wished to reform them. This applied increasingly even to the leading cadres of the system itself. Around 1980 an American research student in Poland noted the total refusal of Polish party functionaries to describe themselves as 'communists'. When, by chance, she was able to ask an important member of the Central Committee whether he was a communist, he answered, after a lengthy pause: 'I am a pragmatist.'[1]

Nor had Marxism (as distinct from the unchallengeable dogmata promulgated from on high) deep roots in the party membership. For most members or aspiring members the important thing about their ideology was not whether it was true, or how it could be applied, but that it was binding. 'What if the line changes, as with Stalin?' a British student at the Moscow Higher Party School asked a Soviet fellow-student. 'He looked at me as if I was politically illiterate. "Then that becomes the current truth."'[2] When the system fell, no doubt its elite had much to regret, including the loss of an all-state ideology, but few had much trouble abandoning its Marxist-Leninist version, unless they belonged to the specific sub-group concerned with doctrine, the equivalent of the Vatican's theologians. At all events they adapted with little difficulty to the combination of state patronage, jungle capitalism and mafia power in post-Soviet Russia.

Nevertheless, the retreat from Marxism cannot be simply ascribed to the collapse or transformation of the Marxist-Leninist and Maoist regimes, since it clearly began well before then. One important element was the gradual decomposition and the change in character of the non-state communist parties in Europe and, in France and Italy where these parties dominated the left, the loss of their hegemony over the post-1945 generations of intellectuals. Nor should we underestimate the gradual exit from the public scene, both in politics and culture, of the age-group shaped by anti-fascism, world war and resistance. The crisis both of the European non-state communist parties and of socialist parties and governments was only too evident by the beginning of the 1980s. In effect, it had been evident for some time that Lenin was off the agenda in the advanced Western countries, though the radicalised student movements had still to discover this after 1968. It was not so clear that in the post-1973 era of a world revival of laissez-faire policies in a transnational economy globalising at express speed this was also true of Bernstein, the champion of Fabian gradual reformism by state action. This became only too evident in the era of President Reagan and Margaret Thatcher and, dramatically, after the failure of President François Mitterrand's programme in 1981. And yet, in the 1970s, though the new era had begun, the Marxist presence in the bookshops and seminar-rooms was at its maximum and both political and labour union militancy scored some of their most dramatic successes.

Leaving politics aside, Marxism was already in regression among intellectuals, although this did not become obvious until the 1980s. And not only Marxism, but the entire current of ideas about human society that had dominated Western thinking since the Second World War, of which Marxism was one component. Even the natural sciences came under attack, not only because of the potential or actual damage caused by technology, but because their validity as modes of understanding the world was questioned.

This was perhaps least marked in economics, where Marxists had always been peripheral, though among the first ten Nobel laureates in this field there were three who were formed or partly formed in the early years of the Soviet Union or who were still active there (Wassily Leontief, Simon Kuznets, Leonid Kantorovitch). However, from 1974, when Friedrich von Hayek received the prize, still balanced by his ideological opposite, the Swede Gunnar Myrdal, and 1976, when it was given to Milton Friedman, it became markedly identified with a sharp turn away from Keynesian and other interventionist theories and a return to an increasingly uncompromising laissez-faire. Cracks in this prevailing consensus did not begin to appear until the late 1990s.

A common methodological rather than political or ideological orientation of Marxists and non-Marxists had long been much more evident in the social and human sciences, at least outside the USA, notably sociology and history. From the late nineteenth century on, sociology, the attempt to understand the operations of society, overlapped with both Marx and the more general aim of changing and not merely interpreting the world. Durkheim, Marx and Max Weber replaced Auguste Comte and Herbert Spencer as its founding fathers in the academy, though there is no reason to believe that Marx himself would have thought of it as a distinct and separate field of enquiry. The extraordinary expansion of higher education since the 1960s had given it unusual prominence – at present forty-five university institutions in the UK have departments of or including sociology – and political radicalisation had made it a subject of choice for many students. Intellectually its prominence declined sharply with the fading of the radical mood in the universities.

History was also associated with student radicalism, but its evolution as a field of study is more instructive. Here the Marxists were part of the modernising current which wanted to fertilise the arid conventional historiography that was hostile to generalisations of any kind, and largely confined to political, military and institutional narrative about chronological successions of events in terms of the actions of prominent individuals – mainly by mobilising the insights and methods of the social sciences, which were then rapidly developing. Converging from very different disciplines and ideologies, the reformers had become a recognised presence by the end of the nineteenth century, but had hardly advanced far in their siege of the fortress of academic history except for establishing an institutional outpost of 'economic and social history' on its outskirts. They made some progress between the wars and especially in the 1930s, but they did not become a major force until after World War Two.

Then, in effect, they inspired and transformed the field of history mainly through journals favouring the marriage between history and the social sciences, notably Marc Bloch's and Lucien

Febvre's celebrated *Annales d'histoire économique et sociale*, a militant adversary of the old conventional history in France since 1929, which became, renamed, the most influential historical journal worldwide under Fernand Braudel, who also established the School of Advanced Study in the Social Sciences (Ecole des Hautes Etudes en Sciences Sociales) in the newly built Maison des Sciences de l'Homme as virtually a rival institution to the old university. The *Annales* school was in no sense Marxist in its intellectual origins or sympathies, but it helped to inspire the journal *Past & Present*, founded by British Marxist historians. In the absence of a formal organ of opposition to the old-style academy, this became a rather more modest Anglophone equivalent. Both influenced the reform of German historiography after 1960 under the programmatic title 'Historical Social Science', which was also reinforced institutionally by the foundation of suitably oriented new universities, notably that of Bielefeld. Max Weber rather then Marx inspired the German reformers. Meanwhile a specific interdisciplinary journal, *Comparative Studies in Society and History*, was founded in the USA, later broadening into a still active 'Social Science History Association'.

There is little doubt that by 1970 the reformers set the tone, leaving the traditional historians very much on the defensive. The vast expansion of an increasingly radicalised body of university students reinforced their influence and made 'social history' as well as the more theoretical sociology into the weapon of choice of the intellectual young. The role of Marx and Marxism in these developments is difficult to assess, but they are far ahead of any other historian or historical school in the index of a survey of the field in 1971,[3] and it was a Marxist work which, for the historian of British historiography of the century 1907–2007, 'at last saw off, even from remoter library shelves, some of those dated textbooks of an earlier era'.[4] But the Marxist minority (except in the countries under communist government, where historians had no option) was always only one component of the great movement of historiographical modernisation, which now seemed to have won.

It is hardly surprising that the self-confidence and (as in France) the polemical simplifications of the progress-minded historical modernisers should leave them open to criticism. To take an obvious example, the neglect of what the French depreciated as 'the history of events', and of what the Marxists side-lined as 'the role of the individual in history', meant that an adequate history of Hitler's Germany or Stalin's Soviet Union could not yet be written.[5] Yet from some time in the early to middle 1970s, we find more than this. It became evident that there was a new scepticism about the attempt to understand the structure and change of human collectivities through the social sciences. Sociology and social anthropology took a similar anti-objective and anti-structural turn at the same time, merging with versions of so-called 'critical theory' to produce some extreme forms of post-modernist relativism. Neo-classical economics reduced society to an agglomeration of individuals rationally pursuing their interests whose end was an ahistorical market equilibrium. The new historians fled from the methods so dear to the social sciences and the interdisciplinary 'big questions' of social transformation, back to narrative (notably political narrative) rather than structural analysis. They moved towards culture and ideas on the one hand, empathy with individual historical experiences on the other. One important strand rejected not only historical and social generalisation and predictabilities, but the very concept of studying an objective reality. This critical turn away from the now predominant 'modernists' had no particular political or ideological orientation. Braudel and his *Annales* were as much victims of it as Marx. Though some aspects of the new revisionism suited traditional conservatives, such as historical indeterminacy (which produced a number of exercises in counterfactual or 'what if?', history), much of it came out of the milieu of post-1968 radicalism. Some of what might be called the historical 'post-modernists' even remained on the revolutionary left.

The retreat from Marxism in the non-communist world was therefore part of a more general mutation in the social and human sciences in the 1970s. It had no obvious connection with the Cold War ideology, hostility to the USSR and dissident denunciation of this or that national Communist Party. Strong as these were in the 1950s and 1960s, as we have seen they coexisted with an impressive upsurge of political radicalism including intellectual Marxism. Still less was it an anticipation of the collapse of the European communist regimes, which was not seriously expected even by those who detested them until shortly before it occurred. Nor can we ascribe it to the developing crises of social democracy whose parties were actually ruling more European governments in the 1970s than ever before or since. With the rarest exceptions, the names most widely associated with intellectual anti-Marxism and anti-communism in the last quarter of the century were not new. Even those who denounced 'the god that failed' had broken with their respective communist parties before 1970. The systematic attempt of Western Cold Warriors to counter the Soviets' 'battle of ideas' by Congresses of Cultural Freedom did not effectively survive the revelation of CIA financing in 1967.

If anything, the retreat from Marxism was generated within the old radical left itself, not least by the clash inherent in the revolutionary versions of Marxism between automatic historical evolution and the role of revolutionary action. If historical development inevitably led to the end of capitalism, and hence, it was assumed, inevitable triumph for socialism, then there could be no decisive role for voluntary action, except when the apple was ripe enough to fall off the tree of history. Even then, could revolutionary action do more than pick it up? In practice this only created problems for entrenched revolutionaries where there were no prospects of social revolution. The radical left in the years before 1914, hungering for action, rejected a Marxism identified with the evolutionary expectations of German social democracy. The young Gramsci even spoke of 'a revolution against *Das Kapital*'. Only World War One and the Russian October Revolution brought their ultra-radicalism back to Marx via Lenin. The new radical left movements of the 1960s, equally given to activism at all costs, occurred at the height of Western capitalist success, stabilised by rising incomes, welfare and the symbiosis of business enterprise and labour unions. They certainly did not dismiss Marx, whose bearded face was by now established as a revolutionary icon, though increasingly replaced by a more suitable image of voluntarist insurrection, Che Guevara.

However, what they disliked about Marxism was not so much the inevitable 'forward march of labour' social democrats read into Marx, but the rigid and centralised party organisation Lenin had imposed on him. In terms of revolutionary history, they represented a reversion from Marx to Bakunin. Everything they hated about Soviet communism derived from its disciplined centralisation, from centrally commanded truths and actions to the hecatombs of Stalin's victims. Spontaneity, rank-and-file initiatives, not to mention unrestricted self-expression ('doing your own thing'), were to be the roots of action; leadership was suspect, decisions were to emerge from the multiple voices of grass-roots assemblies. Conversely, those who continued to pursue the traditional end of Marxist revolutionaries, the transfer of political power, could no longer rely on history generating Leninist 'revolutionary situations' in the society of class oppression. They therefore increasingly put their hopes into planned insurrectionary or terrorist actions by small outlaw groups, such as had been traditionally dismissed by Marxists. These could be justified in poor and undeveloped countries by the assumption that such regions were permanently on the verge of social conflagration, and would burst into flame once 'focused' by the initiative of outside guerrillas like Che Guevara. (In practice this Cuban-inspired theory failed utterly in the 1960s and 1970s in its chosen continent, however elegantly formulated by Régis Debray.)[6] In the rich economies they could only fall back on the old anarchist slogan of 'propaganda by the deed', small-group terrorism, which was to make unexpectedly large impacts in a media society hungry for headlines and dramatic images.

A number of tendencies therefore emerged from the post-1956 ferment of the old (Marxist) left and the new cultural radicalism of the 1960s, which moved away from the traditional Marxist analysis while often, though not always, continuing to situate themselves on the left: notably the *History Workshop* movement and journal in Britain, 'Everyday History' (*Alltagsgeschichte*) in Germany, the 'Subaltern School' in India, various forms of 'critical theory' and a new crop of feminist and other identity histories claiming to represent 'new social movements' that would, they hoped, fill the gap left by the crisis of the traditional labour movements.

At the same time the discovery (dramatised by the Club of Rome from the early 1970s) that the uncontrollable increase in the human capacity to produce laid the basis of future environmental catastrophe, contradicted the appeal of Marxism as a theory of evolution looking forward to a better future. The 'crisis of progress' which Marxists had seen in the 1930s as characteristic of an exhausted bourgeois society now turned against them. The injustices and oppressions generated by the capitalist nature of progress had always been denounced, but now that progress itself came under attack. Increasingly the campaigns of the left aimed to protect and conserve against the advances in the human power over nature which their Marxist predecessors would have hailed or would at least have regarded as inevitable (as with globalisation). Marxism was particularly vulnerable to this reversal of the perspective of 'historical inevitability' from positive to negative.

Possibly a shift to the political left, particularly among the growing and politically significant strata with university education might have revived the fortunes of Marx, since an interest in his theories has so often been historically linked to the political radicalisation of individuals or groups or the emergence of countries from periods of authoritarianism. Nothing like this happened in the West, though there is some evidence that political activism led to a rise in interest in literature with Marxian associations in some non-European countries, such as, at various times since 1970, Brazil, Taiwan, South Korea and Turkey.[7] On the contrary, the crisis of the major reservoir of the Western left, the labour-based social-democratic movements, eliminated any aspirations to socialism within them. So far as I am aware no leader of a party of the European left in the past twenty-five years has declared capitalism as such to be unacceptable as a system. The only public figure to do so unhesitatingly was Pope John Paul II. Moreover, nothing proved easier than to incorporate the rebel generation of 1968 – this time the Situationists – into a flourishing capitalist system that made more allowance than any of its predecessors for variations in personal taste and lifestyle, and which increasingly operated and presented itself as that economy and society of media-driven public spectacle. Increasingly academic success brought money. The 1990s and 2000s were the first era of the billionaires with research degrees. Indeed, at least one humorist observed that the world banking crisis of 2008 was due to the fact that for the first time the smart graduates rather than, as of old, the intellectually less gifted went into finance, thus inventing algorithms too complex for most capitalists to understand.[8] Careers rather than social change were on the horizon for the intellectually liveliest students.

In addition, let us not forget a more general phenomenon: the general retreat of what one might call the ideologies of social change of the eighteenth-century Enlightenment and the rise or revival of alternative inspirations for social activism, notably tacitly modernised versions of traditional religions. While these made no great appeal in Europe, they achieved their first great success in the Iranian revolution of 1979, the last of the great social revolutions of the twentieth century. Even had this not been so, historic and intellectual developments in the second half of the twentieth century visibly undermined the political analyses, programmes and forecasts traditionally derived from Marx. Marx's basic analysis of the development and modus operandi of capitalism retains its force. However, any future revival of interest in Marxism will undoubtedly need to be based on substantial recalibrations of traditional views of his thinking.

Without the collapse of most communist regimes and the deliberate abandonment of their traditional methods and objectives by others, and the simultaneous crises of labour-based social democracy, this would probably not have been enough to account for the twenty years of almost total marginalisation of Marxism in intellectual discourse. Since ostensibly Marxist systems and movements once inspired by Marx had failed to survive or abandoned their traditional purposes, it was no longer politically important nor did it seem intellectually necessary to spend much time on theories that history appeared to have discredited. In any case, the Cold War was over. Paradoxically, indignant denunciation continued even as its objects disappeared, much as antisemitism in Poland survived the disappearance of Jews from that country.

The rhetoric of Cold War anti-communism continued, not so much against a once-feared enemy as in favour of the world-wide superiority and, hopefully, supremacy of Western liberal-democratic capitalism. Increasingly confident, this saw itself, by means of the intervention of armed and soft power justified by an ideology of universal human rights, as the maker of order in a disturbed world. What were denounced – for argument atrophied – were not Marx's theories and analyses but his prospect of revolution, which, it was argued, misled the idealistic young, and the totalitarianism he and any other challenge to liberalism were believed to imply or propound, not to mention the obstacles socialist aspirations raised to the self-regulating rationality of market society. In a word, Marx was typecast as the inspirer of terror and gulag, and communists as essentially defenders of, if not participators in, terror and the KGB. It is not clear how far this rhetoric convinced those not already converted, some from 'the god that failed', in the days of the Cold War. It is difficult to see these exercises in execration long surviving into a century in which even today only those in their thirties and above have any memory of the actual years of Cold War.

However, in the end Marx was to make a somewhat unexpected return in a world in which capitalism has been reminded that its own future is put into question not by the threat of social revolution but by the very nature of its untrammelled global operations, to which Karl Marx has proved so much more perceptive a guide than the believers in the rational choices and self-correcting mechanisms of the free market.

16

Marx and Labour: the Long Century

It seems fitting that a set of studies in the history of Marxism should conclude with an essay on the organised movement of the working class. For Marx, the proletariat was the destined 'grave-digger of capitalism', the essential agent of social transformation. In the twentieth century most organised working-class movements and parties came to be associated with Marx's dream of a new society ('socialism'), and in turn all Marxists, almost without exception, saw working-class parties and movements as their chosen field of political action. Yet neither Marxism nor labour movements can be understood except as independent historical agents, in complex and changing relationships with each other. Nor, indeed, can the impact of either on the history of the twentieth century.

Though any reader of the *Communist Manifesto* knows that labour movements go back much further, nevertheless there is some justification in beginning this survey of labour movements and their ideologies at the very end of the nineteenth century. Serious British labour history began in the 1890s, notably with the Webbs' remarkable studies of trade unionism. The first comparative global survey appeared in 1900: W. Kulemann's *Die*

Gewerkschaftsbewegung. Darstellung der gewerkschaftlichen Organisation der Arbeiter und Arbeitgeber aller Länder. The first histories written from within the new socialist parties began to appear around the same time, e.g. in 1898 the first version of Mehring's history of the German Social Democratic Party.

What is more, the 1890s were the decade when European governments came to recognise the political existence of firmly organised labour movements. The British government published its first *Abstract of Labour Statistics* in 1893–4; the Belgian government began to publish a *Revue du Travail* in 1896. For the first time a British prime minister – Lord Rosebery in 1894 – felt moved to personal intervention to settle a dispute between employers and workers. Five years later the French premier, Waldeck-Rousseau, followed his example, having been invited to do so by the striking workers of the Schneider-Creusot works. And in the same year the French government took a step that shook the political parties of labour, or at least the socialist ones, to the core. It appointed a socialist, the forty-year old Alexandre Millerand, to the Ministry of Commerce. Until then, and indeed for many more years, socialists took it for granted that they would neither form nor take part in government until the revolution or a general strike had laid capitalism low, or at least until an intransigently social-democratic party had won a single-handed electoral victory. Ideologically, this was the crisis that initiated the political history of labour in the twentieth century.

Why did European governments conclude that they had to take labour seriously? Certainly not because of its economic force, even though there were plenty of employers who claimed that trade unions were about to strangle industry. Union organisation was still modest – say 15–20% in Britain and France, rather less in Germany. Nor was labour a major political presence except in Germany, where the Social Democratic Party was by far the strongest electoral force with its 30% of (male) voters. However, if electoral democracy were to be introduced, as seemed likely, labour parties could be expected to become major electoral forces, as indeed they did in Scandinavia and elsewhere in the years before 1914. Nevertheless, what really made governments nervous was not electoral calculation but the evident class-consciousness of the workers, which found its expression in new and overwhelmingly 'red' class parties. As Winston Churchill, President of the Board of Trade in the new reforming Liberal administration of 1906, put it, if the old two-party system of Conservatives and Liberals were to break down, British politics would become open class politics, that is to say politics dominated by the conflict of class interest. In Britain, most of whose inhabitants were or saw themselves as 'workers', this seemed a matter of special urgency, but avoiding the politics of class struggle was a general problem.

The Millerand crisis forced the new labour parties for the first, but not the last, time to consider their relation to the system in which they operated. The time was patently ripe for asking this question, for, almost at the same time (in the autumn of 1899), Eduard Bernstein, one of the earliest pillars of German Marxism, published his manifesto of reformism, *Die Voraussetzungen des Sozialismus und die Aufgaben der Sozialdemokratie*, which was to lead to an acrimonious debate in the international movement. Nor is it irrelevant that this was also the moment when, again for the first time, books were published with titles like *The Crisis of Marxism* (by Masaryk, later President of Czechoslovakia).

The central question behind both the Millerand crisis and the debate on Bernstein's revisionism was: reform or revolution? Given that by the end of the 1890s the immediate collapse of capitalism was not to be expected, at least in the developed economies, what was the historic function of labour movements? In other words, was there a non-revolutionary way to socialism? The cases of Millerand and Bernstein were particularly scandalous, because there was no way of escaping the peremptory form in which they raised this question. Bernstein had to be rejected, because he outraged all sections of the International by actually proposing a frank revision of

Marxism, and was therefore denounced by one and all. The movement handled the Millerand affair with more circumspection, since it concerned a single individual and socialist theory as such was not at issue. A compromise solution was proposed, which in practice made possible the participation of individuals, but not yet parties, in 'bourgeois governments'. As for Bernstein, in practice social democracy accepted the thesis that the improvement of labour's conditions under capitalism was the chief business of the movement, while categorically repudiating his theoretical justification of reformism. In fact, after 1900 even the Marxist labour movements in the main countries of capitalism lived in an unacknowledged symbiosis with capitalism, rather than in a state of war.

While labour and socialism seemed inseparable, the two movements were not identical. Millerand and Bernstein were a crisis of socialism, but not of labour movements. An international conference of labour historians mistakenly debated the theme 'The Labour movement as a project of modernity that failed'. Labour movements and class consciousness are not 'projects' but, in a certain phase of social production, logically necessary and politically almost inevitable characteristics of classes of men and women employed for wages. The term 'project' applies rather to socialism, that is to say the intention to replace capitalism by a new economic system and a new society. Labour movements arise in all societies that contain a working class, except where they are prevented by coercion and terror. Labour movements have played an important role in the history of the USA. They still do within the Democratic Party. At the same time the question 'Why is there no socialism in the USA?' was already being asked – notably by the one-time Marxist Werner Sombart in 1906 – taking for granted the absence or insignificance of socialism there, whether as ideology or political movement. In Britain the Lib-Lab trade union movement looked for political support to the Liberal Party, with which it did not completely sever its connections until after the Great

War. Socialists and communists, long frustrated in Argentina, found it difficult to understand how a politically independent and radical labour movement could develop in that country in the 1940s, whose ideology (Peronism) consisted primarily of loyalty to a demagogic general.

What is more, there have been actively anti-socialist bona fide labour movements such as the Polish Solidarity, and labour movements tied to specific nationalisms or religions, with or without links to other ideologies. Thus the British government's attempt in the 1970s to include the Catholics in the government of Northern Ireland was sabotaged by a general strike of the Protestant working class. Conversely, history records socialist and communist movements which neither had nor sought a class basis, both orthodox and heretical Christian movements and the various community-building 'utopian socialists' of the nineteenth century, paradoxically more popular in the USA at the time than anywhere else.

Of course it is undeniable that from the time of the *Communist Manifesto* to the 1970s, labour movements without a relation to socialism were exceptional. Indeed, in practice it is practically impossible to find any labour movements of whatever kind in which socialists or people formed in the socialist movements did not play a significant part. This symbiosis of labour movement and socialism was evidently not fortuitous. Both sides derived advantages from it, except for the systems of 'really existing socialism' which abolished labour movements in the name of parties claiming to represent the working class and in the name of socialism.

Nevertheless, labour movements and socialism were not necessarily congruent. Indeed, Marxist theorists from Kautsky to Lenin held that labour movements did not generate socialism spontaneously, but that it had to be imported into them from outside. This was perhaps an exaggeration. It may be argued that the age of the American, French and Industrial Revolutions made the possibility of ending the existing order and replacing it with an entirely different and better society part of the general intellectual scene, at least in the West. The struggle of workers for better conditions, essentially collective, therefore implied the potential of such a better, i.e. more socially just, society, and indeed a society based on community and cooperation not on competition. Movements of the poor were likely to approve and favour this prospect. What had to be imported into labour from outside was something else: the specific name and content of the new society, a strategy for the transition from capitalism to socialism and, above all, the concept of a politically independent class party active on a national scale. Organisations like labour unions, mutual aid and cooperative societies might emerge spontaneously from workers' life experience, but not political parties.

The fundamental contribution of Marx and Engels from the *Communist Manifesto* onward was that the class organisation of workers must logically find expression in a political party active throughout the territory of the state, or even beyond. (Admittedly this was possible only in constitutional, liberal or bourgeois-democratic states.) This was a proposition of enormous historical significance, not only for the labour movement, which could not get very far in its objects without mobilising state support against employers, but for the structure of modern politics in general. It also proved realistic, because several such parties, some still bearing their original class affiliation – the Labour Party, El Partido Socialista Obrero Español, Sveriges Socialdemokratiska Arbetareparti, Det Norske Arbeiderparti – emerged after Marx's death, destined to become and remain governing or major opposition parties in much of non-communist Europe. This is a record of almost unparalleled continuity and significance on our continent. Incidentally, it invalidates the belief that labour movements must become or remain revolutionary because they could not get anywhere under capitalism. As for the presumption that by historical necessity the proletariat was or would be a 'truly revolutionary class', it is now evident that this was baseless. Moreover, history has also taught us that revolutions are far too complicated sets of events to be seen simply as transcriptions of class structure. Left-wing theoreticians and historians of labour who, like the Marxists, attempted to explain why most working-class parties stubbornly refused to play the revolutionary role imputed to them might have saved themselves much time, effort and acumen.

In short, the (constitutional) countries of developed capitalism, in which revolutions were not on the agenda for other reasons, contained revolutionaries within or outside labour movements, but most organised workers, even the class-conscious ones, were not normally revolutionary even when their parties were committed to socialism. The situation was naturally different in countries such as those of the Russian and Ottoman Empires, where any political change for the better could only be expected to come through revolution.

So nothing in the core states of developed capitalism seemed to stand in the way of a symbiosis between labour and a flourishing economic system at the beginning of the twentieth century. Neither the breakdown of capitalism nor that of the liberal and increasingly democratised constitutions typical of this region was in sight. The capitalist model of development seemed no more imperilled than the imperialist structure of the globe, for in the 'backward' world the economic, cultural and, not least, the military superiority of the 'advanced' world was evident. Indeed, in 'backward' countries where revolution was a real prospect and not a mere rhetorical device, it was clear to Marxists that bourgeois-capitalist development was the only way forward. Hence in Russia the so-called 'legal Marxists' turned Marxism into an ideology of capitalist industrialisation, but – until 1917 – even the Bolsheviks were convinced that the immediate aim of the coming revolution was a bourgeois-liberal society, since only this could create the historical conditions for further progress to the proletarian revolution and hence to socialism.

World War One seemed to put paid to all such expectations. The 'Age of Catastrophe' from 1914 to the late 1940s lived in the shadow of war, social and political breakdown and revolution – above all the Russian October Revolution. Everything went wrong for the old world. Wars ended in revolutions and colonial unrest. Constitutional bourgeois-liberal and democratic states under the rule of law gave way to political regimes hardly imaginable before 1914 such as Hitler's Germany or Stalin's USSR. Even the market economy of economic liberalism seemed to break down in the crisis of the early 1930s. Could capitalism survive at all except perhaps in a form that abolished both democracy and the labour movement? Only the depth of the troubles of global capitalism can explain why, even outside the Soviet Union, the primitive industrial economy of Stalin's USSR could be seriously regarded as a more dynamic system than that of the West, and a possible global alternative to capitalism. As late as the early 1960s there were still bourgeois politicians, like the British prime minister Harold Macmillan, who shared Khrushchev's belief that the socialist economies could outproduce the Western ones. Even those who were more sceptical of the USSR's economic achievement and potential could not deny its global political weight and military power. The First World War had destroyed tsarism, the Second turned Russia into a superpower. For large parts of the now liberated colonies and other parts of the 'Third World', the USSR, and through it socialism, actually became an economic model of how to overcome backwardness.

The political agenda of socialists and labour movements in the Age of Catastrophe therefore shifted from living with capitalism to ending it. Revolution and the subsequent construction of the new society seemed a better prospect than the slow forward march through reforms here and now towards a distant and not seriously pursued socialism. Sidney and Beatrice Webb, the inspirers of the British Fabians and apostles of gradual reformism – which had actually inspired Bernstein's revisionism in the 1890s – abjured reformism in the 1930s and put their faith in Soviet socialism.

Nevertheless, though things looked very different after 1917, capitalism in its main strongholds was threatened neither with final breakdown nor with a social revolution – revolution being confined to countries on the periphery of the system. Petrograd's Soviet revolution did not establish itself in Berlin, and we can now see that it was unrealistic to expect it to. Hence the foundations of the reformist symbiosis remained strong. Indeed, it became more attractive to politicians and entrepreneurs as a safeguard against social revolution and the spectre of a global communist movement, all the more as there was now a sharp distinction between mutually hostile reformist social-democratic and revolutionary communist parties. All that was often missing between the wars was the prosperity which provided the means for the necessary concessions to labour movements. In any case, even in the worst days of crisis the majority within the labour movements in these countries refused to move from reformist parties to revolutionary ones. Between the wars communist parties enjoyed mass support in only three of the states in which they were legal, and even there they remained weaker than social democracy: Germany, France and Czechoslovakia. Had the CP been legal in Finland there might have been four. Elsewhere communist parties between the wars scored a maximum of 6% of votes (Belgium, Norway, Sweden), and even that only briefly.

After the Second World War the symbiosis was pursued more systematically as part of a policy of structural reform of Western capitalism by means of the deliberate policy of full employment and what became the welfare state, and on the basis of the massive advances of the capitalist economies in the post-1945 decades (1947–73). Would this conscious attempt to integrate labour have emerged without the traumatic experiences of the great inter-war depression and the rise of Hitler's Germany? How much of it was due to the fear of communism, whose forces had dramatically increased during the years of anti-fascist resistance? What stood behind them now was a superpower.

Would Bernstein ('the movement is everything, the final aim nothing') have won without Stalin and Hitler? It is unlikely.

So, in the core countries of capitalism the revisionist model of the labour movement prevailed in the new Golden Age of Western capitalism. Its victory was symbolised by the formal abandonment of Marxism in the 1959 Godesberg Programme of the German Social Democratic Party. Nothing seemed to be lost by ditching it, except sentimental memories, for as the Golden Age (1947–73) drew to its close the objectives of reformism had been in practice achieved, and workers were incomparably better off than even the most optimistic representatives of reform could have imagined before 1914. Nevertheless, the revisionist parties remained rooted in the working class, in spite of renouncing the 'final aim' of socialism, though sniped at by traditional left wings within them. The manual working class, their main electoral base, continued to vote for them. They did not begin to abandon their class parties until later.

In fact, until the end of the 1970s the spectacular expansion of production still required a vast mass of industrial workers, who therefore remained or became a major part of the electorates. In the 1970s there were probably more proletarians, absolutely and relatively, in capitalist Europe than there had been at the end of the nineteenth century, when the new class-consciousness of labour suddenly produced proletarian mass parties. However, it is also now clear that these working-class parties, even reformists and revolutionaries in conjunction, never commanded more than half the electoral votes, and even that not until after the Second World War.

Apart from the period between the wars, the development of labour movements in the core capitalist countries until the era of crisis after the 1970s may be summarised as follows.

Even before World War One the policies of the ruling classes, faced with growing political democratisation (accelerated by pressure from the new labour parties), had begun to shift towards social reform. In the non-fascist countries this process was accelerated between the wars, but it did not become systematic until after the Second World War, under the slogans 'full employment' and 'the welfare state'. Even before 1914 democratisation and economic growth encouraged an open recognition of the value of moderate labour movements, though imperial Germany remained a major exception. In consequence, labour movements and parties became in practice identified with their nation-states. This became only too manifest at the outbreak of war in 1914.

The end of that war saw a spectacular rise in the numbers and power of the organised working class. Though this rise could not be maintained between the wars, it resumed both during and after the Second World War. Except for traditionally weak or unstable industrial countries like France and Spain, organised labour probably reached maximum strength in the 1970s. Labour parties thus became state- and system-maintaining forces. During and after the First World War their representatives joined governments and soon formed governments themselves, though not until after 1945 could they do so without the support of non-socialist parties. This development also reached its peak in the 1970s when at one time or another social-democratic governments ruled in Austria, Belgium, Denmark, Finland, Norway, Portugal, post-Franco Spain, Sweden, the UK and Federal Germany, to be joined by France and Greece in 1981. Then came the crisis.

What part did revolutionaries play in the labour movements of the core countries of Western capitalism? Whatever their theory, in practice they could not be revolutionary, since neither the fall of capitalism nor the transition to socialism were to be expected. On the other hand they were needed, since even non-socialist labour movements depended on the combination of class struggle in the workplace and political pressure on national governments, not to mention ideas expressing their aspirations. Where labour unions were strong, revolutionaries could thus play a significant part, so that tiny minorities of communists could be disproportionately effective in countries like Britain and the USA, where their parties were politically negligible. The peak of Communist Party influence in the British trade union movement was reached in the 1970s, when the CP was already at death's door.

In the dictatorships left over from the Age of Catastrophe – e.g. Spain and Portugal – the illegal communists were still the major force of resistance, and played a significant part in the transition to democracy in the 1970s, but were soon marginalised. In Italy the largest communist mass party in Europe, systematically excluded from government by US pressure, distanced itself from the USSR and moved towards a social-democratic model. In France, the CP pursued a reforming policy for some years in the 1970s as part of something like a new Popular Front initiated by Mitterrand, who had reconstructed the Socialist Party. It briefly entered government under the socialist president in 1981–4 – the first time since 1947 that a Communist Party was allowed to do so – but soon reverted to a traditional hard line. Outvoted and outmanoeuvred by the reconstructed socialists since 1974, its mass support collapsed in the 1980s.

The situation was very different outside the core countries of capitalism, including in those states now under the victorious Leninist revolutions of 1917 and 1945–9. The Russian Bolsheviks had come to power in the name of the proletariat and their Five-Year plans created a huge industrial working class, but they abolished the labour movement as we know it. Until the end the Soviet Union permitted no organisation of the workers not controlled by party and state, a model followed in the post-1945 successor communist states as long as they had the power to do so. It is possible to write the history of the working class in the communist world and even a history of labour conflicts, but not the history of labour movements, with the major exception of Solidarity in Poland in the 1980s.

Elsewhere in the world socialist or other labour movements

(give or take those in Australasia and a few other modest exceptions) only began with the Russian Revolution. The Second International hardly existed in those regions, and there was simply no basis for the social-democratic, let alone the Bernsteinian policies. On the other hand, in some (mainly American) countries we find a phenomenon which, for historical reasons, barely existed in the old world, namely the readiness of demagogic heads of state to favour labour movements as part of their struggle against the older elites of landowners. This was the case in Argentina and Brazil. In Mexico the same role was played by the PRI, the institutionalised state party that emerged after the Mexican revolution. In fact, until the beginnings of real industrialisation in and after the 1970s an organisable working class was hard to find in these regions, apart from in the mining, energy, transport and shipping and textiles sectors. Since then, however, there have been two developments which are comparable to what happened in Europe a century before. They are the rise of a mass trade union movement in Korea and of the Party of Labour (PT) in Brazil, both in the 1980s. The influence of Leninism (orthodox or dissident) was important in such movements, but it was decisive in only a few countries. All the same, whatever ideology or non-ideology stood behind these movements, practically all took place in countries where the military coup, revolution, street-fighting and guns were more familiar than peaceful democratic politics. In China and Vietnam, as in the USSR, mass industrialisation could not lead to independent labour organisation.

Then, after the 1970s, everything changed: both Lenin and Bernstein lost their hopes. Everyone knows that the Soviet system collapsed, while the non-state communist parties faded. What is less familiar is that Bernsteinian social democracy was also swept away. The edifice of reformism rested on a triple foundation. The first was the size and growth of the working class, the consciousness that welded a heterogeneous mass of the labouring and the more or less poor together as a single

411

class, and the readiness of bourgeois-democratic governments, even before 1914, to make concessions to such significant
voting blocs, provided they did not behave too radically. But
since the 1970s the manual working classes of the core capitalist countries (the 'First World') have shrunk both relatively and
absolutely, and lost a good part of their unified and unifying class-
consciousness. This went so far that some groups within them,
unconditionally anchored to the movement in the past, shifted
to parties of economic liberalism, as happened both in Britain
under Thatcher and in the USA under Reagan. In the 1980s we
also note the rise of parties of the radical nationalist right with an
attraction for working-class voters, notably in France (led by
Le Pen) and in Austria (led by Haider). Moreover, the enormous
increase in the wealth of affluent consumer societies, which also
benefited the working classes, undermined the axiomatic belief
that real improvement for the working-class individual could be
achieved only by solidarity and collective action.

What part was played by the decline of the left-wing ideologies, including socialism, rooted in the eighteenth-century
Enlightenment, we can only guess. In Europe it was probably
insignificant, but not so in parts of Asia and Africa, particularly
the Muslim regions. The Iranian revolution of 1979 was the
first major revolution since Cromwell's time that was not
inspired by a secular ideology but appealed to the masses in
the language of religion, in this case the idiom of Shi'ite Islam.
Subsequently, a politicised fundamentalist (Sunni) Islam began
to appear in various regions between Pakistan and Morocco
and gained force. At the same time there was, as we have seen,
a steep decline in Marxism and the social-democratic left and a
general depoliticisation both of workers and of students.

The Russian Revolution had given reformism a second foundation: fear of communism and the USSR. The advance of
both during and after the Second World War seemed, at least in
Europe, to require from governments and employers alike a
counter-policy of full employment and systematic social security.

But the USSR no longer exists, and with the fall of the Berlin Wall capitalism could forget how to be frightened, and therefore lost interest in people unlikely to own shares. In any case, even the spells of mass unemployment in the 1980s and 1990s seemed to have lost the old power of radicalising their victims.

However, it was not only politics but also the economy that proved to require reformism and especially full employment after 1945 – as both Keynes and the Swedish economists of Scandinavian social democracy had predicted. This was to be the third foundation of reformism. It became the policy not only of social-democratic governments but almost all governments (not excluding the USA). This brought the Western countries both political stabilisation and unprecedented economic success. Not until the new era after 1973, when the economy and post-war policy of reform no longer gave such positive results, were governments persuaded by the individualist ideologies of radical economic liberalism which had by then infested the economic faculty in Chicago. For them labour movements, labour parties and indeed public social welfare systems were nothing but obstructions of the free market which guaranteed maximal growth for profits and the economy and thus – the ideologists argued – of general welfare also. Ideally, they should be abolished, although in practice this proved impossible. 'Full employment' was now replaced by labour market flexibility and the doctrine of 'the natural rate of unemployment'.

This was also the period when nation-states retreated before the advance of the transnational global economy. In spite of their theoretical internationalism, labour movements were effective only within the enclosure of their state, chained to their nation-states, particularly in the state-steered mixed economies and welfare states of the second half of the twentieth century. As the nation-state retreated, labour movements and social-democratic parties lost their most powerful weapon. They have so far not been very successful at operating transnationally.

As capitalism enters a new period of crisis, we thus find ourselves at the end of a peculiar phase in the history of labour movements. In the rapidly industrialising 'emerging economies' there is no possibility of a decline in industrial labour. In the rich countries of old capitalism labour movements are still in existence, though largely drawing their strength from the public services which, in spite of neo-liberal campaigns, show no signs of shrinking. Western movements have survived because, as Marx predicted, the great majority of the economically active population depend on their wages and salaries and therefore recognise the distinction between the interests of wage-providers and wage-receivers. When conflicts between the two sides arise, they therefore imply collective action, at all events by the wage-receivers. Class struggle therefore continue, whether or not buttressed by political ideologies.

Moreover, the gap between the rich and the poor and divisions between social groups with divergent interests continue to exist, whether or not we call such groups 'classes'. Whatever the very different social hierarchies from those of a hundred or two hundred years ago, politics therefore continues, though only in part as class politics.

Finally, labour movements continue because the nation-state is not on the way to extinction. The state and other public authorities remain the only institutions capable of distributing the social product among its people, in human terms, and to meet human needs that cannot be satisfied by the market. Politics therefore has remained and remains a necessary dimension of the struggle for social improvement. Indeed, the great economic crisis that began in 2008 as a sort of right-wing equivalent to the fall of the Berlin Wall brought an immediate realisation that the state was essential to an economy in trouble, as it had been essential to the triumph of neo-liberalism when governments had laid its foundations by systematic privatisation and deregulation.

However, the effect of the period 1973–2008 on social democracy was that it abandoned Bernstein. In Britain its leaders felt they had no option but to rely on such benefits as the economic growth of the global free market generated automatically, plus a social safety net provided from above. 'New Labour' became identified with the market-driven society and remained so until its crash in 2008, almost severing its organic link with the labour movement. The case is extreme, but the situation of reformist social democracy in other strongholds (including that of the only remaining mass Communist Party, the Italian) also deteriorated sharply, except perhaps in a now reunited Germany and in Spain. The communists, split between moderate 'Eurocommunists' and hardline traditionalists, declined to the point where communism disappeared as a serious political force in the West.

However, this era is also at an end, as in 2008 the world suddenly entered the most serious crisis of capitalism since the Age of Catastrophe. As it began, the situation of labour was incongruous. Its parties were still in government in a number of European countries, alone or as parts of a 'grand coalition' (Spain, Portugal, the United Kingdom, Norway, Germany, Austria and Switzerland). The sudden financial collapse rehabilitated the state as an economic actor, as both employers and workers appealed to their governments to save what remained of the national industries. Moreover, there were already clear signs of workplace militancy and public discontent, although among the workers the old tradition of 'going on the street' (*descendre dans la rue* as the French say) had been weakened – though it was still alive and politically significant in some European countries and elsewhere, as in Argentina. Important trade union movements were still in existence, and still largely led by men and women who had emerged from the socialist tradition, whether social-democratic or communist.

On paper at such a time a revival of labour movements linked to the ideological left seemed possible. In practice, however, its short-term prospects were less encouraging, even for those who did not remember that the immediate political result of the Great Depression of 1929–33 was a dramatic shift away from labour movements and the left almost everywhere in Europe. The socialists, traditional brains-trust of labour, do not know any more than anyone else how to overcome the current crisis. Unlike in the 1930s, they can point to no examples of communist or social-democratic regimes immune to the crisis, nor have they realistic proposals for socialist change. In the old capitalist countries of the West de-industrialisation had already shrunk and would continue to contract their main basis, both industrial and electoral: the industrial working class. In newly emergent countries where this was not so, labour movements might well expand, but there was no real basis for their alliance with the traditional ideologies of social liberation, either because these were linked to actual or former communist regimes or because the 'red'-linked movements of earlier times had atrophied in the meantime. (Let us leave aside the unusual case of Latin America.)

True, some radical or left-wing thinking emerged during the fragmentation and decline of the old ideologies of the left, but on a much more middle-class basis. Its preoccupations – e.g the environment, or passionate hostility to the wars of the period – were not directly relevant to the activities of labour movements. They might even have antagonised their members. Where the labour movements envisaged social transformation, they represented protest rather than aspiration. It was easy to see what they were against – they were 'anti-capitalist', though without any clear idea of capitalism – but it was almost impossible to identify what they proposed to substitute for it. This may explain a revival in what looks like Bakuninite anarchism, the branch of the nineteenth-century socialist theories with fewest ideas about what was to happen when the old society had been overthrown, and therefore most easily adapted to a situation of acute social discontent without prospect. While this has been effective as a generator of publicity through the media value of riots, confrontations with the police and perhaps some terrorist activities, it has virtually no bearing on the future of labour movements today. We have the equivalent of the nineteenth-century 'propaganda by the deed' but no longer any equivalent of anarcho-syndicalism.

It is not clear how far the void left by the fading of the old ideologies of the socialist left can be filled by the imagined communities of ethnic, religious, gender, lifestyle and other collective identities. Politically ethnic nationalism has the best chance, since it appeals to the grass-roots working-class xenophobic and protectionist political demands that resonate more than ever in an era combining globalisation and mass unemployment: 'our' industry for the nation, not foreigners; priority of national jobs for nationals; down with exploitation by the foreign rich and the foreign immigrant poor, etc. Theoretically universal religions like Roman Catholicism and Islam impose their own limits on xenophobia, but both ethnicity and religion appeal as potential barriers to break-neck capitalist globalisation that destroys old ways of life and human relationships without providing any alternative. The risk of a sharp shift of politics to a nationalist or confessional demagogic radical right is probably greatest in the formerly communist European countries and South and West Asia, and least in Latin America. In the USA the economic crisis may bring a relative shift to the left similar to what happened under F.D. Roosevelt during the Great Depression, but this is not likely elsewhere.

And yet, something has changed for the better. We have rediscovered that capitalism is not the answer, but the question. For half a century its success has been so much taken for granted that its very name exchanged its traditionally negative associations for positive ones. Businessmen and politicians could now glory not only in the freedom of 'free enterprise' but in being frankly capitalist.[1] Since the 1970s the system, forgetful both of the fears that led it to reform itself after the Second World War and of the economic benefits of this reform in the subsequent 'Golden Age' of the Western economies, reverted to the extreme, one might even say pathological version of the policy of laissez-faire ('government is not the solution, but the problem') that finally imploded in 2007–8. For almost twenty years after the end of the Soviet system its ideologists believed that they had achieved 'the end of history', 'an unabashed victory of economic and political liberalism' (Fukuyama),[2] growth in a definitive and permanent, self-stabilising social and political world order of capitalism, unchallenged and unchallengeable both in theory and practice.

None of this is tenable any longer. The twentieth-century attempts to treat world history as an economic zero-sum game between private and public, pure individualism and pure collectivism, have not survived the manifest bankruptcy of the Soviet economy and of the economy of 'market fundamentalism' between 1980 and 2008. Nor is a return to the one more possible than a return to the other. Since the 1980s it has been evident that the socialists, Marxist or otherwise, were left without their traditional alternative to capitalism, at least unless or until they rethought what they meant by 'socialism' and abandoned the presumption that the (manual) working class would necessarily be the chief agent of social transformation. But the believers in the 1973–2008 *reductio ad absurdum* of market society are also left helpless. A systematic alternative system may not be on the horizon, but the possibility of a disintegration, even a collapse, of the existing system is no longer to be ruled out. Neither side knows what would or could happen in that case.

Paradoxically, both sides have an interest in returning to a major thinker whose essence is the *critique* of both capitalism and the economists who failed to recognise where capitalist globalisation would lead, as predicted by him in 1848. Once again it is manifest that the economic system's operations must be analysed both historically, as a phase and not the end of history, and realistically, i.e. not in terms of an ideal market equilibrium, but of a built-in mechanism that generates potentially system-changing periodic crises. The present one may be one of these. Once again it is evident that even between major crises, 'the market' has no answer to the major problem confronting the twenty-first century: that unlimited and increasingly high-tech economic growth in the pursuit of unsustainable profit produces global wealth, but at the cost of an increasingly dispensable factor of production, human labour, and, one might add, of the globe's natural resources. Economic and political liberalism, singly or in combination, cannot provide the solution to the problems of the twenty-first century. Once again the time has come to take Marx seriously.

Notes

2 Marx, Engels and pre-Marxian Socialism

1 See Marx–Engels, *Collected Works*, vol.4, note 242, p.719.

2 Engels, *Beschreibung der in der neueren Zeit entstandenen und noch bestehenden kommunistischen Ansiedlungen*, *Werke* 2, pp.521, 522.

3 *Werke* 3, pp.508ff.

4 Though for Marx the original form of property is 'tribal', there is no suggestion in the early writings that this represents a phase of 'primitive communism'. The well-known footnote about it in the *Communist Manifesto* was added in the 1880s.

5 *Anti-Dühring* (first draft) begins with the following sentence (*Werke* 20, p.16 footnote): 'However much modern socialism originated in substance [*der Sache nach*] with the contemplation of the class contradictions found in existing society, between those owning property and the propertyless, workers and exploiters, in its theoretical form it appears in the first instance as a more consistent continuation and development of the principles propounded by the great French spokesmen of the eighteenth-century Enlightenment. Its first representatives, Morelly and Mably, belonged to this group.'

6 *Werke* 20, p.17.

7 Advielle, *Histoire de Gracchus Babeuf* (Paris, 1884), II, p.34.

8 *The Holy Family* (*Works* IV, p.131; *Condition of the Working Class*, ibid. p.528).

9 *Works* IV, p.666; Engels to Marx 17.3.1845 (*Werke* 27, p.25). However, very soon Marx's attitude to this thinker became distinctly less favourable, though the judgement in *The German Ideology* is still positive.

10 J.P. Brissot de Warville, *Recherches philosophiques sur le droit de propriété et le vol* (1780); cf. J. Schumpeter, *History of Economic Analysis* (NY, 1954, pp.139–140).

11 Advielle, op. cit., II, pp.45, 47.

12 Cf. 'Anti-Dühring', English edn, p.116.

13 For Engels' view, see *Progress of Social Reform on the Continent* (*Werke* I, pp.484–5), written for the Owenite *New Moral World*, 1843; for Marx's view (1843), *Werke* I, p.344.

14 Cf. Engels' 1888 preface to the *Communist Manifesto* (*Werke* 21, p.354ff).

15 The Premier banquet communiste was held in 1840; Cabet's *Comment je suis communiste* and *Mon crédo communiste* date from 1841. By 1842 Lorenz von Stein, in *Der Sozialismus und Communismus des heutigen Frankreichs* – widely read in Germany – first attempted a clear distinction between the two phenomena.

16 See *German Ideology* (*Werke* 3, p.488) for a proud display – presumably by Engels – of his knowledge of 'English communists' as against the ignorance of the German 'true socialists'. The list – 'More, the Levellers, Owen, Thompson, Watts, Holyoake, Harney, Morgan, Southwell, J.G. Barmby, Greaves, Edmonds, Hobson, Spence' – is interesting not only for what it contains but for what it does not. It makes no reference to several of the 'labour economists' familiar to the mature Marx, notably J.F. Bray and Thomas Hodgskin. Conversely, it includes now forgotten figures familiar to those who, like Engels, frequented the radical left of the 1840s, such as John Goodwyn Barmby (1820–81), who claimed to have introduced the word 'communism'; James Pierrepont Greaves (1777–1842), 'the Sacred Socialist'; Charles Southwell (1814–60), an Owenite 'social missionary' like John Watts (1818–87); G.J. Holyoake (1817–1906) – a much less obscure figure; and Joshua Hobson (1810–76), an Owenite activist and publisher of the *New Moral World* and the *Northern Star*. Owen, William Thompson, John Minter Morgan, T.R. Edmonds and Thomas Spence are still to be found in any history of socialist thought in Britain.

17 Franco Venturi, 'Le mot "socialista"' (Second International Conference of Econ. Hist., Aix, 1962; The Hague, 1965, II, pp.825–7).

18 G. Lichtheim, *The Origins of Socialism* (NY, 1969), p.219.

19 The first article on the subject, by the Saint-Simonian Pierre Leroux, bracketed the two terms: 'De l'individualisme et du socialisme' (1835).

20 *Anti-Dühring, Werke* 20, p.246.

21 *Anti-Dühring, Werke* 20, pp.272–3.

22 For the general debt to the utopians, see the *Communist Manifesto* (*Werke* 4, p.491) where the 'positive propositions about the future society' are listed.

23 Engels, *Progress of Social Reform*, *Werke* 1, p.482; Cabet is defended at length against Grün's misrepresentations in *The German Ideology*.

24 Cf. the projected 'Library' in which they already appear together.

25 *Condition of the Working Class* (*Werke* 2, pp.451–2).

26 Marx, *Peuchet on Suicide* (1846) in *Works*, vol. IV, p.597.

27 *Anti-Dühring*, *Werke* 20, p.242.

28 Engels to F. Toennies, 24.1.1895 (*Werke* 39, pp.394–5); *Anti-Dühring* (*Werke* 20, p.23).

29 The young Engels noted that Fourier did not actually write much about the workers and their conditions until very late (*A Fragment of Fourier's on Trade* in *Werke* 2, p.608).

30 *Progress of Social Reform* (1843) in *Werke* 1, p.483.

31 *German Ideology* (*Werke* 3, p.33).

32 *Grundrisse* (1953, Berlin edition), pp.505, 599.

33 *Werke* I, p.482.

34 *Condition of the Working Class* (*Werke* 2, pp.452–3).

35 Marx, *On P.-J. Proudhon* (1865) in *Werke* 16, p.25.

36 *Werke* 1, pp.499–524.

37 *Communism and the Augsburger Allgemeine Zeitung* (*Rheinische Zeitung*, 1842), *Werke* 1, p.108. *Rh.Ztg* 4.1.1843 (New MEGA I, 1, p.417).

38 *Kritische Randglossen zu dem Artikel eines Preussen* (*Werke* 1, pp.404–5).

39 Marx, *On P.-J. Proudhon* in *Werke* 16, pp.25ff.

40 *Kritische Randglossen* in *Werke* 1, p.405.

41 E. Roll, *A History of Economic Thought* (London, 1948), p.249.

42 See *Theorien über den Mehrwert* III (*Werke* 26, iii, pp.261–316) and the references to Hodgskin in *Capital* I, where Bray, Gray and Thompson are also cited.

43 *Umrisse einer Kritik* (*Werke* 1, p.514). Marx also read this author, together with Bray and Thompson, in Manchester in 1845 (*Grundrisse*, 1953 edn, pp.1069, 1070).

44 Tr. 'the petty-bourgeoisie' seems wrong.

45 Wilhelm Weitling lived in Paris 1835–6 and 1837–41 where he read Pillot and various communist journals.

46 Schumpeter, *History of Economic Analysis*, p.506.

47 The section on 'feudal socialism' in the *Communist Manifesto*, which discusses comparable tendencies, makes no reference whatever to Germany but only to French legitimists and Disraeli's 'Young England'.

48 Marx in *News Rheinische Zeitung* 1.1.1849 (*Collected Works* vol. 8, pp.213–25). Cf. S. Avineri, *The Social and Political Thought of Karl Marx* (Cambridge, 1968) p.54.

49 Quoted in Avineri, op. cit., p.55. For similar quotations, cf. J. Kuczynski, *Geschichte der Lage der Arbeiter unter dem Kapitalismus* vol. 9 (Berlin, 1960), and C. Jandtke and D. Hilger (eds), *Die Eigentumslosen* (Munich, 1965).

50 And left traces in the later Marxist labour movement, e.g. through the devoted Fourierist Eugène Pottier, author of the words of the Internationale, and even through August Bebel, who published a work on Charles Fourier, *His Life and Theories*, as late as 1890.

51 Cited in W. Hofmann, *Ideengeschichte des sozialen Bewegung des 19. u.20. Jahrhunderts* (Berlin, 1968), p.90.

3 Marx, Engels and Politics

1 It is true that the original plan of *Capital* envisaged three final 'books' dealing with the State, Foreign Trade and the World Market (Roman Rosdolsky, *Zur Entstechungsgeschichte des Marxschen 'Kapital'* I (Frankfurt,1968) chapter 2), but the one on the State appears to have been intended only to deal with 'the relation of different forms of state to different economic structures of society' (Marx to Kugelmann, *Werke* 30, p.639).

2 Cf. the absence of specific citations in Paschukanis, *Marxism and the General Theory of Law* (French edn., EDI Paris, 1970), which attempted to construct a Marxist theory of law for a socialist state.

3 L. Colletti, *From Rousseau to Lenin*, (NY, 1972), pp.187–8.The tracing of a Rousseau–Marx affiliation was first seriously attempted by G. della Volpe in *Rousseau e Marx* (Rome, 1957).

4 *Werke* 1, p.321.

5 *Werke* 1, p.323; Colletti, op. cit., pp.185–6.

6 *Origin of the Family*, Marx–Engels *Collected Works* vol. 26, p.29.

7 *Anti-Dühring*, Marx–Engels. *Collected Works* vol. 49, pp.34–6.

8 See *First Draft of Civil War in France* (*Werke* 17, p.544): 'Removal of the illusion that administration and political leadership are secrets, transcendent functions which could only be confided to the hands of a trained [*ausgebildeten*] caste . . . The whole deception . . . was swept away by a Commune which consisted predominantly of simple workers who organise the defence of Paris, wage war against the pretorians of Bonaparte, ensure the supplies of this giant city, and fill all the posts hitherto shared among government, police and prefecture.'

9 Lenin, *State and Revolution*, III, 4.

10 In Kreuznach and Paris, 1843–4.

11 See *Holy Family*, *Werke* 2, pp.127–31.

12 *Die moralisierende Kritik*, *Werke* 4, pp.338–9. On the origins of this idea, see H. Förder, *Marx und Engels am Vorabend der Revolution* (Berlin, 1960) and W. Markov, *Jacques Roux und Karl Marx* (Sitzungsberichte der deutschen Akad. d. Wissenschaften zu Berlin, Klasse für Philos., Geschichte, Staats-, Rechts- u. Wirtschaftswissenschaften, Jg 1965, Berlin 1965).

13   The key references are Marx to Weydemeyer 5.3.1852 (*Werke* 28, pp.507–8) and *Critique of the Gotha Programme* (*Werke* 19, p.28).

14   Cf. Wilhelm Mautner, *Zur Geschichte des Begriffes 'Diktatur des Proletariats'* (Grünberg's Archiv), pp.280–3.

15   Marx to Nieuwenhuis 22.2.1881 (*Werke* 35, p.161).

16   *Critique of the Erfurt Programme*, 1891, (*Werke* 22, p.235).

17   Marx, speech on the seventh anniversary of the IWMA (1871), in *Werke* 17, p.433.

18   Engels, preface to Marx, *Civil War 1891*, in *Werke* 22, pp.197–8.

19   Marx, *Civil War*, Draft II, in *Werke* 17, p.597.

20   Marx, *Gotha Programme*, in *Werke* 19, p.19: '*The general costs of administration, not directly belonging to production.* This part [of the social product] will from the start be remarkably reduced in comparison with society today, and will diminish in proportion as the new society develops.'

21   Marx, *Gotha Programme*, ibid., p.21.

22   Marx to Nieuwenhuis 22.2.1881, in *Werke* 35, pp.160–1.

23   Marx, *Civil War* draft I, in *Werke* 17, p.546.

24   Inaugural Address of the IWMA (*Werke* 16, p.11).

25   See chapter 4 and Marx, *Value, Price and Profit* (*Werke* 16, pp.147–9).

26   Resolutions of the London Delegate Conference of the IWMA 1871, (*Werke* 17, pp.421–2); Notes for Engels' Speech, ibid., pp.416–17.

27   Marx to Bolte 25.11.1871 (*Werke* 33, p.332).

28   Marx to Freiligrath, 1860 (*Werke* 30, pp.490, 495).

29   *Werke* 17, p.416.

30   To Sorge 29.11.1886, to Nieuwenhuis 11.1.1887 (*Werke* 36, pp.579, 593).

31   To P. and L. Lafargue (*Werke* 32, p.671).

32   Marx, *Der politische Indifferentismus* (*Werke* 18, p.300).

33   *Civil War*, Draft I (*Werke* 17, pp.544–6).

34   *Civil War*, text and Draft I (*Werke* 17, pp.341, 549–54).

35   The point is made lucidly in G. Lichtheim, *Marxism* (1964 edn), pp.56–7, though the author's fundamental distinction between pre- and post-1850 Marxism cannot be accepted.

36   Engels, Introduction to *Class Struggles in France*, 1891 (*Werke* 22, p.513–14).

37   L. Perini (ed.), *Karl Marx, Rivoluzione e Reazione in Francia 1848–1850*, (Turin, 1976), Introduzione LIV, perceptively analyses the differing historical references in Marx's *Class Struggles in France* and in the *18th Brumaire*.

38   Address of the Central Council (*Werke* 7, pp.244–54).

39   Compare his attitude on the Russian peasantry (drafts and letter to Zasulich, *Werke* 19, pp.242–3, 384–406) with Engels' (*Nachwort zu 'Soziales aus Russland'*, *Werke* 22, pp.421–35), and his extreme concern to maintain the support of peasants and middle strata after a revolution (*Civil War*, draft I, *Werke* 17, pp.549–54) with Engels' cavalier dismissal of the danger of demagogic reactionaries capturing peasants and petty crafts-

men (*Die Bauernfrage in Frankreich und Deutschland, 1894, Werke* 22, pp.485–505). It is hard to conceive that the author of the *18th Brumaire* would have written of small peasants and independent artisans unready to accept the prediction of their disappearance: 'These people belong among the Anti-Semites. Let them go to those, who promise them to save their small enterprises.' (*Werke* 22, p.499.)

40 Bebel to Engels 24.11.1884, in August Bebel's *Briefwechsel mit Friedrich Engels*, ed. W. Blumenberg (Hague, 1965), p.188–9. See also L. Longinotti, *Friedrich Engels e la 'rivoluzione di maggioranza'* (*Studi Storici* XV, 4,1974, p.821).

41 *Konfidentielle Mitteilung, 1870* (*Werke* 16, pp.414–15). Here Engels' analysis went deeper. Even in 1858 his casual phrase about the 'bourgeois proletariat' created by British world monopoly (to Marx, 7.10.1858, in *Werke* 29, p.358) already anticipated some of the main lines of his analysis in the 1880s and 1890s (cf. *England in 1845 and 1886, Werke* 21, pp.191–7); and introduction to *Socialism, Utopian and Scientific* (*Werke* 22, pp.309–10).

42 Introduction to *Class Struggles* (*Werke* 22, p.519).

43 Introduction to *Class Struggles* (*Werke* 22, p.521).

44 To R. Fischer 8.3.1895 (*Werke* 39, pp.424–6); Introduction to *Class Struggles* (*Werke* 22, pp.521–2); to Laura Lafargue (*Werke* 38, p.545).

45 Speech on the Hague Congress (*Werke* 18, p.160). Engels, preface to the English edition of *Capital*.

46 Marx, 'Konspekt der Debatten über das Sozialistengesetz, 1878' in *Briefe and Bebel, Liebknecht, Kautsky und Andre* (Moscow–Leningrad, 1933) I, p.516; interview with *New York Tribune*, 1878 (*Werke* 34, p.515).

47 *Critique of the Erfurt Programme*, draft 1891 (*Werke* 22, pp.227–40, esp. pp.234–5).

48 To Bebel, 1891 (*Werke* 38, p.94), apropos of party objections to his publication of the *Critique of the Gotha Programme*.

49 See *The Future Italian Revolution*,1894 (*Werke* 22, pp.440, 441): 'It is not our business directly to prepare a movement which is not precisely the movement of the class we represent'.

50 See especially *The Future Italian Revolution* (*Werke* 22, pp.439–42), *The Peasant Question in France and Germany* (*Werke* 22, pp.483–505.

51 *Critique of Erfurt*, draft (*Werke* 22, p.234).

52 For Marx's attitude to Bonapartism (formulated chiefly in the *18th Brumaire*, whose argument is continued in the *Civil War*), cf. M. Rubel, *Karl Marx devant le Bonapartisme* (The Hague, 1960).

53 *18th Brumaire* VII (*Werke* 8, pp.196–7).

54 *18th Brumaire* VII (*Werke* 8, pp.198–9).

55 *18th Brumaire* (*Werke* 8, pp.196-7); *Civil War*, Draft II (*Werke* 17, pp.336–8).

56 *18th Brumaire* (*Werke* 8, pp.176–85). To Lafargue 12.11.1866 (*Werke* 31,

p.536); for a more elaborate version, see Engels, 'The real causes of the relative inactivity of the French proletarians last December' (1852) (*Werke* 8, pp.224–7).

57   To Marx 13.4.1866 (*Werke* 31, p.208).

58   'It seems to be a law of historical development that in no European country is the bourgeoisie able – at all events for a lengthy period – to capture political power in the same exclusive manner as the feudal aristocracy maintained it during the Middle Ages' (introduction to English Edition of *Socialism, Utopian and Scientific*, in *Werke* 22, p.307).

59   Engels to Kautsky 7.2.1882 (*Werke* 35, p.269).

60   Engels to Marx 15.8.1870, Marx to Engels 17.8.1870 (*Werke* 33, pp.39–44).

61   *Nachwort zu 'Soziales aus Russland'* (*Werke* 22, p.433).

62   To Bebel 13–14.9.1886 (*Werke* 36, p.526). For the question, see E. Wangermann, introduction to *The Role of Force in History* (London, 1968).

63   Engels to Bernstein 27.8.1883, 24.3.1884 (*Werke* 36, pp.54–5, 128). Of course Engels may have considered merely a brief phase of the future revolution itself: cf. to Bebel 11–12.12.1884 (*Werke* 36, pp.252–3).

64   Cf. S.F. Bloom, *The World of Nations*, p.17ff.

65   Engels in *Neue Rh. Z.* 31.8.1848; see also Engels to Bernstein 24.3.1884 (*Werke* 35, p.128).

66   Cf. Roman Rosdolsky, *Friedrich Engels und das Problem der 'Geschichtslosen Völker'* (Sonderdruck aus Archiv f. Sozialgeschichte 4/1964, Hanover).

67   'Was hat die Arbeiterfrage mit Polen zu tun?' 1866 (*Werke* 16, p.157).

68   Marx, *Civil War in France* (*Werke* 17, p.341).

69   Engels to Bernstein on the Bulgarians, 27.8.1882 (*Werke* 35, pp.280–2).

70   *N. Rh. Z.* 1.1.1849 (*Werke* 6, pp.149–50.

71   Marx to Paul and Laura Lafargue 5.3.1870 (*Werke* 32, p.659).

72   Engels to Bernstein 26.6.82 (*Werke* 35, pp.337–9).

73   Preface to the Russian edition of *Communist Manifesto* (*Werke* 19, p.296).

74   Cf. E.H. Carr, 'The Marxist Attitude to War', in *History of the Bolshevik Revolution* III (London, 1953), pp.549–66.

75   Engels to Marx 9.9.1879, Marx to Danielson 12.9.1880 (*Werke* 34, pp.105, 464); Engels to Bebel 16.12.1879 (*Werke* 34, p.431); Engels to Bebel 22.12.1882 (*Werke* 35, p.416).

76   Engels to Bebel 13.9.1886 (*Werke* 36, p.525).

77   To Bebel 17.11.1885 (*Werke* 36, p.391).

78   Cited in Gustav Mayer, *Friedrich Engels* (Hague, 1934), II, p.47.

79   Marx in *N. Rh. Z.*, 1.118.49.

80   For their expectation of imminent revolution, Marx to Engels 26.9.1856, Engels to Marx 'not before 27.9.1856', 15.11.1857, Marx to Engels 8.12.1857 (*Werke* 29, pp.76, 78, 212, 225).

81   Cf. *On the Brussels Congress and the Situation in Europe* (*Werke* 22, p.243).

82   The debate is summarised in Gustav Mayer, op. cit., II, pp.81–93.

83   Engels to Lafargue 24.3.1889 (*Werke* 37, p.171).

84   Marx to Paul and Laura Lafargue 5.3.1870 (*Werke* 32, p.659).

85   Preface to English edition (1892) of *Socialism, Utopian and Scientific* (*Werke* 22, pp.310–11).

86   Marx to Meyer and Vogt, 9.4.1870 (*Werke* 32, pp.667–9).

87   Marx to Kugelmann 29.11.1869 (*Werke* 32, p.638). More fully: General Council to Federal Council of Suisse Romande 1.1.1870 (*Werke* 16, pp.386–9).

88   Marx to P. and L. Lafargue 5.3.1870 (*Werke* 32, p.659).

89   E.g. to Adler 11.10.1893 (*Werke* 39, p.134ff).

90   To Bernstein 9.8.1882, apropos Egypt; to Kautsky 12.9.1882 (*Werke* 35, pp.349, 357–8).

91   To Bernstein 22/25.2.1882 (*Werke* 35, pp.279–280).

92   To Kautsky 7.8.1882 (*Werke* 35, pp.269–70).

93   E.g. apropos of Alsace and areas in dispute between Russia and Poland; to Zasulich 3.4.1890 (*Werke* 37, p.374).

94   G. Haupt, M. Lowy, C. Weill, *Les Marxistes et la Question Nationale* (Paris, 1974), p.21.

95   Engels to Kautsky 7.2.1882 (*Werke* 35, p.270).

96   To Adler, 17.7.1894 (*Werke* 39, p.271ff). For the infrequency of contacts with the French, except for Lafargue, see the register of correspondence in *Marx-Engels, Verzeichnis* I, pp.581–684.

97   To Adler 11.10.1893 (*Werke* 39 p.136).

98   To Kautsky 7.2.1882 (*Werke* 35, p.270).

99   To Bebel 29.9/1.10.1891 (*Werke* 38, pp.159–63); *Der Sozialismus in Deutschland* (*Werke* 22, p.247).

100 *Capital* I, chapter XXXII.

101 This is particularly clearly exemplified in Engels' *Anti-Dühring*, especially in the parts published separately as *Socialism, Utopian and Scientific.*

102 Cited in E. Weissel, *Die Ohnmacht des Sieges* (Vienna, 1976), p.117.

4 On Engels, The Condition of the Working Class in England

1   Apart from the *Condition* the chief results of his stay were the *Umrisse zu einer Kritik der Nationaloekonomie,* an early though still imperfect sketch of a Marxist economic analysis, and articles about England for various continental papers and about continental developments for the Owenite *New Moral World.* See *Werke* 1, pp.454–592.

2   *Die Lage der arbeitenden Klasse in England.* Nach eigener Anschauung und authentischen Quellen von Friedrich Engels. Leipzig. Druck und Verlag von Otto Wigand. 1845. A second German edition was published in

1892. The standard edition is Marx-Engels *Gesamtausgabe* (section I, vol. 4, pp.5–286), Berlin 1932, where a number of slips and misprints are corrected. The basic English text, used here, is that of the 1892 British edition. The fullest English edition is that of W.O. Henderson and W.H. Chaloner (Oxford, 1958), where all Engels' references have been checked and where necessary corrected, supplementary information added, and the text retranslated. Unfortunately the translation is not always reliable and the work suffers from the editors' strong but vain desire to discredit Engels' book.

3   Notably from Buret. The charge is discussed and dismissed in Gustav Mayer, *Friedrich Engels* vol. I (Hague, 1934), p.195, partly on the ground that Buret's views have nothing in common with Engels', partly on the even more unassailable ground that there is no evidence of Engels' acquaintance with Buret's book before his return from England.

4   The only other works of the pre-*Communist Manifesto* period which Engels regarded as worthy of republication in book form in his lifetime are Marx's *Theses on Feuerbach* and the *Poverty of Philosophy* (1847). The doubt about the priority of Engels' work arises because we do not know exactly when in the spring of 1845 Marx drafted his great *Theses*. It is barely possible that he did so before 15 March, when Engels signed the preface to his book.

5   From the article 'Frederick Engels', written in 1895. See *Marx–Engels–Marxism* (London, 1935), p.37.

6   He may have owed something to Sismondi here, and more to John Wade, *History of the Middle and Working Classes* (1833), a work used in the preparation of his book. Wade suggests a cycle of five to seven years, which Engels adopts, though he later abandoned it in favour of a ten-year cycle.

7   V.A. Huber (*Janus*, 1845 II, p.387); Bruno Hildebrand (*Nationaloekonomie d. Gegenwart u. Zukunft*, Frankfurt, 1848); Henderson and Chaloner (eds), *Engels' Condition of the Working Class* (Oxford, 1958, p.xxxi). For contemporary German reactions to Engels' book, see J. Kuczynski, *Die Geschichte der Lage der Arbeiter unter dem Kapitalismus* vol. 8 (Berlin, 1960), which reprints several reviews.

8   For some discussion of these accusations see E.J. Hobsbawm, *Labouring Men* (London, 1962), chapter 6.

5 On the Communist Manifesto

1   The fullest guide to the Communist League is Martin Hundt, *Geschichte des Bundes der Kommunisten 1836–52* (Frankfurt am Main, 1993); to the background of the *Manifesto*, Gareth Stedman Jones, *The Communist Manifesto: with an introduction and notes* (Penguin Classics, 2000). For the

original edition, see Wolfgang Meiser, *Das Manifest der Kommunistichen Partei vom Februar 1848*; 'Zur Entstehung und Ueberlieferung der ersten Ausgabe' in *MEGA Studien*, 1996, vol.1, pp.66–107.

2 Only two items of such material have been discovered – a plan for section III and one draft page. Karl Marx and Frederick Engels, *Collected Works*, vol. 6, pp.576–7.

3 In the lifetime of the founders they were: (1) Preface to the (second) German edition, 1872; (2) Preface to the (second) Russian edition (1882) – the first Russian translation, by Bakunin, had appeared in 1869, understandably without Marx's or Engels' blessing; (3) Preface to the (third) German edition, 1883; (4) Preface to the English edition, 1888; (5) Preface to the (fourth) German edition, 1890; (6) Preface to the Polish edition, 1892; and (7) Preface 'To Italian Readers' (1893).

4 Paolo Favilli, *Storia del marxismo italiano: Dalle origini alla grande guerra* (Milan, 1996), pp.252–4.

5 I rely on the figures in the invaluable Bert Andréas, *Le Manifeste Communiste de Marx et Engels. Histoire et Bibliographie 1848–1918* (Milan, 1963).

6 Data from the annual reports of the SPD *Parteitage*. However, no numerical data about theoretical publications are given for 1899 and 1900.

7 Robert R. LaMonte, 'The New Intellectuals', in *New Review* II, 1914, cited in Paul Buhle, *Marxism in the USA: From 1870 to the Present Day* (London, 1987), p.56.

8 Hal Draper, *The Annotated Communist Manifesto* (Center for Socialist History, Berkeley, 1984), p.64.

9 The original German begins this section by discussing 'das Verhältniss der Kommunisten zu den bereits konstituierten Arbeiterparteien . . . also den Chartisten' etc. The official English translation of 1887, revised by Engels, attenuates the contrast.

10 'The Communists do not form a separate party opposed to other working-class parties . . . They do not set up any sectarian principles of their own, by which to shape and mould the proletarian movement' (part II).

11 The best-known of these, underlined by Lenin, was the observation, in the 1872 preface, that the Paris Commune had shown 'that the working class cannot simply lay hold of the ready-made state machinery, and wield it for its own purposes'. After Marx's death, Engels added the footnote modifying the first sentence of section I to exclude pre-historic societies from the universal scope of class struggle. However, neither Marx nor Engels bothered to comment on or modify the economic passages of the document. Whether Marx and Engels really considered a fuller 'Umarbeitung oder Ergänzung' of the *Manifesto*

(preface to German edition of 1883) may be doubted, but not that Marx's death made such a rewriting impossible.

12   Compare the passage in section II of the *Manifesto* ('Does it require deep intuition to comprehend that people's ideas, views and conceptions, in one word human consciousness, change with changes in the conditions of their material life, their social relations and social existence') with the corresponding passage in the preface to the *Critique of Political Economy*: 'It is not the consciousness of men that determines their existence, but, on the contrary, it is their social existence that determines their consciousness.'

13   Though this is the English version approved by Engels, it is not a strictly correct translation of the original text: 'Mögen die herrschenden Klassen vor einer kommunistischen Revolution zittern. Die Proletarier haben nichts *in ihr* ['in it', i.e. 'in the revolution'; my emphasis] zu verlieren als ihre Ketten.'

14   For a stylistic analysis, see S.S. Prawer, *Karl Marx and World Literature* (Oxford, NY, Melbourne, 1978), pp.148–9. The translations of the *Manifesto* known to me do not have the literary force of the original German text.

15   In *Die Lage Englands. Das 18. Jahrhundert* (*Werke* 1, pp.566–8).

16   See e.g. the discussion of 'Fixed capital and the development of the productive resources of society' in the 1857–8 manuscripts, *Collected Works* vol. 29 (London, 1987), pp.80–99.

17   The German phrase, 'sich zur nationalen Klasse erheben', had Hegelian connotations which the English translation authorised by Engels modified, presumably because he thought it would not be understood by readers in the 1880s.

18   Pauperism should not be read as a synonym for 'poverty'. The German words, borrowed from English usage, are 'Pauper' ('a destitute person . . . one supported by charity or by some public provision' – *Chambers' Twentieth Century Dictionary*) and 'Pauperismus' (pauperism: 'state of being a pauper' – ibid.).

19   Paradoxically, something like the Marxian argument of 1848 is today widely used by capitalists and free-market governments to prove that the economies of states whose GNP continues to double every few decades will be bankrupted if they do not abolish the systems of income transfer (welfare states etc.), installed in poorer times, by which those who earn maintain those who are unable to earn.

20   Leszek Kolakowski, *Main Currents of Marxism* vol. 1, *The Founders* (Oxford, 1978), p.130.

21   G. Lichtheim, *Marxism* (London, 1964), p.45.

22   Published as *Outlines of a Critique of Political Economy* in 1844 (*Collected Works* vol. 3, pp.418–43).

23 *On the History of the Communist League* in *Collected Works* vol. 26 (London, 1990), p.318.

24 *Outlines of a Critique* (*Collected Works* vol. 3, p.433ff). This seems to have been derived from radical British writers, notably John Wade, *History of the Middle and Working Classes* (London, 1833, p.428), to whom Engels refers in this connection.

25 This is even clearer from Engels' formulations in what are, in effect, two preliminary drafts of the *Manifesto*: *Draft of a Communist Confession of Faith* (*Collected Works* vol. 6, p.102) and *Principles of Communism* (ibid. p.350).

26 From 'Historical Tendency of Capitalist Accumulation' in *Capital* vol. I (*Collected Works* vol. 35, p.750).

27 G. Lichtheim, *Marxism*, pp.58–60.

7 Marx on pre-Capitalist Formations

1 For Engels' explanation of the evolution of man from apes, and hence of the difference between man and the other primates, see his 1876 draft on 'The part of labour in the transformation of the ape into man' in the *Dialectics of Nature*, *Werke* 20, pp.444–55.

2 Marx – unlike Hegel – is not taken in by the possibility – and indeed, at certain stages of thought, the necessity – of an abstract and a priori presentation of his theory. See the section – brilliant, profound and exciting as almost everything Marx wrote in this crucial period of his thought – on The Method of political economy, in the (unpublished) introduction to the *Critique of Political Economy* (*Werke* 13, pp.631–9), where he discusses the value of this procedure.

3 Marx was perfectly aware of the possibility of such simplifications and, though he did not rate them as too important, their use. Hence his suggestion that a study of the historic growth of productivity might be a way of giving some scientific significance to Adam Smith's aperçus on stagnant and progressive economies. Introduction to the *Critique of Political Economy*, *Werke* 1, p.618.

4 This is recognised by the abler critics of Marxism. Thus G. Lichtheim correctly points out that the sociological theories of Max Weber – on religion and capitalism or oriental society – are not alternatives to Marx. They are either anticipated by him, or can readily be fitted into his framework. *Marxism* (1961), p.385; 'Marx and the Asiatic Mode of Production' (*St Antony's Papers*, 14, 1963), p.106.

5 To Joseph Bloch, 21.9.1890 *Collected Works* vol. 49, pp33–7.

6 There are obviously certain limits: it is improbable that a socio-economic formation which rests on, say, a level of technology which requires steam engines, could occur *before* one which does not.

7   *Marx und Engels zur Deutschen Geschichte* (Berlin, 1953), I, pp.88, 616, 49.

8   See Engels to Marx, 18.5.1853, on the origin of Babylonia; Engels to Marx, 6.6.1853.

9   Karl Marx, *Chronik Seines Lebens*, pp.96, 103, 107, 110, 139.

10   Engels to Marx, 6.6.1853.

11   Correspondence 18 May–14 June. Among the other oriental sources referred to in Marx's writings between March and December 1853 are G. Campbell, *Modern India* (1852), J. Child's *Treatise on the East India Trade* (1681), J. von Hammer, *Geschichte des osmanischen Reiches* (1835), James Mill's *History of India* (1826), Thomas Mun's *A Discourse on Trade, from England into the East Indies* (1621), J. Pollexfen's *England and East India . . .* (1697) and Saltykow, *Lettres sur l'Inde* (1848). He also read and excerpted various other works and parliamentary reports.

12   G. Hanssen, *Die Aufhebung der Leibeigenschaft und die Umgestaltung der gutsherrlich-bäuerlichen Verhältnisse überhaupt in den Herzogthümern Schleswig und Holstein* (St Petersburg, 1861); August Meitzen, *Der Boden und die landwirtschaftlichen Verhältnisse des preussischen Staates* (Berlin, 1866); G. von Maurer, *Einleitung zur Geschichte der Mark, Hof, Dorf, und Stadtverfassung und der öffentlichen Gewalt* (Munich, 1854); *Geschichte der Fronhöfe*, etc., 4 vols. (Erlangen, 1862–3).

13   Marx to Engels, 14.3.1868; Engels to Marx, 25.3.1868; Marx to Vera Zasulich, 8.3.1881; Engels to Bebel, 23.9.1882.

14   Engels to Marx, 15.12.1882; Marx to Engels, 16.12.1882.

15   Thorold Rogers is praised as 'the first authentic history of prices' of the period in *Capital* I (Torr edn, p.692n.). K.D. Huellmann, *Städtewesen des Mittelalters* (Bonn, 1826–9) is extensively quoted in *Capital* III.

16   Such as Huellmann, Vincard, *Histoire du Travail . . . en France* (1845) or Kindlinger, *Geschichte der deutschen Hörigkeit* (1818).

17   Engels to Marx, 25.3.1868.

18   A. Soetbeer, *Edelmetall-Produktion und Wertverhältnis zwischen Gold u. Silber seit der Entdeckung Amerikas . . .* (Gotha, 1879), known to Engels.

19   Marx–Engels, *Werke* 13 (Berlin, 1961), pp.135–9, which, incidentally, anticipates the modern critiques of the purely monetary explanation of price rises.

20   *Werke* 3, p.22.

21   *Werke* 3, pp.22–3.

22   There is no adequate English translation of the adjective *ständisch*, for the medieval word 'estate' now risks confusion.

23   *Werke* 3, p.24. For the entire argument, pp.24–5.

24   *Werke* 3, pp.50–61.

25   *Werke* 3, pp.53–4.

26   *Werke* 3, pp.56–7.

27   *Werke* 3, p.59.

28 Chiefly Marx to Engels, 2.6.1853; Engels to Marx, 6.6.1853; Marx to Engels, 14.6.1853 and *Werke*.

29 The disappearance of this name may be due to the fact that subsequent studies of the specialist literature led Marx to doubt whether his earlier picture of Germanic society had been accurate.

30 Cf. G.C. Homans, 'The Rural Sociology of Medieval England', *Past and Present*, 4, 1953, for the different tendencies of development of communal and single-family settlements.

31 As, e.g., in pp.87, 89, 99. The usage in *Capital* III is also in general of this sort, e.g. (Berlin, 1956 edn) pp.357, 665, 684, 873, 885, 886, 937.

32 *Capital*, III, p.841.

33 Even in *Capital* III, where he discusses the subject of feudal agriculture most fully, he specifically disclaims the intention of analysing landed property in its differing historical forms. Cf. chapter 37, p.662, and again p.842.

34 *Capital* III, pp.843–5 (chapter XLVII, section II).

35 P.M. Sweezy, M.H. Dobb, H.K. Takahashi, R.H. Hilton, C. Hill, *The Transition from Feudalism to Capitalism* (London, 1954), p.70.

36 This is not widely denied by Marxists, though it must not be confused with the statement that systems of the production of use-values are also sometimes systems of natural economy.

37 Words such as *würdiges Zunftwesen* ('the dignity of the guild system'), 'labour as half artistic, half performed for its own sake', *städtischer Gewerbefleiss* ('urban craft activity') are constantly used. All carry emotional, and indeed in general approving overtones.

38 Marx here underestimates the differentiation of urban crafts into virtual employers and virtual wage-labourers.

39 Engels records their hopes of a Russian revolution in the late 1870s, and in 1894 specifically looks forward to the possibility of 'the Russian revolution giving the signal for the workers' revolution in the West, so that both supplement each other' (*Werke* 18, p.668). For other references: Marx to Sorge, 27.9.1877; Engels to Bernstein, 22.2.1882.

40 In a letter to Vera Zasulich, 1881. Four drafts of this letter – three of them printed in *Werke* 19, pp.384–406 – survive.

41 *Nachwort* (1894) *zu 'Soziales aus Russland'* (*Werke* 18, pp.663–4).

42 *Capital* III, pp.365–6.

43 E.g. drafts to Zasulich, *Werke* 19, pp.387, 388, 402, 404.

44 G. Lichtheim (*Marxism*, p.98) is right to draw attention to this growing hostility to capitalism and fondness for surviving primitive communities, but wrong to suggest that the Marx of 1858 had seen these in an entirely negative light. That communism would be a re-creation, on a higher level, of the social virtues of primitive communalism is an idea that belongs to the earliest heritage of socialism. 'Genius,' said

Fourier, 'must discover the paths of that primitive happiness and adapt it to the conditions of modern industry' (quoted in J. Talmon, *Political Messianism*, London, 1960, p.127). For the views of the early Marx, see *Das philosophische Manifest der historischen Rechtsschule*, of 1842 (*Werke* 1, p.78): 'A current fiction of the eighteenth century saw the state of nature as the true state of human nature. Men desired to see the Idea of Man with their very own eyes, and therefore created "natural men", Papagenos, whose very feathered skin expressed their naivety. In the last decades of the eighteenth century the primitive peoples were suspected of original wisdom, and birdcatchers could be overheard everywhere imitating the song of the Iroquois or the Indian, in the belief that by these means the birds themselves might be captured. All such eccentricities rested on the correct idea, that *crude* conditions are naive paintings, as it were in the Dutch manner, of *true* conditions.' See also Marx to Engels, 25.3.1868, on Maurer's contribution to history.

45 This was a work which Marx wanted to write, and for which he had prepared voluminous notes, on which Engels based himself so far as possible. See Preface to First Edition, 1884 (*Werke* 21, p.27).

46 Drafts to Vera Zasulich, *Werke* 19, pp.384–406.

47 'Slavery is the *first* [my emphasis] form of exploitation, and belongs to antiquity; it is followed by serfdom in the Middle Ages, by wage-labour in modern times. These are the three great forms of servitude characteristic of the three great epochs of civilisation' (*Origin*, in *Werke* 21, p.170). It is evident from this text that no attempt is here made to include what Marx called the 'Asiatic' mode under any of the three heads listed. It is omitted, as belonging to the pre-history of 'civilisation'.

48 *Werke* 3, pp.29–30.

49 *Anti-Dühring, Origin of the Family*, the little essay on *The Mark*, and *The German Peasant War* are the chief published works, but drafts and notes (mostly incomplete) exist about medieval German and Irish history. See *Werke* 16, pp.459–500; 19, pp.425–521; 21, pp.392–401.

50 *Origin of the Family*, in *Werke* 21, p.144.

51 *Anti-Dühring*, in *Werke* 20, pp.164, 220, 618.

52 *Origin of the Family*, in *Werke* 21, pp.148–9.

53 Ibid., pp.146–8.

54 Ibid., pp.146, 164; *The Mark* (*Werke* 19, pp.324–5).

55 *The Mark*, *Werke* 19, pp.326–7. On the need for urban-made arms, Engels' draft *Über den Verfall des Feudalismus und das Aufkommen der Bourgeoisie* (*Werke* 21, p.392).

56 *The Mark*, *Werke* 19, pp.326–7.

57 Engels to Marx, 15.12.1882, 16.12.1882.

58 *The Mark* – whose object is only in passing to deal with the movements of feudal agriculture – was intended as an 8–10 page appendix to *Anti-Dühring*, and the unpublished *Über den Verfall* as a prefatory note to a new edition of the *Peasant War*.

59 See *Zur Urgeschichte der Deutschen* (*Werke* 19, esp. pp.450–60).

60 *Anti-Dühring*: preparatory notes (*Werke* 20, pp.587–8).

61 Ibid., p.588.

62 Quoted in L.S. Gamayunov, R.A. Ulyanovsky, 'The Work of the Russian Sociologist M.M. Kovalevsky . . . and K. Marx's criticism of the work', *XXV International Congress of Orientalists* (Moscow, 1960), p.8.

63 *Anti-Dühring*, *Werke* 20, p.164.

64 *Anti-Dühring*, *Werke* 20, p.252.

65 'All peoples travel what is basically the same path . . . The development of society proceeds through the consecutive replacement, according to definite laws, of one socio-economic formation by another.' O. Kuusinen (ed.), *Fundamentals of Marxism-Leninism* (London, 1961), p.153.

66 The fear of encouraging 'Asiatic exceptionalism' and of discouraging a sufficiently firm opposition to (Western) imperialist influence was a strong and perhaps the decisive element in abandonment of Marx's 'Asiatic mode' by the international communist movement after 1930. Cf. the 1931 Leningrad discussions, as reported (very tendentiously) in K.A. Wittfogel, *Asiatic Despotism* (1957), pp.402–4. The Chinese Communist Party had independently taken the same road some years earlier. For its views, which appear to be very standard and unilinear, see Mao Tse-tung, *Selected Works*, III (London, 1954), pp.74–7.

67 For the Soviet discussions of the early 1950s, see *Voprosi Istoriti*, 6, 1953; 2, 1954; 2, 4 and 5, 1955. For the Western discussion on the transition from feudalism, which partly touches on similar themes, see *The Transition from Feudalism to Capitalism*. Also G. Lefebvre, *La Pensée*, 65, 1956; G. Procacci, *Società*, 1, 1955.

68 See Guenther and Schrot, *Problèmes théoriques de la société esclavagiste*, in *Recherches Internationales à la lumière de marxisme* (Paris) 2, May–June 1957.

69 E.g. E.M.S. Namboodiripad, *The National Question in Kerala* (Bombay, 1952).

70 D.D. Kosambi, *An Introduction to the Study of Indian History* (Bombay, 1956), pp.11–12.

71 See *Recherches Internationales*, loc. cit., (1957), for a selection of studies.

72 E. Zhukov, 'The Periodization of World History', *International Historical Congress, Stockholm*, 1960: *Rapports* I, pp.74–88, esp. p.77.

73 Cf. 'State and Revolution in Tudor and Stuart England', *Communist Review*, July 1948. This view has, however, always had its critics, especially J.J. Kuczynski (*Geschichte d. Lage d. Arbeiter unter dem Kapitalismus*, vol. 22, chapters. 1–2).

74 Cf. Bogdanov, *Short Course of Economic Science*, 1897, revised 1919 (London, 1927); and, in a more sophisticated form, K.A. Wittfogel, *Geschichte der bürgerlichen Gesellschaft* (Vienna, 1924).

75 O. Lattimore, 'Feudalism in History', *Past and Present*, 12, 1957.

76 E. Zhukov, op. cit., p.78.

77 *The Transition from Feudalism to Capitalism.*

78 Cf. *Zur Periodisierung des Feudalismus und Kapitalismus in der Geschichtlichen Entwicklung der U.S.S.R.*, Berlin, 1952.

79 *Asiaticus, Il modo di produzione Asiatico* (*Rinascita*, Rome, 5 October 1963, p.14).

80 *Recherches Internationales* 37 (May–June 1963), which deals with feudalism, contains some relevant polemical contributions. For ancient society, see the debates between Welskopf (*Die Produktionsverhältnisse im Alten Orient und in der griechischrömischen Antike*, Berlin, 1957) and Guenther and Schrot (*Ztschr. f. Geschichtswissenschaft*, 1957, and *Wissensch. Ztschr. d. Karl-Marx-Univ.*, Leipzig, 1963); for oriental society, F. Tökei, *Sur le mode de production asiatique*, Paris, Centre d'Etudes et de Recherches Marxistes, 1964, cyclostyled.

8 The Fortunes of Marx's and Engels' Writings

1 Bert Andréas, *Le Manifeste Communiste de Marx et Engels: Histoire et Bibliographie 1848–1918* (Milan, 1963).

2 R. Michels, *Die italienische Literatur über den Marximus* (*Archiv f. Sozialwissenschaft u. Sozialpolitik* 25ii, 1907, pp.525–72).

3 *Neudrucke marxistischer Seltenheiten* (Verlag Rudolf Liebing, Leipzig).

4 As late as the 1960s the GDR edition of the *Werke*, while not actually refraining from publishing these works, issued them separately from the main series and not as numbered volumes of the works.

5 The following works of Marx and Engels were textually cited in that inevitably influential work: *Anti-Dühring*, *Capital*, the *Communist Manifesto*, the *Critique of Political Economy* (Preface), *Dialectics of Nature*, *Feuerbach*, *Zur Kritik der Hegelschen Rechtsphilosophie*, *Poverty of Philosophy*, *Socialism, Utopian and Scientific*, *Wage Labour and Capital*, and one or two letters and prefaces by Engels.

9 Dr Marx and the Victorian Critics

1 *Problems of Communism* V (1956).

2 M. Kaufmann, *Utopias from Sir Thomas More to Karl Marx* (1879), p.241.

3 *Nineteenth Century* (April 1884), p.639.

4 W. Graham, *The Social Problem* (1886), p 423.

5   M. Kaufmann, *Socialism* (1874), p.165.

6   See Kaufmann's chapter in *Subjects of the Day: Socialism, Labour and Capital* (1890–1), p.44.

7   J. Bonar, *Philosophy and Political Economy* (1893), p.354.

8   *National Review* (1931), p.477.

9   *Report of the Industrial Remuneration Conference* (1885), p.344.

10 *Contemporary Socialism* (1884), reprinting earlier articles.

11 W.H. Dawson, *German Socialism and Ferdinand Lassalle* (1888), pp.96–7.

12 William Graham, *Socialism* (1890), p.139.

13 Archdeacon Cunningham, *Politics and Economics* (1885), p.102.

14 Cunningham, 'The Progress of Socialism in England' *Contemp. Rev.*, (January 1879), p.247.

15 J. Shield Nicholson, *Principles of Political Economy* I (1893), p.105.

16 William Smart, *Factory Industry and Socialism* (n.d.), p.1.

17 M. Prothero, *Political Economy* (1895), p.43.

18 H.S.Foxwell, 'The Economic Movement in England', *Q. Jnl. Econ.* (1888), pp.89, 100.

19 Shield Nicholson, op. cit., p.370.

20 Kirkup, *History of Socialism* (1900), p.159.

21 B. Bosanquet, *The Philosophical Theory of the State* (1899), p.28.

22 Bonar, op. cit., p.358.

23 Ibid., p.367.

24 Toynbee disagreed with Marx's view that the yeomanry had disappeared by 1760 (1908 edn, p.38). However, later views were with Marx rather than Toynbee.

25 George Unwin, *Studies in Economic History* (1927), pp.xxiii, lxvi.

26 Robert Flint, *Socialism* (1895), p.138.

27 Robert Flint in *Athenaeum* (1887).

28 Cf. *Capitalism and the Historians* and critiques by W.H. Chaloner and W.O. Henderson.

29 Kaufmann, *Utopias*, p.225.

30 Llewellyn-Smith, *Economic Aspects of State Socialism* (1887), p.77.

31 Shield Nicholson, op. cit., p.370.

32 J.R. Tanner and F.S. Carey, *Comments on the use of the Blue Books made by Karl Marx in Chapter XV of Capital* (Cambridge Economic Club, May Term, 1885).

33 Llewellyn-Smith, *Two Lectures on the Books of Political Economy* (London, Birmingham and Leicester, 1888), p.146.

34 Tanner and Carey, op. cit., pp.4, 12.

35 Ibid., p.12.

36 Foxwell, op. cit., p.99.

37 Flint, *Socialism*, p.136.

38 E.C.K. Gonner, *Rodbertus* (1899).

39 Flint, loc. cit.

40 *Econ. Jnl.* V, p.343.

10 The Influence of Marxism 1880–1914

1 For English quotations to this effect, see E.J. Hobsbawm, *Labouring Men*, (London, 1964), pp.241–2; for an authoritative German view, R. Stammler in *Handwörterbuch der Staatswissenschaften* (2nd edn, 1900), article 'Materialistische Geschichtsauffassung'.

2 Cf. Hobsbawm, op. cit., pp.242–3.

3 For a good survey of the available literature, see K. Diehl's bibliography in *Hwb. d. Staatswissenschaften* (2nd edn, 1900), article 'Marx'.

4 It may be recalled that the original phrase of Masaryk who coined it in 1898 was 'the crisis *in* Marxism'; but in the course of the revisionist debate it was very soon changed into 'the crisis *of* Marxism' as Labriola quickly noted. Cf. E. Santarelli, 'La revisione del marxismo in Italia nel tempo della Seconda Internazionale' (*Riv. Stor. del Socialismo* 4, 1958, p.383n).

5 Omitting the USA unions for which no data are given before 1909. Source: W. Woytinsky, *Die Welt in Zahlen* II (Berlin, 1926), p.102.

6 E.J. Hobsbawm, 'La diffusione del marxismo' (*Studi Storici* xv, 1972, pp.263–4).

7 The leading spirits in the Fabian Society broke with Marxist theory, which had originally had some influence in the small circles of the British ultra-left, in the late 1880s. However, the *Fabian Essays* which expounded the group's views (1889) still show a distinct Marxist influence in some parts, notably the chapter by William Clarke.

8 G.D.R. Cole, *The World of Labour* (London, 1913), p.167.

9 A. Gramsci, 'La Rivoluzione contro il *Capitale*' in *Scritti Giovanili* (Turin, 1958), p.150.

10 R. Pipes, 'La teoria dello sviluppo capitalistico in P.B. Struve' in Istituto G. Feltrinelli, *Storia del marxismo contemporaneo* (Milan, 1973), p.485.

11 On a smaller scale the (mainly political) emigration of small numbers of East European intellectuals, male and female, helped to spread Marxist influence in otherwise unreceptive countries – e.g. Charles Rappoport in France, Theodore Rothstein in England. Cf. G. Haupt, 'Le rôle de l'exil dans la diffusion de l'image de l'intelligentsia révolutionnaire' (*Cahiers du Monde Russe et Soviétique* xix/3, 1978, pp.235–50).

12 Richard T. Ely in *The International Encyclopaedia of the Social Sciences* (1968).

13 Cf. E.J. Hobsbawm in *Studi Storici*, 1974, pp.251–2. The roles of the Knights of Labor in Belgium, of the Marxist Daniel De Leon in Britain, and later of the (syndicalist) Industrial Workers of the World in various parts of the globe, are familiar.

14 However, it is worth noting that the school of British economists which tended to show most interest in Marx in the 1880s and 1890s was the defeated minority on the wrong side of the famous 'Methodenstreit', who were largely extruded from the academic field of economics, and became economic historians, social reformers or government servants. Cambridge was on the winning side.

15 See Christophe Charle, *Les intellectuels en Europe au XIX siècle, essai d'histoire comparé* (Paris, 1996), part 2, pp.143–311; but for the dominance of socially uncritical intellectuals see Wolfgang J. Mommsen, *Bürgerliche Kultur und politische Ordnung: Künstler, Schriftsteller und Intellektuelle in der deutschen Geschichte 1830-1933* (Frankfurt, 2000), esp. pp.178–215, and Christophe Prochasson and Anne Rasmussen, *Au nom de la patrie: les intellectuels et la première guerre mondiale (1910–1919)* (Paris, 1996).

16 Such an assessment was attempted by Michels, *Soziologie des Parteiwesens*, who notes the relative hostility (except in France and Italy) of medical men to socialism in Western Europe (Stuttgart, 1970, pp.249–50).

17 Hobsbawm, *Labouring Men*, chapter 14.

18 Michels, op. cit., pp.99–100.

19 Of the numerous Normaliens who became socialists during this period the only Guesdiste of note was Bracke-Desrousseaux, a distinguished classical scholar and Marx translator. Cf. H. Bourgin, *De Jaurès a Léon Blum* (Paris, 1938).

20 The Old Guesdiste Alexandre Zévaès, in *De l'Introduction du Marxisme en France* (Paris, 1947), observes that the 1872–5 translation of *Capital* I 'à l'époque, passa à peu près inaperçue'. Apart from publications in the Guesdiste journal and in a book of bourgeois reportage on socialism (1882, 1886), the *Communist Manifesto* appears to have been published separately only in 1895 (reprinted 1897) until the elaborate academic edition of the university professor Charles Andler in 1901. The first separate publication of *Civil War in France* is given as 1900, of *The 18th Brumaire* as 1891, of *Class Struggles in France* as 1900. A number of translations were published in the second half of the 1890s: *Poverty of Philosophy* (1896), *Critique of Political Economy* (1899), *Value, Price and Profit* (1899), *Revolution and Counter-revolution in Germany* (1901). It is significant that *Capital* II and III (published 1900–2)) were translated not in France but in Belgium (Zévaès, op. cit., chapter. X). Little was published between 1902 and 1914.

21 Michels, op. cit., p.255.

22 Hobsbawm, *Studi Storici*, p.245.

23 R. Michels, 'Die deutsche Sozialdemokratie. Parteimitgliedschaft und soziale Zusammensetzung', *Archiv f. Sozialwissenschaft u. Sozialpolitik* 23 (1906), pp.471–559.

24 There is virtually no correspondence between Engels and any Belgian

socialist leader in this period; the only letter to Vandervelde (1894) is formal in tone.

25 G.D.H. Cole, *History of Socialist Thought, The Second International*, II, p.650.

26 See Marcel van der Linden, (ed.), *Die Rezeption der Marxschen Theorie in den Nederlanden* (Trier, 1992), esp. pp.16ff. and the chapters by H.M. Bock and H. Buiting.

27 The national problem was neglected by socialists, including Marxists, in Western Europe, though it evidently existed. Thus the Belgian Labour Party paid no attention to the Flemish problem, doubtless because Ghent was its strongest fortress. The forty-eight-page bibliography attached to Vandervelde and Destrée's *Le Socialisme en Belgique* (Paris, 1903) contains no section, and indeed no title, on the subject. National/regionalist movements were not only regarded as primarily bourgeois or petty bourgeois, but as politically secondary.

28 In Hungary (1910) 22% of Jewish males, or three times the proportion of any other religion, had undergone four years of secondary education; 10%, or twice the proportion of any other religion, had completed eight years of secondary education. (V. Karady and I. Kemény, 'Les juifs dans la structure des classes en Hongrie', *Actes de la Recherche en Sciences Sociales* 22, 1978, p.35.)

29 In Vienna the demagogic Christian-Social Party, which captured the municipality in the 1890s, was stridently antisemitic, though its leader Lueger was careful to select his targets: 'I decide who's a Jew.'

30 Robert Hunter, *Socialists at Work* (NY, 1908).

31 Michels, *Soziologie*, p.259.

32 Max Adler, *Der Sozialismus und die Intellektuellen*.

33 A.V. Pešehonov, 'Materialy dlya istorii russkoy intelligentsii', cited in M. Aucouturier, 'L'intelligentsia vue par les publicistes marxistes' (*Cahiers du Monde Russe et Soviétique* XIX, 3, 1978, pp.251–2).

34 *Intelligentsia i sotsializm* (1912), cited in Aucouturier, op. cit., p.256.

35 Aucouturier, op. cit., p.253ff.

36 Though the most original theorist and socialist leader, Dobrogeanu-Gherea (1855–1920), was a Russian Narodnik-Marxist émigré.

37 Cf. the two articles on 'Socialism and Darwinism' reprinted in *Neue Zeit* 16/1, 1897–8, p.709n. See also: article by K. Pearson in the *Dictionary of Scientific Biography* X (NY, 1974), p.448.

38 Cf. *Neue Zeit* 9/1, 1891, p.171ff, 'Ein Schüler Darwins als Verteidiger des Sozialismus'.

39 Cf. G. von Below: 'Historians have, with minimal exceptions, rejected the Hegelian evolutionary scheme as much as any other rigid dogmatic system . . . Similarly they show no sympathy for the materialist evolutionary scheme' ('Die neuere historische Methode', *Hist. Ztschr.* 81/1898, p.241).

40 They had also helped to convince the leading members of the Fabian Society of the truth of economic orthodoxy, which is why the new London School of Economics, a Fabian foundation of the 1890s, became a stronghold of orthodox economics and resisted even non-Marxist heterodoxy.

41 Both had been engaged in such arguments since 1870. Curiously, Schäffle's *Quintessence of Socialism* (originally published 1874) was widely regarded as an impartial exposition of socialism and used as an introduction to socialism outside Germany.

42 Cf. E. Gothein in *Hwb. d. Staatswissenschaften*, 2nd edn, art. 'Gesellschaft und Gesellschaftswissenschaft', p.207; H. Becker and H.E. Barnes, *Social Thought from Lore to Science* (3rd edn, 1961) III, 1009: 'a great many Italian academicians seem to identify sociology with the doctrines of historical materialism'.

43 E. Gothein in *Hwb. d. Staatswissenschaften*, 2nd edn, art. 'Gesellschaft und Gesellschaftswissenschaft'.

44 'Socialism in the light of social science', in *American Journal of Sociology* xvii, May 1912, pp.809–10.

45 Becker and Barnes, op. cit., p.889; see also F. Tönnies, *Gemeinschaft und Gesellschaft* (6–7th edns, 1926), pp.55, 80–1, 163, 249.

46 'Uber individuelle und kollektivistische Geschichtsauffassung' (*Hist. Ztschr.* 78/1897, p.60).

47 *Hist. Ztschr.* 64/1890, p.258.

48 Cf. the note on the positivist Breysig in *Hist. Ztschr.* 78/1897, p.522, and G. von Below in *Hist. Ztschr.* 65/1891, p.294.

49 *Hist. Ztschr.* 81/1898, 'Die neue historische Methode', pp.265–6: Lamprecht 'has solemnly rejected the charge of materialism. It is true that he is no Marxist. But nobody has charged him with being one. However, his conception of history is materialist. True, he does not motivate everything by economic motives (*sic*). But even the Marxists do not make economic motives immediately effective everywhere; frequently they see the immediate motives as being political or religious.'

50 G. von Below, op. cit., p.262. For Marxian influences on Lamprecht see also L. Leclère, 'La théorie historique de M. Karl Lamprecht', *Revue de l'Université de Bruxelles* IV (1899), pp.575–99.

51 Cf. the review of Kautsky in *Hist. Ztschr.* 79/1897, p.305. Serious work by Marxists was not, however, so easily dismissed. The jurist G. Jellinek singled out Bernstein's pioneer exploration of the Levellers and Diggers for praise (*Hist. Ztschr.* 81/1898, p.117f), while Robert Pöhlmann, strongly hostile to modern socialism and communism, could not but treat E. Ciccotti's *Tramonto della Schiavitù* (1899) with respect, and even admit that Marxism had helped him. Even more, he admitted that this type of work advanced the study of antiquity (*Hist. Ztschr.* 82/1899,

p.110). Pöhlmann wrote extensively on ancient socialism and communism. He appears to show no awareness of Marxism in 1893, but a great deal by 1897.

52 Bryce Lyon, *Henri Pirenne* (Ghent, 1974), p.128ff.

53 'Une polémique historique en Allemagne' (*Revue Historique* LXIV/2, 1897, pp.50–7).

54 R.H. Tawney, (ed.), *Studies in Economic History*, ed. (London, 1927), pp.xxiii, lxvi.

55 E.J. Hobsbawm, 'Karl Marx's Contribution to Historiography' (*Diogenes* 64, 1968).

56 E. Klebs, *Hist. Ztschr.* 82/1899, pp.106–9; A. Vierkandt, *Hist. Ztschr.* 84/1900, pp.467–8.

57 Hauptmann's *Weavers* and *Florian Geyer* were frankly committed sociopolitical dramas and much admired as such.

58 F. Mehring, *Gesammelte Schriften und Aufsätze*, ed. E. Fuchs, *Literaturgeschichte* II (Berlin, 1930), p.107.

59 Cf. 'Was wollen die Modernen, von einem Modernen', 1893–4, pp.132ff, 168ff.

60 Mehring, op. cit., (1898–9), p.298.

61 For the same reasons a 'people's opera' never developed at all, though at least one operatic composer, the revolutionary Gustave Charpentier, tried his hand at a working-class heroine (*Louise*, 1900), and an element of *verismo* enters opera at this period (*Cavalleria Rusticana*).

62 E.P. Thompson, *William Morris, Romantic to Revolutionary* (London, 1955, 1977); Paul Meier, *La pensée utopique de William Morris* (Paris, 1972).

63 Stuart Merrill, cited in E.W. Herbert, *The Artist and Social Reform: France and Belgium 1885–98* (New Haven, 1961) p.100n.

64 Subscribers to the anarchist *La Révolte* in 1894 included Daudet, Anatole France, Huysmans, Leconte de Lisle, Mallarmé, Loti and the theatrical avantgarde of Antoine and Lugné-Poe. No socialist review at the time was likely to attract such a galaxy. But even so early an anarchist as the poet Gustave Kahn deeply respected Marx and favoured a unity of all leftists (Herbert, op. cit., pp.21, 110–11).

65 Max Ermers, *Victor Adler* (Vienna, 1932), pp.236–7.

66 H.-J. Steinberg, *Sozialismus und deutsche Sozialdemokratie* (Hanover, 1967), pp.132–5.

67 Caroline Kohn, *Karl Kraus* (Stuttgart, 1966), pp.65, 66.

68 Cf. G. Botz, G. Brandstetter, M. Pollak, *Im Schatten der Arbeiterbewegung* (Vienna, 1977), pp.83–5, on Austro-German anarchism.

69 Rosa Luxemburg, *J'étais, je suis, je serai. Corréspondance 1914–1919* (Paris, 1977), pp.306–7.

70 Ibid.

71 L. Trotskij, ed. V. Strada, *Letteratura e Rivoluzione* (Turin, 1973), p.467.

72 G. Plekhanov, *Kunst und Literatur* (Berlin, 1954), pp.284–5.

73 J.C. Holl, *La jeune peinture contemporaine* (Paris, 1912), pp.14–15.

74 Plekhanov, op. cit., pp.292, 295.

75 William Morris, *On Art and Socialism*, ed. Holbrook Jackson (1946), p.76.

76 He first appeared at a socialist meeting (to discuss the building of houses for the people) in 1883.

77 'Considering the relation of the modern world to art, our business is now, and for long will be, not so much attempting to produce definite art, as rather clearing the ground to give art its opportunity': 'The Socialist Ideal' in Morris, op. cit., p.323.

11 In the Era of Anti-fascism 1929–45

1 For the general situation in the communist movement, see Aldo Agosti, *Bandiere Rosse: Un profile storico dei comunismi europei* (Rome, 1999), p.35–40. For the varied origins and ideological complexion of Western communist intellectuals, see Thomas Kroll, *Kommunistische Intellektuelle in Westeuropa* (Cologne-Weimar-Vienna, 2007), which compares France, Italy, Austria and Britain 1945–56.

2 95% of the members of the KPD (German Communist Party) had only an elementary education, 1% a university education (H. Weber, *Die Wandlung des deutschen Kommunismus*, Frankfurt, 1969, II, p.29). For the situation of intellectuals in a very proletarian (illegal) party, see Giorgio Amendola, *Un'isola* (Milan, 1980).

3 *For Peace and Plenty. Report of the Fifteenth Congress of the CPGB* (London, 1938), p.135. There is some evidence that the composition of congresses is not dissimilar to that of the party as a whole. Cf. K. Newton, *The Sociology of British Communism* (London, 1969), pp.6–7.

4 See Georges Haupt, 'Emigration et diffusion des idées socialistes: l'exemple d'Anna Kuliscioff' (*Pluriel* n.14, 1978, pp.2–12).

5 Maurice Dobb had to write his first major work on the Soviet economy, *Russian Economic Development since the Revolution* (London, 1928), with the help of a translator.

6 This was the case with such figures as Karl Korsch, Walter Benjamin, Karl Polanyi, Norbert Elias and others, both Marxist and non-Marxist.

7 P.M. Sweezy, *The Theory of Capitalist Development* (NY, 1942).

8 *Unter dem Banner des Marxismus* (*Pod znameniem marksisma*), which was closer to an international journal of theoretical discussion, disappeared from sight in the mid 1930s and had in any case been increasingly assimilated to Soviet orthodoxy. Moreover, it was available only in German and Russian.

9 Cf. the characteristic casuistry of Radek: 'Is it necessary to learn from

great artists, such as Proust, the ability to sketch, to delineate the slightest motion in man? That is not the point at issue. The point at issue is whether we have our own highroad, or whether this highroad is indicated by experiments abroad.' *Problems of Soviet Literature* (Moscow, 1935), p.151.

10 For a cross-section of this kind of literature, see John Lehmann, *New Writing in Europe* (London, 1940).

11 For a good sketch of this cultural-political atmosphere, see J.M. Richards, *Autobiography of an Unjust Fella* (London, 1980), pp.119–20. The author was editor of the *Architectural Review* in Britain.

12 Thus the (communist-organised) Artists' International Association in Britain (1933–9) organised exhibitions – generally under some such heading as 'Artists against Fascism and War' – of academic artists, constructivists, cubists, surrealists, social realists and post-Impressionists, of German twentieth-century art, of French artists (Gromaire, Leger, Lhote, Zadkine), etc. Its own militants were largely realist, but influenced by Mexican art (Rivera, Orozco) and American art (Gropper, Ben Shahn) rather than by Soviet models. See Tony Rickaby, 'The Artists' International' (*History Workshop* 6, Autumn 1978, pp.154–68).

13 Beatrice Webb, *Our Partnership* (London, 1948), pp.489–91.

14 Absurd not necessarily from the point of view of the state interests of the USSR, but because of the assumption that the interests of world communism, or even of the USSR, would best be served by imposing the new policy uniformly on communist parties everywhere.

15 Apart from the Nazi sympathies of an influential sector of Boer opinion in South Africa.

16 South and Southeast Asia were, as it happens, the only regions in which heterodox communism won some mass support, most notably in Ceylon.

17 George Lansbury, the leader of the British Labour Party 1931–5, was a passionate pacifist.

18 Pascal Ory, *Les collaborateurs 1940–1945* (Paris, 1976), pp.135–6.

19 See Gary Werskey, *The Visible College* (London, 1972); S. Zuckerman, *From Apes to Warlords* (London, 1978); Andrew Brown, *J.D. Bernal: the Sage of Science* (Oxford, 2005); Simon Winchester, *Bomb, Book and Compass: Joseph Needham and the Great Secrets of China* (London, 2008).

20 But under German occupation literature resisted the blandishments of the occupiers better than the visual, and above all the performing arts. Cf. Henri Michel, *The Shadow War: Resistance in Europe 1939–1945* (London, 1972), p.141.

21 For the politics of his journal *Scrutiny*, see Francis Mulhern, *The Moment of 'Scrutiny'* (London, 1979), part II, chapter 2.

22 E.g. Aldo Garosci, *Gli intellettuali e la guerra di Spagna* (Turin, 1959).

23 Cf. the testimony of the fascist police in G. Amendola, *Un'isola*, pp.96–7.

P. Spriano, *Storia del PCI* (Turin, 1970), III, pp.194–201. Thomas Kroll, op. cit., pp.361–6, 382–90, 394–402.

24 Cf. Andrew Boyle, *The Climate of Treason* (London, 1980), chapters 1–4. For the 'public school rebellion', see Esmond and Giles Romilly, *Out of Bounds* (London, 1935), and Philip Toynbee, *Friends Apart* (London, 1954). Miranda Carter, *Anthony Blunt: His Lives* (London, 2001).

25 Stephen Spender, *Forward From Liberalism* (London, 1937).

26 To cite only some where more than one child of such parents took this road: Edward Thompson (a well-known champion of Indian freedom), E.F. Carritt (an Oxford moral philosopher), St Loe Strachey (editor of the influential review *The Spectator*).

27 The author recalls student communists of both sexes who were close relatives of prominent Conservative politicians or judges. For the general British situation, see T. Kroll, op. cit., pp.511–3, 525–33.

28 Among such self-made *agrégés* one may mention G. Cogniot and A. Parreaux, respectively first director and secretary of the review *La Pensée* and A. Soboul, the historian of the French Revolution.

29 Stuart Samuels, 'The Left Book Club' (*Journal of Contemporary History*); John Lewis, *The Left Book Club* (London, 1970). For data on the Club drawn from the publisher's records see Richard Overy, *The Morbid Age: Britain between the Wars* (London, 2009), pp.304–6.

30 Cf. Francis Newton, *The Jazz Scene* (Harmondsworth, 1961), caps 13, 14, App.1.

31 For the impact of the 1930s on Hollywood see the excellent collection of thirty-five interviews by Patrick McGilligan and Paul Buhle (eds), *Tender Comrades: A Backstory of the Hollywood Blacklist* (NY, 1997).

32 The contemptuous catalogue comes from Arthur M. Schlesinger Jr (Harvard, Cambridge and the court of J.F. Kennedy), *The Age of Roosevelt: The Politics of Upheaval* (Boston, 1960), p.165.

33 J. Fauvet, *Histoire du Parti Communiste Français* I (Paris, 1964), pp.267–8.

34 Annie Kriegel, *The French Communists* (Chicago & London, 1972), pp.175–6.

35 Preface to Russian edition of *Communist Manifesto*, *Werke* 19, p.296.

36 This calculation is based on a bibliography compiled by the British Communist Party's Historians' Group in 1955, and includes American work and translations.

37 See Stuart Macintyre, *A Proletarian Science* (Cambridge, 1980) and R. Samuel, 'British Marxist Historians I' (*New Left Review* 120/1980, pp.21–96).

38 Notably the deliberate downgrading of the Hegelian elements in Marx and the elimination of the 'Asiatic Mode of Production' from his analysis. Whether these revisions were defensible or not is a question which falls outside the limits of the present chapter.

39 Cf. K. Wittfogel, *Oriental Despotism* (Yale University Press, New Haven, 1957), p.401ff.

40 M. Shirokov and J. Lewis (eds), *A Textbook of Marxist Philosophy* (London n.d. – 1937), p.183; I. Luppol, *Diderot* (Paris, 1936).

41 P. Anderson, *Considerations on Western Marxism* (London, 1976).

42 C. Haden Guest (ed.), *David Guest: A Scientist Fights for Freedom. A Memoir.* (London, 1939), p.256.

43 H. Lefebvre, *Le nationalisme contre les nations* (Paris, 1937), p.128. Admittedly the author later denounces Bauer in more orthodox fashion, but in phrases specifically annotated as 'directly inspired' by the text of Stalin's 'Marxism and the national question' (ibid., p.225).

44 H. Lefebvre, *Le matérialisme dialectique* (Paris, 1939), pp.62–4.

45 Published, in both cases posthumously, in Paris (1946) and London (1939).

46 'La "philosophie" marxiste connaît aussi une vogue singulière. Lorsqu'il écrivait son *Anti-Dühring*, Engels cherchait avec soin tout ce qui, dans les sciences naturelles et dans la physique et la chimie nouvelles, paraissait révéler dans le monde de la nature cette même "dialectique" que Marx et lui avaient appliquée à l'histoire et à l'évolution sociale. Maintenant des savants, et même des grands savants, leur rendent la pareille, en y découvrant la "philosophie" de leurs sciences particulières.' 'A. Rossi', *Physiologie du Parti Communiste Français* (Paris, 1948), p.335. The book was written in 1942.

47 E.H.S. Burhop in M. Goldsmith and A. Mackay (eds), *The Science of Science* (London, 1964), pp.33.

48 C.P. Snow in John Raymond (ed.), *The Baldwin Age* (London, 1960), p.248.

49 J.B.S. Haldane, a communist biologist of genius, admitted that Lenin's view of space and time was incompatible with relativity theory, but consoled himself with the information that Lenin had accepted relativity while rejecting its idealist interpretations in an article of 1922 of which 'I have been unable to obtain a translation' (*The Marxist Philosophy and the Sciences*, London, 1938, p.60). He compared this with Lenin's acceptance of the New Economic Policy.

50 *Marx-Engels Archiv*, Band II (Erlangen, 1971) pp.140–1. It appears that the German Social Democratic Party had taken no steps to publish the MS on the advice (shortly after Engels' death) of one of the rare natural scientists then associated with the party, but one who, 'strongly committed to empiricism, was hostile to dialectics' (Ryazanov in *Marx-Engels Archiv* II) Ryazanov's own defence of Engels against the charge of obsoleteness is cautious, and the MS was in fact originally published not in the MEGA but in the *Marx-Engels Archiv*, reserved for the *parerga* rather than the actual works of the founders.

51 Personal information.

52 E.g. J.B.S. Haldane, op. cit., and *A la lumière du marxisme* (Paris, 1936).

53 Christopher Caudwell, *The Crisis in Physics* (London, 1939), p.60.

54 Cf. J.B.S. Haldane, 'A Dialectical Account of Evolution' (*Science and Society* I/4, 1937, pp.473–86).

55 Joseph Needham, 'On Science and Social Change' (*Science and Society* X, 3, 1946, pp.225–51); written in China in 1944. Needham – Christian, Marxist, embryologist, historian (of embryology, the English revolution and science and civilisation in China), constant seeker after a view of the world both scientific and non-Galilean – is a particularly interesting example of such dissatisfaction with the nineteenth-century models.

56 Caudwell, op. cit., pp.21, 3.

57 In *Science at the Crossroads* (London, 1931).

58 S. Zuckerman, *From Apes to Warlords* (London, 1978), p.394. Appendix I gives details of the Tots and Quots.

59 Interview in *New Statesman* 28.1.1939.

60 D. Caute, *The Fellow Travellers: A Postscript to the Enlightenment* (London, 1973).

61 B. Crick, *George Orwell: A Life* (London, 1980), pp.310–19, on Orwell's difficulties with *Animal Farm*. Cf. Kingsley Martin, editor of the *New Statesman & Nation*, on his refusal to publish Orwell's articles in favour of the POUM: 'I *minded* more about losing the war in Spain than about anything else that ever happened in my life . . . Both sides behaved with abominable cruelty; but I had to make my decision on general public grounds *to the end that one side might win rather than the other side.*' Cited by P. Johnson in *New Statesman*, 5.12.1980, p.16.

62 Arnold Zweig denounced one of the earliest show trials in 1930. (D. Caute, op. cit., p.279.)

63 Cited in J. Rühle, *Literatur und Revolution* (Munich, 1963), p.136.

64 The International Brigades do not seem to have contained many intellectuals (except those who went as part of their duty as professional revolutionaries), though their presence appears to have been unusually notable among the Americans and the small Czech contingent. Andreu Castells, *Las Brigadas Internacionales de la guerra de España* (Barcelona, 1974), pp.68–9. See also N. Carroll, *The Odyssey of the Abraham Lincoln Brigade: Americans in the Spanish Civil War* (Stanford, 1994); Rémy Skoutelsky, *L'Espoir guidait leurs pas: les volontaires français dans les Brigades Internationales* (Paris, 1998); Richard Baxwell, *Volunteers in the Spanish Civil War: the British Battalion in the International Brigades, 1936-1939* (London, 1994).

65 Among these we may mention in France such journals as *Commune* (*Revue littéraire française pour la défense de la culture*), *Europé*, *La Pensée* and, on an even broader Popular Front base, the weekly *Vendredi*; in Britain the Left Book Club, the short-lived *Left Review*, *Modern Quarterly*, and

during and after the war *Our Time*; in the USA the longer-lived *New Masses*, *Science and Society* and, for a time, *Partisan Review*.

66 Dimitrov at the seventh congress of the Communist International: '*Final salvation* this government [of the anti-fascist united front] cannot bring . . . Consequently it is necessary *to prepare for the socialist revolution*: Soviet power and *only* Soviet power can bring such salvation.'

67 To quote an eminent classical scholar whose days as a communist International Brigader are long behind him: 'The social revolution may have been (for some people) Paradise Now, but it was a fools' paradise; without an efficient army its days were numbered. The people who made it proved incapable of waging the kind of war Franco was waging against them.' Bernard Knox, 'Remembering Madrid' (*New York Review of Books*, 6.11.1980, p.34).

68 The possible critique of the new socialist regimes does not concern us here.

69 The article by Jacques Duclos in *Cahiers du Communisme* (April 1945) criticising the dissolution of the American CP in 1944 was seen as representing authority, and the CPUSA was re-established shortly after.

70 Wolfgang Leonhard, *Child of the Revolution* (London, 1979), p.208.

71 E. Lustmann, *Weg und Ziel: die Politik der österreichischen Kommunisten* (London, 1943), p.36. Dimitrov in 1946, cited in F. Fejtö, *Histoire des démocraties populaires* (Paris, 1969), I, p.126.

72 Fernando Claudin, *La crise du mouvement communiste: du Komintern au Kominform* (Paris, 1972), p.533; Eugenio Reale, *Avec Jacques Duclos au banc des accusés* (Paris, 1958), pp.75–6.

73 'It preserves to each nation the ultimate right to determine for itself, within this framework, the form of government and social organization it desires.' Earl Browder, *Teheran and America: Perspectives and Tasks* (NY, 1944), p.14.

74 Ibid., pp.13–14.

12 Gramsci

1 Gramsci's *Prison Notebooks* have been translated and edited in their entirety into English by Joseph A. Buttigieg (NY, 1992–97). The entire correspondence *Letters from Prison*, Frank Rosengarten (ed), has also been published in two volumes by Columbia University Press (NY, 1993–94). The most convenient access in English is still Q. Hoare and G. Nowell-Smith (eds), *Selections from the Prison Notebooks of Antonio Gramsci* (London, 1971). See also David Forgacs, *A Gramsci Reader: Selected Writings 1916–35*. James Martin (ed), *Antonio Gramsci: Critical Assessments of Leading Political Philosophers* 4 vols (London and NY, 2001) provides a range of

opinions on this thinker. More recent are Anne Showstack Sassoon, *Gramsci and Contemporary Politics: Beyond Pessimism of the Intellect* (London and NY, 2000) and P. Ives, *Language and Hegemony in Gramsci* (London and Ann Arbor, 2004).

2   A Gramsci, *Lettre del Carcere* (Turin, 1965), p.481

13 The Reception of Gramsci

1   P. Spriano, *Gramsci in carcere e il partito* (Rome, 1988).

2   Q. Hoare and G. Nowell-Smith (eds), *Selections from the Prison Notebooks of Antonio Gramsci* (London, 1971), p.175.

3   A. Bullock and O. Stallybrass (eds), *The Fontana Dictionary of Modern Thought,* (London, 1977).

4   Q. Hoare and G. Nowell-Smith (eds), *Selections from the Prison Notebooks of Antonio Gramsci.*

5   'The 250 most-cited authors in the Arts and Humanities Citations Index, 1976–1983' (in Eugene Garfield, Institute for Scientific Information, *Current Comments* 48, December 1986).

6   Q. Hoare and G. Nowell-Smith (eds), *Selections from the Prison Notebooks of Antonio Gramsci.*

7   Gwyn A. Williams, *The Welsh in their History* (London, 1982), p.200.

8   G. Lichtheim, *Marxism* (London, 1964), pp.368–70. See also the same author's *Europe in the Twentieth Century* (London, 1972), pp.44, 218–20.

9   Georg G. Iggers, *Neue Geschichtswissenschaft* (Munich, 1978), p.51.

10 Abelove, Blackmore, Dimock and Schneer (eds), *Visions of History* (NY, 1983), p.38.

11 E.J. Hobsbawm in *Società*, XVI, 3, p.456.

12 Peter Burke, 'Revolution in Popular Culture', in R. Porter and M. Teich (eds), *Revolution in History* (Cambridge, 1986), p.211.

14 The Influence of Marxism 1945–83

1   The only industrially developed countries under such regimes would not have acquired them after World War Two without Russian domination.

2   John Rae, *Contemporary Socialism* (London, 1884).

3   E.g. the article 'Socialism' by Daniel Bell in *International Encyclopaedia of the Social Sciences* (NY, 1968).

4   Introduction by R.H. Hilton to *The Transition from Feudalism to Capitalism* (London, 1954).

5 Ibid., p.41n.

6 Immanuel Wallerstein, *The Modern World-System* (NY, 1974). For an early critique of the Frank thesis, see Ernesto Laclau, 'Feudalism and Capitalism in Latin America' (*New Left Review* 67, 1971).

7 Among influential writers one might mention Eric Wolf, Teodor Shanin and Hamza Alavi. The rediscovery of Chayanov was by the Marxist Daniel Thorner.

8 For a list of some of these libraries, their contents and their 'alumni', see Hywel Francis, 'Survey of Miners' Institutes and Welfare Libraries, October 1972–February 1973' (*Llafur I*, 2, May 1973, pp.55–64).

9 The apparent renaissance of some weak or moribund socialist parties since the early 1970s, as in France, Spain or Greece, should not mislead us. They no longer operated as mass parties with a proletarian base, along traditional lines, but as bodies mobilising a socially heterogeneous electorate united mainly by discontent with existing conservative regimes and a desire for a variety of reforms in state, economy and society.

10 H. Francis, op. cit., p.59.

11 The anecdote is quoted by R.A. (Lord) Butler.

12 As we have already seen, a large sector of the 'new left', and certainly most of its members who took an interest in Marxist theory, initially consisted of former communists (orthodox or dissident) who left or were expelled from parties or groups formed in the Bolshevik tradition, or had been otherwise associated with it.

13 G. Lichtheim, *Marxism* (London, 1961), p.393; P. Baran and P.M. Sweezy, *Monopoly Capital* (NY, 1966), p.3.

14 This is true not only of a number of revolutionary sects and groups, but also of transformed small communist parties such as that of Sweden.

15 Lichtheim, op. cit., pp.393–4.

16 Ibid., p.394.

17 For a useful discussion of the development of the term 'articulation' in Marxist theory since Althusser, see A. Foster-Carter, 'The Mode of Production Debate' (*New Left Review* 107, 1978, pp.47–78).

18 N. Poulantzas, 'The capitalist state: a reply to Miliband and Laclau' (*New Left Review*, 95, 1976, pp.65–6). Poulantzas' main works were *Political Power and Social Classes* (London, 1973), *Fascism and Dictatorship* (London, 1974) and *Classes in Contemporary Capitalism* (London, 1975).

19 Cf. the polite but ruthless critique of Althusser from the standpoint of a veteran Marxist historian: P. Vilar, 'Histoire marxiste, histoire en construction: essai de dialogue avec L. Althusser' (*Annales* 281, 1973, pp.165–98).

20 Georg G. Iggers, *Neue Geschichtswissenschaft* (Munich, 1978), p.157.

21 Paul A. Samuelson, *Economics* (tenth edition, 1976), chapter 42.

22 G.A. Cohen, *Karl Marx' Theory of History: A Defence* (Oxford, 1978), p.ix.

23 For a good example, see O. Kuusinen (ed.), *Fundamentals of Marxism-Leninism* (Moscow, 1960), part III and chapters 22, 23.

24 For an early example, see Oskar Lange, *Political Economy I: General Principles* (Warsaw, 1963), whose chapter on 'The Principle of Economic Rationality' contains an Appendix on 'The mathematical foundations of programming' which refers, among others, to works by Frisch, Samuelson and Solow. Lange was an eminent socialist academic who had returned to Poland after the war.

25 Largely under the stimulus of Piero Straffa's *The Production of Commodities by Means of Commodities* in that year, which led to considerable argument between 'Ricardian' and 'non-Ricardian' Marxists.

26 This phrase comes from a work which opens with the words 'This book is a work of Marxist theory'. B. Hindess and P.Q. Hirst, *Pre-capitalist Modes of Production* (London, 1975).

27 It is not implied that doctrines in the mainstream of Marxism are thereby more true than those on the fringe; only that they are more true to Marx.

28 E.g. Hilferding's *Finance Capital* and Rosa Luxemburg's *Accumulation of Capital* which constantly refer back to Marx.

29 The phrase occurs in *State and Revolution*. One consequence of giving the analysis of the 1970s and 1980s this slim textual authority was that faithful Leninists felt obliged to hold that state monopoly capitalism was already flourishing during and after World War One. (Cf. art. 'staatsmonopolistischer Kapitalismus' in *Wörterbuch der marxistisch-leninistischen Soziologie*, Berlin E., 1977, p.624ff.)

30 In this respect the arguments about the break between the young and the mature Marx, familiar in the form of Althusser's 'rupture épistémologique' – anticipated by the reluctance of orthodox Soviet Marxism to recognise the *Frühschriften* as properly belonging to the corpus of Marxism – are genuinely important. What is at issue is not whether Marx ever abandoned the Hegelian heritage or the arguments of the Paris Manuscripts of 1843. It is certain that he did not. What is at issue is the effect of combining two entirely different ways of envisaging the future.

31 J.A. Schumpeter, *History of Economic Analysis* (London, 1954), p.573.

32 P.M. Sweezy, *The Theory of Capitalist Development* (London, 1946), p.vii.

33 Cf. M. Desai, *Marxian Economic Theory* (London, 1974), a good example of the literature designed for students by a Marxist economist: 'This book treats Marxian economics as an ongoing research programme where many unsettled questions remain to be answered' (p.6).

34 Cf. G. Lichtheim, 'On the Interpretation of Marx's Thought', in *From Marx to Hegel* (NY, 1971), p.69: 'It is plain that for Marx the only "nature" that enters into consideration is man's own, plus his surroundings which he transforms by his "practical activity". The external world, as it exists in and for itself, is irrelevant.'

35 E.g. Sebastiano Timpanaro, *On Materialism* (London, 1975).

15 Marxism in Recession 1983–2000

1   This incident was reported by Norman Davis at a British Academy colloquium on the fall of communism in Europe (15–16 October 2009).

2   Jim Riordan, 'The Last British Comrade Trained in Moscow: The Higher Party School, 1961–1963', Socialist History Society, SHS Occasional Paper 23, 2007.

3   Felix Gilbert and Stephen R. Graubard (eds), *Historical Studies Today* (NY, 1971, 1972).

4   Robert Evans, 'The Creighton Century: British Historians and Europe 1907–2007', in David Bates, Jennifer Wallis, Jane Winters (eds), *The Creighton Century 1907–2007* (London, Institute of Historical Research, 2009), p.15.

5   The broadening of the modernists' social perspective produced a historical masterpiece but not before 1998–2000 – Ian Kershaw's two-volume *Hitler*. We still await an analogous work on Stalin's USSR.

6   Régis Debray, *Révolution dans la révolution, et autres essais* (Paris, 1967).

7   I am using the rate of translation and circulation of my own titles as an indicator.

8   See Calvin Trillin, 'Wall Street Smarts' (*International Herald Tribune*, 15.10.2009, p.6).

16 Marx and Labour: the Long Century

1   The new fashion was pioneered by the US magazine *Forbes* which already described itself proudly as a 'capitalist tool' in the 1960s.

2   F. Fukuyama, 'The End of History' in *The National Interest* (summer 1989), p.3.

Dates and Sources of Original Publication

1   Marx Today
    Not before published in its present form. A brief version of the con-
    versation on which it is based was published in *New Statesman*
    (13.3.2006, Eric Hobsbawm and Jacques Attali, 'The New
    Globalisation Guru?'). © E.J. Hobsbawm 2006, 2011.

2   Marx, Engels and pre-Marxian Socialism
    E.J. Hobsbawm (ed.), *The History of Marxism Vol. 1: Marxism in Marx's Day*
    (Harvester Press, 1982), chapter 1. © E.J. Hobsbawm 1982.

3   Marx, Engels and Politics
    The History of Marxism, chapter 8.

4   On Engels' *The Condition of the Working Class in England*
    Introduction to F. Engels, *The Condition of the Working Class in England*
    (Panther Books, 1969). Introduction © E.J. Hobsbawm.

5   On the *Communist Manifesto*
    Foreword to K. Marx and F. Engels, *The Communist Manifesto: A Modern
    Edition* (Verso, 1998), pp.3–29. Foreword © E.J. Hobsbawm 1998.

6   Discovering the *Grundrisse*
    Foreword to Marcello Musto (ed.), *Karl Marx's* Grundrisse: *Foundations
    of the Critique of Political Economy 150 Years Later* (Routledge, 2008),
    pp.xx-xiv. Foreword © E.J. Hobsbawm 2008.

7   Marx on pre-Capitalist Formations
    K. Marx, *Pre-Capitalist Economic Formations* (the *Grundrisse*), translated by

Jack Cohen, introduced and edited by E.J. Hobsbawm (Lawrence & Wishart, 1964), pp.9–65. © E.J. Hobsbawm 1964.

8   The Fortunes of Marx's and Engels' Writings
    The History of Marxism, chapter 11.

9   Dr Marx and the Victorian Critics
    The New Reasoner 1 (1957). Published in E.J. Hobsbawm, *Labouring Men* (Weidenfeld & Nicolson, 1964). © E.J. Hobsbawm 1957.

10 The Influence of Marxism 1880–1914
    Not before published in English. Published in Italian in E.J. Hobsbawm, Georges Haupt, Franz Marek, Ernesto Ragioneri, Vittorio Strada and Corrado Vivanti (eds), *Storia del Marxismo,* vol. 2 (Einaudi, 1979). © E.J. Hobsbawm 1979, 2008.

11 In the Era of Anti-fascism, 1929–45
    Not previously published in English. Published in Italian in E.J. Hobsbawm, Georges Haupt, Franz Marek, Ernesto Ragioneri, Vittorio Strade and Corrado Vivanti (eds), *Storia del Marxismo,* vol. 3, part 2 (Einaudi, 1979). © E.J. Hobsbawm 1979, 2011.

12 Gramsci
    Not previously published in its present form. A version of this essay was published in Anne Showstack Sassoon (ed.), *Approaches to Gramsci* (Writers and Readers, 1982). © E.J. Hobsbawm 1982, 2008.

13 The Reception of Gramsci
    Not previously published in English. Published in Italian as the introduction to Antonio A. Santucci (ed.), *Gramsci in Europa e in America* (Laterza, 1995). The book was misleadingly published under my name. © E.J. Hobsbawm 1995, 2011.

14 The Influence of Marxism 1945–83
    Not previously published in English. A version in Italian, extensively rewritten for the present work, appeared with the title 'Il Marxismo oggi: un bilancio aperto' in E.J. Hobsbawm, Georges Haupt, Franz Marek, Ernesto Ragioneri, Vittorio Strada and Corrado Vivanti (eds), *Storia del Marxismo,* vol. 4 (Einaudi, 1982). © E.J. Hobsbawm 1982, 2011.

15 Marxism in Recession 1983–2000
    Not previously published. © E.J. Hobsbawm 2011.

16 Marx and Labour: the Long Century
    Not previously published in English. Published in German in 2000. This essay is rewritten from a lecture given in 1999 at the International Meeting of Labour Historians, Linz. © E.J. Hobsbawm 2000, 2011.

Index

Index

Index

Now you can order superb titles directly from Abacus

☐ The Age of Extremes   Eric Hobsbawm   £12.99

The prices shown above are correct at time of going to press. However, the publishers reserve the right to increase prices on covers from those previously advertised, without further notice.

──────────────── ⟨ABACUS⟩ ────────────────

Please allow for postage and packing: **Free UK delivery.**
Europe: add 25% of retail price; Rest of World: 45% of retail price.

To order any of the above or any other Abacus titles, please call our credit card orderline or fill in this coupon and send/fax it to:

Abacus, PO Box 121, Kettering, Northants NN14 4ZQ
Fax: 01832 733076   Tel: 01832 737526
Email: aspenhouse@FSBDial.co.uk

☐ I enclose a UK bank cheque made payable to Abacus for £ . .
☐ Please charge £ . . . . to my Visa/Delta/Maestro

☐☐☐☐☐☐☐☐☐☐☐☐☐☐☐☐☐☐

Expiry Date ☐☐☐☐   Maestro Issue No. ☐☐

NAME (BLOCK LETTERS please) . . . .
ADDRESS . . . .
. . . .
. . . .
Postcode . . . . Telephone . . . .
Signature . . . .

Please allow 28 days for delivery within the UK. Offer subject to price and availability.